Network Administrator's Security Resource Guide

TechRepublic Credits and Copyrights

Member Services Manager
Kenneth E. Tolle

Editors
Joan Harvey, Mike Jackman, David Bard,
Heather Morris, Liz Welch, Nathaniel Cadle

Technical Editors
John Sheesley, Jack Wallen, Jr.

Content Systems Coordinator
Travis Frazier

Senior Copy Editor
Marilyn Bryan

Copy Editors
Kim Mays, Kimberly Thomas,
Erika Render, Kachina Dunn, Sarah Graf-Koto,
Allison Hoffert, Claire Woolston

Graphic Artists
Natalie Strange, Kimberly Wright

Web Design
Bill Johnston, Shawn Morton

CD-ROM Design
David Petersheim

Web Development Manager
Greg Gorman

Web Operations Manager
Jim Ketcham

Content Resources Manager
Elayne Noltemeyer

Membership Manager
Dan Scofield

Vice President, Memberships
Jon Pyles

Vice President for Content Development
Bob Artner

CEO
J. Thomas Cottingham

President
Max Smith

TechRepublic
9900 Corporate Campus Drive
Suite 1500
Louisville, KY 40223
E-mail: customerservice@techrepublic.com
www.techrepublic.com

Table of Contents

Foreword

Welcome to TechRepublic's first-ever Security compilation. Here you will find advice, tips, tricks, and helpful files to bring you closer to that peace of mind every IT professional and network administrator is searching for.

This compilation is put together in specific chapters to guide you along the way. These chapters represent the major topics that fall under the blanket title of security. Within each chapter, you will find related TechProGuild drill downs and TechRepublic content. You may be asking yourself, "What is the benefit of having this when I can get it online?" Well, my friend, one of these days it's going to happen. You're going to be sweating and laboring over your network when it's going to come down right under your eyes. When that happens, you might need assistance, and TechRepublic wants to be there to help you! With this compilation, we can be!

The first chapter in this compilation is, simply put, the basics: philosophies, pinciples, and techniques fundamental to security. This chapter covers things you should know before you begin and techniques to help you get where you're going.

The second chapter is dedicated to Operating Systems. Within this chapter you will find content specific to Windows, Linux, and Netware. Although most of the content will be necessary for most people running a cross-platform network, you may find something completely unique to your situation.

Chapter 3 is a small but very important chapter on firewalls. Although the number of pieces is limited, you may find them to be invaluable tools for your security model.

Chapter 4 is all about attacks. Be it viruses or hackers, we've got you covered. Pay close attention to this particular chapter, for there is very sound advice coming from multiple levels of the security paradigm.

The fifth chapter deals primarily with encryption tools. The sixth chapter is a host of tips that will aid you in your quest for secure computing. Use these tips well, for they often are hit-and-run snippets geared toward getting you locked down fast. And, finally, Chapter 7 includes the latest Gartner security research.

I hope this compilation becomes part and parcel to your security needs. Although not exhaustive, it is a fine resource from which you will learn many important, practical ideas.

Enjoy!

Network Administrator's Security Resource

Chapter 1—Basics

Before You Begin

Principles

Techniques

Chapter 2—Operating Systems

Windows

Chapter 7—Gartner Notes

Basics: Technique

Operating Systems: Linux

Operating Systems: 390

Chapter 1—Basics

Before you begin

Principles

Techniques

Chapter 1: Basics

Chapter 1: "Basics" has three sections:

▶ Before You Begin

▶ Principles

▶ Techniques

This chapter was broken into these sections for obvious reasons. The first section, Before you begin, makes you stop and think about the issues that all network administrators should consider before going about the business of setting up a secure network.

Going beyond the hardware setup, the first section also takes a look at many other issues, such as:

▶ What to ask

▶ When to outsource

▶ The security market

▶ The importance of network security

▶ E-commerce security

▶ Better tools

▶ Legality

We attempt to make you stop and think about what you are getting involved in, and we'll cover the issues relative to your situation.

The next section, Principles, covers the fundamental principles of security. A very strong series by TechProGuild author Chris Dinsmore is a highlight of this section.

The final section is Techniques. Here you will find similar topics from the first section, only this time around we'll get more technical in nature. Topics covered include:

▶ Kerberos

▶ VPNs

▶ Enabling retail payments online

▶ IP masquerading

Ask your ASP tough security questions

By Suman Bolar

ASPs can make your life easier by running and managing cumbersome apps. But there is one aspect of your business that you cannot afford to relinquish to a third-party supplier—data security.

Many managers mistakenly assume that all their security worries are history the minute they sign up with an ASP. You should take just the opposite view, according to Winn Schwartau, chief operating officer of The Security Experts, Inc., an information security consulting firm in Seminole, FL.

"If you use an ASP, you should concentrate on security even more because you are extending your enterprise, broadening its perimeter, including the Internet as part of your networks, and adding an entirely new infrastructure to your existing one," said Schwartau.

Just how safe is your data when you outsource an application? How much control should you retain? How much control *can* you retain?

"That's not easy to answer. It's a very delicate balance," said Sreeram Krishnamoorthy, senior consultant at KPMG Consulting, a professional services firm based in Montvale, NJ. Krishnamoorthy believes that developing a relationship with an ASP can be challenging when you're used to having total control over your enterprise applications.

"You have to do your homework and ask the right questions," he said.

Questions to ask

Here's some valuable advice from Ron Hale, vice president of professional services for Illinois-based Telenisus, an Internet solutions provider that offers information protection services and computer security consulting services. Hale suggests asking the following questions before signing up:

- How secure is your environment?
- Is there any segregation between clients sharing the same infrastructure?
- What types of security controls are in place to protect my information?

- Are you audited, or have there been security assessments completed that certify the protection provided?
- If there is an incident, can you block an attack and recover the infrastructure?
- How deep are the technical skills in your organization?
- Are you depending on a few key people, or is there sufficient depth to ensure quality service under various conditions?
- What security assessment and integrity tools are used and how frequently are they used?
- Is there an outside organization that performs periodic testing and certification, or do you rely on internal quality testing?

Independent research needed

Hale, former director of Deloitte & Touche LLP's Information Protection Consulting practice, also recommends investing in independent research. He says you should require the following:

- Ask for an audit, security report, or an SAS 70-style report from an accounting firm. They should interview the people involved with security.
- The audit or similar form should provide information from the security managers who should detail the security measures in place.

"The manager should be able to review documentation that has been collected to attest to security levels. If the ASP is providing services, the client should be able to run independent tests without notifying the ASP to ensure the protection of information," said Hale.

The ASP market responds to security demands

There are positive indications that the ASP industry is serious about providing a secure environment. Meredith Whalen, program manager for ASP Research at Boston-based IDC Research, says that customers' security concerns are having a definite impact on the ASP market.

"We've done demand studies asking customers what factors would make them more likely to invest in an ASP. Security issues ranked pretty high up there. And when we asked ASPs what their customers typically use to access their services, we found that it isn't the Internet. Customers are using secured lines and VPNs. They are concerned and aware about security risks," said Whalen.

She warns that ASPs that have not focused on this area will need to invest in security infrastructure—or they may go out of business. She added that although many ASPs already have security services in place, they don't always emphasize or publicize them. Unless you ask specific questions about security measures, you risk misjudging prospective ASPs.

The most important reason to ask questions is to protect your business interests. "You are relying on this provider to ensure the security and integrity of your business. Make sure your ASP takes security issues as seriously as you do," said Hale. ◆

Should you outsource your Internet security?

By Mary Ann Fitzharris

Many companies are finding out too late that there's more to Internet security than slapping a firewall on their T1 line. Protecting your corporate knowledge is critically important, and it requires expertise and time that you might not have. Can your IT staff provide an effective security program to prevent unauthorized access to your corporate data? Or should you outsource your Internet security to an ISP that is set up to provide the monitoring that you can't? Here are some answers.

When should you consider outsourcing?

"If your business has had the luxury of the time to put a good security capacity in place, and if you have the technical expertise, obviously it's more cost effective to run it internally," said SRA International's security guru, Tony Valletta, vice president and director of control, communications, and intelligence. "Or are you like the majority of companies that are now realizing you have all this great information technology and, by god, you'd better start thinking about how to protect your assets, or you're going to be subjected to a whole bunch of naughty things?"

Mike Martucci, vice president of marketing for WatchGuard, a security outsourcing vendor for small and midsize businesses, says that a lot of small companies and telecommuters have simple security policies, but as their complexity grows, so does the need for outsourcing. "I always come back to the security polic," Martucci said. "If it's not a complex policy, you probably can do it yourself. But as the complexity increases, you dedicate a person or more than one person to this, and your costs rise. It begins to look more attractive to spend $800 a month or whatever [to an ISP] to say, 'take over control of this box, create a policy for me, update and monitor it, and give me the reports.'"

What are your Internet security options?

Valletta suggests you might want to start out by outsourcing, then build up a capability and bring it back in-house. "At least do something," he urges, "whether you do it internally or externally." There are three options for IT managers to consider:

1. **Do-it-yourself security**. Can your staff assemble all the right components of a security system and put them into place? This assumes you have the in-house expertise and the number of staff to ensure around-the-clock surveillance. This is a big assumption for some companies, Valletta suggests. Also, according to Martucci, "If you think you have a somewhat savvy person on staff, take a close look because we would bet [he or

she's] a network manager and not a security expert. Network managers spend a lot of time configuring Ethernet cables and that kind of thing, but you ask them questions like how do you set up your security policy, should your HTTP proxy be on or off, or what kind of VPN do you want, and they give you blank stares. Now you have to make an educational investment. But does he have the time to be a security guy?"

2. **Subscription service.** With this option, you buy a package that includes a dedicated network security appliance to implement a security policy, and an integrated suite of security software. This enables you to have sophisticated security products to protect your network while managing your own Internet security. Then, through the vendor's Internet-based subscription service, you can get advice and ongoing information to keep you updated. Martucci said, "We send you software updates and threat responses. Like when the Melissa virus came out, we had a team of experts whose sole job was to look at new security threats and urgently send you an update for your firebox to protect you. We're sending it to you, but you have to read it and update the firebox yourself. It's a service, but at a minimal level."

3. **Total outsourced security.** If you decide you don't have the security expertise on staff, you might want to go with a comprehensive, fully outsourced Internet security service from your ISP, assuming your ISP has the data center, network, back-office systems, and the expertise to support your security needs. Your ISP may provide several services, including:

   ▸ Installation of software with security and management features

   ▸ Support for customized security appliances at your site

   ▸ Software updates and threat responses

   ▸ Monthly reporting

IT staff expertise and availability

"You have to decide if you have the security expertise on staff and whether or not you want it," according to Martucci. "It becomes a financial

analysis. The PSInet service is something like $795 a month; you're not going to hire someone for that," he said. "Another issue is that security is around the clock, seven days a week. So it's not one person you're looking for, it's two or three because you're going to need some shifts."

"Some systems or network administrators feel like their turf is being invaded when someone else manages a piece of their infrastructure," said David Bovee, product manager of managed security service at WatchGuard. "I've encountered systems administrators who manage the telephone systems, and all of the servers and clients. They dictate the acceptable use policy for the company. They manage the antivirus, the business database, and all the other things. Well, one person managing all of this is an equation that equals trouble. It means something is going to get missed somewhere. When you're talking about security, things get missed."

"Once I did a firewall installation for a network administrator," Bovee said, "and he was one of these people who didn't want to relinquish control of any part of his network. So, he tried to retain that control and, in doing so, he missed a critical piece of his perimeter infrastructure. He ended up being hacked at one of his peripheral sites, which—because of his lapsed security policy, which he had no experience writing—resulted in a hack of his entire company. He had to rebuild 40 client systems in addition to his server."

Integration of technologies

Another issue to consider is how you integrate new technologies into the platform. "You need to ask potential security vendors, 'Does outsourcing affect my ability to implement new systems I've written or purchased? What are you going to do when I add applications, homegrown or off-the-shelf? If I have to add or change applications, will I be able to do it, or will I get charged an arm and a leg for you to do it?'" said Tim Landgrave, president of eAdvantage.net.

Integration certainly should be a concern, but you should be able to find solutions with your outsourcing partner. According to Martucci, "An ISP will work with us to design the right system for your needs. So putting together the right security package is a big time-saver. We make sure everything you add to the package works with the rest of it. That's all out of your hands now."

Design of a security policy

"Boy, is it a headache to make a security policy, manage it, and keep it current. Big, big job, and it takes a lot of experts to do it," according to Martucci. "One of the advantages you get by outsourcing security is that the ISPs will design your security policy for you. They'll interview you about your business practices, and then they'll fit that into the policies and technology they're going to apply for you to make it happen.

"A security policy is all the rules about how the people in your company will behave while on the Net. Who is allowed to come in (by name, department, branch office, or IP address), where they're allowed to go, what services they can get, what files they can get to, what time of day they might be able to come in, who's on a VPN, and who's not? All these rules have to be designed and need to be written down. They should reflect your business practice," Martucci said.

Policy changes: How often do you need to update?

"Most security experts recommend you update your security policy, at a minimum, two times a year. And really big e-commerce companies do it more often than that," Martucci said. "When policy changes are required, the outsourced service provider can affect the change for the company, thus minimizing the risk that a mistake is made," said Bovee. "When you're talking about using a firewall to access the Internet, a mistake will also affect other servers that the business has, so it could interrupt service to the customer. Most companies, if they make a change on their firewall and it happens to be a mistake, may not recognize right away that they've affected access to business customers." He says that "an inexperienced IT staffer may make a change to the company's firewall policy on Friday, go home at 5:00 P.M. and be out of range of his pager, and all this time the Web site is inaccessible to the customer."

Keep your security system on guard with regular reports

"The only way you know your security system is working for you is when you actually create a report and evaluate it for inconsistencies, errors, or anomalies," Bovee said. Most service providers typically produce a report at the end of the month which can be customized for the customer's requirements. "However," Landgrave cautions, "be sure they will distill all that information and provide a report that's intelligible for you, the customer, not just one that contains IP addresses and numbers."

Proactive notification is critical, according to Landgrave. "I don't want a report that tells me someone stole my data last week. I want to know if and when an attempt is detected, and I want to be notified that someone attempted to get in using this set of credentials, and they tried these 15 passwords. And I want to know they were shut down." Landgrave used an example from a few years ago when a small ISP in southern Indiana had two Russian hackers attempting to break into the system for two days. "Because there was no proactive notification, the hackers eventually shut down the entire business. It took them days to get back up and running," he said. ◆

The information security market space invasion has begun

By A. Dang Van Mien

Leading Information Security Vendors: The evolutionary path that information security management tools vendors are following— from point products to tools suites and major alliances—is reminiscent of the route taken by network and systems management tools vendors. In the security arena, the initial step was the introduction of utilities to fill holes in the burgeoning OS marketplace (e.g., UNIX and Windows NT) or in the network marketplace (virtual private network, or VPN, and firewall) and finally with strong authentication mechanism and antivirus on the desktop. Most of the leading security suite vendors for consolidated service administration began with a key functionality for user administration and then branched out to other areas such as virus protection, VPN, public key infrastructure (PKI), or firewall management. Today, the leading security suite vendors (e.g., Axent Technologies, IBM, Entrust, BullSoft, and RSA Security Dynamics) include a baseline of three to five security management tools.

Security suite vendors are looking toward alliances and integration to expand their offerings. Since security was perceived as a technical afterthought, security market growth has been slow. Pure security vendors are struggling because:

▸ They are selling at a low level in the IS organization. They sell tools that are very focused (e.g., antivirus, firewall, VPN, and authentication mechanism). They sell to chief security officers or security experts who have limited budgets. In all cases, they did not attract business budgets and business managers' attention.

▸ They are faced with new requirements and security in an area that will combine complex technical integration and services to deploy and customize solutions. No information security vendor has enough resources to cope with that demand.

▸ Security market growth was not significant enough for security vendors to develop key security infrastructure technologies such as repositories and dynamic event management console. They are mandatory to deal with the growing distributed/heterogeneous and real-time nature of e-business security. Most of the point solution security vendors (e.g., Axent, ISS, Comdisco, Unisys, and Inacom) plan to integrate their products to event console platforms and standard directory services. ◆

Bottom Line:

Information security vendors have the depth of technical understanding to solve some, but not all, security problems. For transaction incident management (TIM), large NSM vendors such as CA, IBM/Tivoli, and BMC are in a better position than information security vendors. They potentially can leverage their core technology and distribution channels, and make partnerships and acquisitions to change the rules of the security market. By 2003, the TIM market will be dominated by a subset of strategic coalitions between information security vendors and NSM leaders (0.7 probability). Enterprises should not expect more from these NSM suite vendors until they deliver the next-generation of tools in more than 12 months. We recommend that enterprises: **1)** refrain from buying promises of future functional enhancements, **2)** avoid worrying about obsolescence if the tool solves their security problems, and **3)** plan on a life span of two to three years for the tool.

Help users understand the importance of network security

By Jake Necessary

Users don't need to know everything. In fact, most users might never completely understand the complex structure of a network and how network security is organized. Nevertheless, providing users with some basic knowledge of the security process can help them immensely and, hopefully, reduce your trouble calls!

To that end, I prepared a document for my users to explain how security matters are handled on my system. (Keep in mind that before I started disseminating this information to my users, my employer had NO security measure in place.) My user-base is technically challenged, so I tried to present the information in as simple a manner as possible. Please feel free to borrow this format and adapt it for use in your shop.

Introduction to network security

To all end users: We need to do a better job of keeping our network secure. The following information provides the steps you need to log on to the network successfully. Keep in mind, when I say "network" I'm referring to Windows NT. You'll know you're logging on to Windows NT if the first box you see when you turn on the computer says "Press CTRL+ALT+DEL to log on." (This documentation does not pertain to the mainframe users.)

Network Security is composed of three areas:

▸ Intruder detection
▸ Logon restrictions
▸ Password restrictions.

Intruder detection was developed to prevent an unauthorized user from guessing your password. Logon and password restrictions are used to ensure users change their passwords regularly, use unique passwords, and connect to only one computer at a time.

TABLE A: *This table describes the rules that govern access to the network.*

Security Function	Setting	Layman's Terms
Intruder Detection		
Incorrect Logon Attempts	5	If you enter the wrong password 5 times in a 30-minute period, the server will lock you out for 15 minutes or until the network admin removes the lockout.
Logon Restrictions		
Limit Concurrent Logons	'	This means your username can be logged on to only one computer at a time.
Password Restrictions		
Minimum Password Length	5 characters	Your password must have a minimum of 5 characters.
Force Period Changes	Yes, 60 days	Every 60 days your password will expire. You will have to change the password at this point.
Require Unique Passwords	Yes	You cannot use the same password twice.
Limit Grace Logons	Yes, 6	When the password expires, you have 5 more logons to change the password. At the sixth logon the computer locks out the username.

In addition, password restrictions give users the ability to use "grace logons," which are the number of times a user can log on with an expired password. For example, suppose you log on to the network, and the computer advises that your password has expired and four grace logons remain. The system is telling you that you have four more logons until the computer locks you out. Once the remaining grace logons equal zero, a network administrator will have to intervene to allow network access.

Table A describes the Network Security Settings. Please review this table and make yourself familiar with the rules and regulations for passwords and logons.

What to expect?

The first time the computer does something out of the ordinary can be confusing. Here is what to expect during logon when your password expires:

1. After logon, the system advises that your password has expired and you have five grace logons to change your password. "Would you like to change it now? Yes or No."

2. Click Yes.

3. Enter your new password. (Consult the section labeled Summary Of Rules For Passwords below.)

4. Reenter the password.

5. Click OK, and the computer will take a minute and then update your security profile.

Manually changing your network password

Changing your network password is an essential element for network security. The following procedure documents the process of changing your password manually before the server forces a change. Complete this procedure any time you feel your password has been compromised:

▶ After logging onto the network, press [Ctrl][Alt][Del].

▶ When the NetWare Security dialog box appears, left Click on "Change Password"

▶ In the Change Password Dialog Box, enter your old password and press [Tab].

▶ Enter your new password and press [Tab] again.

▶ Confirm your new password and click on OK. A dialog box will report that your password was successfully changed.

If you have any problems with changing your password, please contact your network administrator or I/S help desk.

Summary of rules for passwords

The following network access rules must be followed:

▶ Passwords must be at least five characters in length. A mixture of numbers and letters provides the greatest security; however, this is not required.

▶ Passwords must be unique. You cannot use the same password twice.

▶ Passwords will be changed every 60 days. The computer will prompt you and allow for five grace logons. Please change your password as soon as the prompt appears.

　▶ If you attempt to access the network with the wrong password (five times) the server will lock you out for 15 minutes.

　▶ You can not log on to more than one computer at a time.

　▶ Network passwords are sacred. If compromised, change immediately.

A review of the most common error messages

If you receive an error message when you're logging on or changing your passwords, don't panic. Just take a deep breath, read the screen, and try again. Refer to **Table B** for a description of the most common error messages. ◆

TABLE B: *Here are some of the most common error messages you'll see on logon.*

Error Message	Explanation
"The system could not log you onto the network... check logon	This message is usually displayed after entering an incorrect password. Please re enter your password. If you get this message times, the sixth message will be "You have encountered an unexpected failure..."
"You have encountered an unexpected logon failure..."	Your account has been locked out. Contact the network administrator for action.
"A tree or server cannot be found..."	Although the computer has given you a box to log on, it's not really ready. Click No and wait 10 seconds. Attempt to log on again. Repeat this process 5 times. If the problem persists, contact the network administrator.
"A locally stored profile is newer than the Roaming profile..."	A profile stores your desktop icons and colors. Click Yes, OK, or wait until the computer chooses.

A guide to e-commerce security

By Paul Desmond

Perhaps one of the most daunting aspects of any electronic commerce project is security. Whether you're dealing with a business-to-business application or a business-to-consumer retail site, there are bound to be unseemly types bent on breaking in to your network and stealing corporate assets, or simply wreaking havoc and causing embarrassment.

It's an unsettling thought, but you are far from defenseless. There are myriad software and hardware tools available to help steel your site against most any attack. Vendors are also starting to package products together, delivering a collection of tools that purport to ease your integration chores. And you can also outsource the whole problem, with more and more service providers stepping forward to take on some or all of your security needs.

No matter which route you choose, it's easier to get your arms around the e-commerce security dilemma if you think of the problem in terms of four general requirements:

- Policies and procedures
- Perimeter security, including firewalls, authentication, virtual private networks (VPNs), and intrusion detection
- Authorization, for both data and applications
- Public key infrastructure (PKI), an authorization and encryption setup for those applications where the stakes are particularly high and an audit trail is crucial

Producing good policies

One of the biggest mistakes companies make when it comes to security is failing to come up with good policies and procedures—and to make sure they get followed. Experts agree that security is a moving target. Businesses just can't install a firewall and forget it. Every time there's a change in the IS infrastructure, be it an operating system upgrade or a router reconfiguration, the security implications of that change have to be taken into account.

"Coming up with policies is a whole lot easier than making sure they get followed," says Alan Paller, president The SANS Institute, a coopera-

tive research and education organization that focuses on security.

In a January 1999 report, "Turning Security on Its Head," Forrester Research, Cambridge, MA, says companies need to "shun complexity" and "set dirt-simple policies and use measures that are invisible to users."

While that may be a tall order, the point is well-taken, for if a policy is too complex or burdensome to those who must adhere to it, odds are they won't.

Kicking Off the Series

In this article, you'll learn about improving e-commerce security with the latest vulnerability scanning tools and appropriate alarm thresholds. Other articles in this series will look at trends in firewalls and improving access policies. This content originally appeared in the September issue of Wiesner Publishing's Software Magazine and appears on TechRepublic under a special arrangement with the publisher.

Paul Donfried, chief marketing officer at Identrus, a New York-based company that is developing a PKI service, says the key to good security policy development is inclusion. "What you ideally should do is pull people from all the functional areas that are affected and jointly develop policies and procedures," he says. "Then you've got a high likelihood that they will be followed and implemented."

This is no mean feat because there are innumerable aspects to consider when developing security policies, such as server upgrades, as well as changes to firewalls and even modems. (Do you know about every modem that's attached to a PC in your organization? Doubtful, but each is a potential security risk.)

"One of the biggest areas for security breaches are misconfigurations. Period," says Patrick McBride, executive vice president of the META Security Group, a security consulting firm in Atlanta. Whether a company is dealing with applications, network equipment, middleware, or Web servers, virtually anything can be a security risk if it's not configured properly, with all known patches applied," McBride says. "What you really need is people who understand where those holes are and how to close them."

A good practice is to apply vulnerability scanning tools after any reconfiguration, McBride says. These tools, available from vendors including Network Associates and Internet Security Solutions (ISS), look for known configuration problems and vulnerabilities in operating system, firewalls, and other network elements.

Toward the same end, Paller says SANS is making available a script developed at Xerox's Palo Alto Research Center that helps beef up security for Solaris servers. The tool scans the server for a list of known security loopholes that have been identified by various SANS members, then automatically applies the rec-

ommended fix. SANS has also published a guide to identifying security problems in NT servers, but the fixes must be done manually. (The NT guide is available now for a nominal fee from SANS.)

Another key to good policy development is setting alarm thresholds to avoid too many false alarms. "If a car alarm goes off in New York City, people don't pay attention anymore," McBride says. Letting the same thing happen in your e-commerce security infrastructure is akin to leaving the front door open.

Donfried says companies have to strike a balance and compromise. "You don't want a password policy that says you can use anything you want, but you can't go too far or users will end up writing passwords down, which is worse," he says. "There has to be a cultural fit for policies and procedures or they will never be implemented." ◆

Policing the perimeter

By Paul Desmond

The traditional first and best line of defense to protect the perimeter of your e-commerce site is the firewall. While there are literally dozens of vendors offering firewalls these days with varying features, there are some trends.

In the past, vendors tried to cram all kinds of other services into their firewalls, such as File Transfer Protocol support. Today, most users seem to favor firewall appliances, which are firewalls that perform only security-related functions. The reason for this gets back to the issue of misconfigurations causing most security problems; the less there is to configure, the less chance things will go wrong. Which isn't to say firewalls are doing less these days. In many cases, firewalls are morphing into a new class of device with encryption and authentication features that enable companies to build virtual private networks—secure paths through an otherwise-public network, typically the Internet. Available from the likes of Check Point Software, Internet Devices, NetScreen Technolo-

gies, and WatchGuard, these combination firewall/VPNs enable a company to give authorized remote users access to a site while keeping snoops at bay.

There are also "pure" VPN devices intended more for letting authorized remote users in than keeping everyone else out. Among the vendors offering such products are Check Point, RadGuard, RedCreek, Lucent, and Novell. These products are especially useful for extranets designed for business-to-business e-commerce.

Authentication is another key technology for protecting the perimeter. Shawn Abbott, chief technology officer at Rainbow Technologies, Irvine, CA, which makes an array of Internet security products, says times have changed since users employed electronic data interchange (EDI) technology to conduct electronic commerce. EDI messages were often sent via value-added network (VAN) providers. Given that parties on each end of the transaction had to sign up for the service with the VAN provider and had to agree on the EDI formats to be used, there was a natural prior relationship before the transaction took place.

"On the Internet, all that goes away and you no longer know who you're dealing with," Abbott says. "And there's no security proposition offered by the network service provider anymore."

There are a number of ways to provide authentication. One is a hardware token such as the SecurID from Security Dynamics, Bedford, MA, which generates a unique password every 60 seconds. For authorization to be granted, the password must match that on a central server, which is synchronized with the token.

Another form of token is the smart card, a credit card-size device with memory chips on board that can store passwords, user IDs, and the like. The downside is they require some sort of reader to pull authentication data from the card, making the devices cumbersome for enterprise applications.

Rainbow offers a variation on the smart card called the iKey, a small device that plugs into the USB port on a laptop, PC, router, server, or any other device. Software on the iKey enables it to be programmed with a unique ID. Users insert the iKey into the USB port and enter a password to be authenticated, a process known as two-factor authorization—one factor being the iKey, the other the password.

Authentication is only half the battle, however. Once a user gains access to a Web site, it's likely that some sort of data will be flowing back and forth. When that data is of a sensitive nature, it's got to be protected. That's where encryption comes into play.

VPNs typically provide encryption for data flowing over the wire, but companies also have to think about sensitive data stored in databases, such as a pool of credit card numbers. That's the type of valuable data hackers will spend time looking for.

Another category of product is intrusion detection systems (IDS), which can issue an alert when someone is trying to break in to the network and then thwart the attack. Available from vendors including ISS, Axent Technologies, and Network Flight Recorders, an IDS monitors network traffic, looking for telltale patterns that denote most known types of attacks, such as a repetitious flood of packets typical of a denial of service attack meant to overload a Web site. ◆

Litigation, legislation, and lawsuits: The reality of internal security breaches

By Matthew Osborn

A serious threat to an enterprise's stability is corporate crime. The theft of proprietary information by either dishonest employees or external hackers could have a deep and prolonged impact on a company, making an enterprise's entire infrastructure vulnerable to unwanted intrusions.

According to a 1997 study by the American Society for Industrial Security (ASIS), U.S. companies lose over $250 billion annually to stolen intellectual property. The report said the greatest potential security breaches include employees stealing critical information or divulging secrets to a future employer.

What are the types of internal threats?

In an interview with TechRepublic, David Morrow, the cyberforensics manager at Ernst & Young and a former U.S. Air Force investigator, gave an example of internal corporate crime. "When I was an investigator for the Air Force, we had numerous examples of people in the accounting world setting up dummy companies and writing themselves huge checks because they knew how to write the checks and destroy the evidence," Morrow said.

Security experts classify internal security threats in three categories:

- Bribery occurs when an outside party corrupts or influences a staff member by offering money or gifts in exchange for sensitive information.

- Social engineering is the manipulation of a network administrator or support personnel to obtain information that can be used to steal sensitive data.

- Group collusion is the efforts of several people to breach security by taking advantage and abusing their rights to particular information.

Industrial espionage and the theft of intellectual property may not entail an intricate and carefully orchestrated plan. Morrow noted that stealing information can be simple. Industrial espionage is another example of people putting all kinds of information on a floppy disk and walking out with it, or e-mailing it out, or posting it to a Web site," he said.

What is your defense?

The key to defense is prevention and understanding that internal security poses a real danger to your company. The ASIS survey said that 62 percent of companies have no procedures for reporting information loss, and 40 percent don't have an established response program when a loss is discovered. Admittedly, it's difficult to forecast how a new hire will develop as an employee, but here are some tips for securing mission-critical information.

- Valuation of protected information can help IT strategists determine what resources to allocate.

- Background checks provide employers with a survey of potential employees' work histories, which can discover any misrepresentations.

- Security education makes employees aware of types of techniques that people utilize to obtain sensitive information. For example, if your help desk technician is aware of questions that people ask to get the password for a stolen ID changed, the risk of revealing information could be reduced.

- Separate servers for business-critical information and shared data can limit access to marketing and accounting information.

- A PGP encryption package for select e-mails and documents can shield information from unwanted eyes.

- A temporary account for temporary, external network administrators could prevent contracted assistants from having extended access to data. In addition, IT managers could eliminate their rights and privileges. For example, they may only be able to create accounts or serve basic functions. By creating access levels within your own IT department, you can get a better handle on the situation when an inside job occurs.

- Eliminate opportunities for inside hackers when undertaking large IT projects, such as merging communications computer systems.

As an IT executive, you must establish policies and procedures to address internal security. Although it's impossible to continuously monitor all your employees, especially high-level managers, you can take preventive measures to reduce risk and manage your staff responsibly.

For more information

- A Brief Guide to the Economic Espionage Act of 1996 provides a brief overview of this legislation.

- High Technology Crime Investigation Association, Silicon Valley Chapter (HTCIA) is an organization that is concerned with the methods for investigating and prosecuting crimes involving advanced technologies.

- CERT's Education and Training in Network Computing Security classes and seminars offer personnel of all levels the opportunity to improve their security skills through formal training. ◆

Back to basics: A case for investing in security

By John McCormick

A reminder of security basics can provide ammunition for you to take to management. If you haven't tried it, you'd be amazed how much more attention management pays to published articles than they do to their own in-house experts.

True story: I once proved the power of the press by taking my own review of a product to a company president. He'd ignored my advice for months, but immediately gave the magazine page his attention, never noticing the name of the author. He then took the article to several staff members, pointing out the "new" ideas contained in the piece. Someone later told him that I was the author. Fortunately for that employee, the boss had a sense of humor.

One thing I see repeatedly in many companies is an unwillingness to spend much, if anything, on security. An organization typically has to experience a loss or, at a minimum, see graphic proof of how vulnerable it really is, before the company is willing to invest in security.

The fact is, you may be unknowingly revealing your own security information. For example, did you ever think about what information you disclose when you visit Web sites, or what people can learn about your system just by knowing your Web address?

For this reason, you should ensure that you are making the appropriate investments to protect your network. Still need more convincing?

A real world example

If you're curious about how much information the public can easily obtain relating to your systems, check out www.privacy.net/anonymizer. Test it with a quick visit, and you'll probably be surprised to discover just how much other people can learn about your systems when your company's employees visit other Internet sites.

Each time you visit a Web site, your system announces some of the programs you have installed on your PC. Here's just a small part of the report returned on one of my computers:

```
JavaScript is enabled and working.

The following plug-ins are installed
on your system:

Comet Cursor - Comet Cursor Plugin
v.1.5.0.190 - NP32COMET.DLL

RealPlayer(tm) G2 LiveConnect-Enabled
Plug-In (32-bit) - RealPlayer(tm)
LiveConnect-Enabled Plug-In -

nppl3260.dll

Yahoo! Audio Conferencing Plugin -
Yahoo! Audio Conferencing Plugin -
npyacs.dll

VSCP Module - VSCP COM/Plugin DLL -
npvscp.dll

Shockwave for Director - Macromedia
Shockwave for Director Netscape plug-
in, version 6.0 - NP32DSW.DLL

Netscape Media Player - Netscape Media
Player, Audio Streaming Plugin,
v.1.1.1516 - nplau32.dll

Shockwave Flash 2.0 - Shockwave Flash
2.0 r11 - NPSWF32.dll

Quicken 99 for Windows - IPA Plugin
stub - NPIPA32S.DLL

LiveAudio - Sound Player for Netscape
Navigator, v.1.1.1515 - npaudio.dll

QuickTime Plug-In - QuickTime Plug-In
for Win32 v.1.1.0 - NPQTW32.DLL

NPAVI32 Dynamic Link Library -
NPAVI32, avi plugin DLL - npavi32.dll

Netscape Default Plug-in - Default
Plug-in - npnul32.dl
```

If that doesn't worry you, just how would you like everyone to know what software your Web server is running?

Turning the tables on Privacy.net, I learned that they are most likely running NT 4. How did I obtain this information? Did I spend a day hacking their system? Nope, I simply entered their address at another security-oriented Web site and it returned a report on the software their server is running.

Is your systems information available on the Web?

It's important to try and keep such information confidential. I even wrote a column about it, and many TechRepublic members agreed with me. But I'll bet you didn't know there's a Web site that purports distributing this information to anyone who asks.

It doesn't work for every site, and it isn't 100 percent accurate, but it's accurate enough to be scary. To learn more, just go to www. netcraft.com/whats/ and enter the URL you are interested in. Since the site records the results and adds it to an ongoing Web Server Survey, you might want to think twice before entering your own address.

Pick some sites you are familiar with, however, and I'll bet you'll come up with some interesting results. Although hackers want this data, it can also be a useful management information systems (MIS) tool. For example, if your competitor has a smoothly running site, wouldn't it be interesting to know what software they are using?

Interestingly enough, Microsoft's e-mail site, www.hotmail.com, is reportedly running Apache/ 1.3.6 (UNIX) mod_ssl/2.2.8 SSLeay/0.9.0b.

The report for www.microsoft.com indicates that it is running Windows 2000, as are Dell and NASDAQ.

The search can easily make mistakes, but the errors are usually informative. Since the site examines an HTTP reply returned from the server, it could report on a firewall or a load-balancing device. The site might even provide different results from different searches if the company you are researching uses a number of servers.

The analyzer can also be fooled if the site's Transmission Control Protocol (TCP) stack has been modified. Does this give you any ideas?

I have tested the site against known and unknown systems. I've alarmed some system administrators with the results I've received. The administrators uniformly refused to give out any server information or even confirm my results. However, if the data from Netcraft wasn't correct or at least pretty close, I wonder why they got so upset? ◆

Where's the fire(wall)?

By Mary Ann Fitzharris

Your basic line of defense for your network includes a firewall designed to examine and evaluate everything that passes through it. It also includes security policies that define who can access your network and what services will be allowed.

Firewall

A firewall is a method that combines security policies, hardware, and software to protect a network from unauthorized intrusion. Firewalls are usually set up at a high-level gateway (such as your Web site's connection to the Internet), but they can also be set up at lower-level gateways to protect your network internally (e.g., sensitive financial or personnel records). With a firewall, traffic in and out of the network is

selectively restricted. Employees and other authorized users are given access to the Internet, while traffic from the Internet is not allowed into the internal network. A screening router, or packet filter, will block the traffic based on an IP address or a port number. Other firewall techniques include proxy server, network address translation (NAT), and stateful inspection.

Gateway

A gateway is a network point (or node) where traffic flows between a secure network and an unsecure one. Gateways are often used with routers to form a firewall. An application gateway is a kind of proxy where an application forwards specific application traffic through a firewall. A circuit gateway maps data from one circuit to another (for example, a SOCKS server). A dual-homed gateway is a firewall that uses a bastion host.

Bastion host

A bastion host is a computer with two network interfaces, one of which is connected to the unsecure Internet and the other to the enterprise's protected network. The IP routing is disabled to protect the network from illegal entry, so IP traffic must be specifically forwarded to pass through a bastion host. Bastion hosts include specific roles such as Web, mail, DNS, and FTP servers. Sometimes a network administrator will also use a decoy bastion host that is deliberately exposed to potential hackers. The purpose is to both delay and facilitate tracking of attempted break-ins. A bastion host does not share authentication services within the network, so if it is compromised, the network is still secure.

Socket server

A socket is the endpoint in a connection between a client and a server. A socket server is a circuit-level gateway that forwards traffic through a firewall like a generic TCP/IP proxy. It handles all kinds of traffic (telnet, e-mail, HTTP, FTP, etc.) without being aware of the meaning of the data. It either allows or rejects the requested connection based on the destination or user identification.

SOCKS

SOCKS (or socks) is a protocol that a proxy server uses to take requests from someone on the network, accept the requests, and forward them to the Internet. This protocol uses sockets to keep track of individual connections and is supported by major Web browsers.

ACLs / ACEs

Major operating systems use access control lists (ACLs) to determine the traffic that will be allowed into different parts of a network and what privileges that traffic will have. In Windows NT, an ACL is associated with each system object, such as a file directory. Each ACL has one or more access control entries (ACEs) with the name of a user or group of users or roles (such as "programmer" or "tester").

Screened host firewall

A screened host firewall uses a packet-filtering router that allows only traffic that is destined for a gateway to get through. It is more flexible but less secure than a dual-homed gateway firewall (see below). The screened host firewall has one network interface and does not require a subnet between the application gateway and the router. The gateway's proxy passes services to site systems.

Packet-filtering firewall

A packet-filtering firewall blocks traffic at a gateway based on IP address and/or port numbers. It is also known as a "screening router." It blocks unwanted network traffic based either on its source address, destination, or its type (e-mail, FTP, etc.). Packet filtering is generally performed in a router. It is less secure than other forms of firewalls because it is more vulnerable to IP spoofing. It also does not include password controls or logging; nor does it allow for thorough testing. It is most commonly used for small, simple sites.

Dual-homed gateway firewall

The dual-homed gateway is an alternative to packet-filtering router firewalls. It has a host system with two network interfaces. The host's IP forwarding ability is disabled so it cannot route packets between the two connected networks. As a result, it blocks all IP traffic between the Internet and the secure network. It uses proxy servers on the gateway for access and for services like Telnet, FTP, and e-mail. This firewall can log access as well as attempts to intrude into the system. ◆

Vulnerability to security break-ins stays in the spotlight

By Dana Gardner

Security breaches are a top concern for information technology managers. And no wonder—another vulnerability through which an assault can be waged on corporate networks and applications turns up nearly every day. For example:

▸ The Princeton Secure Internet Programming team and Xerox researchers found a bug in Microsoft's Java virtual machine (JVM) inside the popular Internet Explorer 4.0 and 5.0 browser that could allow a hacker to gain control of the Windows systems beneath the browser.

▸ Hotmail, the popular Web-based, Microsoft-hosted e-mail service was shown to be vulnerable to hacking. The breach could allow e-mails to be surreptitiously sent by a hacker under another user's name.

▸ Internet Security Systems Inc. and its research arm, X-Force, found a bug that allows hackers using a buffer overflow technique to gain illicit entry to Netscape Enterprise Server and Netscape FastTrack Server.

▸ International researchers recently broke the security codes used to guard Internet transactions. RSA Data Security Inc. said a network of 292 computers at 11 separate locations took seven months to calculate the two prime factors in a 512-bit encryption key, the highest level allowed for export in the United States.

Security threats continue to grow, the thinking goes, as the global reliance on computers and networked applications skyrockets. "As computer systems start to become integrated, seamless parts of society's infrastructure, the real threat comes from the cyber-terrorists," said a recent report from the London-based Butler Group consultancy.

All is not bleak, however. Some analysts point out that the cost of computing and accessing the Web would not continue to plunge nor would e-commerce be flowering if substantial sums of money, data files, and productivity were lost to hackers.

"The reality is that we're not seeing a lot of break-ins. No one has ever intercepted an Internet transaction en route. This is a perceived problem," said Jeff Tarter, editor and publisher of the Softletter newsletter in Watertown, MA.

"Certainly there are a lot of smart programmers out there trying to break in to anything they can," said Tarter. Most of the time, he said, the hacker, who is proud of his or her accomplishment, first notifies the host of the problem and offers a fix. That was the case with both the recent Microsoft JVM and Netscape server problems.

What are the real threats?

Keeping an eye on the PC-based office files and managing PC access procedures is probably a better way to protect against the biggest threats: theft, disgruntled employees, and slipshod password use.

"The biggest risk to your systems is not a hacker coming in over the network. It's the loss or theft of the laptop computer at the airport," said Scott McNealy, chairman and CEO of Palo Alto, CA-based Sun Micro-systems. "The biggest security risk is the PC hard drive."

Sun is a major proponent of network centric, Unix-centric, Java-centric brand of computing. Sun describes it as safer than other approaches, including Microsoft's Windows NT server and Windows 2000 platforms. Important data is safer on a central server where it can be protected rather than replicated out on thousands of PCs in the field, according to Sun.

Indeed, Java co-author and Sun evangelist James Gosling claimed shortly after a June 10 worm attack disrupted many sites using Microsoft products that such problems are the result of Windows' and Windows NT's structure, and that UNIX, Linux, and Java environments are far more immune to similar threats.

"Those are Windows viruses, not computer viruses," Gosling said.

McNealy added that postal mail offers a far higher security and privacy risk than information passed over networks. "Out in my mailbox, with a thin metal cover, is all this medical record and credit card information secured only by the spit on the envelope," McNealy said.

"If Internet service providers lose your data, they'll go out of business, just like a bank that loses your money would go out of business," said McNealy.

How to protect the enterprise

Security experts say that due diligence—staying alert and working quickly to thwart potential vulnerabilities—is the best defense.

Recent history shows that the weak security links are more often like a chain link fence, with lots of holes to address at once. And it's often the number, not the severity, of the problems that keeps IT manager up at night, observers said.

Common sense and an ability to manage one's own systems form the key. "Inside break-ins and sabotage are far more of a threat than break-ins from the outside over the Internet," said Daniel Morgan, president of EXE Solutions in Seattle, a consulting firm specializing in product installations, database optimization, and security.

"This is common sense stuff. The real problems are not the high-tech ones. It's the easy stuff of taking an employee off the system when they leave the company," said Morgan, adding that a major defense contractor in the Pacific northwest routinely leaves access open to former employees because it can't manage its access and e-mail directories well.

"Making your systems secure is a nuisance, just like having 10 locks on your front door at home," said Tarter of Softletter. "But it works. You just have to do it and lock them when you leave." ◆

Gnutella: Does it have any legal, practical uses?

By Bryan Pfaffenberger

Gnutella is MP3's latest weapon in the war over copyright infringement, and it's directed squarely against the Recording Industry Association of America (RIAA). Napster, an earlier weapon, had a fatal flaw: It forced users to connect through a central server, which created a trail that RIAA could use to find out who downloaded all those copies of Metallica's latest songs. Gnutella, on the other hand, implements server-free file exchanges within heterogeneous networks. Originally under development by AOL (until AOL management realized Gnutella's legal implications and quashed the project), Gnutella bypasses the server completely. Unfortunately, Gnutella's also a bandwidth hog and a security nightmare.

Introducing Gnutella

Nullsoft, the company that developed WinAmp (the most popular MP3 player for Windows), developed Gnutella. AOL, Nullsoft's parent corporation, pulled the plug on Gnutella—but not before a beta version was released onto the Internet. Hackers quickly reverse-engineered the Gnutella protocol. Now, dozens of Gnutella clones exist. Thus, when I talk about Gnutella, I'm referring both to a specific Nullsoft program, which is no longer available, and to a general Gnutella protocol, which is available in the clones.

Since there's no central server on the Gnutella network, no central site exists, either. Gnutella's home on the Web is the closest thing to an "official" site. From this site, you can obtain all of the available Gnutella clients, and you can read the latest news about Gnutella.

Gnutella has no portal—hence AOL's reaction to this rogue project. Instead, users create ephemeral, peer-to-peer networks among other cooperative users. Within these networks, users find, upload, and download different types of files, including MP3 music files. And that's just what thousands of Gnutella users are doing— to RIAA's dismay. Since Gnutella networks appear spontaneously and have no central tracking mechanism or portal, RIAA don't have the ability to shut down Gnutella like they might shut down Napster. There's no portal, no central distribution point, no central anything.

Setting aside Gnutella's illegal uses, it becomes clear that Gnutella is a very creative software idea, one that has quite an interesting history. Gnutella represents the latest skirmish in an old battle between the proponents of network centralization and users who favor decentralized, peer-to-peer systems. Gnutella erases the distinction between a centralized server and a distributed client; everyone who runs Gnutella can potentially run both a server and a client. To make files available to other Gnutella users, you just identify the directory that will be made public to network users. Then, anyone who connects to the network can access and search that directory. Of course, that means that you can search the public directories of anyone who's connected to the network. Furthermore, Gnutella is an inherently cross-platform protocol, and it's cross-platform in a practical sense, too. Now, Gnutella clients are available for all three major platforms: Windows, Linux, and Macintosh.

Is it possible that this highly controversial tool will turn out to have practical applications? Consider the following scenario: You have a small, internal network that consists of Windows, Mac, and Linux boxes. Implementing cross-platform file exchange isn't easy. Of course, you can always run an FTP server, but you'll be stuck with a central distribution point and all of the associated inconveniences. With Gnutella, network users can create public directories, move shared documents to the directories, and create what amounts to a single, searchable directory space in which cross-platform file exchange is simple, easy, reliable, and convenient. To test the possibilities, I set up a Gnutella file-sharing system on my home network, in which Macs, Linux, and Windows boxes live together (and sometimes even work together). Read on to find out what I've learned.

The clients

Among Linux clients, the best of the lot right now is Gnubile, which is available in a variety of downloadable versions (including Red Hat RPMs and tarballs). Gnubile requires GTK+ (but not GNOME), and it's a very impressive client. You can download a copy of Gnubile. Of the several Windows clients that I evaluated, Gnutella 0.56 seems the most stable. It's distributed in a self-extracting archive. The best Macintosh client is Furi. It's a Java-based client, and it requires Apple's Macintosh Java Runtime environment.

Using Gnutella

Once you've installed Gnutella on your network's clients, you'll need to configure each of the clients and make a local directory available publicly. Into this directory, place some document files that you'd like to exchange among the various machines on your network (such as Microsoft Word documents). Now, try launching two or more of your clients and try a cross-platform file exchange with Gnutella. To connect with another Gnutella client, type the client's IP address, followed by a colon and the default Gnutella port (6346). Here's an example:

`192.168.100.10:6346`

When you've added this client's IP address to your list of connections, you'll see the number of files that are available for download. To download a file, you must search for it. With current versions of Gnutella, you can't view all of the files in a user's public directory; however, this feature probably will be included in future versions of Gnutella.

Searching for files with Gnutella

To search for files in the database of public directories, type a substring to match. For example, to search for all available Microsoft Word documents, type *doc* in the search box. You'll see all of the available files that contain the specified search string. To download one or more of the files, select the files and click the Download button. By default, the downloaded files go to the default download directory, which is one of the Gnutella configuration options. To create more focused searches, you can type more than one search word. By default, Gnutella combines all of the words that you type with the AND operator. Thus, you'll see only those documents that contain all of the search words that you typed. Gnutella doesn't support wildcard searches.

Transparent, cross-platform file exchange

So, how does Gnutella work in a cross-platform network? Brilliantly! Without needing to set up Samba, NFS, or Netatalk, you can implement three-platform file sharing in a matter of minutes. Furthermore, Gnutella provides the only current method of implementing two-way file exchange between Mac and Windows clients without resorting to FTP or to pricey, commercial software. If you tried Netatalk, you probably noticed that your Mac users could access Linux directories but that they couldn't exchange files with Windows users directly. Similarly, Linux users can't access files on Macs unless you're willing to run FTP servers all over the place or to resort to commercial software. On a cross-platform network, Gnutella fills in the gaps in the free software file-exchange picture, and it does so with ease and transparency.

Since Gnutella is an Internet protocol, you might be able to extend file sharing beyond the confines of your LAN; theoretically, you could bring in users who work in branch offices, or you could contact traveling employees who are using notebooks in hotel rooms. Of course, you'd have to accept the risks that come with using Gnutella over Internet.

The drawbacks: Security, legality, and privacy

Just how safe is Gnutella? Let me be as clear as possible. If your LAN is connected to the Internet, it isn't wise to run Gnutella. Your TCP port will be wide open. Although there's no known exploit at the time of this writing, sooner or later somebody is going to figure out how to push one of the Gnutella clients into a buffer overflow. Then, the intruder will obtain access to all of your files (not just the ones that you've made public). This type of exploit has occurred with some of the Napster clones, so the danger is very real.

Of course, we must admit that almost everyone who uses Gnutella uses it for illegal purposes, such as exchanging copyrighted MP3s, pirated software, or pornography. If you install Gnutella on your systems and tell your users how to use the software for internal file exchange purposes, it's only a matter of time before they realize what else is out there. Sure, there's plenty of unethical stuff on the Web, too, but Web users are aware (let's hope) that their actions on the Web can be traced very easily. Many Gnutella users believe that they can use Gnutella networks with anonymity, but they're mistaken.

Gnutella may be decentralized, but it certainly isn't private. When you download a file from somebody else's Gnutella directory, you leave your IP address behind—as a number of unfortunate users have discovered already, to their dismay. ZeroPaid.com recently published a Wall of Shame, which listed the IP addresses of Gnutella users who had attempted to access what appeared to be child pornography images from a secret Gnutella server. The site's author, known only as The Cleaner, makes a good point: Gnutella is fine for data sharing, but anyone who attempts to access child pornography through GnutellaNet is going to be exposed eventually. It doesn't take much imagination to envision future sting operations: Law enforcement agencies will run Gnutella servers in an effort to entrap would-be criminals. In short, Gnutella doesn't give users any more privacy than other means of Internet file exchange do.

There's a bandwidth problem, too. Gnutella's search architecture is innovative, but it isn't scalable—at least, not in its current form. As clients connect with each another, a Gnutella network forms. Eventually, thousands of clients will be able to pool their resources. As the network grows larger, searches take longer and longer to execute. Finally, searches will take so long that they're hardly worth attempting. Various solutions to this problem have been proposed, but the solutions would be difficult to implement without some type of central server architecture. And of course, that's just what Gnutella seeks to avoid.

You also ought to consider what might happen to your network bandwidth if some of your users ignored your advice and started exchanging MP3 files with their Internet buddies. Two or more Gnutella connections can bog down an Internet connection pretty quickly. A dozen of them could shut down your network—unless you're blessed with a high-speed connection.

Conclusion

Gnutella is so genuinely innovative that it's definitely worth a look. It's clear that something like Gnutella would have distinct advantages for cross-platform file exchange among an organization's computer users. What's less clear is whether or not Gnutella could be used safely in an Internet-connected LAN. If your network is connected to the Internet only occasionally and your network is secured by a firewall and a dynamically assigned IP address, Gnutella might be an acceptable means of getting Mac, Windows, and Linux systems to exchange files with a minimum of effort on your part. ◆

Basic principles of network security, part 1: How to stop an intruder

By Chris Dinsmore

For years the cracker credo has been "Information wants to be free." Your company, however, has different ideas about the freedom of its information. Crackers want your information; you don't want them to have it. They have the initiative, and they have the element of surprise. They choose when and how to attack. This puts you on the defensive, which, in turn, puts you at a disadvantage. You'll need to design a security architecture to defend against an enemy with the advantages of initiative and surprise.

This is part one of a series of Daily Drill Downs that take you on a step-by-step tour through the principles of network security. I'll review the security aspects of major operating systems and networking platforms. You will be presented with a comprehensive list of security resources and a good understanding of your options.

I work for a company that produces, sells, and supports network security software, including some of the products that I will speak about. However, I will not make a recommendation that I cannot support. That being said, let's begin.

Planning a security policy

There are four phases in any security project: planning, design, implementation, and enforcement. This Daily Drill Down covers planning a security project and designing a security architecture for your company. I will cover implementation and enforcement in future articles.

The first, and most important, principle in security of any kind is to have a well-defined security policy. To develop a policy, you need to answer these two questions:

1. What constitutes a well-defined security policy?

2. How can I make a security policy without understanding the threats against me?

What is a good Security policy?

A well-defined security policy outlines your requirements and limits your exposure to risk. There are three criteria for creating or evaluating a policy for information security.

1. **Confidentiality:** Your information must be kept private. Unauthorized access must be prevented.

2. **Integrity:** Your information must be protected from tampering. It cannot be modified from its original form without your authorization.

3. **Availability:** Your information must be available to authorized users when they need it.

On your network you probably have a file server, a Web server, a mail server, and an FTP server that have to be accessible from the outside world. You also probably have users needing access to the World Wide Web, their own home e-mail, and maybe some FTP servers. If your network is anything like mine, your users also want ICQ, AOL, PointCast, RealAudio, chat rooms, and other capabilities they don't necessarily need. All of these features may open security holes. And if you are like most employers, you will want to stop all of those services. When designing your security policy, you must balance the wants and needs of your users with the amount of security you want to provide for your network.

Let's say you also have two confidential databases: a credit card database and HR records. No one who isn't supposed to get in should be able to get in, and no one should be able to send out information that shouldn't be sent out.

Now you have your basic requirements for a security policy.

▸ Internal users must be able to share files and access your file server.

▸ Billing users must be allowed to access your credit card database.

▸ HR users must be allowed to access your HR records.

▸ Internal users must be able to access Web sites (HTTP).

▸ Internal users must be able to access FTP sites.

▸ Internal users must be able to access e-mail (POP3, IMAP, SMTP).

- You must be able to exchange mail with the outside world (POP3, IMAP, SMTP).

- External users must be able to access your Web site (HTTP).

- External users must be able to transfer files to you (FTP).

- No users, internal or external, should have access to any other services.

Remember, your security policy determines what you need, not how you are going to get it done. Don't confuse a security policy with a security plan. When you create your security policy, specify what your policy should cover, not how you are going to use it to reach your objectives.

The second question we need to answer in order to make a good security policy, "How can I make a security policy without understanding the threats against me?" suggests the second most important principle of security: That which is not explicitly allowed, is explicitly denied.

That which is not explicitly allowed, is explicitly denied

This principle means that focusing on threats is counterproductive. A properly defined security policy should not allow anything except what is necessary for your business to function. Obviously, if something is necessary for your business to function it should not be hindered. Believe me, you'll have plenty of time to worry about the threats when you get to the implementation phase.

Defense in depth

Think about how government facilities are usually secured. First, you have to go through a gate with a security guard to get into the parking lot. Then, you have to get in the main door, where you'll see another guard or a keypad or card reader or some other security device. To get to the office you are trying to reach, you'll find another guard, card reader, or keypad. To get to your office, you'll pass coworkers who note that you are there. Finally, to get your information, you have to log on to your system using a password. That is defense in depth. It can be expressed in a single sentence: Never trust a single means of protection when multiple means of protection are available.

All systems have their vulnerabilities. Every fence has small holes, every wall has chinks, and every piece of software has bugs. If you depend on any single means of defense, someone will find the bugs or holes in your defense and get through. You can't stop all attacks, from all attackers, at all times.

So what do you do? You certainly don't give up and say, "Here, all my information is free for the taking."

Implementing security architecture: firewalls

Once you've devised a well-defined security policy, it's up to you to design a security architecture, keeping your security policy in mind and using the principle of defense in depth.

Your first line of defense is network access control. Network access control means the process of not allowing unauthorized users or services inside of your network. The most common method of achieving this is with a firewall.

Firewalls refer to barriers erected between a source of fire and what needs to be protected. Your car has a firewall between the engine and the passengers. Internet firewalls (or any other network access control devices) are barriers between all outside traffic and your network. Only traffic you explicitly allow can enter or exit your network. You set up rules on the firewall to control network access. There are dozens of security models that these rules can follow; the most common ones are user authentication, source control, destination control, and protocol control.

User authentication

User authentication means that only authorized persons or groups, presumably using user names and passwords, can gain access through the firewall. It is, in theory, the most secure way of restricting access to information. All network-enabled operating systems, from Windows 3.11 to the OS used on Cray supercomputers, employ a user authentication security model.

There are advantages and disadvantages to this method. An advantage is that, should someone walk into your office and sit down at your computer, that person can't just pretend to be you. Unfortunately, though all network access control solutions allow user authentication, very few do it well. This is especially true when there are hundreds or thousands of users involved.

User authentication has the added complication of not being transparent. Users have to remember a username and password to access the network. And if they have to remember a password, you can bet someone will write it down or lose it. Someone with malicious intent can guess a password.

Source control

Source control restricts access to information to sources that are trusted (e.g., a certain computer, network, or domain). Often this method is known as Trusted Host or Domain Model security. Along with user authentication, this type of control is the basic security model followed by UNIX and Windows NT. Source control ensures that only those computers that should be accessing information are.

When using source control, you don't have any passwords to remember, and you are never prompted to enter any information. This security model is transparent to the user. The problem with this model involves identifying the trusted source. The most common method of identification is via an IP address. However, IP addresses are easily falsified (called spoofing). In addition, many networks use DHCP, which makes it impossible to ensure the IP addresses of a client remain the same.

Identifying sources via other means is possible. Some vendors are now using cookies, and others are using proprietary hardware to ensure that the host gains access. But as of now, no one has found a method that can't be faked.

Destination control

Destination control restricts access to information to destinations that are trusted (again, usually a computer, network, or domain). This security method has similar advantages to using source control. Destination control, like source control, is transparent to the user and requires little or no administration. In addition, there is almost no security risk in allowing traffic through your firewall to the Internet. Destination control is also very good at preventing all access to particular computers or networks.

Problems arise when using this model for access to your internal network. It is possible for the identity of one of your servers to be

spoofed, and information destined for those systems can be redirected. It can also be difficult to restrict access to just a few users if destination control is applied. Destination control also leaves you open for what are known as denial of service (DoS) attacks.

A DoS attack occurs when someone floods your network link, fills up your storage, or sends malformed or malicious information to your servers to try to make them crash, interrupting service for a period of time. This method is considered an attack against the third security criteria—availability.

Denial of service is the most common attack used against public Web and mail servers because, by definition, these servers grant access to anyone. This method is easy for inexperienced attackers to try, but it can be hard to stop without out a network access control device.

Protocol control

Protocol control means that access to information is restricted to particular protocols (i.e., HTTP, FTP, or SMTP), no matter what the source or destination. This is the security model most often used by routers, packet filters, and anonymous public servers of all types. It is very useful for blocking all traffic you know you won't use. For example, if you run an all Solaris network, you won't need NetBIOS (Microsoft Networking) information going through your routers. To prevent NetBIOS authentication from the outside world, you would block TCP port 139.

This method of control is especially useful for Web servers, proxy servers, and any network devices that may be only a hop along a network route. Since you may not know the original source, final destination, or user accessing the information, the only thing left for you to control might be the protocol.

Each of these security models—user authentication, source control, destination control, and protocol control—offers little or no security on its own. The models are nearly always used in concert with each other to provide more complete control.

Let's say that to our all-UNIX network, we added a few Windows NT servers outside the firewall and a few Windows 95 clients inside the firewall. You would need to allow NetBIOS traffic between the NT servers and the 95 clients, but you wouldn't want to allow any NetBIOS traffic from the rest of the Internet to those internal machines. In this case, you would combine controls. Source control would allow communications into the firewall from your NT servers; destination control would restrict that traffic to only the Win95 systems; and protocol control would limit those communications to NetBIOS.

If firewalls don't use source, destination, and protocol control, then they aren't really being used as firewalls, just as packet filters. Most commercial firewalls also include some user authentication and management ability. Unfortunately, most of the freeware or open source firewalls do not because they are intended for use with operating systems that already implement strong user authentication, such as the various UNIX and Linux systems. Windows NT has reasonable, though not great, password protection. Windows 9x, on the other hand, has essentially none. Should user authentication be required, you cannot depend on that OS.

We will discuss choosing and configuring a firewall in "Basic principles of network security, part 4: Getting your network security system started and keeping it going."

Security behind the firewall— they will get in

It is easy to assume that once you have a firewall in place your network is protected. But remember, a firewall cannot protect a network from internal attacks, attacks from segments not behind a firewall but still attached to your network (such as the dialup access server), or attacks from authorized users with malicious intent (such as disgruntled employees).

Also remember my cardinal rule: They will get in. I can't stress that rule enough. Common sense says that you can't prevent a dedicated thief from stealing your car, but for some reason people insist that the same principle does not apply to your data. Believe me, it does.

It's your responsibility to ensure that attackers do the least amount of damage. There are more ways to do this than I could possibly cover in a single article, but we'll look at several options, organizing them by how they relate to our three criteria for information security—confidentiality, integrity, and availibility.

Ensuring confidentiality

How do you keep your files private once someone has accessed your network? I highly recommend using different methods of access control for important internal resources. For example, use a different username and password for sensitive documents. You may also want to use some type of third-party access control system such as SecureID.

Encryption is another method of ensuring confidentiality. It certainly reduces the impact of an intrusion if important information is unreadable by the intruder. It isn't within the scope of this article to discuss the specifics of all the available encryption packages, but I recommend you choose a package that make use of an open encryption algorithm that has been subject to extensive peer review and testing.

Many companies claim their proprietary encryption methods are more secure because they are secret. To put it bluntly, they're lying. Anyone who tells you this should be dropped from consideration immediately. This method is most often known as security through obscurity, and anyone who knows security can tell you it doesn't work.

Ensuring integrity

Though information integrity is difficult to ensure, in many ways it can be more important than confidentiality. How can you be sure your files haven't been altered without authorization when a skilled intruder could alter your data and remove all traces of the intrusion?

Encryption can help ensure data integrity. In addition to keeping your data secret, encryption systems generally include the ability to add a digital signature. Digital signatures place a unique numeric "stamp" on a file. If the file is edited after the signature has been written, the signature is no longer valid and you will know the file has been tampered with.

Most encryption systems use a checksum, a special number that is generated based on the contents of a file, for verification. If you change the contents of a file, the checksum will no longer be correct, and the file cannot be decoded properly. True, that means that you can't get at the data, but if the data has been altered, it's not useful to you anymore. Most importantly, you now know that someone has been doing things they shouldn't be allowed to do.

Another method to ensure data integrity is to use an intrusion detection system (IDS). These systems work though a combination of check-sums, digital signatures, file system cataloging, and enhanced logging. I'm going to make one product recommendation despite my rule not to; I strongly recommend Tripwire. It is quite simply the most comprehensive and effective intrusion detection system available, and it is the only package that I recommend. It is also one of the few IDS packages available for Windows NT.

No intrusion detection systems are foolproof. For example, they aren't effective for data that changes regularly because they work by compar-ing a file's current state to a known, secure state. But IDS packages provide an additional measure of security that can't be discounted.

Ensuring availability

An intruder stopped by your security measures may become annoyed. A possible reaction would be to deny you access to your own information, perhaps through a denial of service attack. The intruder could crash your servers or flood your network with so much traffic that no one could get through. In light of this scenario, the three most important things you can do to ensure information availability are:

1. **Keep complete and current backups.**
   Without a complete, current backup you can't recover from an intrusion or any other disaster. In addition to your standard back-ups, which you should perform nightly, keep a weekly complete backup stored offsite to protect you in case of a facilities intrusion or an accident. All the tape backups in the world won't do you any good if they are stored in a building that burned to the ground.

2. **Have no single point of failure.**
   When equipment fails—whether a firewall, server, or network link—a backup system needs to be ready to take over, preferably without any intervention and without users noticing.

3. **Ensure physical security.**
   Without physical security, nothing else you do matters.

Some cases can help illustrate the need for physical security. In one case, a virtually impenetrable network that used multiple layers of access control, intrusion detection, and live network monitoring at all times was breached. Unfortunately, the servers were kept in a closet in a public area. Someone walked right in and stole several servers, which had the company's intellectual property stored unencrypted on their hard drives, and trashed the remaining servers.

In another case, a building had excellent physical security, limited access, and a secure server room. Unfortunately, the fiber cables coming out of the building ran through an underground conduit in a wooded area. Some-one found an access panel to the conduit and inserted a fiber tap, making it possible to mon-itor all the traffic between the company's main office and their branch offices that went over the secure frame relay network provided by their telco.

Remember: your information is a significant asset to your company. That information needs to be as well protected as your payroll deposits.

Conclusion

The most important aspects of any security proj-ect are having a good plan and having a good design. Here's what you need to remember about planning and designing a security project:

1. Create a well-defined security policy, keeping in mind the principles of confidentiality, integrity, and availability. That which is not explicitly allowed, is explicitly denied.

2. Design a security architecture based on the principle of defense in depth because, no matter what you do, hackers will get through.

3. To create defense in depth: Implement Net-work Access Control with user authentica-tion, source control, destination contro,l and protocol control.

4. Keep complete and current backups.

5. Ensure that there is no single point of failure.

6. Ensure that there is physical security.

Once you understand these points, you will be ready to go on to the next phase and implement your secure network. ◆

Basic principles of network security, part 2: Winning the hearts and minds

By Chris Dinsmore

Have you ever been arrested? Do you know what that's like? Well, first they spin you around and push you up against the wall. Then, they handcuff you, read you your rights, and charge you. They take you down to the station and book you, during which time you are just another number. They fingerprint you, throw you in a cell with nothing to do, and generally ruin your day.

Guess what?

That's how your users are going to feel when you introduce your new security policy. Sure, it may seem like a great idea to you—everything secure, no information going anywhere without permission, everyone authorized and identified—but to your users it's just another thing getting in the way of their jobs, especially if your users are smart and computer literate.

Your worst nightmare

What's the biggest nightmare for a security administrator? His or her own users—if they happen to be UNIX programmers. These people think it's fun to take systems apart and put them back together in ways that you don't even recognize. Believe me, I know; I'm one of them. Security admins are always trying to take away my cool stuff. Like that password-cracking utility I used one weekend to get root on all the local servers when I couldn't be bothered to find the admin. Or that server exploit that lets me remotely control my desktop through the firewall in case I need any files while I'm at home. Now, do you see what I mean about your worst nightmare?

Here's a situation for you. You've just defined the perfect security policy. Nobody in to the network but the admin, nobody out except for e-mail and surfing. Then, over golf one day, somebody tells the CEO how great pcAnywhere is and how he should have it installed so that he can look at his files from home. The CEO thinks it's a great idea and immediately orders all the executives to get pcAnywhere installed on all of their systems, especially their laptops. That way, anybody can get files for and from anybody, anytime, anywhere. After all, it's encrypted, and it will make the sales force a lot more productive.

Then, your CEO's laptop gets stolen. He kept a list of all his passwords on that laptop. (He's always been a little absentminded.) Of course, a few months ago, he asked you to set it up so that his programs remembered all his passwords and he wouldn't have to log in. Oh, and he didn't tell you that the laptop was stolen for two weeks because he was in the Cayman Islands on vacation. Now, you *really* see what I mean about your worst nightmare.

Both of these situations are real, and they happen in companies large and small every day. You may have seen on the news a few months ago that an intelligence agent had some top-secret government files stolen from him. He had apparently left them on the backseat of his car while he was having dinner, and some thieves smashed his window and took all of his belongings. They probably weren't looking for the papers, but who knows? You have to remember that anything can happen. Nothing is impossible—improbable, but not impossible.

Creating a security-conscious environment

I do have a point here. I'm convinced that the only way to help prevent situations like this—and especially to prevent that "imprisoned" feeling that can accompany a major security project—is to create a security-conscious environment.

In "How to stop an intruder: Basic principles of network security, part 1," we discussed developing a well-defined security policy and examined several of the important concepts in creating your defensive strategy. Now, we'll look at what's probably the hardest part (or at least the easiest to screw up): putting it all together and implementing your security project. You have a great security policy and a strategy of defense; now, you need to implement it, putting everything—and everyone—into place to ensure that your information remains secure.

As I said, I think the most important step, and the one that most people miss when implementing a security project, is to create a security-conscious environment first. What that involves is getting your users to think about security. We don't want everyone to be paranoid, walking around like a bad *X-Files* episode; that's just bad for business. What we want is for your users, and especially your management, to understand just how critical security is to your mission, to your business, and to your company. Intelligence agents have a term for this concept. They call it Winning the Hearts and Minds.

I'll be the first to admit that it's a heck of a lot easier said than done—especially here in America, where we don't take kindly to restrictions on what we can do or say. Unfortunately, that's a lot of what information security is all about. Americans as a whole are pretty likely to go and do exactly what you told them not to do, just to show you who's really in charge.

Getting management buy-in

So, how do you deal with all these ideas? What you really need to do before anything gets off the ground is to get *100 percent management buy-in*. And when I say 100 percent, I mean it. If your users find out that their bosses can get e-mail from home and that they can't, you're going to have a riot on your hands. Your security policy has to apply equally to everyone—from the CEO to the office gopher.

But it goes a lot deeper than that. From moment one, you need to involve your company's strategic decision-makers. Help them develop a personal interest in this project and an understanding of what it means to the company as a whole. Remember to keep everything documented in plain English and be ready to explain everything that you are planning or doing. Hold regular meetings to go over the planning and progress of the company and invite anyone who's interested to attend. I know that massive meetings are a pain, but you can ask users to limit their input until you finish your presentation. And by all means, take whatever they have to say to heart. If you don't, they won't follow the policies that you have carefully planned.

And don't forget the other IT staff. If you work for a big company, there's nearly a 100 percent chance that everything you do as a security administrator is going to be cutting across a *lot* of other admin types' territories. Trust me, these people can be your greatest allies—or your worst enemies. You need to have them personally involved every step of the way, or you'll never complete the project. It's going to be difficult for you if you can't convince the server admin to give you the machines that you need in order to set up firewalls and security analyzers. It will be even harder if the router admin won't set up routes to your machines. Treat these people as a vital part of your team, even if "officially" they aren't.

Involving your users

Now that your back is covered with management when something goes wrong and the executive suite isn't going to cry in alarm when you make them remember passwords, what's next?

(Cue scary music.)

Users.

That's right. We mean all those people who actually do the work from which your company derives its revenue. No matter how important you think you are to the company, it's your users who do the work, get the sales, and put the money in the bank. Don't fall into the standard administrative traps. Every time I hear so-called administrators call a user a "luser," I want to smack them. (Read Tuxedo.org's Jargon File Resources if you don't know what I'm talking about…or even if you do. It's hilarious.)

Security people have this annoying tendency of forgetting that there's no point in making the network perfectly secure if it means that your users can't get their work done. Users, on the other hand, tend to look at any inconvenience or change in the way that they work as a prime example of the electronic equivalent of bloody murder. Somewhere, somehow, you need to meet your users in the middle.

Here's how to do it: As you start planning your security project, send an e-mail to the entire company (or whatever division you are responsible for) and ask users to list all the programs that they use and which sites they visit. This list serves three purposes. First, it involves users in the process, making them feel like they have a stake in the results. Second, it helps prevent users from getting angry when you turn on the firewall because you already know what protocols and destinations they need. Third, it gives you a written record. That way, when users start screaming at you because you broke their programs, you can say to them, "But you never mentioned it when I asked what people used." Then, piously show them the e-mail with their names and say, "I don't need anything but e-mail and Web surfing."

Let me tell you, folks, nothing calms angry users more than the realization that they did something slightly dumb and you have proof. This answer is usually followed by the user going away and not bothering you again. It can be a highly desirable thing—as long as the angry, embarrassed user isn't the aforementioned CEO, of course. But seriously, it's very important to understand the needs of your user community before you begin.

Keeping everyone informed

We've covered the first steps in building a security-conscious environment: getting management buy-in and getting the users involved. The next step is *keeping everyone informed*.

Sticking to this policy helps to keep the users involved, giving them an ongoing interest in the project. Distribute regular status updates, in plain English, and a basic outline of the configuration. It helps the users visualize how their information moves from one part of the network to the other. In fact, you'd really be surprised how much a little simple architecture information can reduce your other calls. It helps users figure things out on their own, and they won't feel lost all the time.

But don't just keep users informed about your own project; distribute security e-mails with information about how users can become more secure on their own and in their homes. Send out regular notices about patches and hot fixes. And of course, make sure that people are conscious of things like the last update on their virus scanners.

Training your users

The final and most important step of user prep is also the hardest, the most time-consuming, and usually the most expensive. If you want your project to be a success, you absolutely must train your users thoroughly.

If your users don't know the proper use of the security facilities that you are setting up, not only will they pose a security risk, but they also will get frustrated and angry. They may not be able to get their work done at all, in which case they will either take their aggressions out on

you, find a way around the security (or rip a hole straight through it), or both—possibly at the same time, using heavy weaponry.

A colleague of mine recently implemented a token-based user authentication scheme. He set up the servers and mailed out the key fob tokens that give you your passcode, along with an instruction sheet, and he sent an e-mail the day before the changeover with what he thought were thorough instructions for how to log in to the new system. Within three hours of the cutover, about two-thirds of the company—including the CEO, CFO, and my colleague's supervisor—had disabled their own accounts by trying to log in improperly. He forgot one of the most basic principles of learning: People don't remember what they read; they remember what they do. If he had taken a few more weeks with the project and held ten-minute classes on the new login procedure with a few employees each day, he could have avoided most of that trouble.

It's very important to understand that people retain only about 20 percent of what they read and 30 percent of what they hear. On the other hand, studies show that people retain about 60 percent of what they do and up to 80 percent of what they do and review a few times. (It's too bad that we can't teach by smell because people apparently have a 90 percent retention rate for odors.)

My recommendation is to hold regular classroom-style sessions for a few employees at a time over a period of a few months. If you can, set the schedules so that people who work directly together get staggered instruction. That way, just as one person is starting to forget the material, his or her co-worker is learning and talking about it. Then, when you're ready to go live with the project, hold short review sessions to refresh everyone's memories. Trust me, all the time you spend training your users before the system is in place will keep you from spending three times as long fixing the issues that you could have avoided if you had provided good training in the first place.

Wrapping up

So, what have we covered? First, you need to create a security-conscious environment by getting 100 percent management buy-in and by getting your users involved. Remember that in order to keep your users happy, your security policy needs to apply equally to everyone, with *no* exceptions. Finally, you need to keep everyone informed and train your users thoroughly to gain their help in making this project successful.

In the following article, we'll discuss the actual hardware, software, and wetware (people) that are involved in setting up a security project. ◆

Basic principles of network security, part 3: Stop the fire from spreading

By Chris Dinsmore

In part 1 and part 2 of this series, I've dealt with information security at the intellectual level—defining a policy, planning a general structure, obtaining management involvement, and preparing our users. Now, it's time to get physical.

At this point, you need to determine your specific needs and find the best security solutions for your project. In this Daily Drill Down, I'll cover some hardware and software options and tell you how to wade through them and decide what's best for your project.

What do you need?

Once again, before I get into the details, I'm going to make my full disclosure disclaimer. I work for a company that sells, services, and supports some of the products about which I'll be talking. I promise that I'll always give you my unbiased opinion, and I'll back up any statements I make.

To a large extent, your security policy defines the products that you should purchase. To keep unauthorized external users out, you need some type of firewall system. To keep unauthorized internal users away from sensitive information, you need some type of user access control system. To allow some users here, some there, and some everywhere, you need some type of user management. And of course, if you have multiple locations and/or remote users, you probably need some type of encryption or VPN capability, as well. Within this broad specification, a lot of options are available. There are three major types of firewalls—some of which have user management and access control functionality—from over ten major and dozens of minor vendors. Let's go over some of our options.

Firewalls

A firewall keeps the outside world (Internet) out and the inside world in, but it allows for information exchange between the two, based on a structured set of rules.

There are three major categories of firewall: packet filters, application layer gateways, and stateful inspection firewalls. We'll examine each category.

Packet filters

Packet filters block the passage of information from one side of the firewall to the other by looking at the header of every packet and matching it against a set of simple rules. Essentially a router with security features, packet filters usually can control information flow by protocol, port, source, and destination, and they have little or no authentication, user access control, or user management functionality. Some packet filters have VPN and encryption functionality; however, that functionality is usually very basic and not compatible with systems provided by other vendors.

Packet filter firewalls have a few distinct advantages. Hardware-based packet filters are generally the fastest of all security platforms, having little effect on your network's performance. Packet filters are generally the most stable firewalls. Also, most packet filters are easy to configure and maintain. Although no security platform is "plug and play," hardware packet filters come pretty close to it. Packet filters are often the least expensive security platforms, too.

Unfortunately, packet filters are considered the least secure of the major firewall types because they offer little protection against advanced attacks and have limited features for handling users, custom protocols, remote management, and other options provided by other firewalls. Since packet filters monitor only the network layer, they are highly susceptible to IP spoofing, denial-of-service attacks based on malformed packets (like the "ping of death"), and SYN flood attacks.

Packet filter type firewalls would be typified by the Cisco PIX series of dedicated hardware security platforms and the various security modules for switches and routers. Software-based packet filtering is available for all major network operating systems at little or no cost. IPChains, FW, and the majority of the available firewall software for the Free UNIX-based operating systems (for example, FreeBSD and Linux) fall into this category, though they offer some of the additional functionality of the other two types of firewall.

Application layer gateways

Also known as secure proxies, application layer gateway firewalls are software based and run on general-purpose hardware with popular network operating systems. They are the most common type of firewall, and vendors offer dozens of options.

No generic set of features or functionality exists with an application layer gateway. However, the general market trends show that the more features you have, the more expensive the software gets. Software can range in cost from free to upwards of $30,000, depending on the feature sets and the scale of your installation.

Basic application layer gateway software is available for all popular network operating systems at little or no cost. This basic software doesn't include any support for encryption, remote management, user management, or the features that other firewalls provide. Microsoft Proxy, Black Ice, SSQUID, and several of the freeware UNIX-based firewalls fall into this category.

Advanced application layer gateway software, on the other hand, provides significant additional functionality. It may natively support streaming media protocols, such as RealAudio, and it may be able to provide Web and e-mail proxy services. Typically, user management will be integrated, and encryption and VPN functionality are often available. BorderWare, Axent Eagle (formerly Raptor), and NAI Gauntlet are good examples of advanced application layer gateways.

Application layer gateways offer several advantages over packet filters. A packet filter is only able to enforce rules based on network layer information, such as protocol, port, source, and destination. Since application layer gateways are able to view the contents of a packet, they have a much greater level of control. For example, they can filter Web sites based on content or scan e-mail for viruses. The application layer gateway also can provide enhanced logging services over a packet filter, even to the point of logging network usage per user and logging the Web sites that the user visited.

Unfortunately, these gateways have some disadvantages. In a proxy-based architecture, packets are transported up the network stack, through the kernel, and up into user space. The software then processes the information and sends it back down the network stack. As a result, this type of firewall depends heavily on OS stability, performance, processor utilization, memory, and hard drive speed. It becomes a bigger issue when encryption is involved because encryption adds a large amount of processing overhead. Also, application layer gateways provide no protection against common network layer denial of service or teardrop attacks.

There is an additional disadvantage: A lot more configuration is required on the part of administrators. Since it's a proxy server, all of your users' systems have to be reconfigured to use it for proxy services. Since many applications don't support proxy connections, you must either change applications or open up holes in your firewall to use those applications.

Stateful inspection firewalls

The final type of firewall—and the type that I consider the most secure and the most versatile—is the stateful inspection firewall. This type of firewall provides most of the functionality of packet filters and application layer gateways combined. And stateful inspection firewalls have an additional advantage: They keep information about the state of network connections through them in what is called a state table.

A properly designed stateful inspection firewall operates in an entirely different way from the other two types of firewalls. It's a little difficult to explain, but I'm going to oversimplify it so that you won't have to wade through a 30-page explanation of how stateful inspection works.

Let me try to illustrate it. Say that Bob enters a URL and requests a page from a Web site. A stateful inspection firewall records that Bob's computer has requested a particular file from www.techrepublic.com. It stores this information in a state table and waits for the Web site to respond. Then, when www.techrepublic.com sends the page in response, the firewall will allow it in and forward it to Bob's computer.

To allow this exchange to take place with other types of firewalls, you'd need to make a rule allowing Bob to send out an HTTP request and another rule to allow HTTP responses in to Bob. Since a stateful inspection firewall knows to let the response back in, you don't need to open up an incoming response port.

It may not seem like a very big deal when you're dealing with HTTP, but change that protocol to Telnet, and you have an entirely different picture.

So, how does it work? To explain this question, I'll have to go into a little operating system structure. Bear with me. I'm going to use an explanation that's specific to a particular product, which I usually don't like to do.

CheckPoint FireWall-1 is the leading stateful inspection firewall in the world, with nearly a 100 percent market share. It's considered the industry standard for this class of firewall. And more important, its architecture allows me to illustrate this type of firewall.

In most operating systems, you have a kernel, which is the most highly protected set of processes in your computer. First, the kernel, which operates with the highest priority, is assigned resources. The kernel controls all the other processes, and they interface with it in some way. The kernel also interfaces with your hardware through programs called device drivers.

In the case of an OS that's specifically designed for networking (both UNIX and NT qualify), there is a process called a *network wrapper*, which sits in between the kernel and the device driver for your network interfaces. The network wrapper controls communications between the networking subsystem and the rest of the operating system, and it contains the network protocol stacks and the IP forwarding subsystem for routing.

FireWall-1 modifies this model, with a shim in between the network drivers, the network wrapper, and the kernel. This shim drops, rejects, or accepts packets, providing basic packet filtering services without using a significant amount of the operating system's resources. This shim also interfaces with other processes providing such services as encryption, user management, logging, bandwidth management, load balancing, and high availability.

The advantage to this modification, in addition to performance benefits, is that packets are dropped before they have a chance to take advantage of any bugs in the network stack or core operating system. Those network-based attacks I called vulnerabilities of proxies don't affect this type of firewall. A stateful inspection firewall has much of the stability and speed of a packet filter. Also, since the stateful inspection firewall architecture provides services above the network layer, it can do some of what a proxy firewall can do.

Stateful inspection firewalls have some disadvantages. First, although they are faster than application layer gateways, they don't provide all the speed of a packet filter. And like proxy firewalls, they depend heavily on the stability of the underlying operating system.

Stateful inspection firewalls also don't provide the same proxy services that application layer gateways do. If you have applications that require or work best with proxy services (Real-Audio, for example), you won't be able to do the same things.

Finally, stateful inspection firewalls are complicated and difficult to program, debug, maintain, patch, and configure. Consequently, they tend to be the most expensive firewall systems, both in software cost and in administrative training.

A typical stateful inspection firewall configuration will start at $10,000 and can extend into the hundreds of thousands of dollars, whereas a packet filter will generally max out at $20,000 and an application layer gateway at $30,000. Even more importantly, an experienced and certified firewall engineer for one of these firewalls is paid upwards of $75,000 a year.

Several options are available for administrators who want stateful inspection firewalls. As I mentioned earlier, the market leader for stateful inspection firewalls is CheckPoint software's FireWall-1 series of products. FireWall-1 is available for NT, the popular UNIX operating systems, and soon will become available for Linux. FireWall-1 also provides a very interesting additional function: Client VPN. Through a program called SecuRemote, FireWall-1 can provide a fully encrypted VPN between your firewall and all your remote users.

Nokia provides a dedicated high-performance hardware platform by using FireWall-1 stateful inspection architecture and a specially hardened BSD-based operating system that has been optimized for stability and high availability. As an alternative, NetGuard Guardian firewalls provide stateful inspection through an architecture that's similar to that of FireWall-1 but at a significantly lower cost—though without many of the extra features.

There are also several firewalls that provide stateful inspection. The latest generation of high-end Cisco PIX firewalls, Axent Eagle and NAI Gauntlet firewalls, and the free FW firewall for BSD provide some level of stateful inspection, as do several other products coming to market now.

What a firewall CAN do

A firewall is your first line of defense against the outside world. A properly implemented firewall, enforcing a comprehensive security policy on a secure network with cooperative users, can protect your network from unauthorized users who try to access it via the Internet.

Just as critical as protecting your network from the outside world, a firewall can protect your company's confidential information from unauthorized users *inside* your network. Preventing your programmers from changing their salaries may be as important to you as preventing a hacker from altering your Web site.

What a firewall CAN'T do

Take careful note: A firewall does not provide you with total security—it's only the first line of defense. Too often I hear people say, "Oh we're perfectly secure; we have a firewall." A firewall *cannot* protect your network from malicious authorized users. If a user is allowed access, a firewall can't protect your network from that user.

It's fairly common to have a RAS server that allows your employees to access your network when they're on the road. Unfortunately, it's also fairly common to have that RAS server completely unprotected. Telephone numbers will be disclosed, passwords will be cracked, and someone will gain access to your network through the RAS server eventually. You have to separate the RAS server—along with any other access—from the internal network. If you don't, you're just waiting for a disaster.

Finally, a firewall cannot protect you from someone walking in the door, sitting down at a machine, and taking over your network. That may sound silly, but think about it. There may be a lot of unused network ports inside your building. When the building was wired originally, the electricians and cable layers probably didn't know what your office layout would be. You may not even know about all the ways intruders can access your network physically. I've seen network ports inside closets, in basements, in bathrooms, and in reception areas too many times to ignore this threat. I'm going to say it again and again: Your network is only as secure as your building.

Wrapping up

In this drill down, I've examined the types of firewall, along with their advantages and disadvantages. In part 4 of this series, I'll cover the process of buying, installing, and configuring this security system. I'll discuss dealing with vendors and resellers in an effective and efficient way. ◆

Basic principles of network security, part 4: Getting your network security system started and keeping it going

By Chris Dinsmore

In part 1 and part 2 of this network security series, I explained how to plan a general structure, get management's involvement, and prepare your users for your network security system. In part 3, I described hardware and software options, and I explained how to determine the best options for our project. In this Daily Drill Down, I'll cover the architecture, purchasing, installation, and initial configuration of your network security system.

So, who gets to take your money?

Okay, so you've decided on an external firewall. In fact, you've decided on two, because the Internet is important to your business and you want to have load balancing, load sharing, and failover in case something happens. Let's say you've decided to use two Nokia firewalls and have your remote users connect with SecuRemote. You have a few hundred users internally—and only a few valid IP addresses with which to work.

Now is the time to make that phone call to your friendly neighborhood reseller. These people can be your best friends, your worst enemies, or somewhere in between. An important step in ensuring the success of your security project is to find a good reseller and develop a solid relationship with them.

So how do you go about finding a good reseller? Start by asking around. I'm sure you have colleagues who have gone through this process, and they're usually willing to share their experiences. Unfortunately, more often than not you'll find out which resellers not to use—but that's as important as finding out which ones to choose.

Next step: Crawl the tradeshows. Get cards, talk to people, and see what's going on.

Finally, read the information security magazines. All of the major resellers and service providers advertise in the big information technology and security magazines, and from there you can easily build a list of people to talk to.

The hard sell

Before you start calling people on your list, be prepared. Have at hand information about your current situation and your requirements. A reputable company will get you to the right sales rep for your area immediately. If you like the people you talk to, ask for a meeting with the sales rep and one of their implementation engineers. If the sales rep doesn't agree immediately, that's a sign something is wrong with the company.

When the sales rep and the engineer arrive, talk to them both. Some folks have a tendency to discuss technical details with the engineer and ignore the sales rep entirely. This approach is not the way to begin your sales relationship with the rep. If you're not talking with the rep because you don't like him or her or can't really deal with the person, this is not the company for you, even if the engineer is great. Your sales rep decides how much you pay for your machines and how easy the acquisition process goes, so he or she is the most important part of this deal.

Finally, ask for references from the company. Any good reseller will be able to give you at least a few local references who are willing to talk with you about their experience with the company. If the reseller can't provide any references, they aren't the ones to deal with.

What should you buy, why should you buy it, and why does it cost so much?

Once you've found a good reseller, you need to place your order. At this point, most resellers will attempt to sell you a security audit. Often this is a good idea, and I recommend it for a lot of companies. If you don't have the internal expertise to determine your risks and requirements, a good audit will give you an honest assessment. And it can definitely provide you with an indication of the quality of the reseller. If the reseller sends two engineers to your company for three days, they poke and prod everything, and then give you a thorough report listing the good and the bad, you know you're getting an honest assessment from an honest reseller. If on the other hand, the report is three pages long and looks like a marketing brochure for whatever it is the company is selling, kick them out of there as fast as you can.

Once the audit is done, the reseller will attempt to sell you architecture services. Once again, for many companies this is a good idea. The people who design these systems are very good at what they do, and they deal with networks like yours every day. They know what works—and what doesn't—and what can be made to work in a pinch. Even though architecture services can cost you up to $2,500, they can save you serious money. In the short run, architecture services prevent you from buying too much machine for your network, or from making expensive choices that won't work with your requirements. In the long run, they ensure you have a system that you won't have to replace as you expand or add new applications to.

At this point, you can start ordering the hardware. My advice is to bid the entire system out to one reseller all at once. A good reseller will be able to put all the products you want on a single plan for you, and then start knocking off the retail cost. In general, the more you buy from a single reseller, the better deal you'll get. And you have the added benefit of going to one source for support, parts, and warranty service.

You have the hardware— now what?

So, now your hardware is finally delivered, and it's time to install and configure it. Once again, you have a few options.

The first option is to attempt to put in the system yourself, with no assistance and no training. Obviously, I think this is generally a bad idea. Even a seemingly simple firewall configuration is a very big deal. I have yet to see a firewall that can be dropped in without some tweaking and twisting, and unless you have the experience and training necessary to deal with these problems, your security project will be a total nightmare.

A second option is to have your reseller install and configure the system for you. It's a sure bet your reseller is going to try to sell you on this approach, and it may be the best choice for your company. This is especially true if you know you won't be able to spare the labor to do the job or dedicate someone to maintain the system. The going rate for implementation services is between $2,000 and $2,500 a day, with the average project running three days. A highly trained and experienced engineer will come to your site, set up your system, configure it based on your security policy, and ensure it works. The disadvantage to this approach (other than the cost) is that once the highly trained and experienced engineer leaves, you are either on your own or dependent on the reseller to provide you with support.

A third option is to get trained on the firewall system in question, then do the install. Once again, your reseller will be happy to sell you training for your firewall. Training courses currently range in cost from $1,200 to $2,500 and are probably the single best investment you can make in this process. A good basic training course will cover the installation and basic configuration of the machine in question, along with some simple troubleshooting techniques. Most vendors also offer a more advanced training program covering high-end configuration, advanced functions, and optional extras. Typically, training classes last from two to three days; often a package is available with both the basic and advanced course offered in a single week. There may even be a certification with the training. Your reseller may be able to arrange training on your site, tailored to your specific needs.

I recommend that you take the training and have the engineer come onsite to assist you with the installation and configuration. That way, you get practical experience setting up your system, and someone who knows your security system is there to teach you the tips and tricks not covered in the courseware. I've always had the best results with this method, and I recommend it to almost everyone.

Is there anything else you should think about?

There is one other option, which may be the best choice for a lot of companies: managed security services. What this means is that you call a company and say, "I need a firewall," and the company does it all for you. It sends someone to your site, performs an audit, determines your needs, builds a system for you, buys it, installs it, configures it, and then maintains it, either remotely or onsite. This setup offers some pretty big advantages. For example, you don't need to have any internal expertise. There are no headaches with purchasing, dealing with vendors, and getting support, and you don't need to worry about paying an employee $75,000 a year plus benefits because the company has a bunch of people pre-certified and ready to go. Also, these shops generally provide 24-hour-a-day,

365-days-a-year support. Getting that same support from the vendor of the firewall may cost more than the firewall itself.

Of course, none of this is cheap. That's the only bad thing about this whole scenario. You pay for the convenience of having someone else deal with it. I honestly think this is a worthwhile tradeoff for many companies. If you don't have the labor to handle this project on your own, I recommend looking into a managed firewall solution. ◆

Does your password policy reduce enterprise security?

By W. Malik

Passwords for user authentication will be with us for the next five years. An effective password policy limits its dependency on users and recognizes when additional rules will result in less, not more, security.

There are only three ways to prove you are who you say you are when talking to a computer: something you know, something you have, or something you are. Something you know is a password. Something you have is a token. Something you are is biometric evidence. In low-security environments a simple password may be sufficient. Higher-risk environments may demand two- or three-factor authentication. For instance, when using a cash machine, the personal identification number is known, and the user has the token. The choice should be governed by the degree of risk the organization perceives and its willingness to accept (do nothing) or remediate that risk (spend money).

The principle of using passwords to authenticate end users is predicated on only the user concerned knowing his or her password. The problem with this principle is that it does not consider that a password may be shared, easily guessed, or stolen, either from inside the system while in transit, at the point of verification, or from a physical record such as a slip of paper on a personal computer.

Unfortunately, passwords are not going away. More-advanced authentication mechanisms often still include an element of personal knowledge (e.g., to unlock a private key, to generate a dynamic password, or to open a smart card). Pure biometric authentication is only slowly increasing. Enterprise password policies limit the obvious security shortcomings of password-based authentication through standards and rules. But when information security departments establish and enforce password policies, they meet fierce resistance elsewhere in the enterprise, resulting in irreconcilable positions on what the "correct" password policy should be. Users sometimes seek external published material that recommends a particular password length, format, or change frequency to support one position in the debate.

Good Password Practices

One organization crafted a useful password algorithm: The user selects a favorite phrase from a song or poem and uses its initial letters as the password. For example, a Beatles fan might select "Picture yourself in a boat on a river..." from the song "Lucy in the Sky with Diamonds," giving the password "Pyiaboar"—easy to remember but hard to guess.

In another organization, the security department ordered Post-It Notes with the preprinted message "Please, don't put your password on me."

There is no "correct" password policy. Many policies ignore the risk that a password may be guessed or stolen from an end user. Additional password rules provide diminishing returns. At a certain point, password rules will actually result in a less-secure authentication process. Where that point of diminishing returns occurs will depend on user interest, the organization's security awareness and culture, and the number of systems requiring passwords. An individual having to remember more than four passwords will write them down. If passwords have to be changed often, the limited set of memorable but obscure passwords will be exhausted, and either overly simplistic passwords will be selected or the passwords will be written down. Cracking tools use dictionaries (including slang, jargon, and dialects) and common permutations (replacing vowels with numerals, for instance) to guess passwords. One enterprise found that nearly 70 percent of its passwords were guessed within three minutes using a common tool.

Some sites change passwords every 30 days. This conforms to the guidelines in BS7799 but may prove onerous for the users. Many site expire passwords in 90 days. Most do not formally expire passwords at all unless there is an incident. Some firms automatically disable a user ID if an incorrect password is entered too often. While this can defeat cracking tools, it actually creates a secondary vulnerability—a hacker can create a denial of service attack by simply attempting to log on to any user ID with a series of poor passwords. After a few minutes, users will find their sessions locked down. A better alternative may be not to deactivate the user ID, but to disable it for a fixed time—for example, 15 minutes—long enough to defeat an automated attack (or delay it enough so its activities can be traced), but not so long that users are significantly inconvenienced.

Some single sign-on and password synchronization tools claim to recover some user productivity by reducing the time users spend authenticating themselves to their systems. There is significant soft-dollar justification for single sign-on: improved security by avoiding written passwords and reduced user annoyance at having to re-authenticate oneself.

Bottom Line

Passwords are weak authentication tools. Without adequate end-user support, complex or onerous password policies will be circumvented. Single sign-on and password synchronization tools may simplify the environment, but they can weaken security if the few remaining passwords are too simple. What works with some users and organizations will not work with others. In high-risk environments, consider two- or three-factor authentication. ◆

British Standard BS7799

BS7799 offers the following guidelines in Section 7:

▸ Passwords should be for individual users in order to maintain accountability.

▸ Passwords must be kept confidential.

▸ Passwords should not be kept on paper unless it can be securely stored.

▸ Passwords must be changed whenever there is a chance that the password or the system could be compromised.

▸ Passwords should not contain aspects of a date, family or company identifiers, telephone numbers, the user ID or other system identifiers, more than two consecutive identical characters, or be all numbers or all letters.

▸ Passwords should be changed approximately every 30 days (more frequently for privileged accounts) and cannot be recycled.

▸ Passwords should not be included in a macro or function key to automate login.

▸ Passwords should be stored only as encrypted hash files.

NOTE
The International Information Systems Security Certification Consortium (ISC2) is a nonprofit organization that administers the Certified Information Systems Security Professional (CISSP) certification program. While passing a CISSP exam is no guarantee of performance, it does establish a minimum body of knowledge. The System Administration, Networking and Security (SANS) organization has established a similar program, System Network Assurance Program (SNAP), consisting of a standard series of briefings, courses, and tasks used to demonstrate a more detailed technical body of knowledge.

Internet security advice for small and midsize enterprises

By J. Browning, J. Pescatore

With small and midsize enterprises doing more business on the Internet, their networks are exposed to security breaches. Defensive action is required to protect the enterprise.

Strategic planning assumptions

▸ By 2003, 50 percent of SMEs (small and midsize enterprises) who manage their own network security and use the Internet for more than e-mail will experience a successful Internet attack (0.7 probability).

▸ By 2003, the dominant means of deploying network security technology will be through the use of appliance technology (0.9 probability).

Any server connected to the Internet makes it (and the rest of the network) vulnerable to access from unauthorized and malicious users. An issue for SMEs is that they usually cannot afford, or do not attract, experienced security personnel. As a result, part-time or underqualified staff manage key enterprise servers (i.e., Web, e-mail). SMEs also often use regional ISPs that provide unknown levels of security. By 2003, 50 percent of SMEs that manage their own network security and use the Internet for more than e-mail will experience a successful Internet attack (0.7 probability). More than 60 percent will not know they have been penetrated.

Start with a security checkup: SMEs connected to the Internet should consider contracting with an outside security firm to conduct an audit and risk-assessment of their network. The effort should include an internal network security audit and an external penetration test. Look for consultancies that have certified their security consultants). External vulnerability assessments should be performed whenever an SME makes major changes to its Web site or firewall, at a minimum on a yearly basis. Increasingly, security vendors will offer low-cost "self-service" vulnerability assessments, such as the current offering by mycio.com. These types of tests can be cost-effective for SMEs but will still require experi-

enced support to address reported security problems.

First line of defense: Precautions must be taken to ensure a proper firewall configuration to offer the best possible protection for the enterprise. Firewalls are deployed to prevent unauthorized "external" users from accessing the enterprise network, while permitting "internal" users to communicate with "external" users and systems. Firewalls also provide a central point for logging and auditing Internet traffic. SMEs should focus on firewall appliances such as Watchguard Firebox, Nokia FW-1, and SonicWall that provide a base level of security without requiring detailed security knowledge. By 2003, the dominant means of deploying network security technology will be through the use of appliance technology (0.9 probability). SMEs should also request quotes for managed firewall and intrusion detection services from their own ISPs and companies such as ISS/Netrex, RIPTech, and GTE Internetworking. These services will generally cost less than the equivalent salary of a half-time firewall administrator.

Other safeguards to consider

Boundary services: Virus scanning of incoming e-mail is a critical security control. It can be done by using desktop antiviral protection; but it is often difficult to keep desktop signature virals current. Server-side antiviral protection (e.g., from Trend Micro or FinJan) provide protection against incoming viruses and hostile ActiveX or Java applets. SMEs should also take immediate action to disallow relay and halt the entry of spam into their environments.

Web security: The major vulnerability in Web servers is an attack against CGI scripts and other active code. It is generally impossible for SMEs to assure that active server code does not contain security vulnerabilities. SMEs that develop and host their own Web servers should deploy products such as Tripwire by Tripwire Security or Entercept by ClickNet to detect and prevent hacker attacks.

Consolidated remote access with strong authentication: SMEs that provide dial-in access to e-mail and other corporate systems should eliminate desktop modems and use consolidated modem pools and remote access servers. SMEs should require the use of hardware tokens such as RSA Security SecurID or Axent Defender to authenticate remote users.

Extra Protection: The measures identified earlier will satisfy the security needs of two-thirds or more of SMEs that use the Internet.

SMEs that must manage more highly sensitive environments need to plan for additional precautions.

Bottom line

The amount of security required should be weighed against the degree of risk associated with doing business on the Internet. The sensitivity of information, productivity of users, and impact on revenue should all be assessed to determine the safeguards required. SMEs that fail to pay attention to Internet security issues will experience significant losses as a result of attacks on their network (0.8 probability). ◆

The case against using .doc files

By John McCormick

You use Microsoft Word. I use Microsoft Word. Practically everyone uses Microsoft Word. But that can be a problem.

Why? Many users, and some IT pros, are too trusting. Me? I'm constantly aware of security threats, and therefore I never open a .doc file sent by a stranger. I enforce this practice in my small company to the extent that we don't even save files in .doc format. In fact, I mostly have Word installed only because some of my clients use it to send me documents. Even if they didn't, I have to keep abreast of potential security problems, and these days MS Word is one of the biggest potential threats around.

Do you need all those extras?

Some people will tell you they have to use .doc files to keep all that fancy formatting. Personally, I don't want, need, or like strange fonts, borders, or other unusual formatting in what should be simple text documents. If you really require such formatting, you can share almost everything—minus the prevalent macro viruses—simply by using the .rtf, or Rich Text Format file extension, instead of saving files in .doc format.

Word lists dozens of features not supported by .rtf that would be contained in .doc files, and I suggest you take a look at the list, if only to see an example of things you really don't need. (To find the list, choose Contents And Index

from Word's Help menu, click the Find tab, search for Word 97 & 6.0/95-.rtf format, and then choose the topic "What happens when I save a Word 97 document in Word 97 & 6.0/95-.rtf format?") Office suites have become incredibly bloated, but just because publishers provide thousands of seldom-used features doesn't mean you have to risk virus attacks just to support them all in your business.

Like me, you probably don't need animated text, character borders, or floating pictures with word wrap in every single document you create, at least not badly enough to risk running across a Melissa variant. Of course, you also lose Word macros created in Visual Basic, but that's the whole point!

Adopting another default file format is the prudent thing to do in many situations. Then, when you really need those fancy formatting options saved in a particular file, you can save that file with the .doc extension. Remember: The fewer .doc files you deal with, the smaller the likelihood of macro virus infection.

Changing file formats may seem a bit drastic—and in the vast majority of cases, it will prove unnecessary. Of course, most security steps are unnecessary most of the time; that's why it's so difficult to enforce good procedures. But if you stop creating, sending, and opening .doc files, at least you know you aren't going to get bitten by Word macro viruses.

Macro virus havoc

The biggest problem with macro viruses isn't just that they can clog your own systems the way traditional viruses can, costing you time and money to clear them out and restore your files. Infections from .doc files can be more dangerous than other viruses because they are easily sent accidentally to clients and vendors, which opens you to legal action and damaged relationships. Your victims might even decide that doing business with you in the future isn't a good risk.

Most viruses have to be sent in some executable form, and our daily e-mail communications over the Internet or intranets just don't transmit these infections. But you can infect others with macro viruses just by sending them a simple document.

There is more to the macro virus threat than just the chance you can infect a recipient. Even if you have a policy of never sending .doc files as attachments to external e-mail addresses, merely opening a .doc file can be dangerous. You probably never considered the possibility that something as simple as a Word macro virus might broadcast the most sensitive of internal company documents, but it could happen to you.

Disney Corp. learned just how dangerous macro viruses can be when, in the middle of November, a variant of the Melissa macro virus sent an open Word document containing an internal memo to members of the press. Many companies have never given any thought to this sort of problem. They didn't know it was even possible—but it is.

How would you like to have a document you are still writing sent to everyone on your company's mailing list? How about just distributing a list of potential promotions to everyone inside the company? Or a list of salaries? You probably use Microsoft Word to create rough sketches of numerous memos containing sensitive information, or even just blue sky ruminations that you fervently hope will never see the light of day. People write some strange things in what they expect to be "eyes-only" internal memos, and they can come back to haunt you days, months, or even decades later. Just ask Oliver North or any of the big tobacco companies if you don't believe me.

Because antivirus protection always lags behind the creation of new viruses, a company relying entirely on antivirus software is taking a big risk. Having confidential information broadcast to the press or even vendors can be catastrophic.

If you must use Word and can't enforce a change to the .rtf file format instead of the risky .doc format, there is still a way to protect your secrets, and it works to block even intentional sharing of confidential data. Elron Software's Message Inspector monitors e-mail, FTP sites, and newsgroup message traffic for confidential data and blocks its transmission.

And Message Inspector doesn't just protect confidential information. Because it works by conducting string searches for keywords, you can configure it to help reduce server spam congestion. You can also set it to watch for and block potentially offensive comments, thus reducing legal liability. ◆

Is it time for e-mail surveillance at your company?

By Mary Ann Fitzharris

E-mail surveillance is an important issue in the banking and financial services industry for preventing security leaks. But the technology for e-mail surveillance may soon become your responsibility, regardless of your industry. When should you consider monitoring your firm's incoming and outgoing e-mail? Can you get by with a low-end solution, or will you require an expensive solution?

The answers depend on your specific needs, according to a study by the Tower Group. The research group says the market is currently a cool $12 million a year for e-mail surveillance tools, with an expected increase by 25-35 percent a year over the next three years. Today's high-end solutions are being used almost exclusively by:

- Full service brokerage firms
- Online stock traders
- Bank-brokerages
- Independent brokers
- Registered investment advisors
- Banks

Why surveillance?

Reasons for using e-mail surveillance include:

- To comply with SEC regulations
- To protect against inappropriate dissemination of sensitive data, including medical records, personnel files, insurance claims, and banking information
- To protect corporate proprietary information, such as product design
- To protect a company from potential liability due to inappropriate and offensive language
- To archive a growing part of a company's knowledge
- To protect against incoming computer viruses

To comply with SEC regulations

Emerson Thompson is senior vice president for financial services for SRA International. SRA manufactures a software product called Assentor, which is designed to support enterprises that are concerned with supervision and regulatory compliance on e-mail. Since the SEC approved NASD and NYSE rules regarding e-mail surveillance in 1997, Thompson says "reasonable supervision has to be done on any e-mail communications with customers to avoid violation of SEC rules. That means hyping of stock, downplaying risk, all the various things that registered representatives are beholden to do according to SEC rules. This has to be supervised on e-mail just as it does on written correspondence."

One of SRA's customers is Derek Brooks, manager of applications development at the full-services brokerage firm Scott & Stringfellow. He has used e-mail surveillance since it was developed by SRA in 1997. "We decided to use it for two reasons," Brooks said. "The first was firm preservation, that is, to protect us from discrimination and things like that. The second was the fact that we are regulated to do so in some fashion."

To protect against inappropriate dissemination of sensitive data

Many companies charged with protecting information such as medical records, reports, and other data are vulnerable to having information being sent inappropriately through e-mail.

To protect corporate data and secrets

Sensitive corporate information walks out the door every day—in briefcases, under jackets, and, through e-mail. Can you trap someone who's stealing corporate information via e-mail? "Possibly," Thompson said. "Firms that are using those patterns may find cases where information is being passed in e-mail messages that's not supposed to be."

To protect a company from potential liability

Thompson believes e-mail surveillance will find a wider corporate audience for firm preservation issues. "One of the byproducts of Assentor is that it is quite easy to add patterns for firm preservation involving inappropriate language in messages, harassment, seven dirty words, that type of thing. Some firms have contacted us regarding that capability. In some cases, we have clients that want to use the securities patterns for their registered people, but they want to use the firm preservation patterns for everybody else."

Brooks says that one of the top reasons his firm uses e-mail surveillance is "to protect our associates from harassment, [to watch for] profanity, to sort of keep an eye on things to make sure that the work environment stays clean," Brooks said.

To archive a company's knowledge

"Think about all the information that is stuck in your e-mail system, which no one will ever find because it's all locked up in the text of a message," said Tim Landgrave, president and CEO of eAdvantage. "How many e-mail threads go back and forth in a company on discussion of a single topic in all the internal mail? Now, what if those e-mail threads were saved in an archive and could be indexed and brought up when you are researching an internal topic?"

Why bother? "Because 90 percent of a company's knowledge is trapped in e-mail messages and it never goes anywhere else," said Landgrave. "Think about all the conversations that take place every day via e-mail. That information is trapped. We need a way to index it, filter it, and bring it back out."

Landgrave added, "If you can screen for a phrase like 'sure bet' [as in, that stock is a sure bet], why can't you screen for keywords like, say, 'outsourcing' in internal mail?" Then, if you were doing an internal report on outsourcing security, you could "bring back and read all the internal e-mails that once floated around discussing that topic."

According to Thompson, "It's only a matter of time until all firms will have some sort of e-mail compliance. Whether or not they need or want archiving is another question. Some are very interested in the archiving only, and others are interested in the e-mail scanning and not the archiving." If all your company wants to do is archive e-mail, Thompson said, "you could probably buy other solutions without going to the trouble of having an e-mail scanning engine

and all the different things that Assentor offers." However, he added, "Some companies have to keep archived versions of correspondence in such a way that the archived information cannot be altered."

To protect from viruses

"As a reaction to viruses, vendors are now allowing you to intercept a message from the Internet to the firewall, before it hits the mail server stores," Landgrave said. "You can look at that message, its content, where it's from; you can dissect it programmatically, check it for viruses, check it for keywords, do whatever we want with it. As mail comes in, we'll check it for keywords and decide if we should put it in the store or a pending mail folder, delete it, or return it with an automatic reply saying it's unsuitable. Checking is currently being done at the client level, and sometimes that's too late. E-mail vendors are building that in their products."

What if you want e-mail surveillance?

If your firm decides it needs e-mail monitoring, what are your choices? As the experts see it, you have three e-mail surveillance options:

▶ **Do it yourself**. In-house-designed software is your first option, but Thompson doesn't recommend that approach. "We don't find those to be nearly as effective," he said.

▶ **Use a new e-mail package**. "You can do this in the next versions of Exchange (2000) and Notes," said Landgrave. "Every new e-mail system has added the ability to trap e-mail messages when they go in or out of the stores. They are doing that now to check for viruses."

▶ **Buy an expensive, high-end solution**. According to the Tower Group, four firms have off-the-shelf solutions, which are currently in use at financial services firms:

1. **SRA International**—clients include more than 70 firms using its Assentor product

2. **Worldtalk**—clients include Fannie Mae and Mass Mutual

3. **PaperLess, Ink**—clients include Daiwa Securities and Josephthal & Co.

4. **Amicus Networks**—clients include Sigma Financial and National Planning Corp.

The Tower Group says that SRA is the "current leader" in terms of brokerage clients, but it expects niche markets to open up for the other vendors.

Does surveillance delay the mail?

A delay in communication of important and timely information is a big issue with e-mail surveillance. As a response to customer demand, SRA and others have added a choice of post-review or pre-review of e-mail. The Tower Group report indicates that "the overwhelming majority of e-mails are now surveyed via post-review surveillance, rather than pre-review." As a result, e-mail gets through, but if something is amiss, it will be caught eventually.

Keywords vs. natural language

According to Brooks, "Assentor does both keyword searching and natural language processing. So it'll put words in context." The Tower Group report adds, "Two basic types of surveillance technology—keyword and phrase search, and natural language—are in use in the systems now on the market." SRA's Assentor is the only one that uses natural language search technology, which is "designed to scan and recognize language patterns and to dynamically update its internal lexicon," according to the Tower Group report. "The other three systems rely on variations of the keyword and key phrase search technology and are equipped with databases and rule sets that can pick out words, word patterns, and sequences. One example would be the ability to flag compliance whenever a number of predetermined words ("unique," "opportunity," "get in now!") appear in the same sentence."

Thompson said: "We find that keywords create too many false positives to be useful. So we've incorporated a natural language capability, which reads text somewhat like a human being would read it. It understands the meanings of

How it Works

Thompson describes the process of e-mail surveillance: "Essentially, we process all mail before it leaves the firm and when it enters the firm. We take the messages apart, all the pieces and parts and attachments and attachments within attachments, and so forth, and we scan all the textual information using an artificial intelligence type capability that we've developed over many years at SRA. We examine those messages to see if there are any potential violations." And if they find a violation? "If we find something suspect, we'll assign a probability factor to that item and any other items we discover in the message. Then, depending on the threshold settings that the firm has chosen, we'll check our discoveries against the thresholds. If any thresholds are breached, we'll quarantine the message for human review—performed by a corporate compliance officer. He or she may then send it or return it to the sender.

words and phrases in context." Using the word "free" in an e-mail would be a good example, Thompson said. "If you had a keyword system and that's all it was doing, the word 'free' would likely be flagged as a word that's prohibited. So, if you had a message that said 'We offer free checking' and 'free' was a keyword, it would be flagged unnecessarily. However, 'free checking' would not necessarily be inappropriate; it's very appropriate in banks. So you wouldn't want to quarantine that message. The idea is to minimize the number of messages that are being quarantined and that require human review."

Who does the human review? "A combination of people," Thompson said. "Firms appoint various managers. Sometimes they're compliance officers or branch managers. It depends on how the firm's supervisory process is set up."

Thompson said, "Any firm that's interested in examining message content for regulatory reasons, for firm preservation reasons, or for protecting confidential information, or any other things that the firm wants to deal with in messages and attachments should look at an e-mail surveillance product." ◆

Unlocking lost passwords on protected files

By John Sheesley

Microsoft Word and Microsoft Excel both give your users the opportunity to password-protect sensitive files. The password protection prevents unauthorized users from opening documents. But what do you do if you or your users forget the password? Or, what happens if a disgruntled ex-employee puts a password lock on all of your network's files? Don't panic. Fortunately, there are some actions you can take to unlock password-protected application files.

A tale of two passwords

When you put passwords on data files, both Word and Excel warn you that if you forget your password, you're out of luck. That's not completely true. You have several options for recovering the data depending on the level of password protection placed on the file, how you go about recovering the password, and how much money you want to spend.

If the data file's password was set to Read-Only mode, recovery is fairly simple. Open the data file in Read-Only mode. Select Save As from the File menu. When the Save As menu appears, click Options.

You won't be able to see what the current Read-Only password is, however, you can clear the Read-Only password by highlighting it and pressing [Delete] and then clicking OK. It's very important that you clear the Password To Open field before saving the file in the next step. If you don't, you'll just preserve the current Read-Only password.

Next, in the File Name text box on the Save As dialog box, enter a new name for the file. You can't use the current filename because the program tells you the file is read-only. The best course of action is to use the same name with an _A at the end of the name. This will help you find the file later.

After you save the new version of the file, open it to ensure you're not prompted for a Read-Only password. Then, delete the original file and rename the new file appropriately.

Polly wants a cracker

File Open passwords are a bit harder to circumvent. Unlike Read-Only passwords, File Open passwords won't let you inside the file to change the password. As the name suggests, the File Open password prevents you from opening the file.

Fortunately, two courses of action exist. The first involves the use of password-cracking software. The second option is to hire a firm to do the cracking for you. Either way, the Internet can help.

Although using password-cracking software may sound unscrupulous, it isn't. There are several perfectly legitimate companies on the Internet that provide such tools. Some of the more common sites you can visit that offer password-cracking software include:

▶ AccessData

▶ Crak Software

▶ Elcom

▶ LostPassword.com

All of the sites allow you to download demonstration copies of their software. You can also order full versions at these sites. Prices vary by vendor and start at $45, depending on the version you order.

To Data Files

Word and Excel include two levels of password protection. First, you can use a password to mark a file Read-Only. With Read-Only protection, someone else can open the file, but they can't save the changes. Second, if you want to prevent someone from opening a file, you can set a File Open password.

Word and Excel allow you to set one or both passwords when you save the files. To set a file password, select Save As from the File menu. When the Save As dialog box appears, click Options. In Word, you can set the passwords in the File Sharing options section of the Save dialog box. In Excel, the Save Options dialog box is different from the Save dialog box you see with Word, but the concept is the same. Just set the password you want in the appropriate field.

Password crackers do have some limitations. Most of the programs employ a dictionary attack on the encrypted file. Others just throw passwords made up of random characters at the file until the program finds a string that works. This is known as a brute-force attack. Some programs employ both methods. As you can imagine, this type of password cracking can take time. Cracking speeds will vary depending on the speed of your workstation's CPU, the size of the password that's being cracked, and the program you're using to perform the crack.

If you'd rather let someone else do the cracking, you can employ a service to crack locked files. Most of the services we found guarantee a full recovery of your files within 10 to 30 days. Every one of the sites we listed earlier, except for LostPassword.Com, advertises password-cracking services. Other companies we've found on the Web offering password cracking services include Password Crackers Inc. and Password Service.

Conclusion

Microsoft Word and Microsoft Excel allow you to password-protect sensitive data files. However, the password protection feature can cause problems if the user forgets a password or someone intentionally password-protects your files. Fortunately, you can crack these passwords with a little effort. ◆

Layer protection for cost-effective security on your network

By John McCormick

Data encryption is an important technology; it just isn't sufficient for critical data with a long life. And that's the whole point. No single security measure is completely effective. Thus, you need to develop a layered defense, not just from a security standpoint but also from a cost perspective.

How should layers work?

What makes adequate security possible at all is the ability to apply different layers of security to different data. The least sensitive or most time-sensitive data needs the least protection. Data that should never be known by anyone but a few top management members doesn't belong on any computer. In between these two extremes is a vast array of data with different protection requirements.

Although a computer security specialist can design layers of security, someone else must decide just how secure the various kinds of data need to be. That means management must develop a policy so the IT staff knows how much time and money they should expend on securing certain classes of data.

Basic categories must be defined for things such as trade secrets, client lists, payroll accounting, memos kept only on a local server, Internet e-mail, budget projections, and so on. There must also be a procedure in place to initiate ongoing analysis of new data types.

While management might balk at the idea, it's impossible to provide the highest level of security for all data, except in the smallest businesses. Likewise, it's foolish to ignore all need for security and depend entirely on the kindness of strangers for your protection.

Because security costs money and makes data more difficult for everyone to access, deciding how much protection a particular kind of data requires is not a trivial exercise. To decide which security level is appropriate for a data class, management needs to know the approximate costs of the various levels of security, as well as how important the information is and the life span of that importance.

Will a particular kind of data require different levels of security at different stages of its life? If so, is there a way to reduce or remove protection in stages, making the data more widely available and thus potentially more useful?

For example, a new product concept is highly confidential at first, but as more people in the company need to work with it, access to data must be made easier. After the project is dropped or the product brought to market, the same data may require little or no security.

The government tends to classify everything as top secret and tries to keep things classified forever, but that's not practical for a business. It's not really practical even for the feds.

What tools are at your disposal?

So what tools can you use to build your defense layers? Layered security options include:

- Physical security for terminals, cabling, and backup data
- Encryption
- Password management
- Firewalls
- Detection and reporting of intrusion attempts
- Ongoing maintenance of OS and applications with an eye to newly revealed flaws or bugs
- Antivirus software and policies

If you have to protect a variety of data types at different security levels, the best way is to develop layered protection that can be applied in stages to different files. Even within each category there are different stages of protection. For example, you can use light encryption for some data and rely upon the best encryption available only for critical files.

Even something as basic as antivirus protection has many layers, starting with simple programs that prevent changes to files, through inexpensive antivirus programs updated monthly, to programs that are updated daily, to a non-networked PC with no modem and no removable media drive.

Computer security must be viewed as a spectrum ranging from weak to highly secure, and in most cases, each business needs to have more than one level of protection available so it can be applied wherever and whenever necessary. Of course, network and system administrators will require input from IT managers and CIOs to ensure data receives the appropriate classification.

Hey, if it were simple we could just leave security issues entirely to the computers. But then, how would we make a living? ◆

Admins: Don't get bitten when getting to know Kerberos

By John McCormick

Any protocol named after the fierce mythological three-headed dog guarding hell's gates is bound to be intimidating. But have no fear. All ye who enter need not abandon hope.

You'll be hearing quite a bit about Kerberos (Latin spelling: Cerberus) in the months to come. The protocol plays a major role in Windows 2000's security enhancement efforts.

Kerberos, though, isn't a Microsoft invention. It's the MIT-developed standard network authentication protocol that uses secret-key cryptography to secure client-server applications by proving the identity of the client to the server, and vice versa.

No, Kerberos isn't new. In fact, some network administrators already know about it. But plenty don't—hence this article. And since the protocol is new to the Windows platform, I'll introduce some basic concepts, features, and implications that may be unfamiliar to Windows 2000 systems engineers.

Kerberos basics

With small networks, it's easy to maintain a list of usernames and passwords on a single server for authentication. But, as networks grow, it becomes necessary to store the list on increasing numbers of machines, each of which could be hacked for a list of passwords. Difficulty of administration also grows, as the list becomes larger and an increasing number of users change passwords and authenticate to the network.

On the other hand, if you're running an enterprise network or operating a virtual private network over the Internet, users must know they are connecting to the service they believe they're using. In other words, they need a method of identifying that the server they're connecting to is the one it's supposed to be and not another machine pretending to be it.

The need to manage passwords for thousands (and even millions) of users, as well as many services, drove Kerberos' development.

Here's how it works

Users know their own passwords. Services also have passwords. But, there's also an authentication service that stores both sets of passwords in one central database.

Once you have proven who you are to the authentication service, it issues a ticket containing the information needed to pass your request to the service (printer, e-mail, and so on) you have requested.

These tickets identify the user to the service. And because they are encrypted by the authentication service using the service's own encryption key, if the service can decrypt the ticket, it knows the ticket was originally issued by the authentication service and is valid. You can probably see some holes in this idea, and it's all a lot more complicated in real-world implementations, but that gives you the basic concept.

Hackers are prevented from copying your ticket and using it to impersonate you, since your ticket possesses a time limit and includes a date stamp. Windows 2000 provides support for Kerberos version 5. This version helps foil hackers by maintaining only a five-minute ticket lifetime, which helps ensure it's used only once.

There's one last—but important—point. Due to security considerations and the need to make the authentication scheme user-friendly, users don't actually receive a ticket for services. Instead, they receive a ticket allowing them to get tickets.

When the user logs on to Windows 2000, the client gets and stores a valid ticket-granting ticket (a ticket that lets you get end-services tickets without submitting your password each time) from the key distribution center. In Windows 2000, a domain server fulfills the key distribution center role. The process of receiving a ticket-granting ticket is performed only once during each user session.

To gain access to an actual service, such as e-mail or a print server, the user sends the request with a copy of the ticket-granting ticket to the key distribution center. The key distribution center replies with an encrypted ticket for the actual service. The client then sends this service ticket to the service provider.

Get More Kerberos Information from the Source

If you want background information about the free version of Kerberos from MIT, complete with information about known bugs, check out MIT's Web site. You can read a Kerberos FAQ, maintained by the U.S. Navy, or even take in a play that contains a good description of the tool: Just check the MIT site for a copy of "Designing an Authentication System: A Dialogue in Four Scenes."

Think of it as needing a AAA club membership card, which you must show before you can purchase a AAA club tour—only with secret handshakes thrown in for good measure.

Since Kerberos is a standards-based protocol, you can access non-Windows 2000 servers using Kerberos authentication tickets.

If you read the interesting exchange on MIT's Web site entitled "Designing an Authentication System: A Dialogue in Four Scenes," you'll get an excellent, non-technical explanation of the development concepts behind Kerberos. It might also give you some ammunition when you have to present the case for Kerberos to upper management. And be prepared to make a case for it, as implementing Kerberos in Windows 2000 is no trivial task.

Active directory

To use Kerberos in Windows 2000, you must accept the overhead that comes with the Active Directory. This might be exactly what you've been waiting for, but not everyone will love Active Directory.

Directory services are just what they sound like; they manage the addresses of the various services users want to access. They also manage user access to various services by maintaining a database that indicates what services each user is authorized to access.

Another advantage of Active Directory is its ability to let users log on once per session, rather than requiring multiple password requests for each new task. If this sounds similar to the manner in which Kerberos functions, it's no coincidence. In Windows 2000, Kerberos is integrated with Active Directory.

There are many other advantages to using Active Directory, most of which involve the centralized, simplified management of distributed resources. But along with the usual small inconveniences found in any new product, there is one gigantic disadvantage: the need to migrate to what Microsoft designates as "Native Mode."

Maximizing the new features in Windows 2000 requires that a network's operating systems all be running the Windows 2000 platform. Thus, it will be necessary to integrate all current Windows NT 4 domains under Active Directory management. This will be a major project for some shops.

Migration tools for both Windows NT and NetWare networks are available, but they require careful testing. Even with the help of these utilities, the changeover will be no small task.

Bottom line

Kerberos can provide banking-grade security levels for your enterprise using Windows 2000. However, its configuration and management are complex, in part because you must migrate to Active Directory.

In addition to the other resources already listed, there is a Kerberos RFC, but be warned: It's not for the fainthearted. If you're new to Kerberos, do some other reading first. If you're someone who loves the details, you can download the source code from MIT. ◆

Enhancing network security through packet filtering

By Brien M. Posey

Is your network connected to the Internet? If it is, you're vulnerable to information theft and vandalism from countless hackers around the world. A surprisingly simple way to protect your network is with Microsoft Proxy Server. In this Daily Drill Down, we'll explore several of Proxy Server's security features.

Why Proxy Server?

When many people think of Proxy Server, they often think of a device that allows multiple computers to share a single Internet link. While this is true, Proxy Server does much more than allow port sharing—it also regulates inbound traffic. For example, suppose you're filling out a form on a Web page. After you submit your form, the site will usually send a confirmation page. Proxy Server must be able to route the confirmation page to the person who needs it, while keeping it out of sight from other clients.

As you can see, Proxy Server truly does regulate inbound and outbound traffic.

Proxy Server as a firewall

Since Proxy Server is so adept at managing inbound traffic, it should come as no surprise that Proxy Server makes a very effective firewall. A firewall is a computer that stands between a permanent Internet connection and a local area network (LAN). Its purpose is to protect computers on that network against all the hooligans on the Internet.

How does packet filtering work?

As we mentioned, your Proxy Server stands between your network and the Internet. Naturally, a wide variety of traffic flows through the Proxy Server in both directions. Since some of this traffic could be malicious, you can use packet filtering to examine each packet before Proxy Server passes it on to its destination.

But how does Proxy Server distinguish a malicious packet from a legitimate packet? By looking for various types of behavior. For example, a packet filter should look for packets that are using unusual components of the TCP/IP suite. It may also detect packets that are intended to interface with a Windows NT service.

Enabling packet filtering

Enabling packet filtering is easy. Proxy Server has various filters built-in that are effective for enforcing security in most situations. Before we show you how to enable packet filtering, we must address one major concern. Since the packet filters block certain types of traffic, you may wonder what will happen to traffic on your network. For example, you may be concerned that domain synchronizations or Exchange Server RPC traffic could be blocked by the packet filters. However, every proxy server has two network interface cards: one for connecting to the Internet and another for connecting to your internal network. The packet filters will only affect traffic passing through the Internet connection. Packet filters won't intercept packets that stay within the confines of your LAN.

To enable packet filtering, select Microsoft Management Console from the Start|Programs |Microsoft Proxy Server menu. When Microsoft Management Console starts, navigate to Console Root | Internet Information Server | *your server* | Web Proxy. At this point, right-click Web Proxy and select Properties from the shortcut menu. When you see the Web Proxy Service property sheet, select the Service tab and click Security. The Security dialog box. Go to the Packet Filters tab and select the Enable Packet Filtering On External Interface check box. Also make sure the Enable Dynamic Packet Filtering Of Microsoft Proxy Server Packets check box is selected. When you're finished, the Security dialogshould look like the one shown in **Figure A**.

You might have noticed in Figure A that the word Exceptions appears above the various packet filters. This is because the filters work on the principle of exceptions. Essentially, this means that Proxy Server has set up a rule stating that everything is blocked. You can get

FIGURE A

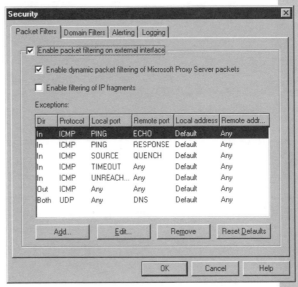

Use the Security dialog to enable packet filtering.

FIGURE B

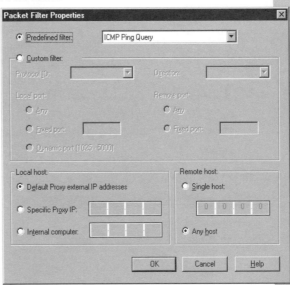

The Packet Filter Properties sheet enables you to modify an existing packet filter.

around this rule by setting up exceptions. If a particular type of packet isn't listed among the exceptions, it isn't getting into your network.

With this in mind, you can see that it may sometimes be necessary to modify the existing filters or add a new exception to the list. To edit an existing packet filter, select it from the Exceptions list and click Edit. When you do, you'll see the Packet Filter Properties sheet, shown in **Figure B**.

It's just as easy to create a new filter. You may want to create a new filter when you need to enable communications between multiple Proxy Servers or when your Proxy Server is running services that aren't normally included in a basic Proxy Server configuration.

To create a new packet filter, open Microsoft Management Console and navigate to Console Root | Internet Information Server | *your server* | Web Proxy. At this point, right-click Web Proxy and select Properties from the shortcut menu. When you see the Web Proxy Service Properties dialog box, select the Service tab and click Security. When you do, you'll see the Security dialog box. At this point, select the Packet Filters tab and click Add. The Packet Filter Properties dialog box, shown in **Figure C** will now appear.

As you can see, you can now create a custom filter to meet your specific needs. However, if you're not exactly sure what you're doing, simply click Predefined Filter, which allows you to choose from a list of the most common types of additional filters. When you've set up your new filter, click OK to add it to the list of existing filters.

An early warning system

So far, we've shown you how to add various packet filters to Proxy Server to help protect your network from the Internet. However, you may be wondering how to tell if your filters are working, or more important, how to tell when your network comes under attack. Fortunately, Proxy Server includes various types of alerts. When suspicious activity occurs, you can instruct Proxy Server to build a log file, create a system event, or send an e-mail message.

What warnings can Proxy Server generate?

There are three basic items that Proxy Server can monitor and alert you to. First, Proxy Server can monitor rejected packets. Rejected packets, as we explained earlier, are IP packets that Proxy Server doesn't allow to come onto your network. Second, Proxy Server can alert you to protocol violations. Protocol violations are attempts at accessing your network via a protocol that you've disallowed. Finally, Proxy Server can monitor your hard disk. If your hard disk fills up, Proxy Server can send an alert notifying you that the disk is full.

Configuring alerting

To enable alerting, open Microsoft Management Console and navigate to Console Root | Internet Information Server | *your server* | Web Proxy. At this point, right-click Web Proxy and select Properties from the shortcut menu. When the Web Proxy Service Properties sheet appears, go to the Services tab. At this point, click Security. to open the Security dialog box. Now, select the Alerting tab.

As you can see in **Figure D**, you can select from the Event drop-down list the type of event that you wish to be alerted to. Then you can set the number of times per second that the event must occur before Proxy Server will generate a system event. To prevent your event logs from filling up and to keep from bogging down your server, you should consider setting Delay Before Next Report to a high value. For example, if you set this value to five minutes, Proxy Server will wait five minutes before testing for that event again in the event that a system event occurs. By default, Proxy Server sets a different wait time for different events.

Finally, you should select the Send SMTP Mail and the Report To Windows NT Event Log check boxes. Doing so allows Proxy Server

FIGURE C

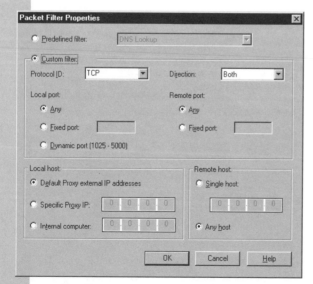

The Packet Filter Properties sheet allows you to create a new packet filter of either a custom or predefined type.

to send an e-mail message and write to the event log when a system event occurs.

Before Proxy Server can send e-mail regarding an event, you must configure the e-mail settings. To do so, click Configure Mail. In the Configure Mail Alerting dialog box,.simply provide the name of your mail server, the port number, and a valid to and from e-mail address. When you've finished, the Configure Mail Alerting dialog box should look similar to the one shown in **Figure E**.

Even after you've entered these settings, don't expect your Proxy Server to be able to send e-mail messages yet. Before it can do so, you must install an e-mail client such as Microsoft Outlook or Exchange Client. You must also create an e-mail account and MAPI profile for the Proxy Server. Finally, you need to configure your e-mail client to auto-start. The e-mail client must be running for Proxy Server to be able to send mail.

Be sure to stop and restart the Proxy services. so that all your new settings will take effect. (You should do this even if you're not using the e-mail option.) Next, return to the Configure Mail Alerting dialog box, and click Test. This will allow you to confirm that the e-mail portion of Proxy Server is working correctly.

Conclusion

In this Daily Drill Down, we've explained how you can increase your network's security by configuring Proxy Server to perform packet filtering. Of course, no network is ever 100 percent secure. Therefore, we've shown you how to put monitors in place that will warn you if someone is trying to break in to your network. ◆

FIGURE D

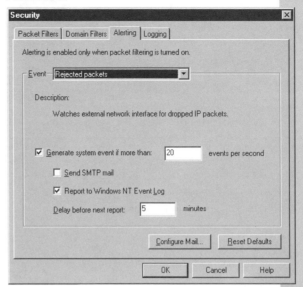

You can set Proxy Server to send e-mail and write to the Windows NT event log when a system event occurs.

FIGURE E

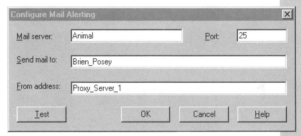

Before Proxy Server can send e-mail regarding an event, you must configure the e-mail settings.

Virtual private networks: The current state

By Scott Lape

Virtual private network (VPN) implementation can make you a corporate hero. It can also make you the company scapegoat.

By definition, a VPN is simply secure access to data and/or resources via private network. This private network connects through public data lines and uses a tunneling protocol and encryption by individuals or machines for whom the data and/or resource is intended.

Over the past few years, VPN has become one of the most used acronyms in the history of the networking industry. Every company that can possibly justify instituting a VPN solution is champing at the bit to do so.

In this Daily Drill Down, I'll discuss the benefits of deploying a VPN and examine the design and technology behind it.

The path of least resistance

They (you know—all of those "experts" out there who know everything) say that VPNs and related services will have a market of greater than $10 billion by 2001. CEOs, CIOs, networking executives, and even the managers below them have become very well read in the area of VPNs. Something about the promise of having secure access to a corporate network from darn near anywhere in the world is tremendously appealing—not to mention it offers the convenience and relatively low expense associated with setting up and maintaining a highly available global network. It seems that in a world of nonstandard standards and rapidly changing technologies, a VPN (which is largely standards-based) is the path of least resistance to a highly available, reliable, and secure network to which you could potentially connect (with the right tools) from a thatched hut in the Himalayas.

On the surface, the high-level benefit of a VPN seems great. But there is one small fact to keep in mind: *Understanding* the benefits and the technologies of a VPN and how it works is very different from *knowing* you need one. The only way to truly reap the benefits is to dig in to the technology and its foundation. Many of the aforementioned professionals have just begun to scratch the surface of the potential of virtual private networking, its services, and its capabilities.

VPN from the clouds

It is only appropriate to touch on the benefits of deploying a VPN prior to delving into its technologies. These aren't all the possible benefits, nor do they apply to every organization and circumstance. Your actual results and benefits may vary.

Cost seems to drive and control many projects in the networking industry. Technologies are available to provide almost any desired or required result, assuming that a company's pockets are deep enough. Realistically, every member of every technology team faces at least some—and often many—budgetary constraints. (If you're a hiring manager and your company's projects don't have *any* monetary or budgetary constraints, please e-mail me and I will forward you a resume.) Members of information technology departments and their managers are paid to find and implement better ways to reach an end. Better can mean faster or more reliable, secure, or available. Generally, a better way to reach a similar end equals—whether directly or indirectly—less expensive. And VPNs may be the answer for many companies.

One of the most well-known benefits of VPNs is access to resources from any point on the Internet. This access could potentially provide companies that currently manage multiple network points of entry with the ability to maintain a single point of entry. A fast connection to the Internet via an Internet service provider (ISP) could take the place of many, if not all, other data lines and remote-access media. A single high-speed line could replace the function of multiple point-to-point connections, Frame Relay, ISDN, and analog modems. Each of these connectivity options requires some piece of unique hardware, which in turn requires unique management and expense. The single link could transport all required traffic to and from remote users and remote sites.

The most apparent benefits from the reduction in the number of entry points to a corporate network are fewer potential points of failure and reduced hardware and administration costs. Another benefit is the ability to take advantage of the inherent redundancy that's built in to the Internet. A properly written service level agreement with an ISP could potentially offload some responsibility and accountability for network uptime. No matter how high your level of redundancy and planning, you can't guarantee that a worker repairing a phone line in Anywhere, USA, won't accidentally slice through the wrong fiber-optic cable and drop one or all of the core backbones of the Internet to its knees. Catastrophic failures are just that. All the precaution in the world can't protect against these types of problems. Luckily, though, situations like these are rare. So, using a VPN to reduce your multiple point-to-point connections is a fairly safe way to save those resources.

All of the resources saved usually equate to dollars. Exactly how many dollars is open to debate. Common wisdom pegs intranational remote-access savings estimates in the area of 50 percent. International estimates of savings are thought to be close to 90 percent over that of conventional remote-access solutions. Site connectivity savings are estimated to be an equally impressive 70 percent over point-to-point. These estimates are very generalized, but clearly, VPNs have the potential to save many companies money. However, to say that implementing a VPN will save every company money would be a misstatement. In the world of technology, there's always an exception.

While potential savings may vary, one statement holds true: Nothing can currently touch an Internet-based VPN in terms of global availability. This is facilitated by the use of the standards-based Internet Protocol (IP).

With the recent explosion of low-cost, high-speed Internet access available to many individuals' homes, VPNs make telecommuting not only an employment alternative but also a selling point to potential employees. The labor market is the tightest it has been in history. Employers are having a hard time finding qualified individuals to fill needed positions. Telecommuting via VPNs affords companies the ability to move outside their local labor market to hire individuals who live virtually anywhere, without incurring relocation expenses.

VPN technology

Assuming that a VPN is a viable solution for a company, the two major concerns that many face are performance and security. While IP was designed to be the standard protocol of the Internet, performance and security were not necessarily factored into its design. In the early days of the Internet, neither security nor reliable performance was mandated. Standards have been introduced to provide the ability to ensure the network performance, security, and availability required of a secure VPN.

The major obstacles of transmitting private information over public or shared lines are familiar to most IT managers. Data transmitted via a VPN must:

▶ Maintain its integrity.

▶ Be tamper-resistant.

▶ Be protected from duplication by unauthorized parties.

▶ Remain confidential until it meets its intended recipient.

VPNs accomplish this by creating tunnels along the Internet from the data's point of origin to the point of delivery. These tunnels are secure paths through which encrypted data can travel without being intercepted by unauthorized parties. Protocol suites have been developed that provide the ability to form VPNs over the Internet and accomplish these goals. Four of these protocol suites are:

▶ PPTP (Point-to-Point Tunneling Protocol)

▶ L2F (Layer-2 Forwarding)

▶ L2TP (Layer-2 Tunneling Protocol)

▶ IPSec (IP Security Protocol)

PPTP is a proposed standard that Microsoft has included with Windows 98, with RRAS for NT4, and in a service pack for Windows 95. PPTP uses PPP (Point-to-Point Protocol) to provide remote-access services across the Internet via a tunnel. PPP packets are encapsulated by using a modified version of GRE (Generic Routing Encapsulation) Protocol. This encapsulation allows other protocols, including IPX and NetBEUI, to be utilized by PPTP. This is one of the main attractions of PPTP. By design, it functions at the Data Link layer (Layer 2) of the Open Systems Interconnection (OSI) model, allowing for transmission of protocols other than IP. In contrast, IPSec functions at the network layer (Layer 3) of the OSI model. The main weaknesses of PPTP are its lack of support of token-based authentication and the inability to provide strong encryption. PPTP relies on PAP (Password Authentication Protocol), CHAP (Challenge Handshake Authentication Protocol), and a Microsoft Windows NT variation that uses NT domain-level security for authentication, MS-CHAP (Microsoft Challenge Handshake Authentication Protocol).

L2F is a tunneling protocol that encapsulates PPP packets within IP packets. It allows the use of unregistered IP addresses by hiding the IP address of the remote user from Internet users. Unlike PPTP, L2F has the ability to work directly with Frame Relay and ATM (Asynchronous Transfer Mode). L2F uses PPP for remote user authentication; however, it supports TACACS (Terminal Access Controller Access System) and RADIUS (Remote Authentication Dial-in User Service). Where PPTP allows only single connections to be made across tunnels, L2F supports multiple connections. Since it functions at the Data Link layer (Layer 2) of the OSI model, L2F also provides the flexibility of being able to handle protocols other than IP.

L2TP was designed to take over where L2F and PPTP left off and become a standard approved by the IETF (Internet Engineering Task Force). It is a Layer 2 tunneling protocol that combines the best of both L2F and PPTP. It supports the transfer of protocols other than IP and is used primarily in remote-access scenarios. Although many believe L2TP to be a security-based protocol, it doesn't provide a secure tunnel. Like L2F, it facilitates authentication of both the user and the connection. For security, L2TP must incorporate IPSec.

IPSec is widely considered to be the best solution for the implementation of a secure VPN. IPSec was originally developed to plug the security inadequacies of IPv4 in the next generation of IP protocols, IPv6. Adoption of IPv6 has been slow, and the current need for securing IP packets is great. These two facts played a large role in the modification of IPSec to make it compatible with IPv4 in an attempt to accommodate the security needs of the current version of IP. Support for IPSec headers is optional in IPv4 but mandatory in IPv6.

In order for current networking applications to use IPSec, they must incorporate special TCP/IP stacks that have been designed to include the IPSec protocols. IPSec is a Layer 3 security protocol from the IETF that provides authentication and/or encryption for IP traffic for transport across the Internet. IPSec affords the sender of IP packets the ability to authenticate and/or encrypt data at the packet level.

There are two methods of using IPSec, which were brought about by the ability to separate authentication and encryption application to each packet. The different modes are referred to as *tunnel mode* and *transport mode*. In transport mode, the transport layer is the only segment that is authenticated or encrypted. Tunnel mode authenticates or encrypts the entire packet, which provides even more protection against unauthorized access, interception, or attack.

IPSec is built around a number of standardized cryptographic technologies to provide confidentiality, data integrity, and authentication. For example, IPSec uses:

▶ Diffie-Hellman key exchanges to deliver secret keys between peers on a public net.

▶ Public key cryptography for signing Diffie-Hellman exchanges, to guarantee the identities of the two parties and to avoid man-in-the-middle attacks.

▶ Data encryption standard (DES) and other bulk-encryption algorithms for encrypting data.

▶ Keyed hash algorithms (HMAC, MD5, SHA) for authenticating packets.

▶ Digital certificates for validating public keys.

IPSec relies on the exchange of secret keys to allow different IPSec parties secure communications. Key management is a "key" ingredient of IPSec. There are two ways to handle these key exchanges and management within the architecture of IPSec: manual keying and the ISAKMP/Oakley scheme, also referred to as IKE (Internet Key Exchange). IKE provides the automation of key management and is the result of the combining ISAKMP (Internet Security Association and Key Management Protocol), which serves as the framework for authentication and key exchange, with the Oakley Protocol, which describes various modes of key exchange. Both manual keying and IKE are mandatory requirements of IPSec.

As with any other management automation tool, the benefit of IKE is easy to see. A VPN with a small number of sites can use manual keying effectively. VPN encompassing a larger number of users and/or supporting many remote-access users will benefit from the automation provided by the use of IKE.

IKE is designed to provide the following capabilities:

▶ It provides the means for protocol agreement between parties, along with which algorithms and keys to use.

▶ It ensures from the beginning of the exchange that you're communicating with the intended party.

▶ It manages the keys that are agreed on.

▶ It ensures that the key exchanges are handled completely and safely.

IPSec is currently viewed as the best solution to support an IP-based environment. It includes the strong security that the other protocol suites lack: encryption, authentication, and usage of keys and their management. While IPSec is designed to handle only IP packets, PPTP and L2TP are better suited to environments requiring transmission of IPX, NetBEUI, and AppleTalk.

VPN design

Aside from the Internet, an Internet-based VPN consists of three pieces: security gateways, security policy servers, and certificate authorities. The Internet is the foundation and groundwork of a VPN. It provides the large pipes for traversal by the small tunnels created by a VPN.

A *security gateway* is the gatekeeper of the private network. It provides security against unauthorized access to the information on the inside. It can consist of routers, firewalls, VPN hardware, and/or software. In many cases, all or most of these functions are provided by the gateway, or vice versa.

The *security policy server* contains the access-list information, which dictates what and who to allow and disallow access to resources. This access list can reside in many places: a router, firewall, VPN hardware, or RADIUS server.

Certificate authorities are the governing body of key verification. This governing body can be a database residing inside the private network or it can be outsourced to a third party. The latter provides the best method of key verification in cases where corporations make use of extranets.

Basic questions that should be answered before settling on the best VPN solution (if any) for your company include the following:

▶ How many users are at each site?

▶ What are the bandwidth requirements for each needed connection?

▶ Does the connection need to be permanent or on-demand (dial-up)?

▶ How much traffic will the site generate?

▶ Are there times when traffic is higher than others?

▶ What are the service-level requirements?

▶ Are there any problems existing in your company that will be solved by the implementation of a VPN?

▶ Why is a VPN better than the next competing alternative?

▶ Should the VPN be outsourced or built in-house?

VPN last word

Tremendous advantages accompany the implementation of a VPN for many companies. In a lot of cases, there are also tremendous savings associated with VPN that could make the project sponsor a corporate hero—not to mention the fact that a VPN and a fast Internet connection at a user's home are a telecommuter's dream. However, as with any relatively new technology, there are numerous questions to be asked and much studying to be done.

The best solutions are always based on knowledge. If a VPN is for you, look to the future. Make sure your choice is as scalable as you think you'll need. Also, pay particularly close attention to any other regulations or requirements that are mandated by much larger bodies, such as the government. A number of options are available, some geared toward small business, some toward much bigger enterprises. If your company is in need of a VPN, there's a solution that's right for you—just make sure you're very aware of the requirements today and, as always, think scalable. ◆

Understanding virtual private networking

By Talainia Posey

Do you have traveling users on your network who wish they could connect to your corporate network from home, a hotel room, or even an airport? Unfortunately, many companies don't have a remote access server (RAS) in place to make this possible. Even if your company does have a RAS, what are the chances that the line will be busy when you call? All these reasons have made doing business on the road difficult. However, by setting up a virtual private network (VPN), you can access your corporate network from anywhere that you have access to an Internet connection. In this Daily Drill Down, I'll explain how VPNs work with Windows 98.

What is a VPN?

A traditional network consists of two computers that must communicate with each other. The two computers are connected by a physical medium, such as an Ethernet connection. A VPN works on the same principle. It consists of two computers that must communicate and a medium. However, unlike with traditional networks, this medium isn't dedicated to the network in question. Often the medium is the Internet. Because both computers are connected to the Internet, it's possible to establish a route through the Internet between the two computers. In the case of a VPN, this route is called a tunnel.

Introducing the Point-to-Point Tunneling Protocol

As you're probably aware, a network connection requires the computers on the network to share a common protocol. A protocol is the language computers use to communicate over the connection medium.

For a standard Internet connection, computers use the TCP/IP protocol over a PPP (Point-to-Point Protocol) connection. In the case of a VPN, this concept is taken a step further. The Windows 98 implementation of virtual private networking relies on a protocol called PPTP (Point-to-Point Tunneling Protocol). As you might have guessed by the name, PPTP is simply an extension of the PPP protocol. PPTP

provides a tunnel through the logical connection medium that allows the two computers to communicate.

Because of the way PPTP works, you can use it regardless of the communications protocol your corporate network normally uses. For example, suppose your corporate network normally uses Internetwork Package Exchange/Sequenced Package Exchange (IPX/SPX). You can set up IPX/SPX on your remote computer and communicate with your corporate network using IPX/SPX packets traveling across PPTP.

Virtual private networking over the Internet

Now that you're familiar with some of the basic concepts and terminology associated with VPNs, let's look at how virtual private networking works in a little more detail. For the remainder of this Daily Drill Down, I'll assume that a remote user dialing into the Internet is making the VPN connection.

When establishing a VPN connection over the Internet, the remote user must make two connections. The first connection is to the user's Internet service provider (ISP) by way of a dial-up session. As I mentioned earlier, this dial-up session uses TCP/IP and PPP to communicate with the ISP. At the time the connection is made, the remote user is automatically assigned an IP address by a Dynamic Host Configuration Protocol (DHCP) server at the ISP's office.

The second connection actually creates the VPN. It uses some of the Windows 98 code that's normally associated with dial-up networking to establish this connection over the existing PPP connection. Packets are sent across the second connection in the form of IP datagrams containing encapsulated PPP packets.

Under normal circumstances, when a remote user tries to access a corporate network via the Internet, the company's firewall prevents PPP packets from entering the network. This means the private network is inaccessible to Internet users. However, when the company loads the VPN services, it can enable certain firewall ports that provide a route across the firewall (or router) and allow Internet users who meet specific security criteria to access the private network from across the Internet.

When a VPN server receives a packet from across the Internet, it disassembles the packet. From this packet, it can derive the name of the computer the packet was intended for. The packet also contains the underlying protocols, such as NetBEUI and IPX/SPX. Once this information has been extracted into a usable form, the packet can be passed from the VPN server to the destination computer residing on the private network. As you can see, the VPN server functions similarly to a gateway.

Because you can imbed standard networking protocols into a packet that's sent across a VPN, all standard networking features continue to work. For example, name resolutions by way of a Windows Internet Naming Service (WINS) server or a Domain Name Service (DNS) server will function just as if the remote host was directly plugged into the local network.

Because name resolution continues to function, you may be wondering about the general DNS requirements. After all, addressing a computer by name across the Internet normally requires the name to be registered and globally accessible. However, in the case of virtual private networking, only the VPN server needs a valid globally accessible DNS name (with a static IP address). When you send packets from the remote computer, they travel only to the VPN server. As far as anything on the Internet knows, the VPN server is the packet's final destination. It's not until the VPN server disassembles the packets that they're passed on to their true final destination. Because the packet already resides at the local level at the time of disassembly, the Internet requires absolutely no knowledge of the name of the computer that's the true final destination of the packet. As a matter of fact, it's a bad idea from a security standpoint to make the name of that computer accessible via the Internet. You should place all local nodes on your network, as well as the VPN server, behind a firewall for protection.

Virtual private networking and routing

As I mentioned earlier, connecting to a VPN involves using two dial-up networking sessions.

The first session establishes your Internet connection. Once you're connected to the Internet, you can establish the VPN connection via the second dial-up networking connection. However, there are a couple of side effects you should know about.

First, when you launch the VPN session, the Internet is no longer accessible for standard access (Web browsing, e-mail, and so forth) unless the network you're connecting to can also get to the Internet. If the remote network doesn't provide access to the Internet, you can't surf the Web or check your e-mail at the same time you're connected to a VPN.

Second, you should know that establishing a VPN session kills your connection to any local networks you might be attached to. For example, suppose you're part of a ten-user workgroup. Now suppose you establish a VPN session to a corporate enterprise network. Once you do, that network will be accessible but your workgroup won't. Consequently, you won't be able to use Windows 98 to route packets between the two networks.

The reason for these routing limitations is because of the way the PPTP protocol affects Windows 98's local routing tables. If you absolutely have to connect to the Internet, to a local network, or to both at the same time you're connected to a VPN, you may be able to do so in some cases by using Windows 98's Route command. The Route command can be used to make Windows 98 aware of other IP networks that you're connected to without the aid of a router.

VPN security

Given the insecure nature of the Internet, security is a big concern with VPNs. After all, you don't want someone to steal your packets as they flow freely across the Internet. And you don't want your corporate network to be compromised. Fortunately, the Windows 98 implementation of virtual private networking is designed to be secure. In this section, I'll discuss some of the aspects of VPN security that you need to be aware of.

The first step in having a secure environment is to have strong passwords. When you dial in to your ISP, it typically asks for a password. However, this password grants you an Internet connection only—it has absolutely nothing to do with your VPN access. Instead, when you establish the VPN session, you'll be prompted for a second password. This is your usual Windows NT (or Windows 2000) domain password. The password is authenticated using the same method that a RAS server uses. You can use Challenge Handshake Authentication Protocol (CHAP), Microsoft CHAP (MS-CHAP), or Password Authentication Protocol (PAP) to authenticate Windows NT passwords.

Once a user has been authenticated into a Windows NT domain, all the usual security mechanisms continue to apply. For example, all NTFS permissions and share permissions apply to a user who's connected through a VPN just as if the user were connected to a network locally.

An added level security comes from encryption. Once a user has specified his or her password, the remote client and the VPN server generate a 40-bit encryption key that can be used to encrypt and decrypt packets. If you're using Windows NT Server with Service Pack 1, 2, or 3, this encryption key changes with every 256 packets. If you're using Service Pack 4 or above, the encryption key changes with every packet. To further enhance security, users in the United States and Canada may use 128-bit encryption as opposed to the standard 40-bit encryption.

Firewalls

You should always place your VPN server behind a firewall. A firewall is designed to block all IP ports that are unused. This prevents attacks on your network by malicious Internet users. Another function of a firewall is to hide the computer names and IP addresses used on your private network from Internet users.

If you already have a firewall in place, you'll have to enable the ports that are used by virtual private networking before the VPN server will be accessible from across the Internet. Remember that virtual private networking relies on the PPTP Protocol. PPTP uses TCP port 1723 and ID number 47. Therefore, you must enable port 1723 and ID 47 (in some cases listed as Protocol 47) before you can use virtual private networking. If these addresses aren't enabled, all VPN traffic will be stopped at the firewall and will never even reach your VPN server, not to mention the rest of your network.

Conclusion

In this Daily Drill Down, I've discussed VPNs as they apply to Windows 98. I've explained a bit about the infrastructure behind a VPN, and I discussed some configuration issues you may encounter when setting up a VPN through Windows 98. ◆

When a stranger calls: Use outsiders to safeguard your e-mail

By John McCormick

The best way to protect e-mail confidentiality is to encrypt each important document separately and place it in an attachment. But, who has time to do that? It's a real pain for both the sender and the recipient.

There are other ways to improve security without creating significant overhead, even if you use public e-mail systems, such as those available from Yahoo!

Interested?

Why, you might ask, would any business that already has an e-mail server want to use one of the Web's portal e-mail accounts? After all, you already have staff or an outside support contract to manage your server, right?

Well, besides anti-spam reasons and the ease of managing an expected, temporary flood of messages, there is another very important reason. Many business users, especially executives or those with confidential management tasks, need an account at Yahoo!, Go.com, Excite.com, or mail.usa.com. Personally, I don't recommend choosing Hotmail.com, unless you want a real flood of "adult" spam as a result of opening an account.

If you doubt the need for a Web-based e-mail account, ask yourself this question: "Do I ever exchange confidential e-memos with other managers about staffing changes, salaries, strategic or tactical planning, new products, or other issues I need to keep secret from employees or MIS system contractors?"

If the answer is "yes," then you need an off-site e-mail account. Such an account eliminates issues related to providing technicians with complete access to your local e-mail server, which they need in order to maintain it properly.

Global strategy shift

Sure, there are people at Yahoo! and other free e-mail services who can see your messages if they want, but they've got millions of messages a day to wade through. Plus, they have no real incentive to crack open e-mails. If you are slightly careful about how you identify yourself when you sign up for off-site e-mail accounts, there will be no way to know whether you are the CIO of IBM, or a six-year-old wanting to trade Pokémon cards.

Since the confidential information exchanged on an anonymous service is often between people who know each other well, there's no need to use full names or titles in the messages. If you want even more protection than anonymity alone provides, some free online services also offer secure e-mail. Most people don't notice, but if you sign on to Yahoo!'s e-mail server manually, an option exists to use standard or secure logon procedures.

If you choose the secure logon option, you will be connected to a Secure Sockets Layer (SSL) server and your messages will be encrypted. Encrypted messages take longer to process, but the security of your messages is enhanced. A big bonus is you don't need to encrypt messages using a separate program. Both Netscape Navigator and Microsoft Internet Explorer can make the secure connection directly. It's the same security protocol you receive when signing on to a secure shopping or banking site.

Remember that SSL services are *more* secure than your own e-mail server, unless you encrypt all messages before you send them to your server. And that's not all you can do on the Web. There's a new e-mail paradigm that promises to significantly improve the level of your Web messaging security.

Internet time lasts forever

This new service, called Disappearing, Inc. addresses what is probably the worst security threat of the Internet—the fact that once you put something on the Web, it just never seems to go away.

A March 1999 Gartner Group, Inc. report titled, "Shredding the E-mail: When Is It Truly Gone?" pointed out the legal liability many companies face due to the persistence of electronic messages. In case you've missed the headlines, the White House is familiar with the issue, as are Microsoft executives.

In a nutshell, what Disappearing Inc. does is provide an electronic shredder for old e-mail at a cost of $4 per user, per month. Disappearing Inc. works with Eudora, Outlook, Netscape Mail, or even Web-based e-mail services, encrypting messages so only the authorized recipient can read the message.

So far it sounds like just another encryption service, but Disappearing Inc. goes much farther by tracking access and destroying the key when you delete your message. This makes it virtually impossible to decrypt even archived or forwarded copies of the original e-mail.

As Disappearing, Inc. CEO, Maclen Marvit, said at the April EMA2000 Conference in Boston, "As the number of incidents involving unanticipated disclosure or inappropriate destruction of old e-mail continues to increase, [there is] a rapidly growing demand for Disappearing E-mail. As the recent events at the White House demonstrate, meeting both the technical and legal requirements of e-mail policy is no easy task."

Since this is a new service, I can't personally guarantee that it actually works, or that there are no important security holes in the service or the manner in which it will be implemented. It's certainly an interesting concept, and I have no reason to believe at this time that it won't work as advertised. ◆

Using biometrics to secure your network

By John Sheesley

If you're like most of us, you have several passwords that you have to remember when you connect to your network and access applications on it. Remembering those passwords can be troublesome. Also, password security isn't the most effective type of security because users inevitably write down their passwords on sticky pads and put them on their computers.

Wouldn't it be nice if you could just do like they do in the movies? All you would have to do is touch a pad or talk to the computer and it would grant you access. Fortunately, what was once just science fiction is now becoming fact. In this article, we'll discuss the growing field of biometrics and what it means to you as a network administrator.

BioWHATrics?

Security systems control access to the things they protect using one or a combination of three basic methods. These methods can be simplified into the following three categories:

1. **Things you have**—These things represent items that you must present to the security system such as keys or ID badges.

2. **Things you know**—These things consist of questions that you must answer or knowledge that you must present to the system to identify yourself. They can include things like passwords, PIN numbers, or phrases.

3. **Things you are**—These are items that are unique to you. They can't be lost, duplicated, or stolen.

As you can probably figure out, the security strength of these methods increase as you go farther down the list. Security strength also improves when you use a combination of the methods. For example, when you go to an automatic teller machine, you can't get any money unless you present something you have—your ATM card—along with something you know— your PIN number. It would be much easier for a thief if all he had to do was steal your card or play guess-the-PIN. Because he must do both, the chances of your money being stolen decreases dramatically.

Biometric security uses the third method of authentication. Biometrics refers to the use of unique physical attributes of a person and the use of those attributes to authenticate someone. These physical attributes can include such things as:

- DNA
- Facial geometry
- Fingerprints
- Hand geometry
- Iris color and patterns
- Palm prints
- Retina patterns
- Signature
- Voice

All of these attributes are unique to each person on the planet. Unlike traditional passwords, these security identifiers can't be lost, forgotten, or stolen. While using this method of identification was once considered to be nothing but science fiction, biometric security has lately become more accepted and widespread.

How do biometrics work?

Biometric security authenticates users by following a fairly simple procedure. First, you must introduce yourself to the system. During this introduction, the system captures the data that it's going to use in the future to identify you. Next, the system takes the sample that you've given it and, based on algorithms unique to each program, produces a template based on a key set of data from the sample.

The program can use only a sample of the biometric data. There's too much distinguishing information for most biological data to include the full information. Databases containing all the information would be too large to search quickly and effectively. After creating the template, the system is ready to identify you in the future. The next time you try to access the system, it compares the new sample with the template created from the original baseline template. Based on comparisons made in the two samples, the system then accepts or rejects your entry.

No matter what biometric measure the vendor has chosen—retinal scan, fingerprint identification, voice patterns, facial geometry, and so on—the basic authentication routine is the same. The only difference is the sampling method that the vendor uses to create the biometric template.

No biometric security program is perfect. Because the templates draw on only key points of biometric data, sometimes they make mistakes. Voices may change due to colds. Fingerprints may be altered temporarily due to cuts and scrapes. If any of the key points in a sample is altered, the security program may fail to recognize the person, even if they are authentic.

Biometric programs are usually judged by two performance measurements that rank the system's level of accuracy. The measurements are known as the false rejection rate (FRR) and false acceptance rate (FAR). Different vendors may use different names for these measurements. The FRR is sometimes referred to as a Type I error rate while the FAR is known as a Type II error rate.

The FRR measures the number of times the system falsely rejects an authorized user. In contrast, the FAR measures the number of times the system falsely accepts a non-authorized user. These measurements are usually listed as a percentage. You should look for programs with the lowest percentage for each value.

What kind of biometric methods can I choose from?

As we mentioned earlier, there are several biometric attributes that can be used to identify people. With the exception of DNA scans, currently you can find security programs that work with all of these attributes. Each of the different methods has its own advantages and disadvantages.

One of the most common methods for biometric security is the fingerprint scan. This method scans the fingerprint of one finger of the user and creates a template based on the curves and ridges of the fingerprint. This method is relatively inexpensive to implement and most popular due to the familiarity people have with fingerprints from law enforcement. Because of the small size of fingerprint scanners, this may be a good choice for biometric security on your network.

Fingerprints do have some drawbacks. Because the area that the scanner must draw the data from is so small, fingerprint scanners are vulnerable to outside interference such as dirt or grime. Fingerprint scanners also aren't effective in places such as manufacturing or shop floors where the user's fingers may be scratched up.

In places like this, hand geometry scanners can be popular. These scanners make note of the user's fingerprints as well as other data drawn from key points the user's hand. The main drawback to these systems is that they are usually large and expensive. Most often, hand scanners are used to control access to buildings or rooms. You probably won't use one to control access to your network.

Another common method of biometric security includes identification drawn from the user's eyes. Blood vessels imbedded in your retina and the color and pattern of your iris are unique. You can purchase scanners that record these differences just like ones that record fingerprints or handprints. Like hand scanners, these methods are relatively expensive. They also don't lend themselves to access control to a network. Finally, your users might object to the thought of having something looking into their eyes for fear of possible damage.

As voice dictation software has become more popular, so too has voice recognition software. Don't confuse the voice recognition programs that do dictation with those that are used for security purposes. Dictation software recognizes only what the person is saying; security software identifies the speaker itself.

Voice recognition software identifies distinct patterns of speech that are unique to each individual. If you've ever seen an oscilloscope in action, you've seen amplitude waves of sound. Each voice has its own amplitude. Even expert impressionists can't duplicate the exact sound patterns of the original speaker.

Voice recognition software doesn't need its own special equipment like other biometric security programs do. It can use the sound card already inside your users' computers. All you need to do is install the software and add a microphone. Compared to other security software, voice recognition is also relatively inexpensive.

Voice recognition software isn't perfect, however. It's more prone to errors than other software. Such things as poor microphones, bad acoustics, or sickness on the part of the user can affect its accuracy.

Where can I find out more?

There are several organizations you can visit on the Web that can tell you more about biometrics. They can also supply you with links to vendors that supply biometric software. Make sure you do a detailed comparison between the features of each program and how it applies to your network before you purchase the software. Some of the best places to find information about biometrics include:

- ▶ **www.biometrics.org**—The Biometrics Consortium, run by the U.S. Government
- ▶ **www.biometricgroup.com**—The International Biometric Group.
- ▶ **www.ibia.org**—The International Biometric Industry Association
- ▶ **www.icsa.net**—The International Computer Security Association ◆

Masquerading's your friend, but don't trust it alone

By Jack Wallen, Jr.

So you have a small network running, you use Linux, and you want to be able to share a single IP address with all your machines. How do you do it? Ladies and gentlemen, I give you IP Masquerading.

There are many sources to guide the novice through the fundamentals of IP Masquerading. Unfortunately, all vary to a great degree in both difficulty and accuracy. Here's the simple—and accurate—scoop.

What is IP Masquerading?

A Linux host with IP Masquerade enabled can provide computers connecting to it with Internet access, even though those clients may have no dedicated IP addresses.

IP Masquerading also offers the opportunity, when combined with a firewall, to better protect critical files and data. Breaking the security of a well-set-up Masquerading system should be considerably more difficult than breaking a good packet filter-based firewall.

Masquerading allows for the average user to benefit from Linux's scalability and security and can be set up simply and

rather quickly by enabling ipforwarding in your kernel and IPV4, setting up basic "firewall" rules, and configuring the gateways of all client machines. It only takes a little tinkering with a few scripts to get your small network up and running online with only a single IP address.

Words to the wise

With IP Masquerading, security is a concern. Make sure to carefully examine the security of your system, or you stand the chance of having your entire network cracked open by some fly-by hacker.

How can this be prevented? In a word, FIREWALLS! For an in-depth look at Linux security, take a trip over to HowTo. There, you'll find the Linux Security How-to. Not a pretty document, nor a simple-to-comprehend piece of art. However, it should be required reading for any aspiring network administrator.

With IP Masquerading, the Linux network becomes an inexpensive solution to a rather expensive problem. Although the security risks can be high, with a little precautionary action, IP Masquerading could soon become the network administrator's best friend. ◆

NEED MORE INFORMATION ON IP MASQUERADING?

Check out these resources:

- ▶ Linux.com
- ▶ Red Hat Software

How to keep users from gobbling up disk space with quotas

By Bryan Pfaffenberger

If the word "quotas" makes you think of the Soviet Union's five-year plans and seldom-met production goals, think again. Quotas are part and parcel of a Linux system administrator's tasks—and that's true even when no other users have access to the system you're using. Sooner or later, you'll set up a server that exists for no other purpose than to provide network users with additional disk space. Lest some of the users fill up the disk at the expense of other users' privileges, you'll need to establish quotas so that each user is apportioned a fixed amount of space.

Although quotas are an essential part of Linux system management, documentation is surprisingly scarce. The topic isn't covered by most entry-or intermediate-level Linux books, and it's missing from the *Linux Documentation Project's System Administrator's Guide*. O'Reilly's *Essential System Administration* provides essential background information, but it's too focused on the Unix utilities. There's a genuine need for an update. Accordingly, this article fully covers all aspects of creating, defining, and managing user and group disk usage quotas on a Linux system, including details about the latest versions of the key underlying utilities. You'll also learn about some user-friendly packages that make quota-setting much easier, including Kmuser, a KDE utility that's currently tracking 200 student users in a German school.

Understanding disk usage quotas

As a system administrator with root privileges on a Linux system, you can establish quotas for any of the users on your system. In addition, you can establish quotas for groups. Whether established for users or groups, you can assign to each user as much or as little disk space as you please; however, you'll probably want to assign the same restrictions to all of the users. In schools that set up accounts for students in a programming class, for example, each student may be given a soft limit of 20 megabytes.

Thus far, we've spoken of quotas as if they pertain exclusively to the amount of disk space a user is allowed to consume-or to be more specific, to the number of 1K *blocks* of disk space. However, you can independently assign a limit on the number of *inodes* a user can create. In brief, an inode is a named entity that's stored on disk; inodes are files, for the most part, but devices and other special files are also inodes. Every Linux file system has a fixed number of inodes; however, this number is so large that it's unlikely to be exhausted. Since most system administrators ignore inode restrictions, this article will focus on setting quotas for disk usage consumption.

For each user and group account, you can create two kinds of quotas:

▶ *Soft* A soft quota generates a warning to the user, but it doesn't prevent the user from exceeding the specified limit—at least, not right away. And that's all to the good, considering that users often perform operations that temporarily gobble up more disk space than they usually consume. For example, consider what happens when you download StarOffice. The download files go in to a temporary directory (so51inst); from there, you run the Setup utility. After you finish the installation, you've eaten up a lot of diskspace, but the amount goes down when you delete the so51inst directory (which is no longer needed). In sum, you assign soft limits on the assumption that users will occasionally exceed them, and often for legitimate reasons.

▶ *Hard* A hard quota establishes an absolute limit, beyond which the system will not permit the user to store additional data. The hard limit should be higher than the soft limit, as much as 25 to 50 percent higher, so that the user has some head room for temporary bouts of inordinate disk usage.

When users exceed the soft quota, they receive a message informing them that they need to bring their disk consumption below the quota level. However, note that the message appears only if the user is working at the console or has a terminal window open within X. Users should be advised to run the quota command frequently; run without options from a user account, this command informs them if they have exceeded the soft quota. Should they fail to do so within a grace period that you can define (such as seven days), the system will prevent them from writing additional data above the soft limit.

Understanding the disadvantages of disk usage quotas

Although disk usage quotas are often needed on multiuser systems, they do have drawbacks. To determine how much disk space each user is consuming, the quota software must scan the disk regularly-and the scan takes time. In addition, users who violate the hard limit (or the soft limit, after the grace period expires) may find that they cannot save data that they've spent time creating. If users cannot save data because they have exceeded the quota, they can switch to a file management program, delete files until their consumption is under the quota, and save their data. Be sure to train users how to perform these actions so that they do not lose data unnecessarily.

Because of the drawbacks to the Linux quota system, you may wish to consider alternatives to disk quotas before proceeding. For a system shared by just two or three users, you could try an honor system, in which users are informed of disk usage limits and asked to observe them. You'll need to keep an eye on actual disk usage, though. For a system with a dozen or more users, there may be no practical alternative to disk usage quotas.

Note that Linux quota support is designed for use with the Second Extended Filesystem (ext2) only. You can't enable partitions that contain filesystems other than ext2.

Enabling quota support in the kernel

To set quotas on your Linux system, you need to make sure that quotas are enabled in your kernel. Linux distributions typically enable quota support by default, but you should check to make sure. To do so, follow these steps:

1. Open a terminal window, and switch to superuser (type *su* and supply your root password).

2. Type cd /usr/scr/linux and press [Enter].

3. Type make xconfig and press [Enter]to display the X kernel configuration utility.

4. Click Filesystems. You'll see the Filesystems options.

5. Check to see if the option is enabled. If not, click Y.

6. Click Main Menu.

7. Do one of the following:

8. If quota support was enabled, click Quit Without Saving.

9. If you had to enable quota support, click Save and Exit. You'll need to recompile your kernel, which isn't as difficult as it sounds.

Obtaining the quota utilities

To implement quotas, you'll also need the following quota utilities:

▶ *quotacheck* Creates the binary quota databases (quota.user and quota.group).

▶ *edquota* Enables the system administrator to define quotas for individual users.

▶ *quotaon* and *quotaoff* Launches or terminates the quota daemon.

▶ *quota* Enables users to check their quota status.

These utilities are provided with most Linux distributions. Should you need to obtain the source code, you'll find it at ftp://nic.funet.fi/pub/Linux/tools for the latest version of the quota utilities.

Implementing disk usage quotas: an overview

You're sold on the quota concept. But how do you implement quotas? Here's an overview of the process:

1. Modify /etc/fstab by adding *usrquota* (for user quotas) or *grpquota* (for group quotas) to the mount options of the filesystems that will have quotas.

2. Run *quotacheck -av* to create the required binary files, quota.user and quota.group, at the toplevel directory of each quota-enabled files ystem.

3. Run *edquota* to create a *prototype* user quota.

4. Run *edquota -t* to define the default grace period.

5. Copy the prototypical quota to other users.

6. Run *quotaon* to enable quotas on the system.

7. Modify your system initialization script to run the quota software automatically.

8. Check quota statuses periodically using *repquota*.

The following sections detail these procedures.

Enabling quotas in /etc/fstab

Quotas can be independently enabled (or disabled) for each partition and file system defined in /etc/fstab. In most cases, though, you will enable quotas only on the partition that contains the users' home directories. If you created a separate partition for /home, enable quotas on this partition. If users' home directories are part of a larger partition, such as the root partition (/), enable quotas on the partition that contains the home directories.

To enable quotas on one of the partitions listed in /etc/fstab, switch to the root user or superuser, and add *usrquota*, *grpquota*, or both to the mount options for this partition. (The mount options are found in the fourth column from the left.)

Creating the quota files

After you have added the quota-enabling options (*usrquota* or *grpquota*) to /etc/fstab, you need to run the quotacheck utility to create the necessary quota files (quota.user and quota.group). These files are created in the top-level directory of each of the quota-enabled partitions.

To create the needed files for all of the partitions on which you have enabled quotas, open a terminal window, switch to superuser (if necessary), and type *quotacheck -av*. The *-a* option tells quotacheck to search all the quota-enabled partitions, while the *-v* option displays status messages.

Defining a prototype user

Quotas are defined individually for each user. On a system with dozens or even hundreds of users, the task of setting up quotas could be quite time-consuming. However, you can cut down the work involved by creating a *prototype user*. In brief, a prototype user quota contains the quota settings that you want to apply to all or most of the other users on the system. For example, if you've decided to give each user 20 MB of storage space, you should begin by set-

ting up a prototype user quota with this amount of storage space defined as the default.

Do your homework before proceeding. Let's say you're setting up a system for a class with 30 students, and you've 1.2 GB of disk space to apportion among them. That works out to a maximum of 40 MB per student, so this figure is a good one to use for the hard limit. As a rule of thumb, begin by creating a soft limit that's 50 percent of the hard limit (20 MB). This figure leaves plenty of room for those occasional spurts of heavier-than-usual disk consumption.

To create a prototype user, do the following:

1. Open a terminal window, and switch to superuser (type *su* and supply your root password).

2. Type *edquota* followed by the name of the user whose disk usage quotas will be typical of users on this system. (If your shell cannot find this command, type *whereis edquota* to locate it.) You'll see the following in the default editor (which will be vi unless you've changed the default editor on your system):

```
Quotas for user bryan:
/dev/hda5: blocks in use:1231756,
limits (soft = 0, hard = 0)
```

3. inodes in use: 6054, limits (soft = 0, hard = 0) If you're using vi, type *i* to enter the insert mode.

4. In the line that contains blocks in use, delete the zero, and type the soft limit (in 1K blocks). To create a soft limit of approximately 20MB, this line should contain *soft = 20000.*"

5. Now set the hard limit by erasing the zero next to *hard =.* To create a hard limit of 40MB, this line should contain *hard = 40000.*"

6. Save the file and exit. If you're using vi, type Esc to exit the insert mode, type *:x*, and press [Enter].

Defining the default grace period

To define the default grace period, type *edquota -t* and press [Enter]. You'll see the default text editor again. This time, you'll see something like the following:

```
Time units may be: days, hours,
minutes, or seconds
```

```
Grace period before enforcing soft
limits for users:

/dev/hda5: block grace period: 0 days,
file grace period: 0 days
```

You'll see a grace period line for each of the partitions for which quotas have been enabled, such as /dev/hda5 in this example. If you enabled quotas on more than one partition, you can assign a unique grace period for each of them.

In the same way that you edited soft and hard limits in the previous step, use your text editor to change these values to those you prefer. A commonly chosen grace period is seven days.

Defining the prototypical user

Now that you've created the prototypical user and defined the grace period, you can easily copy this user's quota settings to other users. To do so, type *edquota -p* followed by the name of the prototypical user and the user whose quotas you want to define. Suppose the prototypical user is named Kyung, and you want to define Suzanne's quota. Here's what the command looks like:

```
edquota -p kyung suzanne
```

Repeat this command for all of the users to whom the prototypical restrictions should apply.

Turning on quotas

To switch quota-tracking on, switch to the superuser, if necessary, type *quotaon*, and press [Enter]. If you'd like to disable quotas, run *quotaoff*. Both of these utilities require root or superuser status.

Running quotas automatically

Once you've implemented quotas, you'll want them enabled automatically when you start your system. To do so, just add the following script to the *end* of /etc/rc.d/rc.sysinit:

```
#Check for quotas and turn quotas on
    if [ -x /usr/sbin/quotacheck ];
then
        echo "Checking quotas..."
        /usr/sbin/quotacheck -avug
    fi
    if [ -x /usr/sbin/quotaon ]; then
        echo "Turning quotas on..."
        /usr/sbin/quotaon —avug
    fi
```

This script should be positioned at the end of /etc/rc.d/rc.sysinit to make sure that the quota utilities run on mounted file systems (the commands that mount the file systems are gen-erally located in the middle of the initialization script). Note that your initialization script may already contain a commented-out version of this script; if so, delete the comment marks instead of adding the script.

Try rebooting your system to make sure the script modifications work correctly. If the script fails, carefully check your typing. Also, make sure the referenced utilities (quotacheck and quotaon) are indeed located in the indicated directory (/usr/sbin).

Checking quota status

Once you've enabled quotas, you should periodically run *repquota* to view the status of the quotas you've enabled. To do so, type *repquota -a* and press [Enter]. You'll see a list of users, their quota settings, and their actual resource usage. You can see at a glance whether any of the users have exceeded their soft quotas.

Quota horizons

If you set and edit quotas frequently, you may wish to explore more user-friendly utilities than the ones we've discussed. Here's the best of the lot:

▶ *Linuxconf* is an X-based system administration utility that enables you to set quotas in an easy-to-use, menu-driven environment. A particularly nice feature of *Linuxconf* is its ability to define defaults for user and group quotas. Once you've set these defaults, you can easily assign the default quotas to individual users. (You can also create custom quotas for each user, if you don't wish to use the defaults.) You can learn more about *linuxconf* at www. solucorp.qc.ca/linuxconf.

▶ For KDE systems, Kmuser is a nicely designed user administration tool that includes quota capabilities. In addition to providing easy-to-use tools for user creation and passwords, Kmuser enables you to define quota defaults. You can then assign the default quotas to individual users, or customize each user's quota as you please. Take a look at the http://kdm. linuxbox.com/kmuser/kmuser.html

Note that both of these utilities require you to enable quotas in the kernel and /etc/fstab; in addition, you need to run quotacheck to create the quota files, as well as quotaon to start the quota software. ◆

Chapter 2—Operating systems

Windows

Linux

Chapter 2: Operating Systems

Chapter 2 covers three of the many robust operating systems that are key to security:

▶ Windows

▶ Linux

▶ NetWare

We'll go deep into the heart of each OS and the applications surrounding it.

Windows

In the Windows section, we will examine the major players within the networking space: Exchange, Outlook, IIS, and a handful of third-party applications.

Linux

The Linux section will focus primarily on firewalling with ipchains and Progressive Systems' firewall appliance. We will also take a solid look at Apache, OpenSSL, and denial of service attacks.

NetWare

Although NetWare isn't typically considered to be the strongest tool for network security, our NetWare coverage will deal with administering NetWare as it functions in a heterogenous network.

Enhancing Exchange Server's security

By Brien M. Posey

In many organizations, e-mail has quickly become a mission critical application. Unfortunately, to send e-mail to and receive it from the outside world, your Exchange server must be connected to the Internet. As you probably know, the Internet is anything but a secure environment. In addition to your business colleagues, those who could harm your server—given the chance—also frequent the Internet. Therefore, one of the keys to successfully running an Exchange server is to never give those people the chance to tamper with your server. In this Daily Drill Down, we'll show you some techniques that you can use to help secure your Exchange Server.

What am I protecting against?

You may be wondering what harm a malicious user could possibly inflict on an e-mail server. After all, Exchange servers aren't usually domain controllers and don't usually contain sensitive application data. However, there are plenty of damaging actions that such a user could perform.

The most common form of attack against an Exchange server is called a denial of service attack. A denial of service attack is performed by flooding the server with mail messages to the point that the server can't keep up and ceases to process legitimate mail messages.

Other security breaches may result in a hacker stealing information. A hacker could do this by breaking in to the server and gaining access to folders containing sensitive information. A hacker could also steal information by using a packet sniffer and intercepting packets as they flow across the line.

Finally, you'll want to protect yourself against spoofing. Spoofing is when a hacker poses as a legitimate user. Although spoofing could be used to steal information, it can also be used to spread false information. For example, a spoofer could easily send notes that appear to be from a legitimate user. These notes could say things like "I quit," "The president of the company is a big, fat, stupid jerk," or "There's a bomb in the building set to go off at 2:00 P.M. if my demands aren't met." As you can see, spoofing can be quite harmful. Fortunately, there are tech-niques that you can use to protect your server against all three types of security breaches.

The basics

Some of the most effective techniques that you can use to protect your Exchange servers are the most basic. However, as you're probably aware, the basics alone aren't good enough. The best security comes from using a combination of basic and advanced security techniques. In the sections that follow, we'll review the basics and discuss some of the more advanced techniques.

Windows NT

As you already know, Exchange Server rides on top of Windows NT. Since Exchange uses many of Windows NT's security features, it's important to make sure that Windows NT is as secure as possible.

The complexity of Windows NT has inspired entire books on the subject of its security. Although space constraints don't permit us to delve deeply into the subject, there are a few pointers that you should keep in mind.

First, make sure that any volume containing Exchange-related files is formatted as NTFS. Many times when someone attempts to hack an NT server, he or she will try to break in through a network share. Although you can't get rid of the default network shares, keep in mind that file permissions (assigned through NTFS) add an extra layer of security to your server. When file permissions and share permissions contradict, Windows NT uses the more restrictive permission. For example, suppose that an unauthorized user gained access to a network share. If this user had full control over the network share but had read only permissions at the file level, NT would see the contradiction and grant the user read-only permissions, since it's the more restrictive of the two.

Service packs

Service packs can go a long way to help increase security. After a Windows NT service pack is released, Microsoft continuously searches for security holes. Patches for these security holes are released in the form of hot fixes, which are posted on Microsoft's FTP site. When a new service pack is released, all previous hot fixes are incorporated into the new service pack. At the time that this Daily Drill Down was written, the current Windows NT service pack was Service Pack 5. The latest Exchange 5.5 service pack was Service Pack 2.

Encryption

Not all service packs are created equal. The service packs that come with TechNet offer 40-bit encryption. This is the maximum encryption strength the U.S. government allows to be exported. Needless to say, 40-bit encryption isn't too difficult to crack.

However, if you live in the United States or in Canada, you can obtain 128-bit encryption in your service packs. To do so, you must download the service pack while connected to a computer that has a domain name that's registered in the United States or Canada. Because many Americans and Canadians have trouble downloading the high encryption service packs, you can order them on CD-ROM directly from Microsoft for a nominal fee.

Virus protection

As with any other application, you must protect your Exchange server against viruses. In many environments, viruses run rampant and spread in record time because of e-mail. For example, who hasn't received a good joke in their e-mail and forwarded it on to 20 of their closest friends. Your friends probably each pass the joke on to about 20 more people. If the message happened to have a file attachment that contained a virus, hundreds of people could become infected in a matter of a few hours.

Every good network administrator knows that you need to have up to date antivirus software on each workstation. However, doing so still leaves room for human error. For example, suppose you opened an e-mail attachment infected with a virus. Many anti-virus programs will give you a choice of repairing the virus, deleting the file, or ignoring the message completely. If a user ignores virus warnings, then the anti-virus software is basically useless.

Fortunately, there's a way around such a problem: installing antivirus software that runs on an Exchange server and scans all inbound messages before it reaches the intended recipient. If the software detects a virus, it immediately quarantines the file. Some packages will even alert the sender of the message of the virus. One such product is Norton Anti-Virus for Exchange by Symantec.

Service account

As you're probably aware, Exchange Server depends on a service account to interact with Windows NT's security system. This service account is a huge security hole, because it has the right to do pretty much anything to Exchange. Unfortunately, you can't disable the service account or decrease its rights without causing problems. Therefore, you should do the next best thing.

When you install Exchange, select a service account name that isn't obvious. For example, you might select a name that blends in with all of the other user accounts. Do you have a close friend that doesn't work with you? If so, consider paying tribute to them by naming the service account after them. For example, you might assign the service account a name like Kendall_Hensley or HensleyK, depending on the format of your other user account names.

It's important to point out that unless you know exactly what you're doing, you shouldn't rename an existing service account. Doing so haphazardly will cause Exchange to malfunction.

You should also use a strong password for the service account. There are a number of programs available on the Internet for cracking passwords. Some of these compare a hash of your password (extracted from the registry) to a dictionary of words and names. Others use brute force to try every possible combination. Therefore, the longer, more obscure, and well encrypted the password, the better. The best passwords mix upper and lower case characters with symbols and numbers.

Your Internet connection

So far we've shown you some basic steps that you can use to protect Exchange on the NT level. However, since the strongest threat comes from the Internet, it's a good idea to safeguard your Internet connection.

Proxy server

One good way to protect your network from Internet users is by using a proxy server. A proxy server requires a "multi-homed" Windows NT Server. This means that the server must have two network adapters. One of these adapters will connect to your Internet connection, while the other adapter connects to the remainder of your network. All traffic passing to and from the Internet must pass through the proxy server. The advantage of using a proxy server is that Internet users can only see one IP address on your network—the address of the proxy server. All other IP addresses are shielded by the proxy server and never passed to the Internet. From the standpoint of an outside user on the Internet, all traffic from your network appears to have been generated from the proxy server. Because all of your IP addresses are hidden, it makes it very difficult for someone to use TCP/IP calls to break into your network. With proxy server, you also have the ability to disable various TCP/IP ports and protocols. By leaving only the needed ports

Figure A

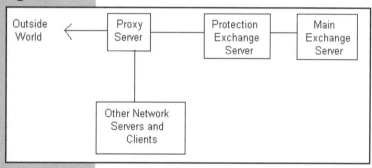

Your network's architecture can be designed in such a way as to make it much more difficult for someone to break into your Exchange servers.

Figure B

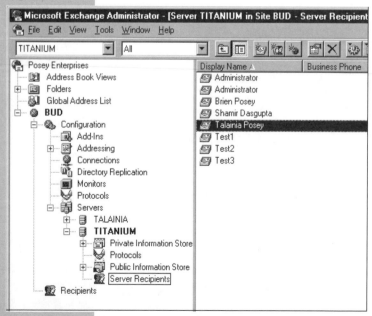

Open Exchange Administrator and navigate to Organization | Site | Configuration Servers | Server Recipients.

and protocols enabled, you reduce the risk of someone using an obscure TCP/IP component to hack your network.

Your Exchange architecture

As we've explained, the best way to protect your Exchange server is to protect NT and shield your network from all of those Internet-dwelling hooligans. However, no matter what you block or filter, there's always the chance that some devious individual will slip through the cracks. Fortunately, there's an easy way to further protect your Exchange server.

To do so, you'll need an extra copy of Exchange Server that will be used exclusively for SMTP routing. Simply load this new copy onto a spare server. Make this new server part of the existing site. The new server should be the only server with an Internet mail connector. All mailboxes and public folders should reside on the other servers in your site.

The new server will automatically pass inbound SMTP traffic to the appropriate mailbox. If someone launches a denial of service attack against you, it will only shut down the protection server. The attack won't have any effect on the servers containing mailboxes and public folders. Setting up Exchange in such a way is also a good safe guard against information theft and spoofing, since inner-office traffic will never touch a server with a direct connection to the outside world.

You may be wondering just how effective such a technique really is. After all, the protective server must be running TCP/IP to connect to the Internet. Likewise, your other servers and workstations are probably also using TCP/IP. Therefore, it would stand to reason that if a hacker makes it past your proxy server and breaks into the protective server, they could probably break into your other Exchange servers as well.

The reason the technique we just described works is due to the types of communications that can be used on various segments of your network. Your firewall will block the majority of the TCP/IP ports. Because of this, a person attempting to steal e-mail, spoof an account, or launch a denial of service attack would probably use SMTP calls to attempt to gain access to the server. Even if they do break into the server, Exchange doesn't use SMTP to communicate between local servers. Instead, it uses

RPC (remote procedure calls). Because of this, your servers containing mailboxes and public folders won't acknowledge SMTP communications. Therefore, your data is protected from such attacks. **Figure A** shows a diagram of what your network will look like with such a layout.

Security settings within Exchange

There are also a couple of parameters you can adjust within Exchange to help prevent a security breach. For example, we mentioned that a denial of service attack is caused by someone flooding your server with more messages than it can handle. Just because you've isolated your SMTP traffic doesn't mean that you want your protective server constantly going down because of such an attack. One way you can prevent such an attack is to place a size limit on inbound messages.

To do so, open Exchange Administrator and navigate to Organization | Site | Configuration Servers | Server Recipients, as shown in **Figure B**. Next, select a recipient and select Properties from the File menu. When you see the user's properties sheet, select the Limits tab. As you can see in **Figure C**, you can use the Limits tab to set the maximum inbound message size for each user. Therefore, you could set a relatively small size for

Figure C

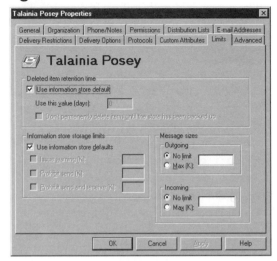

You can use the Limits tab to set the maximum inbound message size for each user.

most users and leave the size set at unlimited for users who frequently receive large attachments.

Conclusion

E-mail systems are often the targets of malicious Internet users. Therefore, it's important to protect your Exchange servers against Internet-based attacks. In this Daily Drill Down, we've explained some techniques that you can use to help enhance Exchange's security. ◆

Constructing an application security architecture using IIS, SQL 7, and NT groups

By Joe Barnes

In a "pre-Web" Windows NT environment, how was application security managed? In most cases, a homegrown security architecture was established on an application-by-application basis. The application buried some type of authentication wrapper around a users table within a database. This database table held a role, or definition, for each user. Or a common database was used specifically for this purpose and not only held user data but rolled it up to a group level. Each user was associated with a group (or groups), and each group had defined

rights within an application(s) and database(s). In essence, an entire group-based security architecture was created and modeled after the existing NT Group Security bundled within the operating system.

Now with Windows 2000 (which is very much Directory Services based) on our corporate heels, we are again pushed to think about how. Microsoft bundled SQL Server 7 with the ability to apply object-level security using NT groups. Prior to this, SQL Server was managed on a user-by-user basis. This meant that each user established within the NT domain who required access to a SQL Server database had to be added twice.

In addition to the SQL 7 security architecture change, Microsoft provided IIS with the ability to manage site security using NT groups via NT Challenge Response. NT Challenge Response is a process by which the IIS Server requests security credentials from the user accessing the site and verifies those supplied by an encrypted token supplied within the browser. The root value of this security method is that the server knows who you are and what you have access to (as defined within the file system security of your site).

In this Daily Drill Down, I'll examine how you can use these features to manage security on an intranet application based on NT group accounts, SQL Server 7, and IIS 4.0.

NT group accounts

The foundation of this security model is the use of NT groups to manage permissions on files and resources within your domain. To demonstrate this concept, I'll show you how to create a few user IDs and groups that will ultimately access your application via IIS.

FIGURE A

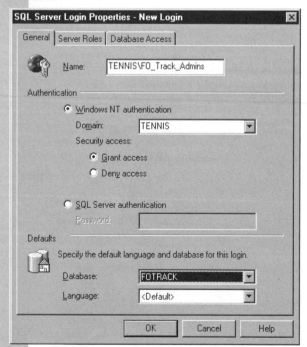

Specify FOTRACK as the default database for your group.

For demonstration purposes, I'll use the FO Track database. FO Track is a consultant's time-tracking tool built on SQL Server 7.

Two types of users will functionally access this application: our FO Track Administrator(s) and the FO Track Consultant(s). To implement access rights (for both the database and the Web site) for these two groups, you must first create the groups within your NT domain.

Begin by opening the User Manager for Domains tool that comes bundled with NT 4.0. Then, select the New Local Group option from the User menu. In the pop-up box that appears, you'll see text boxes for entering the group name and the group description. Name this group *FO_Track_Admins*.

To complete this task, you have to add users or other global groups to your newly created group. For our purposes, we have a global group that already contains all necessary members of our group—the Domain Admins group. The Domain Admins group is a built-in NT account that contains all designated Administrators of the domain. You may be wondering why you need to create a local group when you have a global group that contains all necessary users. The reason is, if you have to add a user as an Administrator of your application, you can do so by adding that user to your FO_Track_Admins group and *not* the Domain Admins group. This concept is the backbone of our security model; we strive to manage security on a group level— even if this means creating local groups and leveraging as much as possible in already functional global groups.

Our next account is application specific: the FO_Track_Consultants group. This group contains all users of the application. You perform the same steps as you did with the FO_Track_Admins account. However, because no predefined global group fills the bill, you have to add specific users to this account.

SQL 7 security

With the domain security model in place, you are now able to map a specific SQL Server database to your newly created NT group accounts. First, you register your groups within your SQL Server (in this case, OFFSRV1). Attach to this server via Enterprise Manager (or the Microsoft Management Console) and add these two groups as user accounts on the SQL Server. Keep in mind that you must have Administrative access to the SQL Server to perform this task.

To begin, navigate to the Security folder on the server. Expand that folder and right-click the Logins icon. Then, click the New Login menu option to open a dialog box containing specific user data. On the General tab, you'll specify how this new login will access SQL Server. Since you're using NT group security, select this option. You will then designate the domain where your user is coming from. (In this case, you are working with the Tennis domain.) Next, type in the user (in this case, group) account name—FO_Track_Admins. To complete the entries on the General tab, specify the FO Track database (FOTRACK) as the default for this group, as shown in **Figure A**. This means that when the user is logging in to your SQL Server, the user will access the FO Track database by default.

You must also configure the server roles and database access associated with this group by clicking the appropriate tab. For this account, you don't need to designate any special rights on the server level. Just assign this group access to the FO Track database and set the permissions on this database as db_owner. This way, you assign Administrative capability over this database to the FO_Track_Admins group.

While on the Database Access tab, add the FO_Track_Consultants group as well. However, keep in mind that the Consultants group will *not* have db_owner access. Assign this group only public access rights, as shown in **Figure B**. Assigning only public access rights gives you the ability to then restrict further the options available to the user or group in the future by creating specific server roles and applying them on a SQL object level. An example of this would be allowing only specific users (or groups) the right to execute stored procedures within a database.

Both groups now have appropriate access within the FO Track database. You have successfully mapped the newly created NT Group accounts to your SQL Server. Next, I'll examine the role IIS plays in completing the connection.

IIS

In order for your Web application to recognize and have the ability to pass the user credentials

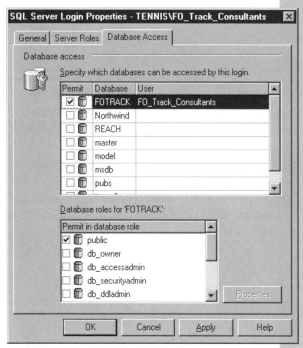

Assign the FO_Track_Consultants group only public access rights.

FIGURE C

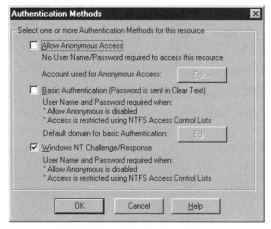

Be sure the Windows NT Challenge/Response option is selected.

from the browser to the calling application, you must configure NT Challenge Response security on your site. This security option, however useful, is applicable only when being used in conjunction with Internet Explorer.

NT Challenge Response performs a couple of critical functions for your application. First, you have the ability to validate your user against the NTFS security permissions applied on the files your application will access. This option plays a great role in creating intra- and extranet systems. Second, you now have captured and sent to the server the username and password. You can leverage this when using application options such as DSN—there are no specific user credentials passed from calling application to database. (I use this type of configuration to limit the amount of security data stored within my code.)

To implement NT Challenge Response within your site, navigate to the Site Properties sheet within the Internet Service Manager (or again, the Microsoft Management Console). Select the Directory Security tab, choose Anonymous Access And Authentication Control, and click the Edit button to open the Authentication Methods dialog box. Deselect the Allow Anonymous Access option and make sure the Windows NT Challenge/Response

check box is selected, as shown in **Figure C** on the previous page.

Conclusion

In this Daily Drill Down, I've outlined a security architecture for your application. By performing this task prior to implementing the model, you draw a map from your calling application and the functionality required to the backend SQL Server database. You leverage this design by applying permissions to resources only on the group level. This will allow you to make changes in one place and affect both the domain and SQL Server architecture.

As you can see, this concept provides both extensibility and manageability from a central location. By making the group account the backbone of your security, you have an easy-to-follow guideline for future applications designed within your environment. ◆

STILL GETTING RID OF WORMS
In what is being considered a bold move by some—and an "about-time" initiative by others—Microsoft is preparing to release a patch that will add greater security to Outlook software. In this article, Exterminator points you to that information and covers a few IIS and Office 2000 issues as well.

Exterminator: Microsoft to patch Outlook in wake of ILOVEYOU worm

By Ed Engelking

Microsoft Security Update

Regarding: Microsoft Outlook 97, 98, and 2000
Posting: soon
Information URL: Go to http://officeupdate. microsoft.com/2000/articles/out2ksecarticle.htm for more information.

In response to the ILOVEYOU worm, Microsoft is preparing a patch for its Outlook software that adds greater security to the program. The soon-to-be-released patch will make it far more difficult to inadvertently launch attachments received via e-mail. The patch will provide a more explicit warning and prevent attached executables from being launched directly from e-mails. Instead, they will have to be saved to a disk and launched in a separate process. Could this spell the end of mass e-mail viruses such as Melissa and ILOVEYOU? More information on this initiative is available from Microsoft. Simply visit the Information URL above for the latest announcement from Redmond.

Microsoft Security Bulletin (MS00-034)

Regarding: Microsoft Office 2000
Posted: May 12, 2000
Patch URL: Go to http://officeupdate. microsoft.com/info/ocx.htm for the patch.
Information URL: Go to http://www. microsoft.com/technet/security/bulletin/ ms00-034.asp for more information.

Microsoft recently released a patch for its Office 2000 suite. The patch eliminates a security vulnerability that could allow a Web site operator to take inappropriate action on the computer of a user who visits his/her Web site. For more information on this patch, visit the Information URL above.

Microsoft Security Bulletin (MS00-031)

Regarding: Microsoft Internet Information Server
Posted: May 10, 2000

Patch URL: Go to http://www.microsoft.com/ Downloads/Release.asp?ReleaseID=2090 for the IIS 4.0 patch.

Patch URL: Go to http://www.microsoft.com/ Downloads/Release.asp?ReleaseID=20903 for the IIS 5.0 patch.

Information URL: Go to http://www. microsoft.com/technet/security/bulletin/ms00-031.asp for more information.

Microsoft recently released a patch for its Internet Information Server (IIS). The patch eliminates security vulnerabilities that could be used to slow down an affected Web server's response or to obtain the source code of certain types of files under very restricted conditions. For more information on this patch, visit the Information URL above.

Microsoft Security Bulletin (MS00-030)

Regarding: Microsoft Internet Information Server
Posted: May 11, 2000
Patch URL: Go to http://www.microsoft.com/ Downloads/Release.asp?ReleaseID=20906 for the IIS 4.0 patch.

Patch URL: Go to http://www.microsoft.com/ Downloads/Release.asp?ReleaseID=20904 for the IIS 5.0 patch.

Information URL: Go to http://www. microsoft.com/technet/security/bulletin/ms00-030.asp for more information.

Microsoft has released a patch for its Internet Information Server (IIS). This patch eliminates a security vulnerability that could be used to slow down the performance of the affected server or temporarily stop it altogether. For more information on this patch, visit the Information URL above.

Trend Micro virus updates

Virus/Worm: W97M_THUS.T
Posted: May 16, 2000
Information URL: Go to http://www.anti-virus.com/vinfo/virusencyclo/default5.asp?V Name=W97M_THUS.T for more information on this virus.

Virus/Worm: W97M_CHACK.BS
Posted: May 16, 2000
Information URL: Go to http://www.anti-virus.com/vinfo/virusencyclo/default5.asp? VName=W97M_CHACK.BS for more information on this virus.

Virus/Worm: W97M_MYNA.N
Posted: May 16, 2000
Information URL: Go to http://www.anti-virus.com/vinfo/virusencyclo/default5.asp?V Name=W97M_MYNA.N for more information on this virus.

Virus/Worm: W97M_PATHETIC.C
Posted: May 16, 2000
Information URL: Go to http://www.anti-virus.com/vinfo/virusencyclo/default5.asp?V Name=W97M_PATHETIC.C for more information on this virus.

Virus/Worm: TROJ_WINCRASH.B
Posted: May 16, 2000
Information URL: Go to http://www.anti-virus.com/vinfo/virusencyclo/default5.asp?V Name=TROJ_WINCRASH.B for more information on this virus.

Virus/Worm: TROJ_SOUTHPARK
Posted: May 11, 2000
Information URL: Go to http://www.anti-virus.com/vinfo/virusencyclo/default5.asp?V Name=TROJ_SOUTHPARK for more information on this virus. ◆

Using Secure Socket Layer with Outlook Web Access

By Ron Nutter

Keeping passwords secure is an important issue for many companies. Accessing e-mail remotely may involve using the Microsoft Outlook Web Access (OWA) component of Exchange. This approach has one small problem: OWA offers no security in terms of keeping the password secure.

With a little bit of work, you can bring the SSL (Secure Socket Layer) technology to Exchange OWA and keep your passwords and e-mail more secure. By using a special file from VeriSign, you can set up encrypted communications between browsers and your Exchange Server. In this Daily Drill Down, I'll take you through the process of enabling SSL on Exchange OWA. I'll also demonstrate the process of getting an SSL certificate from VeriSign.

Getting the certificate

The main three certificate authorities (CA) are VeriSign, Thawte Consulting, and CyberTrust. Other CAs are available. Just be sure to verify that the certificate will be supported by the browsers you intend to support. If it isn't, users will have to install a certificate or other service so they can establish an SSL connection to your Web site.

First, you must decide which level of encryption you need (basic encryption, 128-bit, etc.) and whether you need additional services. You can expect the cost to range from $125 to around $1,300 for one year.

Getting an SSL certificate for your Exchange Server is not something you should put off until you really, really need it. Depending on the CA you use and the level of encryption/service you want, it could take anywhere from a couple of hours to a week or more to get your certificate. One factor affecting the length of time is the amount of background checking the CA must do to confirm your identity.

Preparing for the CA application process

I recently went through this process for my company and had a couple of surprises along the way. We had just moved into new offices and found out that one of the verification steps taken by VeriSign was to check our business information with Dun & Bradstreet, a common source of business-to-business information. The problem we ran into was that our address and contact information was incorrect as a result of our move. The application process for the SSL certificate was delayed for several weeks while we filled out the form twice on Dun & Bradstreet's Web site and then had to follow up with a phone call before getting the changes made.

Just as we started the application process, we found that VeriSign refuses to create an SSL certificate for a site if you don't have a fully

qualified DNS name for the server in question. This means that you must have a DNS record for the server, listing its name and the IP address. VeriSign will not issue an SSL certificate if you have only an IP address. We hit another snag here: The primary DNS server showed the information, but the information we needed to have distributed concerning our e-mail server wasn't showing up on the secondary DNS server. A couple of calls to the ISP hosting our DNS resolved this problem.

VeriSign will send 40-bit SSL certificates to the requesting party, assuming the information you supply checks out. Don't ask to have the certificate mailed to your ISP e-mail account; it will need to go to your company e-mail server. VeriSign will send 128-bit SSL certificates to the administrative or technical contacts for the domain. So if you're hosting your own DNS servers, be sure you're listed as either the administrative or technical contact for the Internet domain(s) for which you'll be getting SSL certificates.

Finally, check the Exchange Server itself. Choose Programs from the Start menu and look for the option NT 4.0 Option Pack. If you see this option, that's a good indication that IIS 4.0 has been installed on the Exchange Server (one of the requirements for using OWA) and that the Outlook Web Access component of Exchange has probably been installed as well. If you don't see this option, you will first need to take the following steps:

▶ Install IIS.

▶ Reapply the NT Service Pack.

▶ Rerun the Exchange setup program.

▶ Add the Outlook Web Access component.

▶ Reapply the Exchange Service Pack (you should be at Exchange SP 2 at a minimum).

I recommend that you use at least Service Pack 5 for NT to avoid some SNMP-level problems.

Starting the certificate process

The first step is generating a certificate-signing request (CSR). This involves creating a text file that you can cut and paste into a form on the CA's Web site so it can begin the process of generating an SSL certificate for you. You start your journey by opening the Internet Service Manager (non-HTML version) to bring up the Microsoft Management Console (MMC).

Once the splash screen disappears, right-click on the Web site name and click the Properties option. When the Web site properties sheet appears, right-click on the Web site you want to add the certificate to. Select the Directory Security tab and click the Secure Communications box. Now, select the Key Manager tab to start the file-creation process. Choose the service for which you want to install SSL (and you thought that SSL was only for HTTP?). Click the Web site to select it and then right-click it. Then, click the Create New Key option. The Create New Key wizard will guide you through the process of creating a certificate request.

Unless you plan to be your own certificate authority (normally only a good idea if you're looking for SSL services on a corporate intranet), you'll go through the wizard to create a text file. You'll then cut and paste that text file into VeriSign's Web site when you apply for the SSL certificate.

When the wizard first appears, the default location and filename is C:\NewKeyRq.txt. Unless you have a compelling need to change the location of this file, click the Next button to continue.

The second window will ask you to supply a name for the key. This step can be important if you'll have more than one certificate on your server. Naming the keys lets you easily identify what certificate is being used for what purpose. Enter the name that you want to use for the key request, and then enter the password you want to use to control the installation of the SSL certificate. Keep the password handy— you'll need it later when installing the SSL certificate. Click Next.

At this point, you have to supply some basic information to help differentiate this certificate from others you may have or others on the Internet. After entering the requested information, click Next. The fourth window will ask you for your country, state, and city. Enter the information as requested and click Next.

Now you're asked to enter your name, e-mail address, and telephone number. This is so that VeriSign can contact you if there are any problems processing your request. Click the Finish button to generate the key request file. You should now see a key entry below the Web site label in the Key Manager window.

Using Notepad or Wordpad, open the key request file you just created. Once you've answered the appropriate questions on VeriSign's Web site, cut and paste the contents of the key request file in its entirety into the appropriate part of the form. Within a few hours or days, you should receive an e-mail from VeriSign containing the SSL certificate.

Once the file is in your possession, return to the Internet Service Manager. Select Start | Programs | Windows NT 4.0 Option Pack | Microsoft Internet Information Server | Internet Service Manager. On the left-hand side, highlight the default Web site on which you want to enable SSL. Right-click, then select the Properties option.

When the properties window appears, click the Directory Security tab. Then, click the Edit button in the Secure Communications box. In the Secure Communications window, click the Key Manager button. Highlight the key request that you created earlier. Then, right-click on the certificate request and select Install Key Certificate. Browse to find where you placed the certificate file from VeriSign, and double-click the filename. Enter the password you used when submitting the SSL certificate request on VeriSign's Web site.

When the Server Bindings window appears, you won't need to do anything unless you're running multiple Web servers on your Exchange Server. If you want to lock the SSL certificate down to operate only with a particular IP address, click the Add button. Then, supply the IP address and port number you want to use for this SSL certificate and click OK.

Regardless of whether you decided to restrict the SSL certificate to a particular address, you'll need to click OK again to continue. Once you return to the Key Manager window, the status for the SSL certificate you just installed should now show as Complete and Useable. Click OK to return to the main MMC console window.

Configuring OWA to use SSL

You've almost finished setting up SSL for your Exchange Server. In the MMC console window, right-click on the directory IISadmpwd, then select the Properties option. In the IISadmpwd Properties window, select the Directory Security tab. Click the Edit button in the Secure

Communications area. Then, select the options Require Secure Channel When Accessing This Resource and Accept Certificates (under Client Certificate Authentication).

Right-click on Exchange (it will have an icon to the left that looks like an open box with a piece of paper sticking out of it), then select Properties. In the resulting window, click the Directory Security tab. Click the Edit button under Secure Communications. Then, select the Require Secure Channel When Accessing This Resource and the Accept Certificates options. Click OK twice to return to the main MMC window. You can now exit MMC.

To achieve even greater security for OWA, you can install workstation-level SSL certificates and configure IIS to look for these. If you do this, OWA and SSL will work only if the user logs in from his or her PC, because an individual certificate is linked to an individual NT login account.

Testing the SSL link to OWA
Now that you've configured IIS to use SSL, you need to perform some tests. First, you must ensure that non-SSL communications will no longer work. In a Web browser, type *http://mailserver.domain.com* (use the actual host

and domain name for your Exchange Server). If non-SSL access has been disabled, you should see an HTTP 403 window. The 403 error indicates that this resource requires the use of SSL for access. Next, reenter the same URL but this time start the URL with *https* instead of *http*. This time, everything should work fine.

You can also test the SSL functionality by replacing the IP address shown with the actual IP address of your Exchange Server. You may see a security alert from your Web browser indicating that the security certificate is valid but that the name on the certificate doesn't match the name of the site. After clicking OK to answer this prompt, you should be able to get an HTTPS session to your Exchange Server via OWA.

Conclusion
In this Daily Drill Down, I walked you through the process of setting up your Exchange Server to handle SSL communications when using Outlook Web Access. Be sure you keep a copy of both the certificate request and the license file you receive just in case you have to replace the files. Good luck, and may all your sensitive information be encrypted! ◆

Exterminator: Microsoft back door causes problems
By Ed Engelking

Microsoft Security Bulletin (MS00-025)
Regarding: Windows NT 4.0 Option Pack, Personal Web Server 4.0, FrontPage 98 Server Extensions
Date Posted: April 17, 2000
FAQ URL: Go to http://www.microsoft.com/ technet/security/bulletin/fq00-025.asp for the FAQ from Microsoft.
Information URL: Go to http://www. microsoft.com/technet/security/bulletin/ ms00-025.asp for information from Microsoft.

Information URL: Go to http://www.msnbc. com/news/396756.asp?0m=-18P for information from MSNBC.

Microsoft recently announced a security hole that affects several of its Web server products. The hole, sometimes referred to as a "back door," could allow a user to cause a Web server to crash or to run arbitrary code on the server if certain permissions had been changed from the default settings. Microsoft suggests deleting the file Dvwssr.dll to close the security hole. For more information, visit the FAQ URL or Information URLs above.

Microsoft Security Bulletin (MS00-024)

Regarding: Microsoft Windows NT 4.0
Date Posted: April 12, 2000
Patch URL: Go to http://www.microsoft.com/ Downloads/Release.asp?ReleaseID=20330 for the x86 patch.
Patch URL: Go to http://www.microsoft.com/ Downloads/Release.asp?ReleaseID=20331 for the Alpha patch.
Information URL: Go to http://www. microsoft.com/technet/security/bulletin/ ms00-024.asp for more information.

Microsoft recently released a patch for Windows NT 4.0 that installs tighter permissions within the Windows NT 4.0 registry. The default permissions could allow any user that is able to interactively log on to a Windows NT 4.0 machine to compromise the cryptographic keys of other users who log in to the same machine. For more information, visit the Information URL.

Microsoft Security Bulletin (MS00-023)

Regarding: Microsoft IIS 4.0 and 5.0
Date Posted: April 12, 2000
Patch URL: Go to http://www.microsoft.com/ Downloads/Release.asp?ReleaseID=20292 for the 4.0 patch.
Patch URL: Go to http://www.microsoft.com/ Downloads/Release.asp?ReleaseID=20286 for the 5.0 patch.
Information URL: Go to http://www. microsoft.com/technet/security/bulletin/ ms00-023.asp for more information.

Microsoft recently released a patch for its Internet Information Server. The patch eliminates a vulnerability that can allow a user to slow a Web server's response, or prevent the server from providing service altogether for a period of time. For more information, click the Information URL above.

Novell issues

Regarding: NetWare 5 Version 7.45
Date Posted: April 17, 2000
Patch URL: Go to http://support.novell.com/ cgibin/search/download?sr&/pub/updates/ nw/nw5/ds7b.exe for the patch.

Information URL: Go to http://support. novell.com/cgibin/show_information?File-Name=ds7b.exe for more information.

Novell recently released a patch that updates its NetWare 5 software. The patch is an NDS update for NetWare 5 servers running Recman (7.x) database. For more information, visit the Information URL above.

Novell issues

Regarding: Host Publisher
Date Posted: April 17, 2000
Patch URL: Go to http://support.novell.com/ cgibin/search/download?sr&/pub/updates/ cp/inwbhpub/ihp232.exe for the patch.
Information URL: Go to http://support. novell.com/cgi-bin/show_information?File-Name=ihp232.exe for more information.

Novell recently released a patch to update its Host Publisher. Novell suggests updating the currently shipping Host Publisher 1.1 "box," as it contains the same code as Support Pack 3. This update contains fixes and enhancements that are more recent than the "red box." For more information, visit the Information URL .

Novell issues

Regarding: Solaris Corporate Edition SP1
Date Posted: April 17, 2000
Patch URL: Go to http://support.novell.com/ cgibin/search/download?sr&/pub/updates/ nds/ndss/n8scesp1.exe for the patch.
Information URL: Go to http://support. novell.com/cgi-bin/show_information?File-Name=n8scesp1.exe for more information.

Novell recently released a patch to update Solaris Corporate Edition. Customers should only use the patch with a valid NDS for Solaris Corporate Edition license. This patch is not meant for Solaris Servers running NDS for Solaris 2.0, NDS for Solaris E-Directory, or any trial version of NDS for Solaris. For more information, visit the Information URL above .

Red Hat Linux issues

Regarding: Red Hat Linux 6.0-6.2 for Alpha, i386, and Sparc
Date Posted: April 16, 2000
Information URL: Go to http://www. securityfocus.com/bid/1111 for more information. SecurityFocus.com recently reported

vulnerability in Red Hat Linux 6.x. According to SecurityFocus, it is possible for a user to cause a denial of service with the X11 Font Server. Due to improper input validation, there is potential for a user to crash the X Font Server, preventing the X Server from operating properly. For more information, visit the Information URL above.

Sun Microsystems issues

Regarding: StarOffice 5.1
Date Posted: April 16, 2000

Information URL: Go to http://www.security-focus.com/bid/1112 for more information SecurityFocus.com recently reported vulnerabilities in Sun's StarOffice 5.1. According to SecurityFocus, a number of buffer overflow vulnerabilities exist within StarOffice 5.1. By supplying either HTML or a native StarOffice document with a long URL, it is possible to cause a buffer overflow. For more information, visit the Information URL above. ◆

THE BURDENS OF ENCRYPTION
As Web appliances move from midsize into larger enterprises, Gartner expects the burden of public key encryption to be too great for the first-generation devices. Servicing large, high-volume retail sites will require the addition of encryption support chips for larger enterprises.

Enterprise management update: Web security outlook from 2000 to 2005

By M. Zboray

Web security will get worse before it gets better, but Gartner expects long-term improvements to appear by 2003 as multiple security technologies are merged into Web security appliances.

An old adage says that imitation is the sincerest form of flattery. That is also true for security technology. Appliance technology for Internet security was pioneered in the firewall space. Its effectiveness as a means of delivering safe Internet access with high value has been unsurpassed.

▶ In practical applications, the appliance approach can supply superior security over PC or workstation implementations of the same security software.

▶ With the appliance approach, the responsibility for platform security is placed in the hands of the designer of the appliance.

▶ The correct integration of the security application and the underlying operating system is completely removed from enterprises.

▶ Easy configuration and operations are maintained by creating Java- or Win32-based administration clients.

As with all security devices, however, theory can deviate from practice. The firewall appliances that have been in use for the last 24 months have a security track record that is at least equal that of NT-based firewall technol-

ogy. Based on theoretical considerations, the security of the firewall appliances will probably equal firewalls running on UNIX workstations by 2002. Firewall appliances will become the dominant form of firewall technology for all user segments by 2003 (0.9 probability).

In addition, Gartner expects that the evolution path described for firewalls will be replicated for secure Web servers. Looking ahead, two new secure Web appliances will likely appear by 2002 that will relieve outsourcers and enterprises of the burden of installing, configuring, and administering secure systems.

Potential contributors to the "trusted Web appliance" include:

▶ Argus Systems Group

▶ Axent Technologies

▶ Cobalt Networks

▶ VA Linux Systems

▶ WatchGuard Technologies

▶ Secure-transaction Web appliances

Trusted Web servers are mandatory for high-value exchanges over the Internet. However, if an enterprise's skills are based in Microsoft technology, it will have no easy solution to finding a trusted NT Web server. A similar situation occurred in the firewall market, but unlike that market, enterprises are being unrealistic if they believe that any vendor outside of Microsoft could possibly make a trusted version of the NT Web server.

Rather, Gartner expects trusted Web server products will quickly bifurcate into a high-end/large-server market and a low-end appliance market. In both segments, enterprises will have the choice of acquiring or using a management service. All aspects of UNIX will likely be hidden by the Web interface integrated into the trusted Web appliance. Enterprises that must customize business logic on the trusted gateway will be able to use Common Gateway Interface or Java servlets. That secure-transaction Web appliance will likely be based on the then-current-generation Intel technology and will have a retail list price of about $5,000.

Secure-information-distribution Web servers

A surefire way to ensure the integrity of an information Web server is to make it "immutable." By setting the executables and the content to "read-only" status, it becomes very difficult—and, if literally implemented, impossible—to corrupt the data that is exposed to the Internet. Currently, this is a difficult approach to creating a secure-information-distribution Web server. Little data is wholly static, and public data is often dynamic (e.g., current stock market quotes).

By year-end 2001, information Web servers will likely use "mailboxes" and digital signatures to ensure the integrity of public data. This technique will create a safe, yet dynamic environment for distributing information. Through the use of read-only mass storage, read-only executables, and intrusion detection systems built into the Web server—all on a preconfigured Web appliance —the security of information distribution Web systems will likely become good enough so that Web administrators who are not security-trained will be able to install, configure, and operate the servers and have full confidence that the Web content on them will remain unchanged.

Bottom line

▶ Through 2001, while the industry waits for this technology to appear, Gartner recommends only short-term outsourcing of secure e-commerce Web systems. This is especially true for enterprises that have stringent security requirements but only modest security skills.

▶ Secure Web appliances, although they will have their own issues, will significantly reduce the cost of secure Web operations.

▶ Through 2001, the option for "insourcing" the secure Web server will likely become more attractive.

▶ Soon thereafter, Web outsourcers will realize that secure Web appliances can reduce the outsourcers' costs of operations and will then reduce their own pricing as well.

▶ In either case, Gartner expects that the cost of acquiring and operating secure e-business systems will be reduced by at least 35 percent by 2002. ◆

How to prevent users from sending external e-mail through Exchange

By Jeff Davis

The Web is full of places where you can get help with support problems, but one of the best resources you'll find is right here in the TechRepublic Forums. When you post a question in one of our forums, you assign a certain number of TechPoints to the question.

When someone answers the question to your satisfaction, you award the TechPoints to that person. (To find out how many TechPoints you have, click the TechPoints link in our left navigation bar.)

Help for e-mail managers

Here's a question that was recently posted in the Messaging/E-mail section of the Support forum with a value of 100 TechPoints. TechRepublic passport owner **Mike C.** wrote, "I have several employees abusing my e-mail policy, and I would like to restrict access to these users and possibly view or print their internal e-mails. My first step is to restrict Internet e-mail for some users. Second, I'd like to view or print internal e-mails and report the findings to our Human Resources department. Some content contains sexual overtones and could possibly be interpreted as sexual harassment."

Here's the answer Mike C. accepted. It was posted by TechRepublic passport owner **DMC-Master**: "You can prevent users from sending external e-mail by doing the following. Go to Microsoft Exchange Administrator. Open Connections, open the Properties of Internet Mail Service, click the Delivery Restrictions tab, and add those users in the "reject messages from" list. ◆

Enhancing Windows 2000 Professional security using ZoneAlarm

By Dallas G. Releford

Okay, so I don't have any information on my computers that the CIA would be interested in. However, I do deal with a lot of big companies, and I have a great interest in protecting their information from prying eyes. In this article, I'll take a look at Zone Labs' ZoneAlarm, which establishes a firewall on your Windows 2000 Professional PC or system.

Building a firewall using ZoneAlarm

Not only do you have to protect yourself from viruses and similar programs, you also have to protect your system from other computers that might put programs on your system that can do major damage. Some of these programs can be installed on your system from a remote location and run transparently. Normally, you wouldn't even know that the program is there. These types of programs are designed to do a lot of damage, such as:

▶ Jamming a Web site by continuously sending files or requests to the Web site's server (also known as a denial-of-service attack).

▶ Taking an inventory of your computer system and use that information to send out data about you and your system every time you log on to the Internet.

▶ Uploading files to the originator's computer.

It's really scary when you find out that your system is under such an attack and your security has been compromised—it's as if you come home one night and everything has been stolen from your home. Luckily, there are many programs that can help protect you from this sort of thing. One in particular that I've found really helpful is a freeware program called ZoneAlarm.

How does it work?

ZoneAlarm establishes a firewall on your PC or system and helps prevent other computers from accessing your ports and installing programs on your system. The firewall controls the door to your computer, helping to protect your data and files.

ZoneAlarm includes four interlocking security services that deliver easy-to-use, comprehensive protection:

▶ **Application Control**—Lets you decide which applications can and cannot access the Internet.

▶ **The Internet Lock**—Blocks Internet traffic while your computer is unattended or while you aren't using the Internet.

▶ **Security Levels**—Automatically configure the firewall and eliminate the risk of improper configuration.

▶ **Zones**—Allow you to grant access rights.

What's it going to cost me?

ZoneAlarm is a great product and it is freeware. It has been checked for virus infection, but when you download it, you should check it again just for peace of mind.

Most of the freeware sites out there have ZoneAlarm for you to download. You can also find it at Zone Lab and ZDNet's Soft-Seek.com. ◆

Managing NT's Remote Access Service

By Ron Nutter

In this article, we'll discuss some ways to handle increased use of RAS once your users become familiar with it. We'll explain how to deploy RAS using both hardware and software methods. The main thing to remember about RAS is that both its implementation and deployment are modular.

Using a dedicated RAS server

At some point, it will become unacceptable for all your RAS users to call into your primary NT Server, due to the high processor load, limited number of modems, and so on. Depending on the number of incoming connections you're managing, you may need to dedicate one or more servers to only handling RAS users.

When you do, you must consider the level of security you want on the network. Security concerns will dictate which of these configurations you choose for the NT Server(s) handling the RAS connections:

▸ Workgroup servers

▸ Member servers in your existing domain

▸ Servers in a resource domain or another separate domain with trusts to the domain containing resources that users will need to access

Each of these options has advantages and disadvantages. Configuring the NT server as a workgroup server with no domain membership really isn't an acceptable option—you'll experience too many management headaches from users accessing resources in a domain to which they haven't authenticated. For most RAS implementations, management will be easiest if the RAS server is a member server in a domain (this option is also simplest for the users).

You can use the Allow Remote Access option in the Remote Access Admin program (under Administrative Tools on the Programs menu) to implement controller dial-up access to the network. In addition, RAS users must know the dial-in phone number. In many cases, these are sufficient security precautions. However, companies that are especially security conscious may want to consider placing the RAS server in another domain. You then establish either a resource domain configuration or two-way trusts between the domain containing the RAS server and the domain containing the resources that users need to access. By placing the NT server in another domain, you can require users to have a dial-in password that's different from the one they use in the office.

In the end, there's no one right way to handle security. The planning process for remote access should involve your company's internal and external auditors, so that any decisions you make will be in compliance with the regulations your company follows during its normal course of business.

Hardware options for handling RAS usage

For four phone lines or less, the regular modems you have now should be sufficient. To alleviate excess processor usage, you should consider using specialized communications boards such as the Comtrol RocketPort Serial Hub (www.comtrol.com). This board comes in both ISA and PCI flavors and in either a four- or eight-port configuration.

As your needs grow beyond a few ports, the cabling mess you must deal with will also increase as you install additional lines. Equinox (www.equinox.com) offers two interesting modem pool products—one for analog use and one for digital use—that can help you prevent such a mess and manage growth. The analog option offers more flexible implementation, due to the way Equinox chose to implement the solution.

The analog modem pool, shown in **Figure A**, uses off-the-shelf internal ISA bus PC modems available for less than $100. The base kit comes with a multiport serial board that can drive either 64 or 128 modems. The cage unit can house up to 16 modems, and you can daisy-chain cages to handle additional card units as your needs grow. I recommend this approach because as modem standards change (and they will continue to do so), you can keep up with the standards by simply changing modems as the need arises. The best part of the Equinox modem pool is that you don't have to power down your entire RAS server to add or change modems. The modem cage unit can power down the slots in groups of four, which lets you add, remove, or replace modems as the situation dictates without adversely affecting your day-to-day operations.

Managing the modem pool

Equinox also offers an EquiView Plus NT Connections Manager software package, which lets you handle the modems in the cage units as if

Figure A

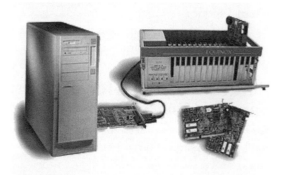

This analog modem pool uses off-the-shelf internal ISA bus modems.

they were external modems—but without the cabling nightmare. Onscreen, you see the modems just as if you were in front of the rack. Equally important are the product's diagnostic capabilities, which let you view the data sent to and from the modem in detail. This capability can be handy when users complain that they can't log in or aren't getting the data they requested.

Depending on the telephone company tariffs in your area, it may be cheaper for you to use a Primary Rate ISDN (PRI) line to bring the phone lines for the RAS users into the building instead of a collection of individual lines. Equinox also offers a digital modem pool unit that gives you the same flexibility of handling RAS users without individual phone lines.

Conclusion

In this article, we've covered both hardware- and software-based options for handling RAS growth. Of course, we've only scratched the surface on the many ways you can handle increased usage. The secret is to keep in mind that RAS, and the service it provides, are like a set of building blocks—you can join and add to the elements in several ways to achieve the result that best suits your needs. ◆

ZENworks tips and tricks

By Ron Nutter

Getting ZENworks up and running is pretty straightforward; the real key is to figure out how to run a problem application or to get an MS-DOS application to work correctly when it needs special drive mappings. In this Daily Drill Down, I'll take you through several scenarios that I've encountered while working with ZENworks, and I'll show you how to get things to work properly.

Getting a problem application to launch

I spent the better part of 1998 designing and implementing a nine-state, 30-office network for a national utility. ZEN was a real time-saver when it came to deploying applications. We encountered two applications that would run

fine when they were launched outside of ZEN, but they wouldn't work when they were invoked from the application launcher.

One of the applications was a terminal emulator that was designed to talk to two different IBM AS/400s over TCP/IP. After installing the program, I noticed a lengthy command-line string that pointed to a session configuration file (it used the .ws extension). I carefully copied this command-line string into the Command Line Parameter field on the Environment tab of the ZEN object with which I was working. When the ZEN object was executed, an error message appeared, indicating that one or more files couldn't be found.

Using the Windows file extension association process to my advantage, I created a batch file that said *Start terminal.ws*. Windows NT realized that this file wasn't an executable, but it recognized the extension and knew that the file could be used by another program. NT took over at that point, started the application that could use the file I was trying to run, and told the application which command-line parameters to use. All I had to do was to enter the drive mapping, including the name of the batch file (for example, f:\apps\terminal.bat), in the Path To Executable File field on the Identification tab for the ZEN object with which I was working. The application then launched normally.

UNC versus explicit file path

When you're creating a ZEN object, you can set the path to an executable file by using UNC (Universal Naming Convention) or by using an explicit path to the file. You'll see UNC on many NT-based networks. Using UNC can save the system administrator from having to set up complex login scripts to map one or more drive letters so that applications can run.

If an application installs itself with UNC, the first step that you should try when you create a ZEN object for that application is to copy the UNC paths to the appropriate areas in the ZEN object window. Then, you need to try running the application. If you get an error, the next step will ask you to use regular drive mappings to get to an application.

When you're using NT as the desktop OS, be careful about what you use for drive mappings. Windows 3.x and Windows 9x will see a drive mapping, such as F:\Public\Client32 and will be able to see files in F:\Public and F:\Home from a single drive mapping. NT, however, will treat this drive mapping command as a map root, and the workstation will see files only in F:\Public\Client32 and the directories below that level. In the past, I've had success with using a generic type of drive mapping in the container login scripts. I map a drive letter to the root of each volume on the server and then add the path to the executable and to the Working Directory field (on the Environment tab). If you have any command-line parameters that reference a configuration or other file, you'll need to edit the Command Line Parameter field to show the explicit path, too.

Mapping and unmapping drives on the fly for problem MS-DOS applications

At some point while working with ZENworks, you'll find that some applications *must* have things their way. MS-DOS accounting applications seem to be at the top of this list. You can accommodate these types of programs by using the Launch Scripts or the Drive/Ports tool. Launch Scripts has been my favorite, and I usually can get it to work with an application that doesn't like the environment that's presented by the Drive/Ports tool. The reason for this fact may be due, in part, to the differences between the two tools.

Launch Scripts offers two text windows—one for commands that must be run *before* the application in question is started and another for commands that must be run *after* the program is terminated (to restore the environment for use by other applications). If you remember the NetWare 2.x/3.x days, you'll quickly see what you need to do. In the Run Before Launching text box, you enter the map commands and/or printer capture statements in order to set up the environment you need. In the Run After Termination text box, you delete the drive mappings and release the printer capture commands.

If you choose the Drives/Ports tool, the environment appears to be setting up as the application starts, rather than before it starts. Another drawback is that you can't remove the changes you've made if you want to restore the environment for other applications.

Documenting how you set up the ZEN objects

Keeping good documentation on how (and why) you set up a particular ZEN object can be important when you're troubleshooting. The Administrator Notes tool allows you to keep this information with the object itself so that you can retrieve the information easily.

Reporting application problems to the SNMP console

Knowing that an application isn't working correctly means making a lot of calls to the help desk. Using the Reporting function in the ZEN object for an application can give you an idea that a problem exists without your having to pour thousands of dollars into yet another specialized management package that will give you that information.

You can choose either to log events to a file or to generate an SNMP trap. Either one or both of these options can be used with any of the ZEN application objects. Logging to a file is a good option to start with. That way, you establish a record in case users complain that an application isn't working; the log file will give you some idea of when the problem started. The problem with this option is that it requires you to check the log file periodically or to create a program that will look for this file, and any additions to it, automatically and alert you to the problem.

Using the Log Events Via SNMP Traps option, you have a little more control over the situation. You can record specific events (for example, a failure to launch or distribute the program). This information is sent to the destination that's specified in the SNMP policy in a container package. When setting the SNMP Trap Target Policy in the Container package, specify how often the policy should be acted on—every certain number of days, hours, minutes, and/or seconds. Unlike with some management systems, you have the ability to specify a Trap Target address by IP or IPX address. For those of you who haven't worked with SNMP much, if the console to which the trap is being sent isn't turned on, the trap (or error message) is thrown away and not re-sent while the workstation is up. For this reason, you'll want to have at least a UPS on the management workstation so that it can always receive the error message. Better yet, have two management consoles operational so that one system is always available to record the problem.

Controlling application availability with Schedule

There are times when you'll want to prevent users from accessing a certain application. Before ZENworks, you pretty much had to rely on the honor system, or you had to disable login to the server and prevent the workstations from accessing any resources on the server until you had finished the task at hand.

Using the Schedule tool of the ZEN application object, you have the option of restricting

access to an application object over a series of days or on certain days every week. To do so, click the Set Schedule In drop-down arrow and select Range Of Days. You'll notice that the days under the Days Available label appear to have a pushed-in appearance. Click on the days for which you wish to restrict access.

The next step will be to restrict the time of day that the applications will be available. You need to click on the small clock icon to the right of the Start Time label. A Time Input window will appear that will allow you to set the start and stop times for the application. Drag the arrow on the time line to set the earliest time that you want the application to be available to users. Repeat the process by using the bottom-sliding arrow to set the latest time that you want the application to be used. Then, click OK to return to the previous window.

The start and stop times for the application should be entered for you. Depending on how resource heavy the application is when it starts (that is, the number and size of files that you must access when you initialize the application before users can open it), you may want to think about staggering the availability of the application once its start time arrives. If you enter a start time of 15 minutes, the times at which the application becomes available to users will be staggered over 15 minutes. That way, the server and/or network won't slow to the point where almost all work comes to a stop until the applications have finished the initialization process. If you have a small number of users (less than 15), it may not be a problem.

Controlling application availability with specific system requirements

You're probably using one or two applications that will run correctly only if another application has already been installed (a situation that's also known as application dependency), a certain amount of disk space is available, or a certain environment variable has been set on a system. Not meeting one or more of these requirements can mean that an application may fail on a random basis or, worse yet, that important information being recorded in a file is not being recorded correctly. Using the System Requirements tool in the ZEN application object with which you are working will allow you to specify certain criteria that must be met before the application will be allowed to start.

For example, suppose you use an accounting application that must have at least 20 MB of disk space available. You begin by clicking the Add button in the System Requirements window and clicking Disk Space. When the Disk Space Requirements window appears, you can check the available disk space in the Windows System Directory, Windows Directory, Windows Temp directory, or a specific drive letter— depending on where your application is looking for free space so that it can run correctly. After selecting the drive letter to watch, you need to choose the qualifier for checking for disk space. The default selection of Greater Than Or Equal To probably will work in most situations,so stick with that option.

The last step is to specify how much available disk space you need. Enter that value in the entry field to the left of the MB label and click OK to return to the System Requirements window. While there is no limit to the number of conditions that you can specify, I suggest entering only those criteria that you know will become a problem if they don't exist.

Keeping the number of icons manageable

As you grow more comfortable with how ZENworks can help make your job easier, you will start using it for more and more applications. To keep things neat and easy to manage, you may want to think about where the ZEN application objects are stored in the NDS tree. You can establish an NDS container called Applications in which to store all of the ZEN application objects. This approach will keep you from confusing those objects with usernames and will make the applications easier to access.

If you have more than a few Organization or Organizational units in your tree, you may want to think about putting those applications that are used by a certain NDS container in the same container as those users. This arrangement will make granting access to the application object easier since you can grant rights based on container membership automatically. This approach also can make user setup a little less of a hassle, depending on the amount of employee turn-

over that your company experiences. If you have applications that several departments use, you'll probably want to place these applications in the base of the tree so that they are equally close to all user objects.

Depending on how often you make changes to an application object, consider making a backup copy of all ZEN application objects in a special container. That way, if the object becomes corrupted or if changes are made to the object that aren't recorded and problems start occurring, you can restore the settings for that object. There is no right or wrong way to approach this situation. You have the option in NWAdmin to move the objects to a container at a later time, should your needs change.

Options for running NAL at the workstation

The main job of deploying applications at the workstation is handled by Application Launcher (affectionately know as NAL). There are several methods of running this program at the workstation. The easiest method is to put the following line in the container login script:

```
@F:\public\nal.exe
```

Make sure that you replace the drive letter with the one that you have mapped to SYS.

You also can put a link to NAL.EXE in the startup folder of the workstation. However, users will receive an error message when they turn on their workstation and NAL tries to start (especially if the workstation is a portable) but they are not attached to the network. It's also possible to bypass the startup folder when you start Windows. Novell TID (Technical Information Document) #2937365 describes the pros and cons of each option in detail.

Keeping up with the latest info on ZENworks

Novell has done a really good job of showing administrators how to use ZENworks properly for their companies. One site that you should visit on a regular basis is ZENworks Cool Solutions. This site is updated several times a week with little nuggets of information on how to use the software that you have effectively and how to make it work for you.

Another good site to visit is the product support page for ZENworks. Here, you'll find the latest TIDs and fixes from Novell without having to go on the proverbial treasure hunt. This site is updated on a daily basis, and you have the option of looking at the TIDs posted in the last seven, 14, or 30 days without having to use specific keywords to search.

As you should begin to see, ZENworks is a very flexible and versatile package. Since beginning its life as a proof of concept as to what was possible from NDS, it has become a very versatile and flexible application and workstation management tool. ◆

Dealing with denial of service attacks in Linux

By Vincent Danen

Recently, malicious hackers struck down a number of well-known and popular Web sites, including Yahoo, Amazon, and eBay. Since then, speculation has been running rampant, and many papers have been written on the subject of denial of service (DoS) attacks. In this Daily Drill Down, I'll discuss denial of service attacks, and I'll tell you how you can prevent DoS attacks from harming your Linux server.

What is a DoS attack?

In its most basic form, a denial of service attack is an action that's initiated by a person or any other system that incapacitates your server's hardware and/or software. It renders your server unreachable and causes the server to deny service to users. DoS attacks originate from attackers who want to knock your server(s) off of the Internet. DoS attacks are always malicious and illegal, except for those instances when security teams test consenting systems.

DoS attacks are a persistent problem for several reasons. First, they are one of the easiest attacks to perform, and they achieve immediate results. They are the most common attacks that an administrator with a system that's always connected to the Internet can expect. DoS attacks also exploit errors, limitations, or inconsistencies in TCP/IP stacks and programs until the author fixes and releases a corrected version of the offending program. While the author is scrambling to fix the program, however, the vulnerabilities exist, and someone is going to exploit those weaknesses eventually.

You would think that Linux users, who have the source code for most of their used applications at their fingertips, would be less affected by DoS attacks. Such is not the case. Certainly, Linux users might find themselves patching software after a new DoS attack surfaces, reconfiguring hardware, or filtering TCP or UDP ports. Unless these Linux users are programmers, however, they must rely on someone else to provide the patches or updated programs that will fix their applications. Thus, Linux systems are just as vulnerable as any other operating system that hosts Internet servers.

Now, you can understand why a DoS attack can wreak such havoc on any server. For some systems, the effects will be trivial; the attacked service can be stopped and restarted easily. For others, however, there may be far-reaching implications. Since the Internet is home to thousands of commercial organizations that produce revenue, a well-timed (or ill-timed, depending on your perspective) DoS attack can greatly reduce profit. To thousands of e-commerce vendors, this possibility poses a serious problem. Of course, with the variety of mission-critical servers and applications that are available on the Internet, DoS attacks can reduce more than revenue. They can hamper your ability to work and gather information. Simply put, denial of service attacks are irritating and time-consuming for everyone involved.

Types of DoS attacks

There are several different types of DoS attacks, including attacks against network hardware, base Linux networking, and Linux applications. Let's take a look at some of these types of attacks.

Hardware attacks

Attacks against network hardware are pretty generic. One common attack occurs when attackers send connection requests from forged or nonexistent IP addresses. Since these IP addresses aren't reachable, the receiving system can't resolve them. The session may hang, which can affect a single service or port or possibly the entire server. Another attack occurs when an attacker exploits overflows in login routines (usually called buffer overflows); this attack causes the server to crash or reboot. Finally, attackers can flood the server with improperly formed or strange packets. The server will lock up because it can't process them correctly.

Networking attacks

Attacks against base Linux networking capabilities are more prevalent, especially when a known exploit exists. There have been a number of cases in the past in which problems in networking code have been exploited and subsequently fixed. Since I can't list all of them, I'll discuss some of the consequences that have resulted from these exploits.

The most common exploits occur because of improperly written source code. One exploit is the IP fragmentation cache attack, which can kill IP connectivity. It usually happens when a 0-length IP fragment is received and confuses Linux. Linux won't release the fragment; instead, it keeps the fragment in the cache. The IP cache is limited to 4,096 simultaneous entries. When the cache is full of these IP fragments, Linux can no longer process incoming packets. Linux begins to deny services. There are a number of other exploits that are based on IP fragmentation. Some exploits are based on IP packet size or on oversized IP packet fragmentation.

Another type of exploit is the ICMP flood attack. It's not limited to Linux; it can affect all other operating systems. Here, the attacker sends a storm of ICMP packets to the server from a forged IP address (which is usually the target's own IP address). Then, the ICMP request is broadcasted to multiple hosts on the server's network, which, in turn, will flood the server with replies. This type of attack can become particularly devastating if the server's network has a number of other hosts. The number of replies would increase dramatically. Eventually, the high volume of responses would shut down the target server.

A very popular DoS attack is known as the Ping of Death. Some previous versions of Linux were susceptible to oversized ping packet attacks that would crash the system. Typically, the ping utility sends out 32-byte packets, which can be handled easily. Most servers can handle packet sizes from 0 to 65,500 bytes. Some will reject packets that are larger than 65,500 bytes, but some won't. If not, they provide the attacker with a successful Ping of Death attack. This particular attack isn't dangerous to recent Linux versions, but they still become problematic. If this flood of ping packets doesn't shut your server down, it will certainly slow the server down. Imagine a high-speed source that delivers packet upon packet to a slower-speed server. The high-speed source has plenty of bandwidth to work with, but the slower server doesn't. Thus, the server will have reduced bandwidth and won't be able to establish any other connections.

Application attacks

Finally, there are the Linux network application attacks. These exploits are based on faulty end-user applications, such as Netscape or FTP clients. Usually, these exploits don't pose much of a problem, and the author of the affected package can fix the problem quickly.

What can you do?

So, how do you defend against denial of service attacks? Unfortunately, there's no generic or foolproof way to protect yourself from a DoS attack. There are some very good guidelines that will reduce the possibility of being susceptible to such an attack, but they're not guaranteed working methods. The first thing that you can do is disable broadcast addressing by issuing:

```
ifconfig eth0 -broadcast
```

Second, you can filter incoming ICMP, ping, and UDP packet traffic with the firewall code in the Linux kernel. This code is called ipchains in the most recent version. Ipchains provides you with several ways of building a firewall to keep unwanted or suspect packets out of your system and of preventing your system from ever initiating an accidental attack (like a Ping of Death) on another system. For example, accepting error ICMP packets is a good idea, but they might be all that you want to accept. To make that distinction, you would type something like the following:

```
ipchains -N icmpacc
ipchains -A icmpacc -p icmp —icmp-type
destination-unreachable -j
ACCEPT
ipchains -A icmp-acc -p icmp —icmp-
type source-quench -j ACCEPT
ipchains -A icmp-acc -p icmp —icmp-
type time-exceeded -j ACCEPT
ipchains -A icmp-acc -p icmp —icmp-
type parameter-problem -j
ACCEPT
```

Creating and using ipchains

First, you'll want to create a new ipchains chain, which we'll call icmpacc. The next four commands (as shown above) add rules to our new chain. These rules tell ipchains to accept the specified ICMP error packets (which are useful in pro-

grams like ping). If any ICMP packets come through that don't match any of these rules, control will be passed back to the calling chain (usually the input chain). If you want to deny all incoming ping and ping replies, you could type:

```
ipchains -A input -i eth0 -p ICMP —
icmp-type ping -j DENY
ipchains -A input -i eth0 -p ICMP —
icmp-type pong -j DENY
```

If you have a router that supports TCP interception, use it. The TCP interception feature allows the router to intercept and validate TCP connections. Connections that fail to resolve after a reasonable time frame are dropped—as are connection requests from unreachable hosts. In either case, the server will be reached only by valid and fully available connections. Finally, use the filtering code in ipchains to drop suspicious source addresses; it will provide you with a defense against spoofed IP addresses. Your server should never accept packets from the Internet that claim to originate from inside your own network, and you might want to prevent

WEB SITES ABOUT DoS ATTACKS THAT YOU MIGHT FIND USEFUL

There are many sites on the Internet that deal with preventing DoS attacks on Linux servers and building proper firewalls that will secure your system from a DoS attack. The sites listed below will provide you with several good starting points for securing your Internet server and protecting yourself from any kind of attack (whether DoS or otherwise).

▶ **Denial of Service Attacks on any Internet Server Through SYN Flooding:**
Tom Kermode offers an overview of SYN flooding and makes some suggestions for preventing the problem.

▶ **Strategies to Protect Against Distributed Denial of Service (DDoS) Attacks:**
Cisco provides a good overview of DoS and DDoS attacks and suggests ways of preventing them.

▶ **Preventing Smurf Attacks:**
NORDUnet provides an overview of Smurf attacks and how to prevent them. (Smurf attacks are another form of DoS attacks.)

▶ **Linux IPCHAINS-HOWTO:**
Paul Russell wrote a standard HOWTO document that explains how to make the most use of the ipchains code in the Linux 2.2.x kernels.

▶ **Firewall and Proxy Server HOWTO:**
Mark Grennan wrote another standard HOWTO document that details firewall and proxy configuration and installation. It contains a lot of good information that will help you set up a proper firewall and prevent your system from being hit by various DoS attacks.

▶ **BugTraq:**
This mailing list about Linux security is one of the most important mailing lists to which a systems administrator can subscribe. BugTraq will alert you to any security holes in your Linux system, and it will give you the information that you need in order to repair the problem.

▶ **CERT Coordination Center:**
This site is an excellent source of information on security. CERT studies Internet security vulnerabilities and provides incident response services to sites that have been attacked. To improve site security, CERT also publishes a variety of security alerts, security research, and developments in information.

incoming connections from reserved addresses like 172.16.0.x and 192.168.x.x, as shown below:

```
ipchains -N no-local
ipchains -A no-local -i eth0 -s
192.168.1.0/24 -l -j DENY
```

This code creates a new ipchains rule called no-local. To this rule, add a command that logs and denies packets on the eth0 interface from the source address of 192.168.1.0/24 or 192.168.1.0/255.255.255.0 (which is a range of IP addresses from 192.168.1.0 to 192.168.1.255). Of course, I'm assuming that your local network uses the 192.168.1.x reserved IP address range.

For more information on ipchains and protecting your system, take a look at the manual pages (man pages) for ipchains by typing *man ipchains*. These pages will give you a good idea of the commands that you can use in order to build a good firewall on your Linux server and to protect yourself from attack.

Conclusion

Since new DoS attacks surface on a regular basis (usually one or two every few months), the best way to protect yourself is to keep up-to-date on security advisories and patches for your programs. You may want to learn about new program ver-sions; however, doing so can become a double-edged sword. New versions may fix past exploits, but they introduce new ones. Paying attention to security announcements from the vendor of your Linux distribution is more effective.

If you find out about a new attack and then you upgrade to a new version or patch level for a particular service, pay close attention to security mailing lists and newsgroups for at least three weeks after the attack is announced and fixed. That way, you'll give the various communities of hackers and crackers enough time to study the new attack's code and modify it further; sometimes, they create new modified attacks on the same application.

The best advice for preventing DoS attacks is to stay alert. Know your system and know what you're running. Keep your eye on the available security sources and know what does and doesn't affect you. Minimize your services to only those services you need. You can't be attacked on a service that you don't run. Administrators who don't pay much attention to their systems and environments will eventually fall prey to some kind of DoS attack. Administrators who understand their systems, however, are much less likely to be affected by these malicious attacks. ◆

E-commerce on the e-cheap: Apache and OpenSSL

By Vincent Danen

The Internet is a budding marketplace of information and e-commerce. In the last few years, the growth of the Internet has been incredible, and today there's a growing trend toward shopping online. A few years ago, people were wary of providing credit card information over the Internet. What has changed the way people view shopping online? Most likely, it's an increased awareness that shopping online is safe and secure—the chance of someone stealing your credit card number is greater when you phone in a pizza order than when you order an item over the Internet.

SSL

Encryption and secure Web sites make shopping online feasible and reliable. Most Web sites use the Secure Sockets Layer (SSL), developed by Netscape Communications Corporation. SSL is a three-tiered encryption method that employs RSA and DES authentication and encryption, as well as additional MD5 integrity checking. This means that using SSL is pretty much guaranteed to be safe, and it allows people to shop easily with their credit cards online. SSL works by defining and exchanging a secret key at connection time between the client and

EDITOR'S NOTE
Should the release version you are installing be more recent than the sample, make sure you insert the correct numbers in the commands.

the server. The secret key is then used to encrypt data. SSL also supports public key cryptography, so the server can authenticate users using schemes like RSA and DSS (the Digital Signature Standard). By using SSL, the server can verify the integrity of ongoing sessions using message digest algorithms like MD5 and SHA. When performing an integrity check, SSL en-sures a secure session by making sure the data in transit isn't being modified by a third party.

As a Linux Web administrator, you may be investigating e-commerce on your own. Perhaps you want to set up your own Web server that provides SSL encryption and authentication to provide your customers with the ability to shop online. Nowadays, this isn't a ridiculous notion.

The tools you want, the tools you need

There are two methods of setting up a secure Web server with Apache, which is a popular Web-serving program for Linux (and many other operating systems). The first method is to patch Apache with the Apache-SSL patches. In order to do this, you need a copy of Apache, the Apache-SSL patches, and a copy of SSLeay, an SSL library that's free for non-commercial use.

The second method, and the one I'll explore in this Daily Drill Down, is to use Apache in conjunction with OpenSSL using the mod_ssl modules for Apache. Since the recent versions of Apache are modularized, it makes sense to use SSL as a module, as opposed to patching the Apache source code and re-compiling the program. You'll need a recent version of Apache (which can be obtained from the official site), the mod_ssl modules (from the mod_ssl official site), and the OpenSSL program (from the OpenSSL official site).

Many distributions provide these programs as RPM or DEB packages, making installation extremely easy. If you're running a distribution that doesn't provide packages for all or some of these programs, download the source TAR/GZip archive(s) and unpack them using:

```
tar xvzf apache_1.3.12.tar.gz
tar xvzf mod_ssl-2.6.0-1.3.12.tar.gz
tar xvzf openssl-0.9.4.tar.gz
```

Next, you need to build the OpenSSL package first. Do so using:

```
cd openssl-0.9.4
./config
make
make install
cd ..
```

Then build Apache with mod_ssl support compiled in:

```
cd mod_ssl-2.6.0-1.3.12
./configure —with-apache=../apache-
1.3.12 —with-ssl=../openssl-0.94 \
—prefix=/usr/local/apache
cd ../apache_1.3.12
make
make certificate
make install
```

Modules, modules, modules

As an alternative, you can build Apache with mod_ssl as a regular Apache module. If you already have Apache installed, it's easy to build the mod_ssl module and use it as a "plug-in."

To do this, use the following:

```
cd apache_1.3.12
SSL_BASE=/usr/local/ssl ./configure
... —enable-module=ssl
```

You can also enable the Dynamic Shared Object (DSO) support for mod_ssl by using:

```
cd apache_1.3.12
SSL_BASE=/usr/local/ssl ./configure
... —enable-shared=ssl
```

For either method, you still need to build Apache using:

```
Make
make certificate
make install
```

The advantage of building mod_ssl as a DSO as opposed to a static module is it allows you to achieve more run-time flexibility than you would otherwise have. You can decide whether you want to use SSL at run time instead of when you're building the program. (This is true, of course, if you build Apache from the source code yourself.) Whatever method you choose, following the code examples above will configure Apache with mod_ssl support, compile it, make a test certificate, and install the program.

Keep in mind that the certificate you create is only a test certificate. This is one way of ensuring that everything is set up and configured correctly. Creating the test certificate will also help you become more familiar with how SSL works with Apache.

Once you have Apache, mod_ssl, and OpenSSL installed, you can create your site's real certificate. To do this, you will need to use the OpenSSL command-line tool called *openssl*. The first step is to generate your certificate. A good way to do this is to use RSA and encrypt the key with TripleDES by using:

```
openssl genrsa -des3 -out server.key 1024
```

This will create a 1,024-bit RSA key encrypted with TripleDES. OpenSSL will prompt you for the information to use while generating your key, similar to when you created your test certificate earlier.

You will be asked to enter the PEM passphrase to your encrypted RSA key. Should you ever need to make changes or administrate your certificate, you will need to know this passphrase. Make sure this is a strong password, because if anyone obtains your certificate, they can make changes to it and compromise your Web site's security. You will be asked to reconfirm the passphrase.

Privacy Enhanced Mail (PEM) is a Base64-encoded Distinguished Encoding Rule (DER) with header and footer lines. DER is a binary way of encoding the certificate for any SSL-based Web site. Since some browsers are incapable of understanding and handling binary certificates, PEM is used to simplify the process of transporting the certificate using encoded ASCII text.

You will now have a *server.key* file in the directory. This is the private key used to encrypt and decrypt data being transferred from the client to the server and vice versa. You must generate the certificate request and use your new key to create it. At the command line, type:

```
openssl req -new -key server.key -out server.csr
```

You'll be asked to answer several questions that determine how to create the certificate request. You'll provide a country name, state or province name, city name, organization name, organization unit name, your common name, and your e-mail address.

You'll also be asked for any extra attributes you want to send with your certification request, such as a challenge password or optional company name. You'll probably want to leave these fields blank.

Certificates

OpenSSL allows you to generate your own certificate to use on your Web site. However, most companies want to have their certificate generated by a certificate authority (CA). If you are going to use this secure Web server for encrypting data sent via forms or during user logins on an interactive Web site, you can get away with generating your own certificate. However, if you plan to use your secure Web server for e-commerce, you'll want to have the certificate generated by a recognized CA.

CA are trusted third parties that issue certificates and verify their authenticity. By using a certificate generated by such a company, you can greatly enhance the credibility of your Web site and help the site meet any requirements you may need to fulfill to become an e-commerce firm.

Certificate authorities establish the validity of your company by requiring you to provide legal proof that you're authorized to use your company's legal business name in transactions. You can provide this proof by using a valid business license, articles of incorporation, notarized partnership papers, registration records, and so forth.

Some recognized certificate authorities are:

▶ EnTrust Technologies

▶ EuroSign

▶ Baltimore Technologies

▶ The Thawte Consulting Certification Division

▶ VeriSign

▶ Xcert International

These sites, and most other recognized CAs, charge a fee for providing a one-year certificate. Most will do this only for valid businesses or governments, but some will provide certificates for individual users for personal use. Regardless of your needs, it's best to look around for competitive rates and for which CA best provides for your needs.

You can easily build your own certificate for your Web site with OpenSSL. Unfortunately, the generated certificate isn't created by a reputable source. Otherwise, generating your own certificate works just as well as paying a CA $200 per year to do it for you. On the command line, issue the following:

AUTHOR'S NOTE
The common name must be the fully qualified domain name of the site for which it will be used. For example, if your domain name is mydomain.com and the secure Web site will be available at https://www.mydomain.com/, you'd type *www.mydomain.com* in the common name field.

```
openssl genrsa -des3 -out ca.key 1024
openssl req -new -x509 -days 365 -key
ca.key -out ca.crt
```

In order to create your own CA, you must generate a new 1,024-bit RSA key—just like we did for your secure Web site's RSA key. The second command creates a self-signed CA. It creates the CA using the X509 structure with the new CA RSA key. The certificate will be valid for 365 days from the date created, which is the typical amount of time certificates are valid. The output is PEM-formatted. If you wish to see the details of your certificate, issue:

```
openssl -x509 -noout -text -in ca.crt
```

The next step is to prepare a script for signing certificate requests. The reason for this is because the *openssl ca* command currently has some strange requirements and the default OpenSSL configuration doesn't allow you to easily use the *openssl ca* command directly. Packaged with the mod_ssl distribution is a script called *sign.sh* located in the pkg.contrib/ subdirectory. Using this script is the simplest way to sign certificate requests and generate your site's certificate.

To create your certificate, type *./sign.sh server.csr* on the command line. This uses your new CA to sign your server's certificate request and creates a real SSL certificate to use with Apache. The result is seen in the newly generated server.crt file in the current directory. The only thing left to do now is to configure Apache to use the new certificate.

In your Apache configuration file, httpd.conf, you must insert these directives:

```
SSLEngineon
SSLCertificateFile/etc/httpd/conf/ser
ver.crt
SSLCertificateKeyFile/etc/httpd/conf/
server.key
```

These directives tell Apache where to find the files to encrypt and decrypt data on your secure Web site, and they tell Apache to turn on the SSL support.

You may encounter a problem when restarting Apache. Since you've encrypted your keyfile with TripleDES, Apache will ask you for your PEM passphrase prior to loading. If you want extra security, leave things as they are. However, if Apache doesn't ask you for the passphrase and simply refuses to start (which happens if you start the server in the background), you must provide Apache with an un-encrypted key-

file. As long as you have your keyfile in a secure place with appropriate permissions (I suggest making the keyfile readable only by the user running Apache, typically httpd or no one, and making it writeable for no one), you can decrypt your RSA key and use it by issuing:

```
mv server.key server.key.des
openssl rsa -in server.key.des -out
server.key
```

In the shop for a tune-up

There are more configuration options available to fine-tune how Apache works with SSL. I recommend creating a new configuration file called mod_ssl.conf in your Apache configuration directory and linking it to your existing configuration by adding to httpd.conf:

```
Includemod_ssl.conf
```

The contents of mod_ssl.conf should look similar to this:

```
LoadModule
ssl_module/usr/lib/apache/libssl.so
# listen to the standard HTTPS port
(443)
Listen 443
# Some MIME-types for downloading
Certificates and CRLs
AddTypeapplication/x-x509-ca-cert
.crt
AddTypeapplication/x-pkcs7-crl .crl
# configure the SSL session cache
SSLSessionCacheshm:logs/ssl_scache(51
2000)
SSLSessionCacheTimeout300
# Semaphore:
# Configure the path to the mutual
exclusion semaphore the
# SSL engine uses internally for
inter-process synchronization.
SSLMutexfile:logs/ssl_mutex
# Pseudo Random Number Generator
(PRNG):
SSLRandomSeedstartup builtin
SSLRandomSeedconnect builtin
# The home of the dedicated SSL
protocol logfile:
SSLLoglogs/ssl_engine_log
SSLLogLevelinfo
```

Restart your Apache Web server. In Red Hat and similar distributions, you can accomplish this by running:

```
/etc/rc.d/init.d/httpd restart
```

At this point, you should be able to connect to your Web site, and your browser should prompt you as to whether you want to accept the certificate. Congratulations! You now have a fully functional secure Web server.

Conclusion

There are a number of excellent sources of information that can teach you how to get more out of your secure Web site and fine-tune it further. The best site I have found is the mod_ssl homepage, which contains instructions for installing all of the necessary components (Apache, mod_ssl, and OpenSSL) and a detailed How-to and FAQ section for a number of different scenarios. It also provides a great deal of information on SSL itself and the types of encryption that can be used on an SSL-enabled Web server.

A secure Web site is ideal, and software has progressed to the point where it's easy to install and configure everything to meet your needs. Gone are the days of patching source code or spending large amounts of money to invest in a commercial SSL library that provides the same functionality as the free OpenSSL implementation. Combine the obvious advantages of running a Web server under Linux with the tools to provide a truly secure Web site, and it's no wonder Apache is one of the most widely used Web serving programs on the Internet. ◆

Setting up a secure FTP server with ProFTPD

By Vincent Danen

One of the most important services available on the Internet today—with the exception of Web serving—is the ability to exchange files via File Transfer Protocol (FTP). FTP sites are a cornerstone of the Internet, and no one can dispute this. Because of the popularity of FTP, a number of FTP server packages have been released for a variety of platforms. In the Linux world, probably the most popular of these FTP servers is the wu-ftpd server.

While wu-ftpd is a good product and provides excellent performance, it lacks a number of features found in newer products. It also has a poor security history. A number of people felt that the only way to get wu-ftpd up to spec was to completely redesign it from the ground up. It was at this time that a new FTP server, called ProFTPD, was born. In this Daily Drill Down, I'll introduce you to ProFTPD.

Features

Unlike other FTP servers, ProFTPD is designed to be lightweight, secure, and configurable. (If you're familiar with Apache, you should have no trouble adapting because the configuration for ProFTPD is based on a similar syntax.) Other FTP servers may provide an extremely secure setting at the expense of configurability. ProFTPD doesn't do this. It provides an extremely capable FTP service, with a high level of configurability and security. Currently, ProFTPD offers some attractive features that I'll quickly outline for you.

ProFTPD features per-directory *.ftpaccess* configuration files similar to Apache's *.htaccess* files. ProFTPD makes it simple to configure multiple virtual FTP servers and anonymous FTP services. It can be run either as a standalone server or from *inetd*, depending on your needs. The anonymous FTP service it provides doesn't need a specific directory structure or other system files like the *anonftp* package for wu-ftpd (no more */home/ftp* if you don't want it!). ProFTPD allows for hidden directories and files based on user/group ownership and UNIX-style permissions. It can run as a configurable, non-privileged user in standalone mode in order to decrease the chance of attacks that might exploit its root capabilities (like Apache running as user *nobody*). It provides multiple forms of logging compatible with the wu-ftpd logging standard, and it provides extended paranoid logging. It also supports full shadow password-ing, including support for expired accounts.

Installing ProFTPD

The first thing you must do is install ProFTPD. Because ProFTPD is a full FTP server, it conflicts with wu-ftpd, you must remove wu-ftpd from your system. To do this on a Linux Mandrake or any other RPM-based system, use the following:

```
rpm -e anonftp
rpm -e wu-ftpd
```

The *anonftp* package provides anonymous FTP services for wu-ftpd and must be removed first because it depends on the wu-ftpd package. Finally, you have to remove wu-ftpd itself.

At this point, you can install ProFTPD. Some distributions provide a packaged version of ProFTPD, usually via user contributions. If your distribution does provide this, it would be easiest to install the ProFTPD RPM. If that isn't possible, you'll have to download the source code from the ProFTPD site and compile it yourself.

To download and compile ProFTPD, grab the latest tarball from the downloads page of the Web site (*216.24.5.22/pub/proftp-1.2.0pre10.tar.gz*). Currently, the latest version is 1.2.0pre10. Move the downloaded file to the */usr/src* directory and issue

```
tar xvzf proftpd-1.2.0pre10.tar.gz
cd proftpd-1.2.0pre10
```

This will place you in the top-level directory of the source distribution. To compile and install the package, issue the following:

```
./configure —prefix=/usr —
sysconfdir=/etc —
localstatedir=/var/run \
—with-
modules=mod_linuxprivs:mod_ratio:mod_
readme
make
make install
```

The first command will set up the *make* environment. Here you tell it to use the */usr* directory as the top-level directory for the installation, and it will place binaries into */usr/bin*, manpages into */usr/man*, and so forth. You also tell it to look for the *proftpd.conf* file in the */etc* directory and to provide localstate files (PID, or Process Identification files) in the */var/run/proftpd* directory. Finally, you tell it to include three modules:

▶ **mod_linuxprivs**—Provides ProFTPD support to use Linux privileges.

▶ **mod_ratio**—Provides user upload/download ratio support.

▶ **mod_readme**—Provides support for displaying readme status information.

Next you make the binaries, and then you use *make* to install everything to its proper location.

A walk-through of the /etc/proftpd.conf configuration file

The main configuration of ProFTPD is done in the */etc/proftd.conf* file. Open the *proftpd.conf* file in your favorite text editor, and let's look at a few directives that will create an effective FTP server with several good security options enabled.

The first thing you want to do is define defaults for the server. The following will define some of the server information ProFTPD needs. These should be the first entries in your *proftpd.conf* file. Like with most configuration files, you place the hash symbol (#) at the beginning of a line to place comments in the file.

```
# Server info
ServerName      ?My Server?
ServerType      standalone
ServerAdmin
mailto:myemail@mydomain.com
DefaultServer   on
```

The *ServerName* keyword defines the default name of the server. The *ServerType* keyword specifies whether ProFTPD is to be run as a standalone or *inetd* service. In our example, ProFTPD is running as a standalone server. If you want to run ProFTPD from *inetd*, change *standalone* to *inetd* and place the following in your */etc/inetd.conf* file:

```
ftp   stream   tcp   nowait   root
/usr/sbin/tcpd   in.proftpd
```

The *ServerAdmin* keyword defines the e-mail address to the administrator of this FTP server, and the *DefaultServer* keyword specifies whether this is the default server in the configuration. Since ProFTPD also supports Virtual FTP servers, you should define one server as the default server. Otherwise, any connections to an IP address not defined will receive a *no server available to service your request* error message. For example, if you do a *ftp localhost* command on the system ProFTPD is running on and don't explicitly define a server for the IP address 127.0.0.1, that error message will be returned if *DefaultServer* is off. With *DefaultServer* on, any connections to unknown IP addresses will be forwarded to the defined default server.

Next you want to define some server defaults. These values must be defined outside any <VirtualHost> or <Global> directives, so we'll put them right after the server information:

```
# Some basic defaults
Port                   21
TimeoutLogin          120
TimeoutIdle           600
TimeoutNoTransfer     900
TimeoutStalled       3600
MaxInstances           30
```

The *Port* keyword defines the default port ProFTPD should listen to (this has no bearing on *inetd*-started servers). The default FTP port is 21, so set it to that value.

The *TimeoutLogin* keyword defines how long the server will wait for a user to log in before timing out when a connection has been initiated. Setting the value to 120 means you give users two minutes to fully log in before disconnecting them.

The *TimeoutIdle* keyword defines how many seconds ProFTPD will wait to disconnect the client if no data is received in either control or data mode. A value of 0 will disable this, but it's generally a bad idea because if a TCP connection dies, the server will never terminate the disconnected session.

The *TimeoutNoTransfer* keyword is used to define the maximum number of seconds a client can sit idle after logging into the FTP server without initiating a file upload or download or without retrieving a directory listing.

The *TimeoutStalled* keyword defines the maximum number of seconds to wait during an active data connection between the server and the client in which no data is sent (in other words, the connection has stalled). The default is 0 (indefinite).

Finally, the *MaxInstances* keyword defines the maximum number of child processes the stand-alone server can spawn at any given time (this has no bearing on *inetd*-started servers). Because each child process is an active connection, this also controls how many users can be logged in simultaneously. Any connections beyond the configured maximum are written to the syslog and silently refused. The default is 0 (unlimited), but this generally isn't a good idea. Reducing the number to a reasonable amount (depending on your system, you may want to configure anywhere from 10 to 100) will prevent denial-of-service attacks that may attempt to fork-bomb your server. This is typically accomplished by repeated connections to the FTP port, which cause ProFTPD to spawn a new child process until it's unable to spawn more and simply gives up.

The next thing you want to define is what user the FTP server will normally run as in standalone mode. When ProFTPD starts, it initially starts as root so it can grab control of the standard FTP port (only root has the power to bind to TCP ports below port 1024). However, it will switch to a defined user as quickly as possible. To accomplish this, add the following to your *proftpd.conf* file:

```
User    ftp
Group   ftp
```

The *User* and *Group* keywords tell ProFTPD what UID/GID to switch to. These keywords can also be used within <VirtualHost> and <Anonymous> directives, allowing ProFTPD to switch to different UID/GID settings if you require them. In the above example, I set both the UID and GID to the user *ftp*, which is a non-privileged user. You could also use the user *nobody* (Apache uses it by default).

Defining permissions and logging options

Now you can start defining some permissions to the server. First, you want to allow all users to log in-to the server, so we have to use a <Limit> directive. Because this is outside a <Global> or <VirtualHost> directive, this setting applies to all defined servers:

```
<Limit LOGIN>
AllowAll
</Limit>
```

The <Limit> directive takes a number of arguments. Some of these arguments are:

▶ **LOGIN**—Allow or deny users from logging in to the server

▶ **READ**—All commands dealing with file reading (RETR, STAT, etc.)

▶ **WRITE**—All commands dealing with file or directory writing/creating/deletion

▶ **DIRS**—All commands dealing with directory listings (NLST, LIST, etc.)

▶ **ALL**—All FTP commands (identical to READ WRITE DIRS)

<Limit> will also take, as an argument, any valid FTP command, like STOR, RETR, DELE, CWD, and so forth. This way, you can either use a command group to limit (like WRITE) or limit a specific command itself.

The precedence of <Limit> directives is defined by which one comes first. The configuration file is basically read from top to bottom, so the first <Limit> directive will control all the servers unless other <Limit> directives are used within <Directory> or <Anonymous> directives that change the behavior. For example, this is the first <Limit> directive you use, so by default all users may log in to the FTP server. You could place, further down in the configuration file, another <Limit LOGIN> to deny everyone except a handful of specific users for a defined <VirtualHost>.

Next, you want to place a global <Directory> directive that allows all files to be overwritten. If you want to upload a new file with the same name as an existing file, you'll have to delete the old file first if you fail to include this particular directive. So this directive saves us a step:

```
<Directory /*>
 AllowOverwrite        on
</Directory>
```

Next, we want to deny writing to the base server. This will prevent users from making their own directories, uploading files, and so forth:

```
<Limit WRITE>
DenyAll
</Limit>
```

Finally, we want to define some logging options. The *TransferLog* keyword defines the log file to write transfers to. You can use multiple *LogFormat* keywords to define different logging styles for different things. The general syntax for *LogFormat* is *nickname string*. The nickname can be referenced via the *TransferLog* and *ExtendedLog* keywords. Here I've defined the default log format, as well as two nicknames, auth and write:

```
TransferLog
/var/log/proftpd/xferlog.default
LogFormat default "%h %l %u %t \"%r\"
%s %b"
LogFormat auth "%v [%P] %h %t \"%r\"
%s"
LogFormat write "%h %l %u %t \"%r\" %s
%b"
UseReverseDNS off
ScoreboardPath /var/run/proftpd
```

You also need to specify whether to use reverse DNS lookups on data connections. Since this can be time consuming, set *UseReverseDNS* to off. You must also define *ScoreboardPath*, which is where ProFTPD will place its PID

file and scoreboard files (these files are necessary for the *MaxClients* keyword to work properly). In addition, this allows us to use some utility clients like *ftpwho* and *ftpcount* that come with ProFTPD.

Next, you need to define some global settings that are shared by the main server and all defined virtual hosts. These settings must be enclosed in the <Global> and </Global> tags as shown:

```
<Global>
 Umask 022
 DisplayLogin welcome.msg
 DisplayFirstChdir readme
 DisplayReadme README
 DeferWelcome on
 IdentLookups on
 ExtendedLog
/var/log/proftpd/access.log
WRITE,READ write
 ExtendedLog
/var/log/proftpd/auth.log AUTH auth
 ExtendedLog
/var/log/proftpd/paranoid.log ALL
default
</Global>
```

The settings I've defined here are quite simple. The *Umask* keyword defines the permissions new files and directories will have, in octal format. The *DisplayLogin* keyword tells ProFTPD what file to display when users first connect to the FTP site. This file must exist in the defined root directory for the FTP site to be displayed. The *DisplayFirstChdir* keyword will display the contents of the defined file if it exists in the new directory a user changes to. And the *DisplayReadme* keyword will display a message that asks users to read the defined file (in this case README). This keyword will also display how long ago the file was modified.

The *DeferWelcome* keyword specifies whether the server will delay transmitting the server name and address to new connections until after the client has logged in. For the security conscious, this is a good option to enable. This way, no extra information is given out on the server for simple probes, only for valid logins.

The *IdentLookups* keyword specifies whether *ident* will be used to identify the remote host name. Because this can be time consuming, some people prefer to turn it off, but again, for the security conscious, this will provide you with more information on clients connecting to your FTP site.

Finally, the *ExtendedLog* keywords define what you're logging. The first instance of the keyword tells ProFTPD to log all WRITE and READ command groups to the file */var/log/proftpd/access.log* using the *write* format (remember the *LogFormat* keywords you defined previously?). The second instance tells ProFTPD to log all AUTH commands to the file */var/log/proftpd/auth.log* using the *auth* nickname format. Finally, the last instance is a catch-all paranoid logging, which will log everything using the *default* format to the file */var/log/proftpd/paranoid.log*.

The next thing you'll define is the anonymous portion of your FTP site. All valid users will be able to log in to their home directories using their regular username/password, but in order to allow anonymous FTP clients, you'll need to define a section enclosed in <Anonymous> and </Anonymous> tags, like this:

```
<Anonymous ~ftp>
 User ftp
 Group ftp
 UserAlias anonymous ftp
 RequireValidShell off
 AnonRequirePassword off
 MaxClients 10
</Anonymous>
```

This section tells ProFTPD to place all anonymous connections into the */home/ftp* directory. (You can use any directory you like; you don't need to use */home/ftp* at all, unlike wu-ftpd and the anonftp package.) Here again you define the *User* and *Group* keywords to tell ProFTPD to run all anonymous FTP connections with the UID/GID of the FTP user. The *UserAlias* keyword tells ProFTPD to map the anonymous user to the FTP user. Since you don't have an actual Linux user by the name of *anonymous*, in order to allow that as a login name, you need to map it to an existing login-user, such as *ftp* or *nobody*. The format of *UserAlias* is

```
<login-user> <userid>
```

where *<login-user>* is the name we want to allow (in this case, *anonymous*) and *<userid>* is the name of the real user to use for the login (in this case, *ftp*).

The *RequireValidShell* keyword specifies whether the user needs a real shell (like */bin/sh* or */bin/csh*) to log in. Since the user ftp should have a shell of */bin/false* or */dev/null* on security-conscious systems, you should turn this off; otherwise, anonymous users will never be able to log in.

The *AnonRequirePassword*, if set to on, will force the client to enter a valid password. In an anonymous environment, clients are expected to enter their e-mail address as the password, so you turn *AnonRequirePassword* off. If you were defining a guest account that you wanted to force using a valid password, you'd turn *AnonRequirePassword* on.

Finally, let's add a little extra security for existing real users. Since, by default, a real user will connect to the FTP site and be placed in the */home/username* directory, tell ProFTPD to *chroot* that home directory. This prevents users from moving outside their home directory tree. In any other FTP environment that doesn't *chroot* the home directory upon login, users can change to directories like */etc* or */usr/bin*. When you tell ProFTPD to *chroot* the home directory, the user will be placed in / instead of */home/username* when they connect, and */home/username* will be treated as an absolute root directory. If the user then tries to change to */etc*, ProFTPD will attempt to change to */home/username/etc*. Although this should not be the complete basis for FTP security (it can be circumvented), it is usually enough for the average FTP site. Trying to break out of a *chroot* environment via FTP is time consuming and difficult. To enable this feature, use:

```
DefaultRoot /home/bob bob
DefaultRoot /home/jim jim
```

This means that when user *bob* logs in, his root directory is */home/bob*, and the same for user *jim*.

Conclusion

While securing an FTP site is not the simplest thing, ProFTPD has made it much easier and more intuitive by providing configuration directives that allow you to tighten the hatches on potential exploits of your system. Beyond the security itself, ProFTPD is an excellent replacement for the traditional wu-ftpd that ships by default with most Linux distributions. Not only is it far more secure, it's also much more versatile and configurable. The keyword directives, if used together, will provide a fully functional FTP server with anonymous login capabilities and a fairly high level of security. To provide even more security, you can use the <Limit> directives liberally to secure various areas of your site.

For more information on the many configuration keywords and directives, I suggest visiting the ProFTPD Web site and reading the man-pages that come with ProFTPD. ◆

A guide to NetWare 5 security and control

By Charlene A. Dykman, Cindy Cook, and H. Van Tran

All standard security measures for any EDP environment, such as ensuring file system backups, apply to NetWare 5. In this article, however, only those measures specific to the NetWare 5 network are discussed. Novell Directory Services (NDS) security, directory and file system security, login security, new security technology, the enhanced auditing system, server console security, and software licensing are all areas of interest.

Novell Directory Services security

Concepts and Defaults NetWare 3.x is a server-centric system in which users, groups, network resources, and network security are defined and managed server by server. Typically, security administration of each 3.x file server is entirely managed by people with supervisor or supervisor-equivalent login names.

NetWare 4 and 5, on the other hand, have a network management feature known as Novell Directory Services (NDS) that manages users, groups, network resources, and network security globally. Users, groups of users, business

units, subunits, and network resources such as file servers, volumes, and print servers are represented in NDS as objects.

These objects are defined, tied together hierarchically, and stored in a single global database called an NDS database. The hierarchical structure pulling all network elements together is known as the NDS tree. This is an upside-down tree with its root at the top.

In the NetWare 5 environment, the ability to administer network security depends on the administrator's level of access to the NDS tree. In a centralized security administration environment, LAN administrators are given all access privileges to the entire tree or its root to administer the entire network of all users and servers.

In a decentralized administration environment, LAN administrators are given limited access to parts of the NDS tree to administer selected groups of users or resources. In addition to tying together all network elements ranging from users to file system volumes residing on file servers, the NDS is also used to store security-related data, such as:

▶ User security attributes (e.g., login name, password, login restrictions).

▶ Network management capabilities (e.g., who can manage users or other resources).

▶ File system access data (e.g., how files and directories can be accessed and by whom, actually stored in volumes' directory entry tables, but linked to object IDs in NDS).

Objects and properties

Externally, the NDS structure is hierarchical; it is configured as an upside-down tree with the root object at the top.

The terminal objects are called leaf objects and typically consist of users, print servers, and file servers, which can be further expanded into volumes, directories, and files. Objects between the root and the terminal points are called container objects. Container objects are objects that can contain other objects, and include the country, organization, and organizational unit.

Figure A

EXHIBIT 1 Object Rights

Rights	Explanation
Supervisor	Implies all other Object rights and all Property rights to the object's properties.
Browse	Gives the right to see the object in the NDS tree.
Create	Gives the right to create a new object in the NDS tree. (Valid only for containers.)
Delete	Gives the right to delete the object.
Rename	Gives the right to change the name of the object.
Inheritable	Enables an object trustee of a container to inherit the assigned object rights to objects and sub-containers within a container. (Available only for container objects and granted by default.)

Object Rights.

Internally, an NDS object is like a record in a database with many properties, which are like the fields associated with the record. NDS properties contain values, like fields contain data. There are two types of objects: container and leaf.

The ability to access the NDS tree to manage network resources is governed by NDS security. Access to these resources is directly granted to the same trustees and is controlled by two separate sets of rights: object rights and property rights. Rights originating from different sources are additive.

Object rights are described in **Figure A**.

Only those with network administrative responsibilities should be given object rights beyond Browse. In cases of sensitive objects, such as the container with the administrative user objects, even the Browse right could be restricted, after first granting explicit rights at the container object to the administrators. This would effectively create a hidden container with "stealth" users that could be seen only by the administrative users.

Object rights given to an administrator at a given container object flow down to subordinate objects. In other words, the administrator inherits the same administrative rights at subordinate objects as those object rights explicitly granted at a parent container object.

The inheritance of object rights may be blocked in three ways. First, they may be blocked by the use of Inherited Rights Filters (IRFs). However, this method of blocking rights has a high "Whoops!" factor, because IRFs are global in nature, affecting all users, not just certain users. In general, IRFs should be avoided in favor of granting a new trustee assignment to the same trustee at a lower level to change rights assignments.

This second method would affect only that one trustee, rather than globally affecting all users in the entire tree. If used, IRFs should be carefully planned and heavily documented.

Third, the inheritable right may be revoked to accomplish the same end. Using these methods allows different sections of the NDS tree to be administered by different administrators These administrators could completely block out object rights that had been granted to other NDS administrators at higher-level container objects and that would otherwise be inherited. ◆

Managing virus outbreaks on your network from your server

By John Sheesley

Sometimes it seems that not a week goes by when you don't find out about some new computer virus waiting to strike the computers on your network. To help prevent virus outbreaks, you've probably already deployed some type of virus detection software on your users' computers. But in a networked environment, is running virus detection on your client workstations enough? Not necessarily. In this Daily Drill Down, we'll show you how you can control viruses on your network more effectively by using a server-side protection scheme.

Computer viruses 101

Just in case you aren't familiar with the kinds of viruses that can infect your computers and how the viruses work, let's review them. There are thousands of different computer viruses that can infect your workstations. Current estimates of the actual number of viruses in existence vary widely. Some experts and virus protection software vendors claim that there are over 13,000 viruses in existence. However, most of these viruses exist only in the vendor's labs.

The Wildlist Organization maintains a list of viruses that have been discovered by people on their computers. Since the organization began tracking computer viruses in 1993, contributors to the list have encountered fewer than 1,000 unique viruses.

That low number doesn't mean that you should ignore the threat of viruses to your computers and network. However, at the same time, don't let yourself be confused by vendors who claim to be able to detect tens of thousands of viruses. If you get a virus on your system, it will probably be one of the big ones like Melissa or Chernobyl.

Computer viruses normally fall into one of the following major categories:

▶ **Boot-sector viruses**—Boot-sector viruses corrupt the boot sector of your computer's hard drive by overwriting the sector with bad information. They prevent the computer from booting properly, if at all.

▶ **Executable viruses**—Executable viruses infect your files by attaching to executable programs (.exe and .com files) when you launch them.

▶ **Macro viruses**—Macro viruses are the newest breed of viruses. Macro viruses infect Microsoft Word documents in particular, but newer versions of macro viruses can also infect Microsoft Excel spreadsheets. These macro viruses can infect data files, taking advantage of the application's built-in programming language. The people who create macro viruses turn this feature against software owners. These virus makers can hide a complex macro virus in any document or spreadsheet. When you load the infected file, your application program will spread it to any other data file that you open. Originally, macro viruses wouldn't destroy data on your hard disk. However, newer strains are more deadly.

▶ **Memory-resident viruses**—Memory-resident viruses avoid detection by loading into different areas of your computer's memory. The virus waits there until you launch an application. Then, it infects your computer and the files on it. Some of these viruses place their memory-resident code into memory normally allocated for command.com. Others place their code into unallocated memory. Viruses may also incorporate their code into the video-card buffers between 640 KB and 768 KB (A0000h and C0000h).

▶ **Partition-table viruses**—Partition-table viruses infect your hard disk's partition table. These viruses can either move or destroy your hard disk's partition-table information.

▶ **Polymorphic viruses**—Most viruses have a set code pattern that never changes, no matter what files they infect. Polymorphic viruses can alter their own code, making them harder to detect.

An ounce of prevention, a pound of cure

Your first line of defense in the war against viruses begins at your workstations. If you don't already have some form of virus protection running on the workstations on your network, then you're in trouble. Although virus infection may be rare, if protection software isn't running on your client workstation, a virus can run amok on your network easily.

Unfortunately, since Windows 3.1, Microsoft hasn't included any virus prevention software with its operating systems. That means that you're on your own when searching for protection. To fill this void, several vendors have produced software that you can use on your client workstations. **Table A** lists some of the more popular virus software vendors and their products.

Besides installing the software on your client workstations, you also must ensure that the software has the latest virus signature files. The virus signature files contain the information that the software needs in order to detect new viruses. If you haven't updated the signature file for your virus detection programs in several months, you may as well not have them on your workstations. The virus detection programs won't know about new viruses and will be ineffective.

Server-side virus protection

While it's technically possible to write a virus that would infect NetWare's core operating system, I haven't found any evidence of one existing that

TABLE A: *Popular virus software vendors and their products*

Vendor	Product
Computer Associates	InnocuLAN
Symantec	Norton Antivirus
Network Associates	McAfee VirusScan
Panda Software	Panda Antivirus Platinum
Data Fellows	F-PROT Professional

you have to worry about. Viruses can infect the files that are stored on your NetWare server, however.

Your second line of defense in the war against viruses resides with your servers. Unfortunately, it's often a line of work that network administrators fail to deploy. Sometimes, network administrators work under the assumption that they don't need to deploy server-side virus detection because their workstations' software will eventually block any viruses. Why is this assumption a potentially fatal mistake?

Server-side virus protection can provide several benefits that a workstation-only based protection scheme does not. Some of the benefits of server-side virus protection include:

▶ Centralized file scanning of shared files

▶ Automatic pushing of updated signature files to users

▶ Automatic scanning of backups

▶ Logging of virus outbreaks and scanning of results

▶ Immediate alerting of virus outbreaks

▶ Lower network overhead

The main reason that you have file servers in the first place is to provide a central location for storing and accessing files. You can run virus scanners constantly on your workstations, but if you haven't scanned your servers, files that reside on your servers can re-infect the workstations.

Additionally, you have the problem of maintaining up-to-date signature files throughout the workstations on your network. Unless you have only a few clients on your network, you must either spend lots of time visiting each workstation on your network to update the virus signature files or rely on your users taking the time to update their own files. Most of your users may be able to figure out how to do it on their own, but virus protection is a lot like a chain—it's only as strong as its weakest link. If one user fails to update on a regular basis, the entire network can become susceptible.

You should perform backups of the data files on your server. However, if you deploy only workstation-based virus scanners, your backup software probably will back up viruses with your data. If you ever restore data from your backups, you'll likewise restore the viruses unknowingly—thereby starting the whole infection cycle over again.

As you can imagine, virus scanners add overhead to your workstation's CPU in order to process the files as they're being read. You also know that it takes longer to load files across the network than it does loading them locally. Therefore, as you probably can deduce, running workstation-based virus scanning to detect files loading from the network can potentially slow down processing at the workstation level. If the server has already scanned the file, it can deliver it virus-free to the workstation quickly. The workstation's scanning software can be used to scan the faster-loading local files.

If you rely only on workstation-based virus protection, you have no way of knowing what your virus scanning software's doing. It's possible that a user has disabled the software. It's equally possible that the program isn't scanning the proper files. Server-side scanners can log the virus scanning activity for both your servers and your workstations in a central location, which allows you to keep tabs on what the software's doing and what it has detected.

In a similar vein, you don't want to rely on your users to notify you of an outbreak. While logging may show you after the fact that a virus has been found, you probably want to know as soon as possible when a virus hits. Unfortunately, workstation-based virus scanning won't let you know when a virus hits. You'll have to rely on your users to tell you that they've encountered a virus—when they get around to it or when they're able to get in touch with you. Server-side virus protection software immediately notifies you of a virus with e-mail, pager alerts, or network broadcasts.

Most of the vendors mentioned in Table A sell some sort of server-side virus protection program. For the rest of this Daily Drill Down, we'll focus on one of the programs that you can deploy on your NetWare servers—InoculateIT by Computer Associates. We'll show you some of its features, and we'll demonstrate how you can use it to tighten your network's defenses against virus outbreaks.

Inoculating your NetWare server

InoculateIT is Computer Associates' virus protection solution. It replaces CA's older virus protection software for NetWare called Innocu-LAN. CA sells server versions of InoculateIT that run on Windows NT and NetWare. The client versions run on MS-DOS, Windows 3.x, Windows 9x, and MacOS. InoculateIT gives you a central point of administration over your entire network's virus defense. InoculateIT's key benefits include:

▶ Detects boot-sector, memory-resident, macro, and polymorphic viruses

▶ Updates virus signature files on servers and workstations automatically

▶ Uses Heuristic Virus Detection Engine to detect unknown macro viruses before they impose damage on the network

▶ Scans each file in the background from the server as a client accesses it

▶ Scans compressed files, such as ZIP and ARJ files

▶ Installs Windows 95, Windows 3.1, and MS-DOS clients remotely from the server

▶ Forces logoff remotely for clients who aren't running virus protection software

▶ Integrates with NDS

▶ Provides virus-free backups when used with CA's ARCserve IT

▶ Sends automatic virus alerts to selected users via e-mail, pager, SNMP, network broadcast, or printed trouble ticket

Like most NetWare programs, InoculateIT runs as an NLM (more specifically, a group of NLMs) on your NetWare server. It runs under NetWare 3.x, 4.x, or 5.x; all you need is 2 MB of disk space and 16 MB of RAM on your NetWare server.

Installing InoculateIT

Although InoculateIT runs on your NetWare server, you install it from your administrative workstation. Make sure that you've logged onto the server where you want to install InocolateIT either as Admin or as a user with Admin-equivalent rights. The installation program runs under Windows 9x or Windows NT. However, if you run the installation program from a Windows NT machine, you won't be able to install the InoculateIT Manager.

To begin the installation, insert the Inoculate-IT CD into your workstation. The installation program should begin by itself. If it doesn't, explore the CD and run the SETUP.EXE program. Setup begins by displaying the NetWare Edition Product Explorer. This window lists the available programs that you can install in the Please Select A Component To Install list box. Select InoculateIT 4.5 for NetWare and click Install.

Now, the Setup program for InoculateIT 4.5 for NetWare will begin. First, you'll see the license window. Read the license carefully to make sure that you can comply with its terms. Click Accept to accept the license and to continue with the installation. If you click Not Accept, Setup will terminate.

After you click Accept, Setup asks you to provide the InoculateIT license information.

Danger, Will Robinson!

Although you're supposed to be able to use any Windows 9x client to install InoculateIT onto your NetWare server, I've run into trouble when installing InoculateIT from a Windows 9x client running Novell's client 3.1—even with Service Pack 2 for the client installed. The installation program locks up mid-way through the installation and disconnects the client from the server. Thinking it

may have been a client issue, I also tried installing it with Microsoft's NetWare client. The same thing happened. I encountered the problem using Windows 95, 98, and 98 SE. Windows NT installations went without a hitch. (Except, as noted, you can't install the InoculateIT Manager.)

To get around this problem, you can download the ITLITNWUP.EXE file. It contains a newer build of

InoculateIT than is on your Inoculate-IT CD. The Setup program for the update runs the same way as the Setup program on the CD. You can use the same CD-Key for the update that you use for the regular CD version. I didn't encounter any problems installing InoculateIT with the update file.

You should have either a license floppy disk or a key code on the back of your CD-ROM's jacket. If you have a license floppy disk, click the File Type radio button and enter the file path to the license information. If you have a CD-Key, enter the key in the Enter Key field. Be careful to type the key properly. If you make a mistake, you'll have to retype the entire 20-key string. To continue, click OK.

Next, Setup displays a summary window, which gives a brief description of what Setup is about to do and lists the minimum requirements you must meet on your workstation and server to run InoculateIT. Click Continue.

Setup then asks for your name and your company's name. Enter the information in the appropriate fields and click Continue.

Setup then asks you which kind of installation you'd like to perform: Express Setup or Custom Setup. As you can probably guess by the names of the types of installation, Custom Setup gives you more flexibility; you can select individual components to install. Express Setup makes most of the decisions for you. For the purposes of this Daily Drill Down, we'll select the Express Setup installation. Make sure that the Express Setup radio button is selected and click Continue.

Next, you must select the server on which you want to install InoculateIT. Setup displays the list of NetWare servers to which you're currently attached. You can view a list of all of the servers on your network by clicking the Show All Available Servers button. Select the server you want and click Continue.

Setup asks you where on the server you want to install the files. By default, Setup copies the InoculateIT files to the SYS:INOCULAN directory and the Alert files to the SYS:ALERT directory. If these directories don't exist, Setup will create them. You can specify a different volume and path by entering the information in the appropriate fields. After you select the target directory, click Continue.

If you're running Setup from a Windows 9x computer, Setup asks you where you want to install the InoculateIT Manager. If you're running Setup from a computer that runs Windows NT, you won't see the InoculateIT Manager installation window.

By default, Setup suggests installing the InoculateIT Manager to drive C: of your workstation

in the INOCULAN directory. If you select the Install Manager To Your Host Server, you can install the Manager to your server rather than directly onto your workstation. You may want to install the files to your server rather than your workstation if you use several different computers or if you have limited space on your workstation. For the purposes of this Daily Drill Down, we're going to install the InoculateIT Manager to the server. When you select the Install Manager To Your Host Server radio button, Setup specifies the SYS:INOCULAN\MANAGER directory. After you decide where to install the Manager, click Continue.

Before installing InoculateIT to your server, Setup displays a summary window that shows your selections up to this point. You can confirm the server and directory locations where the InoculateIT components are going to be copied. If the locations are correct, click Continue to copy the files. If not, you can click Back to work your way backward through the previous windows to make any necessary changes.

When you click Continue, Setup begins copying the files. Then, it asks you to back up the key system files on your workstation. You should go ahead and run the backup. The backup will make it easy to recover quickly in case a virus outbreak damages your boot sector or CMOS.

After you make the backup floppy disk, Setup displays a window informing you that you're finished. Click OK to close the installation. If you want to review a log of what Setup installed, you can click the Notes button. You're now ready to start InoculateIT on your NetWare server.

Starting InoculateIT

You can start InoculateIT from your server's console, or you can start an Rconsole session to your server from your workstation. Don't try to start InoculateIT by loading the NLMs one at a time. Fortunately, InoculateIT comes with a startup NCF that you can use to start InoculateIT.

To start InoculateIT, type *istart4* at your server's console prompt and press [Enter]. Istart4 then launches the NLM launcher that loads all of InoculateIT's NLMs. When it's done, it displays the InoculateIT Available Options window, as shown in **Figure A** on the following page.

On this window, you can check InoculateIT's current status. Don't misinterpret the Server Up Time indicator as referring to the total up time for your server. It only represents the amount of time that InoculateIT has been running.

Also, don't misinterpret the Domain Name entry as referring to a Windows NT domain. Like a Windows NT domain, an InoculateIT domain refers to a group of InoculateIT servers, whether or not they belong to an NT domain. The Master Server Name field refers to the Master Server of the InoculateIT domain. Don't worry if these fields are empty. You'll use them only if you have multiple copies of InoculateIT running on several servers.

FIGURE A

This window enables you to view InoculateIT's status on your server.

FIGURE B

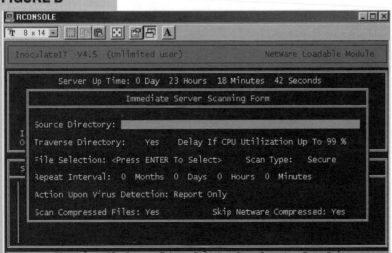

You can create special virus scanning jobs to run on your server.

The Real-time Scan field displays how InoculateIT scans files. By default, InoculateIT scans files as the server reads and writes them to its hard disks. Later, we'll show you how to change that method.

The Last Virus Detected and Last Virus File fields are fairly self-explanatory. They tell you what viruses, if any, InoculateIT has encountered and how many files it has scanned.

The Available Options menu allows you to reconfigure or turn off InoculateIT. To turn off InoculateIT, highlight Deactivate InoculateIT and press [Enter]. You then will notice the Deactivate InoculateIT menu choice change to Activate InoculateIT. As you can probably guess, you can turn InoculateIT back on by highlighting Activate InoculateIT and pressing [Enter].

If you select Job Queue Operation from the Available Options menu, you can create custom scans of files on your server. To add a custom job, highlight Job Queue Operation and press [Enter]. You'll then see a blank job queue appear. Press [Ins]. You'll see the Immediate Server Scanning Form window appear, as shown in **Figure B**. The form allows you to specify when the job runs, how often it runs, and what files it scans. You can even have the job postpone itself, if you tell it to run at a time when the server's CPU is too busy.

The Configuration selection from the Available Options menu lets you customize the way that InoculateIT works on your server. If you highlight Configuration and press [Enter], you'll see the Configuration menu. Here, you have two choices: Realtime Monitor and NLM Information. The NLM Information option displays basic information about the version of InoculateIT that you're running. It provides such details as the version of InoculateIT, the date of the virus signature file, and the program serial number.

The Realtime Monitor option enables you to change how InoculateIT operates on your server. You can select when InoculateIT scans files by changing the value of the direction field. Other directions you can choose include:

▸ **Incoming/Outgoing**—Scans files as they are read from and written to the server.

▸ **Incoming**—Scans files only when they are written to the server.

▸ **Outgoing**—Scans files only when they are read from the server.

▶ **Disabled**—Turns off real-time scanning.

By default, InoculateIT scans all files as the server processes them. You can tell InoculateIT to scan only certain file types. Unfortunately, you can't control it down to the file extension level. You can only tell InoculateIT to scan all files or just executables.

On the Realtime Configuration window, you also can change the type of scan that InoculateIT performs. By default, InoculateIT does a Fast scan, which scans only the beginnings and endings of files for virus signatures. While this type of scan will save the server a great deal of processing time (especially with large files), the fast scan may miss some viruses that are embedded in the center of the files.

Alternatively, you can set InoculateIT's scan type as Secure or Reviewer. A Secure scan checks the entire file as it's written to or read from the server. However, as you can probably guess, this type of file scan can slow down server processing.

Likewise, the Reviewer scan can slow down processing because it scans the entire file as it goes to and from the server. However, unlike the Secure scan, the Reviewer scan searches for virus-like behavior within the files. While this method can be helpful in identifying unknown virus types, it may generate false alarms.

Finally, the Realtime Configuration window enables you to specify what you want InoculateIT to do when it detects a virus by using the Action Upon Virus Detection field. After detecting a virus, InoculateIT can do the following:

▶ Report only (generate a report about the virus but leave the file intact)

▶ Delete file

▶ Rename file

▶ Cure file

▶ Move File

▶ Purge File

▶ Move and Rename (move the file to a safe location and change its name)

▶ Copy and Cure (copy the file to a safe location and disinfect the copy, leaving the original in place in case the disinfection breaks something)

As you can probably guess, the View Activity Log choice from the Available Options menu allows you to view InoculateIT's activity log. The log contains a record of what InoculateIT has been doing since the last time you erased the log. Highlight View Activity Log and press [Enter]. InoculateIT displays the log with the oldest entries at the top. When you press [Esc] to exit the log, InoculateIT asks whether you want to delete the log. After reviewing it, you may want to delete the log if there's nothing important in it. If you don't delete the log, the next time you view it you may find yourself scrolling through many screens of older entries to get to relevant information.

The Lock Screen option on the Available Options menu prevents anyone who uses Rconsole to get to the server's prompt or who accesses the console directly from making changes to InoculateIT's settings. Don't confuse this screen locking with the screen lock function from the server's Monitor console. Unlike the screen locking with Monitor, you can switch screens away from the InoculateIT configuration screen when it's locked. When Monitor is locked, you can't do anything. InoculateIT's screen lock prevents you from making changes only, not from switching screens.

Finally, if you select Exit from the Available Options screen, you can shut down InoculateIT. When you exit this menu, InoculateIT unloads its NLMs from your server's memory. You can then restart InoculateIT.

Using InoculateIT Manager

With the InoculateIT Manager, you can use a Windows interface from the comfort of your administration workstation to perform all of the tasks that we've discussed above. The InoculateIT Manager gives you the added benefit of being able to manage multiple servers from a central location and a single program, rather than having to run from server to server or having to run multiple Rconsole sessions.

The InoculateIT Manager was installed on your workstation when you installed InoculateIT on your first server. To start it, click Start | Programs | InoculateIT | InoculateIT For Windows. The InoculateIT Manager begins by displaying the Quick Access window. The first thing that the program asks you is if you want to use the Domain Manager, perform a local scan, or perform a quick backup of the critical areas of your computer's disks. Click the Domain Manager button.

When the Domain Manager appears, you'll see a list of InoculateIT servers in the Domains/Servers pane, as shown in **Figure C**. The Summary For Domain pane displays a summary listing of the information on your domain and servers, depending on whether you've highlighted a domain or an individual server.

If you've selected a Domain, the Summary For Domain pane lists all of the servers in that domain. It shows the server name, its status, any jobs that are scheduled, the InoculateIT version, and the virus signature version.

If you haven't created any domains or selected an individual server, the Summary For Domain pane displays detailed information about the server. You'll see the server's name, NetWare version, InoculateIT version, virus signature date, serial number, and InoculateIT status.

Clicking the Configuration button, you can do the same InoculateIT configuration tasks from the Domain Manager that you perform at your server's console. Clicking that button will reveal the Configuration window, which is shown in **Figure D**.

The Configuration window gives you the same choices that you have when you use the text-based interface at your server's console. It uses a Windows interface to do so. As you can see, it breaks down your choices into several panes.

The DOS File Selection pane allows you to select what type of files InoculateIT will scan. By default, InoculateIT scans all DOS files. You can force it to choose only executable files by selecting Executable Files from the DOS File Selection drop-down list box. If you select Executable Files, you also can tell InoculateIT which files to scan by specifying the types of file extensions.

By default, InoculateIT doesn't scan Macintosh files. You can change that by making a selection from the Macintosh File Selection drop-down list box. You can scan all Mac files, all application files, or files that use a resource fork.

The Options pane controls what InoculateIT should do when it encounters a virus and how to scan the files on your server. Selections in these panes closely mirror those that are found at the server console and that use the Real-time Monitor and Real-time Configuration windows. Again, the biggest difference is that you can select items from Windows-style drop-down list boxes, rather than from text-based menus.

If you click the Server tab on the Configuration window, you'll see the window shown in **Figure E**. This tab allows you to control basic settings on the server. You can turn InoculateIT off by clearing the Server Active check box. You can turn off alerting on the server by clearing the appropriate check box. Other options on this window include:

FIGURE C

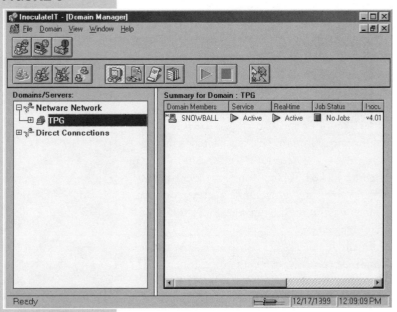

You can use the Domain Manager to administer InoculateIT from your workstation.

FIGURE D

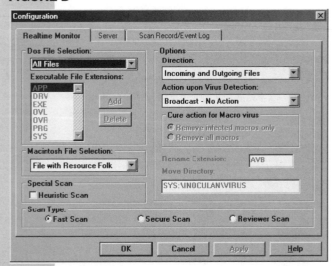

The Configuration window allows you to configure your server from your workstation.

- **Update Domain Interval**—Specifies the amount of time between each update of domain information.
- **Grace Period**—Specifies the amount of time that users have to load WIMMUNE or IMMUNE on their workstations before being disconnected from the server. It's supposed to be used in conjunction with InoculateIT's Enforcement function, but it didn't work for me (see below for an explanation). Values in this field seemed to have no effect on my workstations.
- **NCOPY Delay**—Sets the number of milliseconds that InoculateIT waits before using the NCOPY command to scan files that are copied to the server.
- **Completed Job Hold Time**—Specifies the amount of time that a completed job remains in the Job Queue record.
- **Scan Queue Poll Interval**—Controls the amount of time that passes between each check of the scan queue. When the scan queue is checked, updated information is passed to the Domain Manager.

Not only did I find that some menu choices, such as Grace Period, have no effect, I also discovered that the scroll boxes were rather quirky. You can't enter the values that you want by typing them directly into the fields. Instead, you must use the arrows to scroll to the value that you want, which can be quite annoying if you want to set a value that is very different from the displayed defaults.

If you select the Scan Record/Event Log tab on the Configuration window, you'll see the window shown in **Figure F**. This window controls the way InoculateIT tracks and stores its logs. InoculateIT stores two kinds of logs: the Scan Record and the Event Log. The Event Log tracks everything that InoculateIT does while it's running, including such items as the time that it loaded, any viruses that it has encountered, and the times that you update the virus signature file. The Scan Record maintains only the scanning history. On this window, you can set the amount of information that InoculateIT retains. The choices are self-explanatory.

You can also use Domain Manager to maintain /create custom job scans on your server. To

FIGURE E

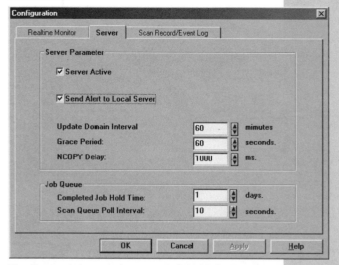

The Server tab controls several of the default values for InoculateIT.

FIGURE F

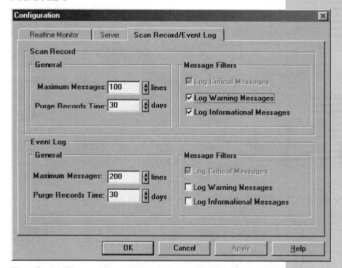

The Scan Record/Event Log tab controls InoculateIT's logging.

Hey! Where did that go?

If you click the Help button while displaying the Configuration window, you may notice that several features described in Help don't exist on your screen. Don't Panic. I was equally confused and confounded when I tried to review some of InoculateIT's "features." I couldn't find such features as Enforcement and Auto Update, even though they were described clearly in Help and in the Features documents for InoculateIT. After much digging, I called CA's Tech Support line for InoculateIT. The support person seemed equally confused but informed me that there are several features in Help that are no longer included as feature sets of InoculateIT. So, the bottom line is: if you can't see it, it isn't there.

create a custom scan, click the Add/Re-Schedule A Scan Job button, which resembles the Play

FIGURE G

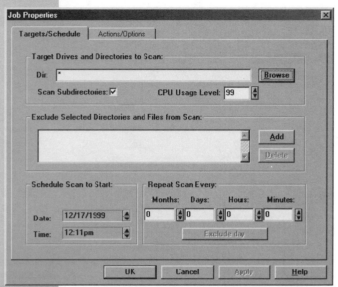

You can use Domain Manager to create custom scan jobs.

button on a VCR. You should see the Job Properties window, shown in **Figure G**. The Targets/Schedule tab allows you to specify which files and directories to scan. You can also specify if and when you want the job to repeat. The Actions/Options tab allows you to control what happens when InoculateIT detects viruses and what type of jobs to run.

Conclusion

If you are a network administrator, one of your most important jobs is to make sure that you keep the information on your network secure. This task includes ensuring that you have effective virus protection running on your network. Just having virus protection software on your workstations isn't enough. You should also run virus protection software on your server. In this Daily Drill Down, we have examined one example of the available server-based virus software for NetWare—InoculateIT. ◆

All is not lost: Reset that missing NetWare Admin password

By John Sheesley

What do you do if you've lost the Admin password for your NetWare server and don't have any users with Admin rights? Don't panic. You can use the SETPWD utility to reset the Admin password on your NetWare server.

Old Faithful

The SETPWD utility has been around for quite a while. The utility is a NetWare Loadable Module (NLM) that can run on any version of NetWare after 3.11, including NetWare 5. It allows you to reset any password on a NetWare server. You'll be glad you have it if you've forgotten your Admin password or been given administrative duties over a NetWare server without being given the Admin password.

You can find SETPWD.NLM by going to http://www.nmrc.org/files/snetware/index.html. This site also contains several other handy NetWare security utilities. To get SETPWD.NLM,

download the SETPWD.ZIP file. The file is only 10K, so it will download almost instantly. Extract the archive file's contents to a blank floppy disk using PKUNZIP or WinZIP.

On the floppy, you'll see five extracted files. The most important one is SETPWD.NLM, the actual utility. The other files are Readme files that contain information about the program and the source code for SETPWD.

You should copy the program to a disk rather than to your server for two reasons. First, this technique makes the program easier to transport if you have to fix multiple servers. Second, having the program on disk avoids a security problem posed by storing the powerful tool on the server. If it's on the server and users know the path to it, they can execute it from the server at any time and change passwords on you without your knowing or being able to do anything about it.

Running the program

Using SETPWD is very easy. Because SET-PWD runs as an NLM, you must run it at your server's console rather than from your administrative workstation. Take the disk from your workstation and place it in the server's drive A. From the dedicated server's command console prompt, type:

```
LOAD A:SETPWD ADMIN newpassword
```

And then press [Enter]. The variable newpassword represents whatever string you want the Admin password to be.

After you enter the password, your server's screen will briefly turn black with a copyright screen for SETPWD at the top. If SETPWD successfully changes the password, it will display a message saying so. This message also redisplays the password you entered, so make sure no one's watching you when you do it. After the message displays, press any key to return to the console prompt.

When you're finished, you can either use SETPWD to set the password for another account or take the SETPWD disk out of the floppy drive and store it for future use. Make sure that you store it someplace secure. You don't want it to fall into the wrong hands. ◆

Notes

Notes

Chapter 3—Firewalls

Firewalls

Chapter 3: Firewalls

Chapter 3 takes a look at firewalls. With the help of Linux, *ipchains*, and Progressive Systems, you'll be able to set-up a rock-solid firewall for your network.

The primary focus of this chapter is an introduction to network firewalls with a tutorial on beginning *ipchains*. This particular tutorial takes advantage of *ipchains'* flexibility and simplicity and includes a fairly complete *ipchains* script that only requires minimal configuration for your own network use.

This chapter also gives those with less knowledge of security a means for choosing the best firewall for their needs. This content should be key reading for any network administrator.

How to select a firewall

By Marcus Ranum

The concept of creating a firewall as a basic means of protecting information assets was introduced by William Cheswick and Steven Bellovin in their 1994 book, *Firewalls and Internet Security: Repelling the Wily Hacker.* They described a firewall as a logical IS security mechanism that was designed to protect information: this was done by keeping potential intruders out of information by erecting a barrier to it.

The risks of Internet connection

Since 1994 , the explosive growth in the number of organizations that have access to the Internet has made a firewall a critical element in IS security. The security of an organization's Internet access should be seen as a small fraction of its entire IS security requirements.

What is needed is a comprehensive approach to these requirements within the organization. Without this enterprise-wide view, the organization may end up with a secure firewall product that is protecting a wide-open network behind it. Above all else, an organization should be consistent in how IS security is handled across the entire enterprise. The organization and its executives should realize that they are as likely to be attacked by means of dial-up access, social engineering, dumpster diving, and toll-fraud attempts as they are to be attacked through the Internet.

It is unfortunate when an organization invests an immense amount of money and effort in securing its Internet connection but still has such things as unprotected modem pools that do not even have passwords or dial-back capabilities. Such a situation can allow intruders to have access to the network behind the firewall. And such a break-in can be a disastrous problem when it occurs.

The cost of downtime

Probably the greatest expense associated with a break-in will be due to processing downtime. The time of IS staff will be diverted to cleanup. In some cases, public embarrassment may be a significant factor. Before anything is done that may affect the security of an organization's information, it is important to ask first:

▶ What is it necessary to protect?

▶ How likely is it that someone will want to break in to it, alter it, or steal it?

▶ How badly will the organization be hurt if such an assault succeeds?

In some instances, it may be concluded that the potential damage that may result from a break-in is so high that no justification for connection to the Internet exists. But in the process of making such a conclusion, it will be wise to examine the organization's existing IS security practices. Frequently, enterprises that have decided on a policy of no Internet connectivity ever permit dial-in access or have other practices that are every bit as risky—and often more perilous—than a well-secured Internet connection.

Often, organizations that have implemented very restrictive firewall products or have mandated adherence to no Internet connectivity policies have dial-out modems scattered around their networks, as individuals who need access simply obtain it through Internet service providers (ISPs). These links are potential avenues of attack, just as any other Internet links are.

The level of attacks examined

Many organization executives do not understand the level of sophistication that attackers are showing. As a result, they either overestimate or underestimate the likelihood that the organization's existing IS security will be compromised. (That is, if they have any IS security.) In recent years, computing activities have been subjected to increasingly sophisticated attacks, including those that capitalize on protocol level and cryptographic flaws and those that utilize sophisticated social engineering.

A pattern has emerged wherein highly skilled attackers (who are sometimes termed ueberhackers) develop tools for exploiting specific IS security weaknesses. Eventually, these tools find their way into the hands of less skilled or completely unskilled novices (who are called ankle biters). These latter individuals can employ the tools, however, to penetrate sophisticated defenses. Also, attackers are persistent. They understand how to exploit the often-tangled interconnections among an organization's networks, the modem pools, and other X.25-based networks and telecommunication mechanisms. For instance, there have been numerous cases of firewalls being compromised from the inside by attackers who gained access to networks by means of dial-in modems that had been left unattended on users' desktops.

What does this indicate for the connected site? If there is a firewall in place, it does not mean that the organization is invulnerable to attack. Other routes of attack into the network must be secured as well, and constant security awareness is mandatory. Organizations with extremely critical data should put it behind internal firewalls. Further, the organization should compartmentalize its networks to make it harder for an attacker to succeed once a successful break-in has been made. In some cases, if there is data that is extremely sensitive or is part of a mission-critical information-processing application, it may be desirable to have no Internet connection to it at all. Or it may be desirable to place this data only on a site that is isolated physically from the organization's backbone computing mechanism.

The likelihood of attack

A number of organizations have concluded that IS security is not a problem for them because "nobody will bother attacking us." Unfortunately, when an attacker is choosing a target to assault, usually this person does not bother researching the target to see if it may contain valuable information.

Rather, most of these people conclude that it is easier to smash in and look around. As a result, the attacks seem to be pretty much random. Those information-processing applications that have important data may be ignored in favor of those applications that simply catch the attacker's eye.

Recently, attackers who broke into a financial database application were observed to ignore completely the financial data they had exposed (which was worth millions of dollars) in favor of exploiting a back-door connection they discovered during the intrusion to a local university's computing center.

The problem is that the unpredictable nature of such attacks makes it very hard to place a value on defending the information assets involved. Thus, one site with a very strong firewall and no important data might come under ferocious attack, while another that has installed no security at all in front of several mission-critical information-processing applications may be ignored completely. It is not realistic for an organization's IS security provisions to rely on the idea that it will be ignored by potential attackers. Such an idea would be true only when the data that the organization processes and maintains is unimportant and the positions of its IS auditor and IS security specialist are absolutely secure.

Mission-critical processing

An organization that is considering connecting its network to the larger world should first ask, "If something happens to our network, will this event put us out of business?" Connecting to the public networks increases greatly that chance of something happening, and the IS auditor or security specialist who is involved in a firewall implementation project must weigh that in the design.

The next question is, "What will be the cost of the kind of business damage that downtime or system cleanup might cause?" Those organizations that possess intellectual property or private data must consider, also, the potential for the disclosure of trade secrets, or the liability that may accrue if, say, a customer's private information is divulged. If the organization handles patient records, customer financial or credit card information, personal data, customer home addresses, and demographic information, it is advisable to consult the organization's legal counsel and to protect that data in accordance with the best business practices in the environment of which the enterprise is a part.

Service-oriented requirements analysis

One effective approach in determining what a firewall product should do for the organization is the process of service-oriented requirements analysis. Rather than simply jumping into the technical details about what features a particular firewall product should provide, the conduct of such an analysis involves taking a step back and listing the network services that the organization may want to take advantage of. A typical set of these services might include:

- Access to the World Wide Web (WWW), including being able to use the File Transfer Protocol (FTP)
- Electronic mail
- USENET connection to the massive network of user forums on the Internet
- Telnet terminal emulation capability to communicate with a wide assortment of remote sites

Defining IS security requirements for services

Based on the list of the actual network services that the organization wants to provide to the network's users, consider whether there are any special requirements that may mandate providing additional IS security activities. For example, what kinds of audit trail and related records may be required to account for and control transactions that move through the network on which the firewall product will be installed? Fashion these requirements on those of other real-life services that the organization uses. Try to assure that the IS security policies that are applied to the various services are consistent. For example, if the organization has a security policy that users cannot use FTP to move data out of the enterprise, then it should also require that its employees not use electronic mail to send data out or send diskettes that contain data by way of the postal system. The key to effective IS security is consistency.

One other important thing to consider when approaching IS security is the growth plan for the organization's network. If the organization installs a firewall product or Internet connection that provides a few services today, will this arrangement work effectively, say, three years from now? That does not mean that the organization will be using the same physical computing hardware three years in the future. (The lifecycles of network equipment for Internet connections are fairly short.) But be certain that the basic firewall architecture that is put in place is likely to be viable for the long term.

Different types of firewalls

Essentially, a firewall should be thought of as a gap placed between two telecommunication networks. This gap is filled with something that lets only a few selected forms of traffic through. The designers of the firewall product should be able to explain the mechanism that enforces the separation, as well as the mechanisms that carry the data back and forth between the area that is being protected and the outside environment. Another important aspect of a firewall is how well it protects itself against attack. The actual firewall product should not be easy to break in to, since breaking in to the firewall will give an attacker a foothold on one or both of the networks that the product has been installed to protect.

Firewall designs

The simplest and most popular form of firewall design is one that implements router screening. Most commercial router products have some kind of capability built in to them to restrict traffic between destinations, while permitting other traffic to move through the gaps. Screening routers operate only at the network level and make all of their permit or deny traffic access decisions based on the contents of the Terminal Control Protocol/Internet Protocol (TCP/IP) packet header. These arrangements are very fast, very flexible, and quite inexpensive. But they lack the ability to provide detailed audit information about the traffic they transmit. Screening routers often have proven to be vulnerable to attack since they also rely on the software being configured correctly on the hosts that are behind them. Many IS security experts prefer, for this reason, to avoid relying on screening routers as a sole defense.

A second form of firewall design is the dual-homed gateway. It is a mechanism with two network interfaces that rests on both the protected network and the public network. Because the gateway can communicate with both networks, it is an ideal place to install software for carrying data back and forth between the two. Such software agents are called proxies. Usually they are customized for the service that they are intended to provide.

For example, a dual-homed gateway that has a proxy for WWW traffic will have some form of agent running on it that manages the making of requests to the remote networks on behalf of the user. Proxy firewalls are also known as application firewalls. These are attractive to many sites, since the proxies are able to perform a continuing detailed audit of the data that is passing through them.

Also, proxy firewalls are felt by many IS experts to be more secure, since the software proxies can be customized to deflect specifically known attacks that the host software behind the firewall might be vulnerable to. The two main disadvantages of using proxy firewalls are that, sometimes, they are not completely transparent, and they do not support protocols for which a proxy has not been developed.

Some firewall products are based on dynamic packet filtering. A dynamic packet filter firewall is like a cross between a proxy firewall and a screening router. To the end user, it looks as if it is operating only at the network level, but in fact the firewall is examining the traffic as it passes by, just like a proxy firewall's proxy application does. When a user connects out through the firewall, it records that fact and allows data to come back in to the user for the duration of that session. Dynamic packet screening firewall products are an attractive technology that is continuing to evolve. This technology shows a great deal of promise for the future.

Trade-offs inherent in firewalls

Firewall products, like many other IS security mechanisms, are not perfect. Usually, the trade-off that they represent is between ease of use and security. The more rigorously the firewall checks the user's identity and activity, the more likely the user is to feel interrupted, pestered, and resentful. The selection of a firewall product should not discount as a decision factor the possible user resentment of the restriction being imposed. Many sites have installed firewalls but also have networks that are festooned with uncontrolled dial-in/dial-out modems. Typically, these devices have been installed by users in an attempt to bypass the firewall product's restrictions by subscribing to some sort of online services. If the IS security mechanism that is chosen is not useful and easy to use, the affected end users will find some way to bypass it.

Proxy firewall products provide better IS auditing and more tightly defined access control capabilities than do screening router firewall products. But many of the latter do not have sufficient capacity to support telecommunication network connections that perform at faster than Ethernet speed. If the organization is planning on using Asynchronous Transfer Mode (ATM) networks or Digital Transfer Rate 3 (T3) telecommunication techniques, it may have no other choice available to it than to use a screening router type firewall product.

Different types of organizations

These trade-offs are complicated, typically, by the type of organization that will be using the firewall product. To illustrate this, here are situations in three different types of organizations.

The experience of an academic organization

Academic organizations such as universities have the most freedom in the environment in which computing is done. The academic user community usually wants to experiment with a wide variety of network features. These people will tend to resent or to actively circumvent a firewall product that is perceived as interfering with this experimentation.

Additionally, academic organizations often have independent departmental budgets and semi-autonomous use of the campus network, which makes it difficult for the institution to enforce a common IS security approach. If one department in the university installs a security system that interferes with the others, they can and will purchase new network links to bypass it. One approach that seems to work for academic situations is to isolate critical computing mechanisms behind internal firewalls. Those information-processing applications in which student records, loan information, and paychecks are processed should be isolated from the main campus networks by placing these sensitive applications behind screening routers or commercial firewall products.

The problem in a research laboratory

Often, research laboratories are another difficult case. Scientists expect to use the network for collaboration and to research access to late-breaking information. In many cases, however, the research may be significant economically and should be protected. Those information-processing applications in which such things as patent applications and the designs for propriety products reside should be isolated and protected specifically. Or, consideration should be given to adding a second network that is Internet accessible and keeping it separate physically from the internal research network. Research laboratories suffer many of the same problems academic organizations do. These enterprises tend to have user communities that want to be on the cutting edge of technology and will not tolerate interference with their work by an IS security mechanism such as a firewall product.

Perhaps more than anything else, it is important to persuade the laboratory's employees to recognize the need to protect the intellectual property they are working with. Many research laboratories are connected to the Internet behind commercial proxy-based firewall products of fairly conservative design, which permit the user to have access to the Web and other sources of information. Other research laboratories rely on segregated networks or isolated computing mechanisms for storing proprietary information.

An electronic commerce application

As electronic commerce becomes more important, the need to pass commercial traffic into and out of firewalls will become more crucial. Service-oriented requirement analysis is a useful tool for designing and implementing such systems. Suppose an organization wants to put a Web server on an external network and provide database access of some sort to a system behind a firewall. In this case, the design requirement is to move data back and forth for use by a form of structured query language (SQL). The organization might choose to install a screening router firewall product. It would be configured to allow for the movement of just this SQL data between the outside Web server and the inside. A commercial firewall product that permitted the operation of some kind of generic proxy or which supported an SQL service might be another option.

Other issues

Other issues to be addressed include how much manpower is needed to maintain the firewall,

whether it is better to buy or build, and how to know that the firewall is secure.

The effort to maintain typical firewalls

Typical firewall products require about an hour a week to maintain once their installation is complete. That is true only if one does not count the other Internet-related time that the firewall administrator (or some other responsible individual) will spend on the project. For instance, achieving Internet connectivity brings with it the requirement for someone to act as the site's postmaster for handling electronic mail traffic, as well as its probable Webmaster, its FTP maintainer, and its Usenet news manager. All these things are time consuming and, taken together, they can become a full-time job for a single person. Often, the firewall administrator winds up being responsible for a lot of tasks in addition to maintaining the firewall. Usually, this individual is the first person who is called or interrupted when someone detects a problem, cannot get his or her Web browser to talk to the firewall, or is trying to resolve some comparable difficulty.

Building a firewall

There are a number of tools available for building one's own firewall. The Internet Firewall Toolkit (FWTK) of Trusted Information Systems (TIS) is a freely available reference implementation of a set of firewall application proxies. It is available by means of anonymous FTP from ftp://ftp.tis.com/pub/firewalls/toolkit. If an organization is building its own firewall using a router or a router and the toolkit, it will find it helpful to take advantage of the router's built-in screening. Brent Chapman and Elizabeth Zwicky's book, *Building Internet Firewalls*, describes some approaches to setting up a screening router. (The book is available from O'Reilly & Associates, 101 Morris St., Sebastapol, CA 95472. Its price is $32.95 in the United States. Elsewhere, inquire as to the local price and verify the shipping charges; include U.S. funds with the order.)

When deciding whether to build or to buy a firewall product, it is important to consider the actual cost of the employee time that will be committed to this venture. Having an employee spend a week building a firewall may not be cost effective unless this person's time is free. Also, when this is done, the result will involve the organization in providing its own support for maintaining the firewall in the long term. This situation will further increase the costs involved in this venture. Before there was such a variety of commercial firewall products available, many organizations hired consultants to build their firewalls. Nowadays, that is not a cost-effective option, since entering into a contract arrangement with a consultant costs more, eventually, than installing a commercial firewall product. And the individual who is engaged for this project may not be able to support or enhance the firewall product over time.

Knowing that it is secure

Whether an organization decides to build or to buy its firewall, a basic consideration is knowing if the firewall is secure. How does one know this? This is a very difficult question to answer. There are no formal tests that can be applied easily to something as flexible as a firewall. A safe rule of thumb is that the more data traffic that the firewall lets in and out, the less likely it is to be resistant to attack. The only firewall that is absolutely secure is one that is turned off.

Costs and delivery

A common misconception in dealing with firewall products is that you get what you pay for and, therefore, the more expensive a firewall is, the more secure it is. That is not necessarily true. The sale of microcomputer and workstation hardware is a commodity marketplace. However, the firewall product market has not settled down enough, yet, for consistent and competitive pricing to evolve. Most commercial firewall products cost from $10,000 to $20,000. And the more expensive offerings can cost as much as $80,000 and up.

An organization considering the acquisition of a firewall product should demonstrate some healthy skepticism when it comes to assertions of product cost versus value. If a particular firewall product costs twice as much as another offering, the organization that is offering this product should be able to explain clearly why its product is twice as good as that of a certain competitor.

What a typical firewall product installation is like

Most firewalls used to be sold as consulting packages. When a firewall was sold, part of its cost included the product's installation and support. Usually, this involved the arrival of a consultant from the vendor who assisted on site with the installation. In those days, many of the organizations that were being connected to the Internet did not have an employee who was competent in using TCP/IP. Thus, the firewall product installer's job often also encompassed configuring the routing of data and such tasks as setting up internal Domain Name System (DNS) and send mail software products. Some vendors continue to provide such a level of service, while others ship a power-on-and-configure turnkey solution product.

Typically, when an organization reaches the point of installing a particular firewall product, the Internet connection must be ready but not yet connected to the protected network. Then, the firewall installer will arrive, test the machine's basic function, and may lead a meeting in which the participants will work out the details of how the firewall will be configured. This meeting will consider such things as what type of access control policy is to be put in place, where electronic mail will be routed, and to what address logging information should be forwarded. Once the installer has a good idea how the firewall product is to be configured, it is connected to the Internet side and tested for correct operation with the network. Then, the firewall's access control rules are installed and checked and it is connected to the protected network. Typically, some additional basic interoperation tests are performed, such as Web access and electronic mail sending and receipt. At that point, everything should be ready to go.

What vendors typically provide with a firewall

Most vendors provide some kind of support period for basic questions pertaining to the firewall. Many provide an installation service similar to that described earlier in this article. Such a service is valuable since it provides the organization with an opportunity to tailor the firewall product in a way that makes sense for the information-processing environment in which it will be used. Meanwhile, the organization has access to qualified vendor support that is equipped to help with this tailoring. Often, a difficult part of setting up a firewall is getting various software packages that must operate behind it to talk correctly to it. Some vendors provide direct support as far as hooking a microcomputer local area network or intranet mail mechanism into the firewall product's mailer or configuring the DNS. If an organization does not already have an employee who has technical skills in these areas, having a vendor that is able and willing to support these aspects of the firewall configuration is an important time and energy saver.

Some ISPs offer a supported firewall as part of their connectivity service. For those organizations that are new to the use of TCP/IP or that are in a hurry to put a firewall product in place, this is an attractive option. In such a situation, the network support, the leased telecommunication line support, and the firewall support are all available through the same vendor.

The single most important thing a vendor can provide with its firewall is an understanding of how to create a sensible IS security policy. Unless an organization is sure that it understands exactly what it is allowing to move into and out of its network, it may not be safe to just install a firewall that allows users to point and click and decide what to allow through. Some firewalls can be configured to allow through things that they should not allow normally, on the assumption that the user organization knows what it is doing. Support from the vendor in getting everything set up with a reasonable baseline helps prevent having a firewall that has unintentionally been configured to allow an attack.

What vendors typically do not provide with a firewall

Typically, a vendor does not configure a customer's internal legacy systems to work with the firewall product. For example, the design of most firewall products assumes that they are talking to the Internet on one side and a TCP/IP network on the other. Usually, it is the customer's responsibility to have TCP/IP-capable information processing applications on the inside network for the firewall to interact with. For electronic mail,

firewalls mostly support only Simple Mail Transfer Protocol (SMTP). It is the customer's responsibility to have an SMTP-compatible mechanism located someplace on the inside of the firewall arrangement. Often it is the customer's responsibility to know of any application-specific configuration changes that are necessary to make that internal SMTP mechanism forward all of the Internet outbound mail to the firewall. Unless an organization is buying its firewall product from an ISP, it is the customer's responsibility, usually, to have both a Class C IP network address and domain name allocated.

Other considerations

There are questions to ask firewall vendors other than just those that deal with product price and delivery times. These questions relate to the security aspects of the firewall product itself, the vendor's credentials, its support and engineering capabilities, the documentation for the product, its audit reports, and its operational features.

Security aspects

▶ What are the security design principles of this firewall product?

▶ Why does the vendor think that the firewall is secure?

▶ What kind of third-party expert review has it been subjected to? By whom? When? (Will the vendor provide a report of the results of this review?)

Vendor credentials

▶ How long has the vendor been selling this firewall product?

▶ What is the size of the product's installed base?

▶ Will the vendor provide contacts with reference accounts that the organization can communicate with?

Support and engineering capabilities

▶ How many full-time support engineers does the vendor have?

▶ During what hours does this support activity operate?

▶ How much does technical support and maintenance of the product cost?

- What is the vendor's product patch and upgrade policy?
- Does the product offering include any type of warranty for the hardware or the software?

Product documentation and audit reports

- Request a copy of the product documentation for review from the firewall vendor.
- What kind of audit reports does the firewall product generate? (Ask that the vendor provide a copy of an audit report for review.)

Operational features

- Does the firewall product include hardware or just software?
- What kind of network interfaces does the firewall product support? (For example, will it be necessary to install token ring to Ethernet routers along with the firewall product?)

- How does the executive interface of the firewall product function?
- Can the firewall product be administered remotely?
- How is this remote administration function protected?

As these questions suggest, selecting a firewall product is much like choosing an automobile. One assumes that selecting a car is easy because, by the time most individuals can afford to acquire an automobile, they already have much of the information that is needed to be able to assess quickly and easily the cost and benefit and performance and convenience tradeoffs that operating different models of vehicles represent. The best way to make sure one obtains a suitable firewall product is to learn enough about the topic to facilitate choosing wisely. ◆

Phoenix Adaptive Firewall: You've tried the rest; now try the best

By Jack Wallen, Jr.

You've seen those cute little Cobalt cube servers on television, in magazines, and in your dreams, but you haven't taken the time to give one a test run. Why? Who really knows what they're for? Web servers? File servers? Print servers? The little blue cubes are an enigma, and they have a reputation for being incredibly reliable and powerful for their size and cost. But what do they do? Well, I'm not sure. However, I do know what Progressive Systems has done to the Cobalt hardware. They've made it into the single best piece of security equipment I've ever had the privilege of using. What this little cube can do in minutes would take an administrator hours to pull off.

I have to admit that when I first received the cube, I was a bit skeptical. The tiny appliance (7.25" x 7.25" x 7.25") looks, for all intents and purposes, more like a micro space heater than a network appliance. With its black finish and hacker-esque green power light shining across the front, Progressive Systems' Phoenix Adaptive Firewall looks more like a toy than a powerhouse

security system. Looks, in this case, are most certainly deceiving. Somehow, Progressive has managed to pack into this minuscule cube more features than most full-sized firewall appliances and software packages could ever dream of.

Specs and such

According to Progressive Systems, the Phoenix firewall uses Adaptive Firewall Technology to secure your network. Adaptive Firewall Technology consists of security features and applications working together to protect and hide network assets. Adaptive Firewall Technology includes:

- **Adaptive State Analysis (ASA) firewall engine**—ASA is a network-level firewall technology that goes beyond the simple packet filtering that's most commonly implemented to protect networks. Packet filtering examines only a portion of the network packets that traverse between your network and the global Internet. ASA examines all aspects of incoming packets to ensure their validity.

- **Anti-attack features**—You may not realize it, but an unprotected network can have literally thousands of open holes, or ports, for network traffic to flow in and out of. A "port scan" is a common way to attack networks; the scan searches for all the possible holes in your network to exploit. Port-scanning applications are available for free on the Internet and have become very easy to use. The Phoenix firewall closes these ports and, depending on the security policy you set, dynamically opens and closes these ports based on the packet information provided by the ASA engine. Furthermore, the anti-attack features of this firewall recognize a scanning attack and will actually hide the Phoenix firewall and the network from the attack, maintaining business as usual for your important network applications.

- **Network Address Translation (NAT)**—The Phoenix firewall uses one-to-many NAT to hide your internal network behind the firewall protection of ASA. NAT can also be used to help conserve IP addresses, which is useful when Internet connectivity provides only a few routable IP addresses.

Additional features not listed on the Web site include:

- Access logging and monitoring
- Authentication secure remote management
- Packet firewall

What Progressive Systems has done, in effect, is to write a group of programs that function independently on top of a standard Linux kernel. The individual programs include:

- **pafserver**—Using an encrypted tunnel, the Secure Management System (SMS) allows remote administration via a Web browser (port 8181).

- **paflogd**—This is the logging daemon that's used by the firewall appliance and that also rotates logs when they become large enough to cause a lag.

- **thttpd-phoenix**—A specialized Web server used for remote graphical user interface (GUI) management.

- **pafnanny**—Monitors the three critical programs (pafserver, paflogd, and thttpd-phoenix) and instantly restarts them if they come

down. Without pafnanny, it would be possible for one of the critical programs to crash, thereby rendering remote management impossible.

- **e-conduit**—Provides the tunnel for SMS to communicate to pafserver.

- **phoenix kernel module**—A user-loadable kernel module that contains the firewall.

- **firewall template files**—User-configurable firewall applications and protocols.

The list of supported predefined applications is lengthy and covers nearly all the common applications that run over IP-based networks.

The physical appliance is laid out in a very straightforward manner. On the backside of the cube, you'll find:

- A few buttons (for inputting information)
- Three Ethernet jacks (one for the external network, one for the internal network—each with a status indicator light—and one for a DMZ network connection)
- A serial port (so the appliance can be connected to a console terminal)
- A cooling fan port
- A power switch
- An AC jack
- An LCD screen
- A keyhole button (which allows access to additional features)

Although the machine is designed to be set up and forgotten about (being the Linux champ that it is), the aesthetically pleasing design, as shown in **Figure A**, will surely become a trophy that most admins will want to display.

Figure A

Here's the front view of the Microserver.

Setup

My setup of the Phoenix Adaptive Firewall went off with only one small glitch. Out of the box, the cube should be set up to allow IP masquerading so that a machine within the firewall can use the remote administration tools or SMS.

Somehow, however, the test machine I received had IPV forwarding set to off, so I couldn't open the remote GUI. Fortunately, tech support was only a phone call away, and the agent I spoke with solved my problem very quickly.

Other than that issue, the setup is as simple as:

▶ Powering on the appliance

▶ Opening the Network Configuration menu

▶ Entering the internal IP address (the address of the NIC that will serve inside the firewall)

▶ Entering the subnetmask of the internal IP address

▶ Entering the external IP address (the address used to serve outside the firewall)

▶ Entering the subnetmask of the external IP address

▶ Entering the gateway

▶ Saving the changes

▶ Rebooting the machine

Once the appliance itself is configured, you're given a pass phrase for remote administration. (Remember to write down this password.) Now all that's left for you to do is configure the machines within the firewall. For testing purposes, I had two machines running Red Hat Linux 6.1: one inside the firewall and one outside the firewall. The test machine inside the firewall was my personal desktop machine, and the one outside the firewall was my Linux test box running a simple server.

The private IP address I chose was within the 172.22.1.* range. The firewall's internal NIC was set up as 172.22.1.1. The machine behind the firewall would have an IP of 172.22.1.2 and a gateway of 172.22.1.1 (hence the need to enable masquerading on the firewall box itself). The final machine, outside the firewall, would have a public IP address assigned by the network administrator (or the DHCP server).

Once I entered the numbers correctly for all the machines, it was time for me to take a look inside and see what this baby was all about!

The first look

Getting to the remote GUI is as simple as pointing a Java-enabled browser (Linux Netscape 4.06 or better) to the internal IP address on the firewall appliance at port 8181. So by entering http://172.22.1.1:8181/, I was greeted first by

Figure B

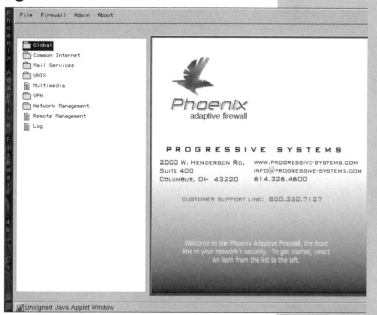

In the post login window, the Progressive contact information appears on the right.

the Progressive splash screen, followed by a smaller login screen. (I should probably warn you that sometimes the Java script can take a bit of time to load.) Regardless of connection speed, the Java client can take anywhere from five to 25 seconds to load (and that's on a base 10 LAN connection). Note: The same speeds applied when I was connected with my cable modem. This time issue is not really a problem because it is absolutely the *only* waiting you'll do with this system.

According to both the beta user manual and the tech support representative I spoke with, the Progressive GUI has a problem with certain desktop environment/Window manager combinations. Apparently, the most stable combination is KDE/Enlightenment. However, I didn't have any problems running a GNOME/AfterStep combination. The GUI didn't crash or lock up on me in over three weeks of testing the application—a fairly good track record.

Once the GUI was up and the login window was available, I entered the passphrase and logged in to the remote management system.

The first look at the progressive remote management system shows the post login window, shown in **Figure B**. The Progressive contact information is displayed smartly on the right, the navigation window is on the left, and the main menus appear as drop-down menus at the top.

The main window (the large window with the Progressive contact information) is where you'll do all the configuring. Once you either select a service (from the left navigational menu) or open an existing firewall file, the contact window disappears and is replaced by the window shown in **Figure C**.

In this window, you'll notice the change in both the main window and the left navigational window. The newly displayed main window is where nearly all the configuration will take place. Within this window, all firewall rules will be edited (with a click of a button or the entry of an IP address), and each service will display a very simple help file to aid the user in understanding what the service is all about.

As far as configuring the firewall rules through this interface goes, it couldn't possibly get any easier! For the network administrator migrating from a Microsoft environment, Progressive Systems' user interface will feel like home. Everything is well explained, well designed, and simple to follow.

Example configuration

Figure C shows Progressive Systems' remote administrative tool (through Netscape) config-uring the HTTP secure firewall rule. In the main window (on the right side), you'll notice three check boxes (Incoming, Outgoing, and Enable), two main boxes (Local Servers and Remote Clients, which change as you click between Incoming and Outgoing), and the Firewall Assistance window. For this particular firewall rule, I'll look at both incoming and outgoing traffic.

The incoming traffic is, for most situations, the most important traffic to monitor/block with firewall rules. For incoming traffic on secure HTTP, set it up to only allow certain IP addresses through the firewall. So, for this example, allow the IP address A.B.C.1 (obviously, this is not a real IP address) into the port assigned to secure HTTP, and allow that IP access to all IPs within the firewall. To do this, click Incoming, enter * in the Local Servers box, and enter A.B.C.1 in the Remote Clients box. If outgoing traffic is permitted and secure, you can then click the Outgoing button and enter * in both boxes. (This will allow anyone within your firewall to use secure HTTP to reach any outside server.)

Once you've set this specific rule, save your firewall file under a specific name, such as test. In order to save a new file, open the File menu, click Save Firewall File As, and enter the name. Once you've saved this file, you can then activate it by going to the Firewall menu and clicking Activate Firewall File or by pressing [Ctrl]F. Note: The firewall file you just saved has but one firewall rule—activating the file you've just created is a very insecure process. Use caution!

Out of the box, there are two basic types of firewall files: Passall and Outgoing Only. The names are fairly self-explanatory. The Passall file allows all traffic in and all traffic out. The Outgoing Only file allows all outgoing traffic and no incoming traffic. Both of these files have their advantages, but they are rather limited. The best idea is to take the Outgoing Only file and modify it to suit your needs. With the Outgoing Only file, outgoing traffic is wide open, whereas incoming traffic is nonexistent. Depending on your needs, you'll want to allow certain services in and not allow certain services out.

I suggest that one of the first things you do with this file is configure port forwarding. Port forwarding takes an incoming request (say, FTP

Figure C

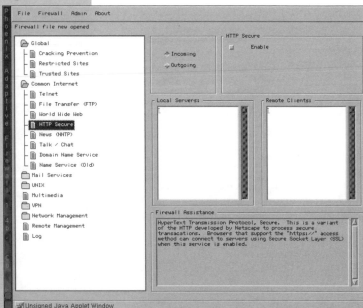

For the network administrator migrating from a Microsoft environment, Progressive Systems' interface will feel like home.

on port 21) and tells the firewall system that when an incoming call for FTP comes in on port 21, send it to this machine instead. So, with the external IP address of A.B.C.1 associated with the firewall appliance, you can redirect services to whichever private IP address you wish. With one machine (inside the firewall) set up for FTP services on 192.34.5.1, follow these steps:

▶ Choose Port Forwarding Configuration from the Admin menu.

▶ Click Add.

▶ Enter the new name for the service (call it FTP).

▶ Click Enable.

▶ Click Forward TCPE.

▶ Enter the firewall's IP in the Interface IP box.

▶ Enter *21* in the Port box.

▶ Enter *21* in the Port box for the destination IP.

▶ Click OK.

Once this is configured, select Save And Activate Current from the Firewall menu. Now the firewall will re-route FTP traffic to the desired machine.

It was the ability to configure port forwarding services that sold me on this machine. Within two minutes of having the Progressive Systems' firewall appliance up and running, I had FTP and ssh re-routing to my desktop machine. In order to do this on most other software or appliances, I'd have to jump through a multitude of obstacles and read a forest's worth of books and a gig of how-tos! Not so with Progressive Systems.

The mysterious keyhole

The keyhole on the back of the appliance allows the administrator access to advanced functions of the system. These advanced functions include:

▶ **Reset GUI Passphrase**—Select the Reset GUI Passphrase option. Once you confirm this action, you'll see a new GUI passphrase displayed on the back LCD screen.

▶ **Enable Telnet**—This is not really an advanced feature since it's also enabled through the GUI interface.

▶ **Display MAC Address**—This feature allows the administrator access to the hardware address of the appliance.

▶ **Reset To Factory Defaults**—This feature resets the appliance to its out-of-the-box state.

Logging

The Phoenix Adaptive Firewall has a built-in logging system, as any good security system would, that features a modicum of configurability. A typical log file from the PSF looks like:

```
3/13-19:47:46 eth1:: udp
255.255.255.255/67 <- 0.0.0.0/68 328
!pass (560)
3/13-19:49:20 eth1:: udp
255.255.255.255/67 <- 0.0.0.0/68 328
!pass (560)
3/13-19:49:20 eth1:: udp
255.255.255.255/67 <- 0.0.0.0/68 328
!pass (555)
3/13-19:49:23 eth1:: udp
255.255.255.255/67 <- 0.0.0.0/68 328
!pass (555)
3/13-19:49:29 eth1:: udp
255.255.255.255/67 <- 0.0.0.0/68 328
!pass (555)
3/13-19:49:33 eth1:: udp
255.255.255.255/67 <- 0.0.0.0/68 328
!pass (555)
3/13-19:49:33 eth1:: udp
255.255.255.255/67 <- 0.0.0.0/68 328
!pass (555)
3/13-19:52:54 eth1:: udp
255.255.255.255/67 <- 0.0.0.0/68 328
!pass (560)
3/13-19:52:54 eth1:: udp
255.255.255.255/67 <- 0.0.0.0/68 328
!pass (555)
3/13-19:54:42 eth1:: udp
255.255.255.255/67 <- 0.0.0.0/68 328
!pass (560)
```

This file shows a small snippet of incoming traffic that's not allowed to pass (indicated by !pass). I'll break this log down:

3/13-19:47:46	time stamp
eth1	interface being filtered
udp	transport protocol being used
255.255.255.255/67	IP address and port number of the local machine
<-	direction of traffic (in this case, incoming)
0.0.0.0/68	IP address and port number of remote host
328	size of packet transmitted (in bytes)
!pass	message indicating that the packet was denied
(560)	line number within the firewall file where the rule was triggered

Another very nice feature is the ability to download log files from within the system. Using the same menu that you use to view the log files (Admin | Logging), you can opt to download the log file to the local machine that's being used to administer the firewall. The downloaded file is named phoenix.log and is much more complete than the information you can view from the remote GUI. You should keep tabs on this downloadable file for more in-depth monitoring of the firewall's functioning.

Although you might be hesitant to hand over the security of the system you've spent hundreds and thousands of hours setting up and parenting to a point-and-click firewall device, Progressive Systems' firewall will quickly change your mind and prove that Linux has reached well beyond the user-friendly stage. The price of the appliance is a bit steep—running approximately $3,200—but it's well worth the cost. Such tight security that can be configured remotely, quickly, and without taking down a running system is worth much more than its weight in gold… and Progressive Systems' firewall is the cream of the crop from this writer's point of view.

If you're interested in purchasing one of Progressive Systems' firewall appliances, you can contact the company through its Web site. You won't regret this purchase. ◆

ipchains: A painless way to ensure networking security

By Jack Wallen, Jr.

Linux does a lot of things as an OS, and it does them well. Linux develops well. Linux plays well with other OSs. Linux does incredible GUIs. Linux does office suites well. Linux networks well. And above all, Linux is king of security. In this Daily Drill Down, I'll take a look at ipchains, an incredibly handy tool for cheap, efficient network security.

Finding out whether your system supports *ipchains*

For the longest time, the Linux kernel dealt with security through *ipfwadm* and the Linux IPv4 firewalling code (stolen from BSD). The older method was a bit clunky. It didn't deal with fragments; had 32-bit counters (on Intel); didn't allow for the specifications of any protocol other than TCP, UDP, or ICMP; couldn't make large changes automatically; didn't deal with inverse rules; and was prone to user error. Starting with the Linux 2.1.102 kernel, the switch was made to *ipchains*, and making a network secure couldn't be easier. With any of the latest Linux distributions, the kernel is already compiled with *ipchains*, so it's simply a matter of writing

your own *ipchain* rules (or downloading any of a number of GUI front ends—more on that later). If you aren't sure whether your particular distribution works with *ipchains*, run the command

```
ls /proc/net
```

and you should see something similar to:

```
arp dev_stat ip_fwnames netlink route
sockstat udp
dev igmp ip_masq netstat rt_cache tcp
unix
dev_mcast ip_fwchains ip_masquerade
raw snmp tr_rif wireless
```

The entry you're looking for is *ip_fwchains*. If this entry is listed, you are in luck, and *ipchains* will be your friend. If *ip_fwchains* doesn't appear, you'll have to remake your kernel and add in support (or upgrade to a newer distribution).

Now that you know whether your system supports *ipchains*, it's time to begin looking into the why and how of the system.

Security, logging, and portability

Like most Linux users, you'll probably want to know why *ipchains* are better. The primary (and obvious) reason is security. Most machines sitting on a network pipe are open and vulnerable to exploitation, hacks, cracks, and prowling, so it's best that they find their way to some semblance of security. Using a Linux box on a network is much different than using a Windows box, because the security of the system is under the complete control of the administrator. When I say complete, I mean just that: The admin can make the system as open or closed as desired and can do so without third-party software or a certification course. With *ipchains*, the admin configures each rule by hand (unless a GUI is used), so each rule can be customized and specified to that particular system's needs.

Logging is essential to any good security model, and with *ipchains*, logging is as simple as adding the proper flag (-l) to the command line. It's very important that you watch your syntax when you're running commands with *ipchains*. Although you probably won't do any damage, you might assume you have a secure system when in fact you don't.

What more could you ask for than a security tool that's usable on all your Linux boxes? You write a set of rules that are tight, and you can use them at work and at home, then distribute them to your friends and family. (I'll present a very good downloadable *ipchains* ruleset at the end of this Daily Drill Down to show you how easy it is to install a working set of rules onto a different machine.)

The needs of the few...

The first thing to remember is that *ipchains* can be done two different ways:

▶ You can enter the rules at a console, one at a time.

▶ You can run an existing *ipchains* file that contains all the necessary rules for your system.

Both methods have advantages and disadvantages. The former allows better means of testing, debugging, and customizing with a one-rule-at-a-time approach. The latter allows simplicity, efficiency, and portability. (Note: When I refer to *portability*, I don't mean cross-platform portability.) In this Daily Drill Down, I'll introduce the idea of *ipchains* with the one-rule-at-a-time approach and eventually move to a much stronger script approach.

You'll also want to take into consideration just how the *ipchains* function deals with an incoming/outgoing packet. As a packet comes in (or goes out), the header is compared to the first rule in the input chain. If the header matches (it's an incoming FTP request to a port that has FTP blocked by *ipchains*), the packet will be dropped and no further action will be taken. If the packet doesn't match, it will move on to the next rule. If the packet makes it through all the rules (or matches a rule that allows it through), the packet will make it into/out of the system. As a result, you should design your ruleset carefully. Make sure your more specific rules are above the general rules. For example, keep your *catchall* rules toward the bottom, which will catch any packets missed by the previous rules.

The structure of a rule

Let's take a look at the parts of an *ipchain* rule. The basic structures of *ipchains* are:

▶ *ipchains* -[ADC] chain rule-specification [options]

▶ *ipchains* -[RI] chain rulenum rule-specification [options]

▶ *ipchains* -D chain rulenum [options]

▶ *ipchains* -[LFZNX] [chain] [options]

▶ *ipchains* -P chain target [options]

▶ *ipchains* -M [-L | -S] [options]

This list doesn't include all the options. I'll focus on the most widely used structures.

The parts of the rule are:

▶ ipchains: The actual command itself.

▶ -A: Tells *ipchains* you're going to append a new rule to the bottom of the chain.

▶ input: Tells *ipchains* that the rule is for the *input* chain.

▶ output: Tells *ipchains* that the rule is for the *output* chain.

▶ -s: Specifies where the packets are coming from.

▶ -d: Specifies where the packets are going.

▶ -p: Tells *ipchains* what protocol of the rule or the packet to check.

▶ -j: Tells *ipchains* to jump to DENY or do something else if the packet matches the rule.

▶ -N: Creates a new chain.

▶ -X: Deletes an empty chain.

▶ -P: Changes the policy for a built-in chain.

▶ -L: Lists the rules in a chain.

▶ -F: Flushes the rules out of a chain.

▶ -Z: Sets the packet and byte counters on all rules of a chain to 0.

▶ -I: Inserts a new rule into the top of a chain.

▶ -R: Replaces a rule in a chain.

▶ -D: Deletes a rule in a chain.

▶ -I: Specifies an interface to be used (that is, eth0).

▶ -l: Logs all instances when a packet matches a rule.

▶ -v: Provides verbose output.

The first rule I'll look at is a very basic rule that will deny a ping to the local machine. I'll call this local machine *willow* (and it will have an entry in the /etc/hosts file) with an IP address of 172.22.1.4. The actual rule looks like

```
ipchains -A input -s willow -p icmp ↪
-j DENY
```

and is run from the command line as root. When you run this command, it places the rule into the input chain and will remain present until the chain is flushed (by entering the command *ipchains -F* or by reentering the same chain and replacing -A with -D) or the machine is rebooted.

A normal ping attempt to willow will look like:

```
> ping willow
PING willow.tech (172.22.1.4) from
172.22.1.4 : 56(84) bytes of data.
64 bytes from 172.22.1.4: icmp_seq=0
ttl=255 time=0.1 ms
-- willow.tech ping statistics ----
1 packets transmitted, 1 packets
received, 0% packet loss
round-trip min/avg/max = 0.1/0.1/0.1 ms
```

which is successful. Once the above rule is entered, the ping will not succeed and, when you press [Ctrl]D, it will return:

```
PING willow.tech (172.22.1.4) from
172.22.1.4 : 56(84) bytes of data.
-- willow.tech ping statistics ----
2 packets transmitted, 0 packets
received, 100% packet loss
```

As you can see, the ping failed this time. A very simple test!

Now to get your ping back, you can do one of two things: You can flush the ruleset or you can delete the ruleset. To flush the ruleset, you simply run (again as root):

```
ipchains -F
```

Now rerun ping and it should be successful. However, if you created more than one ruleset and you want to delete only one rule (instead of all of them), you simply mirror the original rule and replace the Append flag with the Delete flag. So the new command will look like:

```
ipchains -D input -s willow -p icmp ↪
-j DENY
```

and the rule is gone. Simple.

A bit more practical

Let's face it—denying ping is not horribly impressive or effective (in fact, Linux is now immune to the ping of death), so we'll have to look deeper into *ipchains* and write some more useful rulesets. The following rules are pretty basic, but they are fairly inclusive (we're using our test machine willow for these rules to simplify the writing) and list some of the most commonly exploited ports.

Set default output policy to ACCEPT (this will allow all packets to leave willow):

```
ipchains -P output ACCEPT
```

Set default input policy to DENY (this will deny all packets coming into willow):

```
ipchains -P input DENY
```

Deny all access of type tcp into willow:

```
ipchains -A input -p tcp -s ! ↪
172.22.1.4 -j DENY
```

Deny FTP access into willow:

```
ipchains -A input -p tcp -d willow ↪
20 -j DENY -l
```

Deny telnet access into willow:

```
ipchains -A input -p tcp -d willow ↪
23 -j DENY -l
```

Enable loopback (interface = lo) traffic (this lets you run any local networking service you or your system might need):

```
ipchains -v -A input -i lo -s 0/0 ↪
-d 0/0 -j ACCEPT
ipchains -v -A output -i lo -s 0/0 ↪
-d 0/0 -j ACCEPT
```

The next few rules are used to deny access ports that shouldn't be exposed to the network. Many of these particular ports are frequently scanned and easily abused.

Port 0, a reserved port with no legitimate use:

```
ipchains -A input -p tcp -d willow ➥
0 -j DENY -l
```

Ports 0-5, used for sscan signature (ports 0 and 5 will have two entries):

```
ipchains -A input -p tcp -d willow ➥
0/5 -j DENY -l
ipchains -A input -p icmp -d willow ➥
5 -j DENY -l
ipchains -A input -p udp -d willow ➥
0 -j DENY -l
```

Port 7, echo, used for UDP attack (here you'll have two entries, one for TCP and one for UDP):

```
ipchains -A input -p tcp -d willow ➥
7 -j DENY -l
ipchains -A input -p udp -d willow ➥
7 -j DENY -l
```

Port 11, systat, used for User process information (ps):

```
ipchains -A input -p tcp -d willow ➥
11 -j DENY -l
```

Port 15, netstat, used for network status, open connections, routing tables, etc.:

```
ipchains -A input -p tcp -d willow ➥
15 -j DENY -l
```

Port 19, chargen, UDP attack (again you'll have two entries):

```
ipchains -A input -p tcp -d willow ➥
19 -j DENY -l
ipchains -A input -p udp -d willow ➥
19 -j DENY -l
```

Port 21, 20, FTP service:

```
ipchains -A input -p tcp -d willow
20/21 -j DENY -l
```

Port 22, ssh, secure shell service (again two entries):

```
ipchains -A input -p tcp -d willow ➥
22 -j DENY -l
ipchains -A input -p udp -d willow ➥
22 -j DENY \-l
```

Port 23, telnet:

```
ipchains -A input -p tcp -d willow ➥
23 -j DENY -l
```

Port 25, smtp, SPAM relay and older vulnerabilities:

```
ipchains -A input -p tcp -d willow ➥
25 -j DENY -l
```

Port 53, domain, TCP zone transfers and DNS spoofing:

```
ipchains -A input -p tcp -d willow ➥
53 -j DENY -l
```

Port 69, tftpd, Insecure FTP alternative:

```
ipchains -A input -p udp -d willow ➥
69 -j DENY -l
```

Port 79, finger, user information:

```
ipchains -A input -p tcp -d willow ➥
79 -j DENY -l
```

Port 87, link, tty link, which is very commonly used:

```
ipchains -A input -p tcp -d willow ➥
87 -j DENY -l
```

Ports 109, 110, pop-3, one of the most exploited ports:

```
ipchains -A input -p tcp -d willow ➥
109/110 -j DENY -l
```

Port 111, sunrpc, the most exploited port (two entries):

```
ipchains -A input -p tcp -d willow ➥
111 -j DENY -l
ipchains -A input -p udp -d willow ➥
111 -j DENY -l
```

Port 119, nntp, public news feed for SPAM relay:

```
ipchains -A input -p tcp -d willow ➥
119 -j DENY -l
```

Port 143, imap, one of the three most exploited ports:

```
ipchains -A input -p tcp -d willow ➥
143 -j DENY -l
```

Port 144, NeWS, window management system:

```
ipchains -A input -p tcp -d willow ➥
144 -j DENY -l
```

Port 161, 162, snmp, remote network administration and queries:

```
ipchains -A input -p udp -d willow ➥
161/162 -j DENY -l
```

Port 177, xdmcp, X Display Login Manager:

```
ipchains -A input -p udp -d willow ➥
177 -j DENY -l
```

Port 512-520, various, intranet only (two entries):

```
ipchains -A input -p tcp -d willow ↪
512/520 -j DENY -l
ipchains -A input -p udp -d willow ↪
512/520 -j DENY -l
```

Port 540, uucp:

```
ipchains -A input -p tcp -d willow ↪
540 -j DENY -l
```

Port 635, mount, mountd exploit:

```
ipchains -A input -p udp -d willow ↪
635 -j DENY -l
```

Port 1080, socks, SPAM relay, proxy server exploit:

```
ipchains -A input -p tcp -d willow ↪
1080 DENY -l
```

Port 1114, sql, sscan signature:

```
ipchains -A input -p tcp -d willow ↪
1114 -j DENY -l
```

Port 2000, openwin, Open Windows:

```
ipchains -A input -p tcp -d willow ↪
2000 -j DENY -l
```

Port 2049, nfs, remote file access (two entries):

```
ipchains -A input -p tcp -d willow ↪
2049 -j DENY -l
ipchains -A input -p udp -d willow ↪
2049 -j DENY -l
```

Ports 6000-6003, X11, X Windows System:

```
ipchains -A input -p tcp -d willow ↪
6000/6003 -j DENY -l
```

Flush and set the byte/packet containers to 0:

```
ipchains -F input
ipchains -F output
ipchains -Z input
ipchains -Z output
```

Enable all ICMP:

```
ipchains -v -A input -p ICMP -s 0/0 -d
willow -j ACCEPT
```

If you're doing any IP masquerading:

```
echo 1 > /proc/sys/ipv4/ip_forward
ipchains -A forward -s
172.22.1.0/255.255.0.0 -j MASQ
```

This is a fairly exhaustive list of rules and may be a bit on the side of overkill for a single *ipchain* ruleset. However, better safe than sorry. You may also notice that one of the final lines in the downloadable *ipchains* script will cover many of the above rules:

```
ipchains -v -A input TCP -i $OUTWARD_IF
-d LOCAL_IP 0:1024 -l -j DENY
```

However, with this rule you'll block services that may be needed for certain hosts. Therefore, the script includes loops that open certain ports and services for all hosts listed in *$TRUSTED_LOCS*. This approach keeps down the size of the script (imagine having to hardcode all the lines for each trusted location!).

The ipchains script

Now that you understand the individual pieces, you can probably see that running each of them separately would be quite a chore. Granted, using all the above rules probably won't be necessary. However, as the saying goes, an ounce of prevention is worth a pound of cure. So, let's focus on using all the rules for our *ipchain*.

To properly put this chain together to run in a script, you need to think, for the moment, like a programmer. As you can see, there's a lot of room for IP number entry, and the above rules, as written, apply to a specific machine. To change the entire script, you'd have to change each line (such as each instance of *-s willow*). You can do this easily by using *global variables*. Global variables let you apply a variable in one location, within a script or code, and that variable will be applied to all locations where the variable name is found.

For our *ipchains* script, use the following global variables:

▸ LOCAL_IP

▸ OUTWARD_IF

▸ INWARD_IF

▸ DNS 1, 2

▸ ANYWHERE

▸ SERVE_TCP

▸ SERVE_UDP

▸ TRUSTED_SERVE_TCP

▸ TRUSTED_SERVE_UDP

▸ TRUSTED_LOCS

▸ TRUSTED_NTP

We'll also include DNS numbers within the declaration of the above global headers (even though they won't technically be global).

The script will be in sections, which will include the following:

▸ header

▸ variable declaration

- ▶ flush and zero section
- ▶ set policy
- ▶ enable loopback
- ▶ deny ports
- ▶ enable special services

Using this outline, you can put together a fairly tight *ipchains* script. I've written the script, with comments, and left the variable declaration up to you. Download the script (ftp://216.24.5.22/ pub/ip_chains_script) and then I'll describe its use.

The script

To use the script, first log on as root (with *su*) and create a /*root*/*bin* directory. Then, move the *ip_chains_script* file into that directory (*mv ip_chains_script* /*root*/*bin*). With the file properly in place, go through and fill in the global directories. Here's a brief description of each variable:

- ▶ LOCAL_IP—External IP address of the machine being used.
- ▶ OUTWARD_IF—Interface used for external network traffic.
- ▶ INWARD_IF—Interface used for internal network traffic (for example, if IP masquerading is to be used).
- ▶ DNS 1, 2—Primary and secondary DSN numbers for your network.
- ▶ ANYWHERE—A simple way to keep from having to type 0/0 or 0.0.0.0 all the time. It means all locations.
- ▶ SERVE_TCP—TCP services offered to all.
- ▶ SERVE_UDP—UDP services offered to all.
- ▶ TRUSTED_SERVE_TCP—TCP services offered to trusted locations.
- ▶ TRUSTED_SERVE_UDP—UDP services offered to trusted locations.
- ▶ TRUSTED_LOCS—The trusted locations.
- ▶ TRUSTED_NTP—NTP services offered to trusted locations.

With the global variables all filled in, you'll need to take care of one little detail before you run this script. Some distributions of Linux do not have /*sbin* in root's $PATH. In order for this script to run as is, you'll have to add /*sbin* to

root's $PATH. The simplest way to do this is with the export command (run as root):

```
export PATH=$PATH:/sbin
```

and you should be good to go. Log off your machine and log back in (so the new $PATH will take effect). Now all you have to do is make sure the script has executable permissions (with *chmod u+x ip_chains_script*) and you're ready to run.

In the /*root*/*bin* directory, type the following:

```
./ip_chains_script
```

and you will see a lot of text scroll by. If you want to see what this text is, you can run:

```
./ip_chains_script > testing
```

which will *cat* the output to the file *testing*.

Now that you've run your first *ipchains* script, you can test your network connection to make sure you're still getting out. A good way to do this is to go to http://grc.com/x/ne.dll? bh0bKyd2 (Gibson Research Corporation's Shield's Up site) and test your machine's vulnerabilities. Or you could grab a copy of nmap (ftp://216.24.5.22/pub/nmap-2.30BETA18.tgz) to get a better feel of how well your script stands up to port scanning. The output of an nmap portscan on a machine running our script should look something like this:

```
[jwallen@giles nmap-2.30BETA18]$ nmap
willow
Starting nmap V. 2.30BETA18 by
fyodor@insecure.org (
www.insecure.org/nmap/ )
WARNING! The following files exist and
are readable:
/usr/local/lib/nmap/nmap-services and
./nmap-services. I am choosing
/usr/local/lib/nmap/nmap-services for
security reasons. set NMAPDIR=. to
give priority to files in your local
directory
Note: Host seems down. If it is really
up, but blocking our ping probes, try
-P0
Nmap run completed — 1 IP address (0
hosts up) scanned in 54 secondss
[jwallen@giles nmap-2.30BETA18]$
```

Note that we didn't use the -P0 switch, which says "Do not try and ping hosts at all before scanning them." This allows the scanning of networks that don't allow ICMP echo requests (or responses) through their firewall.

AUTHOR'S NOTE
As stated in the comments of the *ipchains* script, our script is based on one written by splanky@nym. alias.net.

Making it a bit more permanent

As it stands, you now have your *ipchain* rules running on your machine. However, when you reboot that machine, you'll lose those rules and, as a result, find yourself wide open again. How do you make the rules more permanent? There are many, many ways to keep your ruleset running. I'll show you one very simple method.

Cron

Let's create a cron job that will always rerun your *ipchain* file. With this method, you can rest assured that at a certain time your ruleset will be run fresh and your machine will be secure.

To create this cron job first (as root) cd to */etc/cron.daily* and open your favorite editor. The file we'll create will be called *ipchains_daily* and will contain the following text:

```
#! /bin/sh
/root/bin/ip_chains_script
```

Once you've entered the text and saved the script, change the permissions to the following:

```
-rwx------
```

with the following command:

```
chmod 700 ipchains-daily
```

Once you've finished, your *ipchains* will run every morning at 4:00. This time is fairly safe, since little work will be done that early in the morning.

What about startup?

What if you restart your machine before 4 A.M.? You'll certainly want your long-awaited security measures in place—but how?

The simplest method of ensuring your new security will be in place upon boot is to place an entry in your */etc/rc.d/rc.local* script. The entry

```
/root/bin/ip_chains_script
```

will cause the *ipchains* script to run at boot.

Another method, and a more solid one, is to add an entry with *chkconfig*. To do this, first download *chkconfig* (ftp://216.24.5.22/pub/ packetfilter) and then run the following steps:

▸ *su* to root.

▸ *mv* the file to */etc/rc.d/init.d*.

▸ Assign executable permission to the script with *chmod u+x packetfilter*.

▸ Run the command *chkconfig -- add packetfilter*.

▸ Run the command *find .. | grep pack*.

The final command is simply a means to check to see whether the setup was successful. You should see something like this:

```
../init.d/packetfilter
../rc0.d/K90packetfilter
../rc1.d/K90packetfilter
../rc2.d/S09packetfilter
../rc3.d/S09packetfilter
../rc4.d/S09packetfilter
../rc5.d/S09packetfilter
../rc6.d/K90packetfilter
```

which will inform you that the packetfilter script has been entered in your startup routines.

Other aspects I didn't cover

There are many other aspects of the *ipchains* utility I didn't cover in this Daily Drill Down. For instance, you can generate and use additional *ipchains* (beyond *input* and *output*). With the command

```
ipchains -N test
```

you create a new *ipchain* called *test*. (Note: *ipchain* names cannot exceed eight characters.) This is primarily useful for organizational purposes and makes debugging a much less painful task.

Another helpful tool to use with *ipchains* is *ipchains-save*. The *ipchains-save* utility prints the firewall chains to stdout, which will allow the administrator to see a list of all the rules (without comments or confusing script) for debugging or archiving purposes.

Conclusion

Although I didn't cover every aspect of the *ipchains* utility, I've tried to bring you a simple means of locking down your network without having to earn an engineering degree in the process.

One thing you'll want to consider: This is certainly not the most advanced *ipchain* ruleset. There are better, more detailed, and more inclusive scripts that would require days of class time to explain and understand.

Regardless of depth and breadth, what you've learned from this Daily Drill Down (and the script included) should enable you to breathe a bit easier knowing that your network has more security than it ever did before. ◆

Chapter 4—Attacks

Intruder Alert

Viruses

Chapter 4: Attacks

Chapter 4 takes a look at a hot topic these days: attacks. Within this particular chapter, you will find two sections:

▶ Intruder alert

▶ Viruses

The first section deals with hackers, crackers, and general break-ins; whereas the second section deals specifically with viruses.

Intruder alert takes a close look at how you can be attacked and how you can prevent these attacks. In this section, we will examine topics such as:

▶ TCP hijacking

▶ Hack encouragement

▶ Security tricks

The viruses section focuses on the ever-present threat of virus attacks. This section helps you to train your users and patch your software. Either way you go, you're going to improve your overall security with Chapter 4.

Don't let others mine your data; guard it with Tripwire 2.0 for Linux

By Sean McPherson

Security should always be on your mind when it comes to important data. After all, you wouldn't consider the data important if it weren't worth something, would you? If your data matters, then Tripwire 2.0 for Linux might be worth checking out. I did, and I found quite a lot to like, although there are a few "gotchas" you should know about.

The latest version, Tripwire 2.0 for Linux, can be downloaded for free from the manufacturer's Web site at www.tripwire.com. Tripwire has been available as an Internet download for years, and many UNIX/Linux admins have used it on servers as a security tool.

What is Tripwire?

The Tripwire introduction page describes Tripwire 2.0 as "a file system integrity checker for UNIX networks." The idea behind the software is that if you have a database of checksums for the files on your server, you have the ability to detect intrusions or unauthorized changes. You can also monitor changes made to files by other software you have installed, which can be a lifesaver.

The test

I tested Tripwire 2.0 on a Celeron 400 with 128 MB and a 2.5-GB system disk. Although the software only requires a 486 and 32 MB of RAM, I knew the majority of today's users would be using a beefier machine.

My test PC is reasonable for both desktop/workstation use and small office servers. The machine has a "comfortable" install of RedHat 5.2, meaning that I installed about 500 MB of software both from the install CD and from the Internet. The intent was to create a machine with critical data as well as files and directories that users would be changing constantly. To me, this seemed a reasonable test environment.

The software's initial installation was simple. I just mounted the CD and ran the included shell script. The script asked a few simple questions and set up the site keys that are used to cryptographically sign all databases and reports.

Remembering these keys is vital, since without them you cannot create, update, or query the Tripwire databases.

After the installation is complete, you'll need to review the default policies, which determine the files and directories monitored by Tripwire. The policies are stored in an easily modified text format, and the documentation explains what each type of rule means and provides the proper syntax to use. These rules are very flexible, and they can be used to monitor file sizes, permissions, and modification times. Just edit the file and initialize the databases with your values. All errors will be displayed, allowing you to learn what problems might exist. But you'll need the passphrase you configured at setup to update the databases. (I TOLD you they were important!)

When you are satisfied with the rules you've written and your databases are loaded, all you need to do for a basic security audit is run the tripwire binary from a 'cron' or 'at' script on a regular basis. Tripwire will happily e-mail the results of a certain report. This feature is great for servers that have multiple administrators, each of whom is responsible for a specific group of files. One example might be a multi-purpose server with both FTP and HTTP access. The FTP administrator would receive a custom report that only described files pertaining to the FTP site, while the Web administrator could be sent a different report for Web files.

As files change on the machine and reports are generated, you can open Tripwire in an interactive mode and add these changes to the database to prevent them from being reported again until the next time they change. This is a simple interface that basically runs as if you had opened the file in your default text editor, and it makes it easy to quickly confirm changes to the machine.

The "gotchas"

What kind of "gotchas" did I find? The one that stands out is the fact that all of the system documentation, including the user manual, is in PDF format. I may just be picky, but I have a *lot* of headless UNIX servers and machines with a slimmed down install. XPDF or Adobe's Acrobat may not be installed. Is it too much to ask for a text version of the documentation? Oh, and just so you don't waste too much time, the version of pdftotext that's part of RedHat 5.2 mangled the file terribly when I tried that.

I did find it amusing that while the documentation required a PDF viewer, most of which run under X, the program itself is completely commandline driven. I was hoping for some kind of GUI interface to make it a bit less daunting for users on a workstation or for admins who just like to point and click.

Aside from that, the software was easy to install, the documentation (while a bit hard to access, and VERY dry and technical) was complete and accurate, and the programs ran quickly and efficiently. Creating the databases took approximately five minutes, and after the third or fourth run, I had a firm grip on creating the rules. Reports can be created nearly instantly, and the disk usage for the whole shebang was under 10 MB.

Overall, I was very pleased with the Linux version's ability to detect system changes. If the documentation can be made a bit more flavorful and easier to access in the next version, I expect even more people will add it to their personal set of required software tools used to protect important data. ◆

Are you encouraging hackers to attack your network?

By John McCormick

Many federal agencies have just instituted a draconian, keep-quiet security policy that should probably be adopted in your company. The move makes a lot of common sense, and we all know how uncommon common sense really is in business!

Don't ask, don't tell

I learned about this policy change a month ago. I was reporting on a new security software release and needed to verify that a government agency was, in fact, using the product. The vendor was anxious to get this information to me, but its public relations department ran into stonewalls at every agency using the software.

No one in the government would discuss this product on record. Only one user would even confirm that he knew what the software was used for, let alone whether his agency actually used it.

Up until a few months ago, the situation was very different. During many years of reporting on government computer installations, I routinely telephoned or e-mailed various agency contacts and chatted about their latest hardware and software acquisitions. Not only did agency workers freely discuss generalities, they would often explain how the entire system was configured and which versions of programs were being used. I've even been offered tours of the Central Intelligence Agency's CD-ROM library.

Such open discussion of computer-related topics made it easy to track the latest developments. However, when I published the information, it inadvertently made it easier for crackers to attack Web sites and servers, as they now knew which operating systems, applications software, and even firewalls an agency was using at a particular location.

The new policy in many agencies, which absolutely forbids any discussion of many network products on pain of demotion or dismissal, makes my life as a consultant and columnist more difficult. But, I applaud the change, since it plugs an incredibly large security hole.

The question for you is just how talkative are the members of your MIS and public relations department? How about your vendors?

I bet you have a policy about not disclosing company secrets or taking confidential files home on floppy disk, but have you ever considered just how useful even general information (such as your operating system version) can be to potential computer vandals?

Whether you are discussing new acquisitions with reporters or just talking at home where little ears can overhear and pass the information along to local cracker groups, do your computer people know just how much important information they are making available to potential computer vandals?

Don't be a target

Even without this information, a dedicated cracker can get into your system and snoop around or plant a virus, but why make it easier?

It's the same principle as home or automobile security. If your car is the only one in the parking lot without an alarm sticker, guess which driver's window the car thief will break first? When all your neighbors have security lights and trim their hedges, but your darkened house offers a nice place for a burglar to hide while breaking in, who do you think will get robbed first?

The same goes for your computer systems. If you institute a general policy of not discussing company operating systems, servers, and security programs, but others issue press releases (or allow vendors to do so), then guess which company will be the first cracker target?

This secrecy will displease your vendors, who like to promote the use of their products. But what's more important: your system security or some vendor's image? You make the call.

If your company is big enough to have a PR department, its personnel will chime in with objections, too. Once again, someone must decide where your priorities lie. Seeing that you're reading a column about computer and network security, my guess is you'll decide protecting your files and keeping your network online is more important than distributing 1,000 press releases. ◆

TCP hijacking

By Alexander Prohorenko and Donald Wilde

"To kill the Enemy, you should know him as well as you know yourself."
—Anonymous

Not long ago, Transmission Control Protocol (TCP) hijacking was one of the most popular techniques for intruders to gain unauthorized access to Internet servers. Even now that almost every systems administrator knows about this potential vulnerability, TCP hijacking is still common because many systems administrators don't understand the principles behind this method. They just can't stop wily hackers who know their stuff. To build an effective defense, you need to understand all of the details about TCP hijacking. That's why I suggest that you start with a brief review of the TCP protocol.

An overview of TCP

Transmission Control Protocol (TCP) is one of the basic protocols of the transport layer of the Internet. This protocol makes it possible to fix errors during packet transfers. It sets up a logical connection—a virtual link that we can assume is free from error. Low-level algorithms control the packet queue and request that damaged or incorrect packets be resent. TCP processes packets by sequence number as they are received, and it puts out-of-order packets back into place. All of this is transparent to the virtual link, which disappears when the connection session ends. The TCP protocol is the only protocol from the TCP/IP protocol family that has additional packet and connection identification and authentication mechanisms. That explains why application level protocols, such as SMTP, FTP, and Telnet, use TCP to gain remote access to other hosts.

For TCP packet identification, the TCP header consists of two 32-bit fields that are used as packet counters. They are named Sequence

Number and Acknowledgment Number. Another field, named Control Bit, is 6 bits long, and it carries the following command bits:

- URG: Urgent pointer field significant
- ACK: Acknowledgment field significant
- PSH: Push function
- RST: Reset the connection
- SYN: Synchronize sequence numbers
- FIN: No more data from sender

Sample TCP connection setup scheme

Let's suppose that host A wants to set up a TCP connection with host B. In this case, host A sends host B a packet like this:

```
A -> B: SYN, ISSa
```

In the message that host A sent, command bit SYN is set, and Sequence Number has an initial sequence number ISSa that's 32 bits long. After receiving this packet, host B generates a reply:

```
B -> A: SYN, ACK, ISSb, ACK (ISSa+1)
```

This reply sets the SYN and ACK command bits. Host B sets the Sequence Number to its initial sequence number ISSb, and the Acknowledgment Number is set to ISSa (from host A) and increased by 1. To finish the handshake, host A sends:

```
A -> B: ACK, ISSa+1, ACK (ISSb+1)
```

This packet sets ACK. The Sequence Number ISSa is increased by 1, and the Acknowledgment Number ISSb is increased by 1. After sending this packet to host B, host A ends the third-level handshake. A TCP connection between these hosts (A and B) is set up. From now on, host A can send data packets to host B through this new virtual TCP link:

```
A -> B: ACK, ISSa+1, ACK (ISSb+1); DATA
```

You can follow the entire TCP connection setup scheme in **Figure A**.

How an intruder generates an attack

In the sample TCP connection setup scheme described above, the only identifiers of TCP clients and TCP connections are Sequence Number and Acknowledgment Number—two 32-bit fields. To generate a fake TCP packet, the only things that an intruder must know are the

FIGURE A

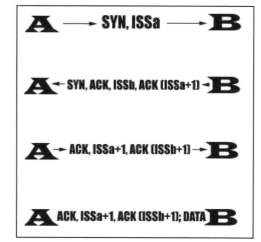

This sample TCP connection setup scheme details the connection between host A and host B.

current identifiers for definite connection: ISSa and ISSb. The possibility of TCP packet substitution is becoming much more important because analysis of the FTP and Telnet protocols, which are based on the TCP protocol, shows that the problem of identifying FTP and Telnet packets is handled only by the transport layer protocol and nothing else. All an intruder has to do is get the current values of the identifiers of a TCP packet for a defined TCP connection (like a Telnet connection). Then, to have the intruder's packet recognized as valid, the intruder can send a packet from any Internet-connected host, as long as the packet is masked as a packet from any host that's part of the connection (such as a TCP connection client host).

Neither FTP nor Telnet protocols check the source IP addresses of the hosts from which they receive packets. When these protocols get a fake packet from an attacker, they assume that it's a valid one from the connected host and send a reply to the IP set in the fake packet. Then, the true connected host loses its connection because the counters in the reply don't match!

As I mentioned, for an attack like the one depicted above to occur, the only pieces of information that an intruder is required to know are the two current 32-bit parameters (ISSa and ISSb) that identify the TCP connection. How can someone learn that information? When an attacker is in the same segment as the target or when the target's traffic comes through the attacker's segment, the task of getting ISSa and ISSb numbers becomes trivial. All the hacker must do is grab and analyze network traffic. The TCP protocol allows us to have secure connections only when the attacking side can't grab (sniff) network traffic.

Multi-segment attacks

More difficult is the multi-segment attack—when the attacker and his target are located in different network segments. In these cases, the task of getting ISSa and ISSb numbers isn't so trivial. Hackers have two ways in which they can proceed: the first involves mathematically guessing the initial number of the TCP connection identifier by extrapolating its previous values, and the second involves using the habits of the identification process of the TCP connection parties for performing an rsh server attack.

Method 1: Guessing ISN values

How does the network operation algorithm form the initial ISSa number (the Initial Sequence Number, or ISN)? Obviously, from a security standpoint, the best answer would be to generate an ISN randomly through a software or hardware random number generator with a very large period. Thus, each new ISN wouldn't depend on a previous value; consequently, it wouldn't be even theoretically possible for an attacker to find a functional ISN generation dependence.

However, it appears that such obvious rules of ISN random generation weren't obvious to the TCP protocol description (RFC793) authors or to kernel developers of the different network operating systems. For example, the TCP protocol description recommends that the value of this 32-bit counter be increased by 1 every four microseconds. What do we see when this practice is implemented? Unfortunately, we see very poor results. In early Berkeley-compatible UNIX kernels, the value of this counter increased by 128 every second and by 64 with every new connection. Analysis of the Linux OS sources shows that the OS generates the ISN value not randomly, but as a dependent variable of the current time:

$$ISN = mcs + s * 1000000$$

(where mcs equals time in microseconds, and s is the current time in seconds from the Epoch: 0 hours, 0 minutes, 0 seconds, January 1, 1970, Coordinated Universal Time)

Do you think that this problem disappears in other OSs? No! In the Windows NT 4.0 OS,

the value of ISN increases 10 times about every millisecond:

$$ISN = ms * 10$$

(where ms is time in milliseconds)

More impressive is a UNIX OS that's certified to a B1 security level and that runs on a multi-processing (SMP) high-uptime server and works as a fully functional firewall. It seems to be the most protected network OS, but it has a simple time-dependent ISN generation algorithm, too.

If the network operating system uses a time-dependent ISN generation algorithm, an attacker can guess the necessary function and close in on workable ISN values. As it comes from the practical OS explorations one can suggest a common form for the ISN generation function:

$$ISN = F (mcs, ms, s)$$

(where mcs equals time in microseconds—usually the shortest time period counted, depending on hardware—ms is time in milliseconds, and s is time in seconds)

You can shorten this formula to:

$$ISN = F (m\acute{0} s)$$

That's the common formula, and we can assume that the ISN generation function depends on microseconds. The function that's most likely to be used will be a simple linear function.

When we've figured out which units of ISN measurement matter and what the functional dependencies are, we're much closer to solving the problem of getting mcs arguments for the network operating system. First, you can try to analyze the sources of the operating system's kernel. Usually, you can't because the OS kernel's sources aren't available. The exceptions include Linux and the three BSD variants, which come with open sources.

That's why the intruder will need to find another way of getting the relationship between ISN generation functional dependence and the mcs argument. Often, the intruder will use the network operating system as a "black box" and will implement a "request-answer" testing method. Many normal requests for TCP connection setup are sent to the victim network OS; after that, the intruder receives the same number of answers, with current ISN values in every moment of time. The intruder records the time periods of the answers in microseconds. As the result, the intruder will get a table of discrete ISN values and corresponding time values:

```
ISN0 ISN1 ... ISNn
t0 t1 ... tn
```

(where *ISNn* is an ISN that was received at time *tn* after the experiment started; the time when the experiment started is defined as 0)

Now, someone easily could use one of the known mathematical methods to derive the ISN function that depends on t:

```
ISN (t) = F (t), with time interval
which varies from 0 to tn
```

This formula can get us another value of ISN from a previous value if we know the ISN generation function. Using this formula, an attacker can predict the next possible value of ISN, depending on the time interval.

The closer an attacker's location is to the victim OS, the better the chance is that this attacker will get a valid function. The key is the time intervals. An attacker who is located far away from the victim OS will get much longer time intervals than a closer attacker and will have to account for variances in the packet transmission time. The attacker doesn't need to perform any experiments directly on the victim host. All the attacker needs to do is detect the type of OS that's on the server. Then, the attacker can find a sample server with the same system and perform ISN function detection experiments on it.

Now for a few words concerning practical results taken from practical tests of the Linux and Windows NT 4.0 OSs. Here are the sample results that were received from the Linux OS during the definite time periods:

```
dISN 65135 134234 202324 270948 338028
t 2759 5685   8560   11462 14303
```

The graph in **Figure B** was based on the results from the table for the Linux OS. The graph demonstrates the particularly linear dependence of the ISN values:

After figuring out the ISN generation function in the operating systems on the server and client, the attacker will start to watch the server's OS and wait for the connection request from the client. When the connection is created, the attacker can count the possible range of ISN values that were used during the setup of the TCP link. Since the attacker can count ISN values only in the definite range (and even then, not exactly), the attacker

FIGURE B

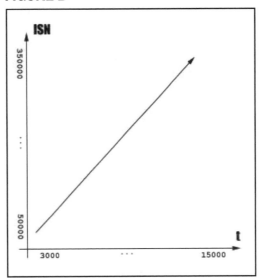

ISN values have a particularly linear dependence on time periods.

can't avoid making guesses. If an attacker didn't perform the analysis that's depicted above, however, the attacker would have to send 2^{64} packets, which is unrealistic. Once the attacker has used the analytical techniques that I've described, the attacker has to send only about 100^2 packets to close in on the answer.

Method 2: Using the habits of the identification process to perform an rsh server attack

There's still another way in which an attacker can get ISSa and ISSb values: by using the habits of the identification process of the TCP connection parties to perform an rsh server attack. All UNIX-like OSs have concepts of a "trusted" host. Any host that can gain access to the server without an authorization and identification process is considered a trusted host. To access a server from a trusted host without an authorization process, you have to use remote service (r-service) protocols. Most UNIX-like OSs have rhosts files, which list the names and IP addresses of trusted hosts. Each program that's part of the r-services (such as rlogin and rsh) uses this file to determine whether a host is trusted or not. The only identification parameter of the trusted host is the IP address. (Almost every program from r-services uses TCP protocol as a basic protocol.)

One of the r-services programs is the remote shell program (rsh). It gives an attacker the possibility of gaining unauthorized access to a host. rsh gives any trusted host the opportunity to send any command to a shell on the victim server. What's important in this case is that it's enough just to send a request and never to get a reply. For an attacker, the biggest problem in the r-service attack is that the attacker needs to send a packet from the name of a trusted host; the source IP address field should have the IP address of a trusted host. Obviously, the reply would be sent directly to the trusted host and never to the attacker's host.

R.T. Morris was the first person to describe this remote attack scheme. Let's examine the details of such an attack, which is diagrammed in **Figure C**.

Host A is supposed to be a trusted host for host B. Host C is the attacker's host. Host C opens a real TCP connection with host B to its TCP ports (mail, echo, etc). As a result, host C gets the current value of ISNb. Mimicking host A, host C sends a TCP connection request to host B:

```
C (A) -> B: SYN, ISSx
```

When host B receives this request, it analyzes the IP address of the source host and thinks that this packet came directly from host A. Of course, host B sends the new value of ISNb' to host A as a reply:

```
B -> A: SYN, ACK, ISNb', ACK (ISSx+1)
```

Host C would never get this packet from host B. Using the previous value of ISNb' and the attacker's scheme for getting ISNb', however, host C can send a new packet to host B:

```
C (A) -> B: ACK, ISSx+1, ACK (ISNb'+1)
```

FIGURE C

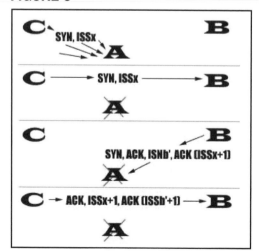

Host C attacks the r-service by pretending to be trusted host A.

To send this packet, host C would have to try several possible values of ACK (ISSb'+1) but would never need to try ISSx+1 values because host C has already received this parameter of the TCP connection from host B in the first packet.

If such an attack is possible, the attacker is ready for the next problem. When host C (using the name of host A) sends the packet to host B, host B will reply to host A. Since host A never sent any packets to host B, however, host A will send a packet with the RST bit set to host B. It's a request to host B to close the connection. Of course, this request doesn't suit the attacker (host C). Host C needs to blast host A with a Denial of Service (DoS) attack to prevent it from responding to host B.

As a result, the rsh server on host B supposes that it has a connection with the user of trusted host A; in reality, it's the attacker from host C. The attacker from host C will never get replies from host B but can still execute commands (r-commands) on host B.

Conclusion

The technique of TCP hijacking is rather old. After Kevin Mitnick, the famous hacker, used it in 1995 to gain access to Tsutomu Shimomura's workstation and the details of this event were published, TCP hijacking became a very powerful weapon for hackers. To implement such an attack, a hacker must be a highly qualified specialist. However, the biggest developers of operating systems have found different ways to defend against this attack strategy—or at least to design some workarounds.

Supposedly, this technique is rarely used anymore. Still, I would say that even nowadays about 35 percent of Internet-connected servers are still vulnerable to this kind of an attack. The main problem isn't the weakness of the OS (though this problem still exists); rather, the problem is trusted hosts and trusted services, such as rsh, rlogin, and rcmd.

An OS upgrade won't save a systems administrator from headaches caused by a hacker's attacks. All too often, one attack leads to others, and at least one will hit the target. The solution is to build a defendable security system that's based not on the tremendous variance of passwords between different servers, but on the principles of service distribution and access control by physical and administrative methods. So, be safe and take care. ◆

Would you risk hiring a hacker?

By Mary Ann Fitzharris

Hackers have made quite a name for themselves: They break in to countless corporate and government Web sites and computer networks on a regular basis. In the summer of 1999, hackers broke in to the computers at the Pentagon, as well as the Web sites of the Army, NASA, and the National Oceanic and Atmospheric Administration (NOAA).

Within their skills set is the ability to annihilate files and shut down or even obliterate networks. But those same hackers can bring much-needed firepower to your cyber security team, according to one of the nation's top cyberterrorism experts. Is the risk of hiring a hacker worth the potential reward? Find out what two specialists say.

I hire hackers, but only the good guys

Tony Valletta would hire a hacker. The top security official at SRA International, Valletta is vice president and director of the command, control, communications, and intelligence (C3I) systems business unit. Valletta said, "When I joined SRA, one of my top initiatives was to set up a critical infrastructure protection capability here, and to staff it with some of the best people that I could find." As part of that initiative, he said, he hired some hackers, "because hackers are some of the best people to bring to our side. They help us defend against the people they know and are used to dealing with." Valletta also chose several top-level IT staffers that he knew from the federal government, where he spent 29 years working in IT and became a cyberterrorism expert.

Valletta added, speaking about hackers: "We have two already, and hackers are being hired by a bunch of other companies as part of their teams that we all put together to help businesses as well as government agencies perform vulnerability analyses." In fact, reports are that hackers who are ready to act responsibly are working for most, if not all, of the Big Five accounting firms.

It's a matter of ethics

Tim Landgrave, president of eAdvantage, an ASP in Louisville, KY, said, "I wouldn't hire someone to work for me that I didn't trust. And I would have a hard time trusting a hacker." Landgrave added, "There are certain things that are right and certain things that are wrong, and hacking is wrong."

Landgrave thinks that the goal of hacking is more often to challenge authority than it is to perfect a skill, or it might simply be the challenge of doing it in the first place. "After all," Landgrave said, "What's the value to the skill? It's illegal, immoral, and unethical."

So, would Landgrave hire a hacker? "Well," he admitted, "There are some circumstances when I might hire a hacker. [For example] if he was an admitted hacker in high school or college, but now is settled down and wants to manage a secure environment that he understands, and if the challenge to him now is stopping hackers." But, Landgrave said he'd still be wary. "My problem with hiring a guy who is still a hacker is that the things he will learn about my system leaves me exposed forever. Can you trust the hacker you hired to tell you everything he found?"

How do you find them?

If you want to hire one, how do you find a hacker? Valletta said, "It's very difficult. It's mostly by word-of-mouth, by people who know people. Certainly, a lot of people don't want to put [on their resumes] 'hey, I'm the hacker who broke into this system.' They'd be worried about the next knock on their door."

When looking for a job, do hackers admit to this skill? "No," Valletta says. "However," he adds, "the people who we look at, we screen very carefully, as do the other companies. We don't hire criminals. That is not what these technical people are."

Who are the hackers who are hirable? "These are people who grew up with video games, and they just love this stuff," Valletta said. "Some of them have their master's and Ph.D.s in computer science. We have [some] of them here today that are just the smartest people that I've ever dealt with. We don't go after the people who were bad. We try to find the great people who decided to make this their obsession and to make it their skill area. They're very highly sought after. These people get top dollar in [the] industry." ◆

Good hackers, bad hackers, and hackers-for-hire—a look at the lingo

By Mary Ann Fitzharris

Some words are simple, like cracker; some sound more exotic, like samurai. But knowing the difference between the two—and acquiring some familiarity with other hacking terms—can help you understand potential security threats to your computer systems.

Hacker / hack

The term hacker originally referred to a good—even expert—programmer who could solve programming problems when there was no built-in function to do it. The solution was called a hack. However, both terms developed negative connotations after the press began using them to describe illegal computer break-ins. When hacks are taken to an illegal or malicious level, the hacker finds and exploits weak spots in the security system of a Web site or network. Journalists call these malicious persons hackers, but IT insiders often refer to them as crackers.

Cracker

A cracker is someone who attempts (perhaps successfully) to break in to someone else's network or otherwise uses programming or expert knowledge to act maliciously. Crackers break in to computer systems or networks to expose security holes, to steal information, to cause trouble, or just for the challenge of it. The results are generally expensive and damaging. Crackers may destroy files, steal financial information, leave behind viruses, and so on.

Hacker ethic

Hacker ethic is a set of principles that hackers often live by. It asserts that all technical information should be free to everyone, so gaining unauthorized entry into a system is not unethical if all you're going to do is gain information. However, it *is* unethical—even to hackers—to do it for malicious reasons. Altering, removing, or destroying data or otherwise causing problems, injury, or expense to the network is considered unethical.

Hoover

A hoover is a hacker who can suction a lot of information out of a network's computer.

Samurai

A samurai is an expert programmer who is hired to break in to a company's computer system or Web site to test for security holes.

Port-scanning

Port-scanning is a favorite way for crackers to break in to a security system. They use administration and downloadable hacking tools to send messages, one at a time, to ports in order to find out what ports are open and which computer services are running on those ports. Types of scans include the entire network (vanilla) or selected ports (strobe). Crackers try to hide their tracks by doing a *stealth scan* (which conceals their attempt to log on) or an *FTP bounce scan* (directed through an FTP server to disguise their location). They may send *fragmented packets* to get past a firewall, and they may do a *sweep*, which is a scan of the same port on many computers.

Sniffing

Sniffing is hijacking information intended for other computers as it goes over a shared network. Once a cracker obtains access to a network's root (see below), the cracker puts that machine into promiscuous mode, which accepts all the packets running across the network, or into non-promiscuous mode, where it will capture sessions only from the machine it is running on. Sniffing is a very popular attack used by hackers.

Root / root dance

The Golden Fleece to a hacker is to gain root user status, since a root is the system administrator with unlimited access privileges. They can perform any and all network operations, which gives them unlimited power. In a UNIX system, crackers gain the ability to access password files and to override file permissions. They can also freely roam through the computer's file directories. When crackers gain root user status, the door is wide open for them. No wonder they reportedly do a celebratory "root dance" when they finally succeed at gaining root access. ◆

The best defense for hacker attacks: An interview with Alan Bishoff, network security expert

By Mary Ann Fitzharris

Been hacked lately? Or are you worried that an attack on your system is just a matter of time? Want to find and fix your security holes? Who doesn't? Securing your company from cyber-evils isn't as impossible as it sounds. You just need to find an expert to point you in the right direction, which is why we've found Alan Bishoff. In this interview, security guru Bishoff provides some detailed answers on how to protect your network from the lurking menace of a hacker attack.

TR: There's been a debate recently among TechRepublic members about hiring hackers. Would you hire one?
Bishoff: Yes. You'd have to, to stay on top of everything.

TR: Would you be able to trust them?
Bishoff: If you hired a hacker and the relationship turned sour, that could be a bad thing. You'd almost have to have someone who knew more than the hacker did to [keep your system safe], I suppose. But, I've never heard of anything like that happening, and I've known lots of people who've switched over from the "dark side." They seem to make good employees.

TR: What is your definition of a cracker as opposed to a hacker?
Bishoff: I've never met anyone who actually broke in to a computer and called themselves a cracker. It's used by people who really hate hackers, but that's about the only kind of people who use it. Hacker is a better term to use to describe someone who breaks in to computers.

TR: How can you really know if your network is protected from hackers?
Bishoff: Well, you do different things to protect different kinds of computers. Basically, if you are running a computer that has old services on it that are able to be connected over the network, then you would be at risk. Say you installed a UNIX machine three years ago and never upgraded it, and it's not behind a firewall, and you can connect through all the ports; then that would really be a risk.

A Windows machine installed three years ago—maybe with a mail server on it, like a mail gateway, and with a Web service on it that's three years old and never upgraded—would get taken over. From there they could take over the rest of the secure network. Once they're in a little bit, there's really no turning back. They've got you. For most companies, that's the way they're usually set up.

TR: Assuming everything is behind a firewall, what else might they still look for?
Bishoff: Well, the firewall has to let something through. So let's say you run a Web server and you only let Web traffic through the firewall, which would be a good way to set it up. Some Web servers are old and they have vulnerable CGI scripts on them. So someone could actually send commands through port 80 (the Web port), which would go through the firewall, and then execute some kind of back door on the machine on the other side of the firewall.

If they can run code on the other side of the firewall, then they can have the machine connect backward out of the firewall, effectively making it useless. So if you're letting something in through the firewall and it's not secure, people could subvert the whole thing.

CGI scripts are the most common example. I'm sure you've heard of all of the government defacements with the RDS bug. RDS is a bug that came out in Microsoft Windows NT about six months ago, which allows you to execute code remotely on a Windows NT machine. That's how most of these government sites are getting hacked, because they have not been upgraded. But you could have a machine like that running behind the firewall, and all of the attacks can be executed over port 80, so the firewall won't help you.

TR: How do you secure your Web server?

Bishoff: Well, most Web servers have a lot of different ports open and that's a real bad thing. You want to set it up so the only port you have open is port 80. If you have a secure Web server that does the credit card number stuff, you need port 443 open as well. Otherwise, you only want port 80 open.

Also do a CGI scan. There's an excellent freeware program called Whisker that you run against your Web server. If Whisker doesn't come up with anything and the only port open is port 80, then you have a darn secure Web server, and no one is going to be able to break in unless they break in to other computers on your network and then work their way over to your Web server.

TR: What else might you do to make sure you are totally secure?

Bishoff: What you want to do is run the least number of services that you can, because network services give hackers an attack point in your network. The number of network services that you have open to an attacker is the number of machines you have publicly addressable on the Internet (the number of machines that have external Internet addresses), multiplied by the number of services running in each machine.

Say you have a firewall and you have 100 people behind the firewall, then they all have fake IPs [Internet protocols], so they're all relatively safe from people directly attacking them. What you need to do is find out how many real IPs you have on the Internet and how many services those real IPs are running.

Each IP address has a lot of different ports and different services running different ports. I was talking about port 80 being the Web port, but machines typically have a Web server running on port 80 and they have other kinds of servers running on different ports.

They take mail in through port 25, but if they're running an old mail server—maybe something three years old that they have never upgraded—someone is going to be able to subvert them through port 25 and gain access to that machine. From there they can take over the whole network.

Most places hackers can break in to can be tightened down by turning off the service. Check what services you have and turn off all of the ones you don't need. Then, for the services you do need, decide how you can provide them in the most secure manner possible.

TR: What are some examples of services that are vulnerable?

Bishoff: Finger is a largely unused service. Finger will allow other people on the network to see who is logged in to the machine and how long they've been idle, but that's real good information for hackers.

For e-mail, there's lots of different mail programs. Some of them are really secure. Some of them aren't. If you decide you need mail, you need to only run one mail program on one of the servers and have all of the mail go through there. Then run a really secure [server inside the firewall] and then no one is going to be able to break in.

Subverting a network through an old IMAP or POP server is a really common thing that

About Packet Storm & Securify

Packet Storm is currently the world's largest Internet security repository. Its Web site contains security tools and daily alerts about security developments and hacker threats. The site is popular with security experts because it collects detailed technical information about how intruders exploit network security holes, and provides information about fixes. It is created by contributions from Packet Storm staff and other IT security experts, including some hackers.

Located in Palo Alto, CA, Packet Storm's provider, Securify, is currently held by Kroll-O'Gara. Its security consultants are experienced in network assessment, cryptography, secure systems and software, Public Key Infrastructure (PKI) digital certificates, and computer system defense.

happens hundreds of times a day. When your Internet browser goes out to get the mail, it connects to an IMAP or a POP server. So companies need IMAP and POP servers so people can read their mail through the browsers. However, they don't need everyone on the whole Internet to be able to connect to their IMAP and POP servers. So what a company would want to do is first upgrade to the newest version and second, make them only accessible to users within their network.

TR: If you have few services running, and they're secure, what else can you do to protect your network?
Bishoff: You can't have people coming in from other sites and logging in remotely, because the other site could get taken over. Let's say someone has an account on their home ISP and they come from their home ISP to your computer. A hacker who hacked over the home ISP would now own the company too, because they would have the password to the remote login. You can use programs to keep the password from being sniffed, but you need to use encryption if you connect to your network from another network.

[Let's say] you go to a different company's site, and you check your e-mail at your company. If the other company is taken over by a hacker, then all of a sudden both companies will be, because the password will get sent. Most employees don't know this. A lot of user training is needed. And, if you can't provide user training, you have to take away the power of the users to log in remotely unless they understand the implications.

TR: What other software is available to help protect our networks?
Bishoff: There are so many thousands of threats to the network. Running some of the scanners out there will pick up most of the threats. There are a lot of free scanners and there are a lot of them that you have to pay to use. At Packet Storm Security, we have a lot of free software that people can use to check the network for that kind of thing. That's actually what we do here: We give out free security tools to help protect networks from hackers. On our site, we actually have all of the hacker tools and we have all of the tools to defend against them. ◆

Download our virus protection checklist
By Lisa Kiava

A recent FBI report found that 70 percent of all companies in the U.S. have been hit with either a virus or a denial of service attack.

You may have created a comprehensive response plan to recover after a virus has infected your corporate system—but have you done everything in your power to prevent a virus before it wreaks havoc in the first place?

TechRepublic readers sent us their tried-and-true methods of virus prevention. We compiled their suggestions—and added a few of our own—to create this valuable security resource.

Download our "Virus Prevention Checklist" at www.techrepublic.com\article.jhtml?id=r00620000331kia01.htm to review your options when developing a virus prevention policy.

Give users e-mail attachment awareness training

By Jeff Davis

The other day I saw the episode of "Seinfeld" where Jerry refuses delivery on a package because there's no return address. "Could be a bomb," he reasons.

In light of the recent rash of computer virus attacks, we need to train our users to treat all e-mail attachments with the same respect Jerry treated that package. (Uncle Leo found out the hard way that you should *never* open something that has an unknown sender.)

Beginners and veterans beware

I've always had problems trying to teach new users how to deal with e-mail attachments. If they can find the attachments, they always want to double-click on them instead of saving them to disk first. Recently I've seen veteran users—people who should know better—double-click on attachments and unleash a virus because they were fooled by the e-mail Trojan horse.

The upshot is we've all become too complacent about e-mail. Fortunately, something can be done about it. First, we can invest in enterprise-wide anti-virus software—tools that examine and disinfect any and all attachments coming into the company's pipeline. That solution works if you're networked and you can afford it.

Forewarned is Forearmed

Get the word out to your users: Don't open e-mail attachments without thinking, saving, confirming, and scanning first.

Second, we could fire anybody who opens an infected e-mail attachment. Granted, that approach is a little extreme. So how about providing e-mail attachment awareness training for beginning and veteran users alike? Here are my suggestions.

Think first, open later

Teach your users to think before they open any file attached to an e-mail message. Remind your users to get out of the habit of automatically clicking on attachments. Here are the questions your users should ask themselves:

▸ **Do I know this sender?** If the sender isn't known, *don't open the attachment.*

▸ **Is this attachment normal?** If the sender *is* known, is this attachment the kind of file that person *normally* sends? If someone normally sends you Word documents but today you get a .zip file, *call the sender for confirmation.* "Did you send me this zip file?" "Did you mean to send me an .exe file?"

▸ **Has the attachment been virus-scanned?** If your company's e-mail server scans incoming attachments for viruses, the e-mail should include a stamp saying "file scanned and is okay." If it doesn't, *don't open the attachment.*

▸ **Have I saved and scanned the file?** Make sure your users know how to right-click on an attachment and save it to disk. Create a "Files to scan" folder on your users' desktops and have them save attachments in that folder. Then make sure your users know how to run the anti-virus software on the files in that folder. ◆

The IT doctor is in: A primer on viruses

By Bruce Maples

It seems that every day we hear about another computer virus and its potential for destruction. Some computer users respond to this threat with virus paranoia, believing that every problem they encounter on their system is caused by viruses lurking somewhere on their hard drives. Other users prefer the big yawn approach: "It's all just hype to sell more copies of McAfee and Norton."

Neither approach is correct, and both are foolhardy. Not every problem on every system is caused by a virus—but *some* are, and it is foolish to believe you are immune. It's even more foolish to be ignorant about viruses or to fail to practice "safe computing."

What the bug does

A virus either attaches itself to some existing program code or completely replaces the code. Then it redirects the computer to execute the virus code in addition to, or in place of, the original code. Let's suppose, for example, that your Format.com file is infected. The original FORMAT routine follows these steps:

- 001 Check to see if the disk to format exists.
- 002 If it doesn't, display an error message and quit.
- 003 Check to see if the disk to be formatted is a hard disk or a floppy.
- 004 If it's a hard disk, get permission to format it.

Once infected, the FORMAT routine might follow this process instead:

- 001 Jump to 100.
- 002 Check to see if the disk to format exists.
- 003 If it doesn't, display an error message and quit.
- 004 (rest of the code is the same).
- 100 Copy lines 101 to 103 to another place in memory.
- 101 Check for floppy disks in all floppy drives.
- 102 If floppy is found, delete every fifth byte of any file on it.

- 103 Set up a timer so these lines keep executing over and over.
- 104 Jump back to 002 and finish the format as usual.

You can see how difficult this would be to detect. Every time you format a disk, you would unknowingly load the code into memory and execute it.

If you change line 102 to include a random condition, such as, "Only delete bytes if it's Friday the 13th," you've got something that would be almost impossible to find. That's where antivirus software comes in.

Of Trojan horses and polymorphism

With such a large variety of new viruses, you'll want to keep up-to-date on the latest bug buzzwords. Here are some of the major virus categories and a few other terms you'll need to know.

- **Executable file virus**—This virus attaches itself to an executable file, such as an .exe or .com file, and runs whenever the executable file is run. Our example above fits this description; it infected a .com file.

- **Boot sector virus**—This virus infects the boot sector of a disk, where it is executed whenever the disk is used to boot from. If you boot from an infected floppy, the virus infects the hard drive's boot sector. Every floppy that you put into your infected machine will also pick up the virus. Boot sector viruses are particularly dangerous, since they run every time the computer is turned on.

- **Trojan horse**—This virus masquerades as something desirable when its real aim is destruction. That cool game your brother-in-law gave you on a floppy might actually be a Trojan Horse virus. When you play the game you are also infecting all your boot sectors. It's just another reason to avoid your brother-in-law.

- **Polymorphic virus**—This virus changes on the fly—making it difficult to detect. A polymorphic virus has a unique sequence of bytes in its code, known as its "signature."

▶ **Stealth virus**—Stealth viruses escape normal anti-virus detection efforts because they contain a unique code. The stealth is a type of polymorphic virus. For example, a boot sector virus may copy the original boot sector to somewhere else on the hard disk, then wait for attempts by other programs to look at the actual boot sector. If the virus detects such an attempt by, say, an anti-virus program, it intercepts the attempt and redirects the anti-virus program to the original boot sector sitting out on the hard disk. The anti-virus program then reports that all is well with the boot sector, and the virus goes undetected.

▶ **Trigger event**—Some viruses do their dirty work immediately upon execution. More commonly, though, the virus lies in wait, biding its time until some event chosen by its author causes it to "wake up" and deliver its "payload." It may be a date, or a time. It may be a certain number of boot ups, or a certain number of times a command is executed.

▶ **Payload**—Just like in missiles, the virus payload is whatever damage the virus ultimately delivers. It may be fairly innocuous, like a message appearing on your screen. It may be annoying, like letters falling to the bottom of the screen. Or, it may be horribly destructive, like deleting every file it can find on both your computer and the network. ◆

Dealing with the ILoveYou virus on a GroupWise system

By John Sheesley

Unless you've been off the planet recently, you've probably heard of the ILoveYou e-mail virus and all of its mutations. You may have even received a few of the infected e-mails or had the virus affect your network. If you use or are considering using GroupWise as your messaging system, you may be curious to know how the ILoveYou virus and its ilk affect GroupWise systems. In this article, I'll show you how the ILoveYou virus affects GroupWise and what you can do to deal with it.

How safe are you?

You may think that just because you aren't running Microsoft Exchange, you're safe. Unfortunately, this isn't the case. Like the Melissa virus outbreak of last year, the ILoveYou virus exploits features in Microsoft Outlook (the e-mail client portion of Exchange) that are supposed to simplify the process of integrating e-mail messages with other data.

I won't go into great detail about how the ILoveYou virus does its dirty work. The Reader's Digest condensed version is that when you open the .VBS attachment in the e-mail message, the virus attaches itself to your workstation's registry, deletes files from your workstation, reads your Outlook Address Book, and finally e-mails itself to everyone in your Address Book.

Therefore, if you're using Outlook as the e-mail client for your GroupWise server using the GroupWise Enhancement Pack, then you'll have just as many problems with the ILoveYou virus as your Exchange-running counterparts. However, if you only use the GroupWise clients for your workstations, you'll be in better shape.

If one of your users opens an ILoveYou virus-infected attachment when using a GroupWise client, his or her machine will still become infected. The Visual Basic Script will still run, infecting the user's workstation and deleting files. However, the virus will go no further, because the script can't make the necessary calls to read the GroupWise address book from the client, nor can it use the GroupWise client to e-mail itself to anyone else. In effect, the user catches the virus and the virus does its damage, but it goes no further on your network.

Making sure all of your users only use the GroupWise client is an effective way of minimizing the potential damage that the virus can cause. Unfortunately, it may not be a politically popular choice. Users and/or management may rebel at the thought of dropping Microsoft Outlook for the native GroupWise client. Therefore, you need to have other means of dealing with the virus and possible infections.

Dodging the bullet

You've probably already done the first and most important thing to prevent the virus from affecting your network: warning your users not to open .VBS attachments to e-mail messages. If your users simply delete the messages before opening the attachment, then the virus won't go anywhere.

However, why should your users do all the work? Although GroupWise won't natively filter messages for content, you can install third-party scanners to filter the messages for you. One of the most popular GroupWise scanners is called Guinevere.

With Guinevere and a virus scanner, you can intercept and kill virus-infected messages before they hit your server. Your users won't have to worry about deleting the messages or becoming infected because they won't see the messages in the first place.

Mopping up after an attack

If you've already been attacked by the virus, you can use Novell's GWCheck utility to clean the GroupWise message store of virus-infected messages. GWCheck comes with GroupWise 5.5. You'll find it on your GroupWise 5.5 CD in the Admin\Utility\GWCheck directory. If you're running GroupWise 5.2, then you must download GWCK524.EXE from Novell's Web site.

GWCheck allows you to purge items from users' mailboxes based on the contents of the subject line. You must be very careful when using this utility because when you use GWCheck to delete messages, you can't get the messages back. You may want to make sure you have a complete backup of your Post Office directory structure, even though it still contains virus-infected files.

To use GWCheck, you must first create a text file called ITEMPURG. The easiest way to do this is to go to an MS-DOS prompt on your administration workstation, type *COPY CON ITEMPURG*, and press [Enter]. You'll notice the cursor drop below the MS-DOS prompt.

Next, type the subject line of the e-mail message you want to purge. You can only type the first 27 characters of the line. If you type more than 27 characters, the purge won't find any matches. GWCheck works from left to right and doesn't match substrings in the middle or end of the string. Don't press [Enter] when you're finished. Instead, press [F6] and then press [Enter] to save the ITEMPURG file. Copy this file to your GroupWise server's Post Office directory.

Next, launch the GWCHK32.EXE file. When the GroupWise Mailbox/Library Maintenance window appears, you must make a few adjustments. First, make sure that the Post Office radio button is selected in the Database Type box. Next, enter into the Database Path field the path where the WPHOST.DB resides. You then must enter the NDS name for the Post Office in the Post Office Name field. Next, select the Post Office radio button in the Object Type box.

On the right side of the window, the Analyze/Fix Databases should be selected in the Action drop-down list box. You should also make sure that only the Contents and Fix Problems check boxes are selected under the Action drop-down list box. Finally, at the bottom of the screen, only the User Database check box should be selected.

After you've configured GWCheck, click Run. If the check runs successfully, you'll find a log file named GWCHK32.LOG in the directory where you ran GWCheck. This log file will contain lines for each user who was e-mailed an infected message, or more precisely, was e-mailed a message that matches the scan you indicated in ITEMPURG.

Don't forget that several mutations of the ILoveYou virus exist, each having a different subject line. You must edit the ITEMPURG file, reenter the particular subject line to search for, save the file, and rerun GWCheck for each mutation.

Conclusion

The ILoveYou e-mail virus and its relatives have been the most damaging e-mail viruses in history. In this article, I've shown you how the ILoveYou virus reacts in a GroupWise environment. ◆

Defense against the enemy: A virus protection guide

By Bruce Maples

In the past, we could take some comfort in knowing that we had some inherent protection against viruses. Writing virus code required a certain level of programming expertise, as well as some understanding of such things as low-level DOS calls and memory allocation. And since data files were not executable, a shared data file couldn't infect your machine. Today, it's a more dangerous virtual world we live in—and those safeguards are gone.

It's easier than ever to create a destructive bug. Macro languages are now included in the major office productivity products, and users have the ability to tie the execution of a macro to the opening of a file or template. Suddenly, anyone who knows how to write an AutoOpen Word macro can become a virus author.

In this article, we'll look at some methods to keep your computer system out of harm's way.

Medicine that's hard to swallow

Microsoft now includes macro detection in the File/Open code for its Office products, although the code is fairly unsophisticated. If the file has any macros at all, you'll receive a dialog box telling you there are macros in the file. The macros may be dangerous, or they may be harmless. The dialog box asks if you want to enable the macros or not. If you have a number of custom templates used throughout your business, it's likely you're uncertain whether the macros in question are legitimate office automation macros or malicious outsider macros. You can't see the macros until you answer the dialog box and open the file.

An ounce of prevention

The best prevention method is so obvious that it's often overlooked: Purchase an antivirus product and use it. Popular products include Norton's AntiVirus and McAfee.

Antivirus software use many different virus detection methods. Here are the three top ways they seek and destroy a virus.

1. File scanning

This compares the contents of the files being scanned to an inventory of virus signatures. If a match is found, the antivirus software alerts the user to a possible virus infection. Some products can remove the virus from the infected file, while others can only detect the virus and alert

HOW TO AVOID BECOMING A VIRUS VICTIM

▶ Start with a clean system. Boot from a floppy you know is clean so that those boot-sector viruses can't activate. Scan your system with a good anti-virus product that can scan both executable and data files and that can find macro viruses.

▶ Run regular scans. Scan all your files at least once a month. Use the inoculation feature as well.

▶ Run monitoring software. My monitoring software has saved me countless times. It's worth the investment.

▶ Scan every incoming file. Scan every download, without exception, to avoid the headache of recovering files from your backups.

▶ Don't open mystery e-mail. Use the preview feature in Outlook. If the sender is unknown, it's time to delete. Remember, with HTML e-mail it is now possible for someone to write malicious code within an HTML message and send you a virus.

▶ Update your knowledge. Don't think computer security is for the Pentagon. Log in to TechRepublic regularly to stay informed about the latest virus.

you to the problem. File scanning is usually fairly fast and can find the majority of viruses actually "in the wild."

The biggest disadvantage to file scanning is the need to update the inventory. The level of protection is only as good as the latest virus included in the inventory. Many users are not diligent about updating, so they compromise their protection. (I've seen many computers with two-year-old virus inventories.)

2. In-memory monitoring

This method loads a small program into memory, where the program continuously monitors what is going on in the computer. Every file that is opened, every floppy that is accessed, and every message to the hard disk are all checked for possible virus activity.

If the monitor sees something suspicious, it stops whatever is happening and alerts the user. Some monitor programs are quite sophisticated and are able to detect stealth and polymorphic viruses.

However, a monitoring program may place a load on a system. It may also sound an alert to a false positive. If users are frustrated from either of these disadvantages, they may shut off the in-memory monitoring.

3. Inoculation

Inoculation is a variation on the file-scanning approach. The antivirus program scans each file and creates a *checksum*, which is based on the bytes in the file as their order and value are combined to create a unique number. These checksums are then stored for later comparison. If the checksum has changed, then the bytes in the file have changed. While it is common for data files to change, executable files normally do not change. This is an excellent line of defense, though it requires the user to understand which files should change. ◆

Ten things you can do to protect your network against viruses

By John Sheesley

With the recent outbreaks of viruses like Melissa and Chernyobl-CIH, you're probably wondering what you can do to keep your network safe. Virus prevention needn't be complicated. In this article, we'll show you ten basic things you can do to stop or minimize virus outbreaks on your network.

From our home office in Louisville, KY

1. **Use virus scanning software on your server and workstations.** Your first line of defense in protecting against viruses is a virus protection program. It's not enough to just load virus software on your client workstations—you should also load it on your servers. The servers can use idle time to scan all the data and program files that they have. This can lighten the load on your clients.

2. **Keep your virus scanning software up to date.** Unfortunately, several hundred new viruses appear every month. If you have a virus scanner with a signature file more than a few months old, then you might as well not have a virus scanner at all. It won't protect you. Most companies update their virus signature files monthly. They also provide emergency files within a day should a major virus like Melissa suddenly appear.

3. **Scan all disks before you use them.** This is especially true if you don't know where the disks came from. Viruses can spread just as easily from disks as they can over the Internet. In fact, it's more likely you'll get a virus from a disk a friend gives you than you will from the Internet. You can't even trust disks that are factory sealed. You should format new disks, even if they come preformatted from the factory.

4. **Enable macro virus protection in Microsoft Office.** In the good old days, viruses only infected program files. New viruses like Melissa and Popa infect data files. Fortunately, Microsoft has built virus protection into its Office products. You should enable it, but make sure you double-check it on a regular basis. Melissa and her progeny disable it if they successfully infect your workstation.

5. **Disable macros from unknown senders.** When you enable Macro Virus Protection in Microsoft Office, it asks you if you want to disable macros when you open files. When you receive data files from outside sources, especially unknown ones, disable the macros.

6. **Set the file attributes of .exe and .com files on your server as read-only or execute-only.** This won't necessarily stop all viruses from infecting your system because some viruses will change the file attributes before infecting them. It will, however, block most viruses.

7. **Develop a virus disaster recovery plan.** If you do get hit with a virus, you should have a plan in place to recover from it. This should include a priority list of data files and programs to check for infection, ways to recover data, contact lists of vendors who can help, and a list of users who can help you double-check outbreaks throughout your organization.

8. **Back up your server and clients.** Make sure you back up your server and clients frequently. Don't just use one set of backups and continually rotate through them. Instead, you should maintain several layers of backups. Remember that some viruses are time-released—you may be backing up time bombs. If you have several layers, you may be able to restore an uninfected file.

9. **Prepare an Emergency Kit.** Make a bootable, write-protected disk containing your virus scan removal software. This will allow you to boot machines virus-free and possibly remove viruses from them. You should also keep original copies of all your programs, either on CD-ROM or write-protected disks, in a safe location and organized in case you need to reinstall from them.

10. **Educate users.** Your users are your first line of defense. They're also the ones who'll get hit first. You should educate them about viruses and what they can do to prevent viruses. Describe the symptoms of virus infection to them and give them detailed procedures for dealing with suspected infections. Teach them how to distinguish possible infections from general hardware and software errors. Also, educate them about virus hoaxes that they may encounter. ◆

Editor's Note

If you've been hit by a virus before, you know there's nothing funny about it. With that in mind, we're serious about these 10 things. This isn't a Letterman-esque takeoff.

Virus jockeys: You're missing the point

By Jack Wallen, Jr.

I sat there, staring at my computer screen and reading the headline, "Cult of the Dead Cow Threatens Attack," knowing that, for the time being, I'm relatively safe from these attacks. But for how long? Linux has survived with relatively few attacks from outsiders. But how long will it be before the mass of virus writers grows tired of their current target, Microsoft? When will doomsday come for Linux?

I should hope never.

Let me first set the record straight. I understand the minds of virus writers, but not their intentions. I know the desire to climb the mountains of intellectual challenge that rewards the 3lit3 (pardon my hacker-speak, that's 'elite' for those of you not in the know), but I do not understand the need for destruction. I understand the compelling force that prods the backs of the minds of the script kiddies and keyboard cowboys (with a nod to William Gibson), but I do not understand the willingness to risk a prison sentence.

Most people look at what's happening to innocent computer users and corporations and see only criminal behavior. They just don't get it.

But virus writers are missing the fundamental principle of being a true hacker. The Mentor, the father of the Hacker movement, wrote the Hacker's Manifesto to bring to the hacker movement a credo.

The Mentor was reacting to a nation—nay, a world—tearing down the intellectual freedom that hacking brought to life in the computing industry. Curiosity was never meant to be a crime. From curiosity, many brilliant ideas were born. But was the Mentor telling everyone to sit

THE HACKER'S MANIFESTO

"This is our world now, the world of the electron and the switch, the beauty of the baud. We make use of a service already existing without paying for what could be dirt cheap if it weren't run by profiteering gluttons, and you call us animals. We explore—and you call us criminals. We seek after knowledge—and you call us criminals.

We exist without skin color, without nationality, without religious bias—and you call us criminals. You build atomic bombs, you wage wars, you murder, cheat, and lie to us and try to make us believe it is for our own good—yet we are the criminals. Yes, I am a criminal. My crime is that of curiosity. My crime is that of judging

people by what they say and think, not what they look like. My crime is that of outsmarting you, something that you will never forgive me for. I am a hacker, and this is my manifesto. You may stop me, but you can't stop us all."

The Mentor

in the dim light of the moon and write such toxic codes as CIH and Worm99? The hacker manifesto was a call to bring about the freedom of the intellect—not the freedom of destruction. Hackers have developed a bad reputation and with good reason: They can destroy.

But writers (such as Cult of the Dead Cow) of the malicious code we now call a virus are threatening to take down what the industry (and the hackers) have fought so dearly to keep: freedom. Freedom of speech and freedom of knowledge.

It isn't hard to predict a gloom and doom outcome for the Web, should the writers of these codes go unchecked. I can see a day when the Net will no longer be an arena in which the common man can exchange ideas with the world. The recent past has given birth to such a horrendous crop of malicious viruses that, should the pattern continue, the only choice will be to close the roads that allow the traffic. This cannot be. The Net is a freedom that we not only deserve but need.

I am not speaking of putting the proverbial child over the knee of the public and giving it the spanking of its life. I'm suggesting more positive solutions.

If corporations would hire the best of the best as "exploitation experts," both hackers and corporations would benefit. Imagine a hacker being able to put his best virus on a floppy, send it to MS attached with his or her resume, and land the job of his or her lifetime. But who would do it? What large corporation has the wherewithal, the intelligence, and the sheer guts to consider such a strategy? And overlooking wherewithal, what company would want to hire people who spend their lives attempting to bring down the systems that corporations have come so desperately to depend upon?

When does Linux come under fire?

What about Linux, the OS of choice to most hackers? When are hackers going to start flooding the data streams with kernel exploits? And why? Why would someone want to take down the very institute they helped create? Why would someone threaten to destroy the thing that threatened to destroy the thing that was threatening to destroy all the other things? The intention to write a virus for Linux just doesn't make sense!

The computer industry has come such a long way in the last decade only to have been brought to its knees by some irreverent coders—who are either ticked off that society has neglected their higher intellect or enjoying it because *they can*.

Make money, not war

OK, virus writers. You've played your game. You've proven yourself worthy in the PC battleground. Now drop your guns and pick up your keyboards and do something worthwhile.

The majority of you are talented enough (generally speaking) to write some fairly stable code. Join the revolution, and help your fellow man by jumping on the Linux bandwagon. Groups like the Gnome project could certainly use your talents.

The computing industry is currently against you. It threatens you, yet it cashes in on you. Why bother? Why waste your time so they can succinctly profit from what you consider cleverness. You're writing malicious code and risking prison sentences when you could be writing the next best Gnome applet and risking one great big hurrah! You do the math (shouldn't be too hard for someone like you)—end up in jail or end up on someone's desktop. Which will it be? After all, it's only going to be a matter of time before the government slaps down an amendment or two protecting society's rights to safety in the PC arena. ◆

Groovy Tip

This is a very simple tip that goes along with our topic du jour: Be cautious of using SETUID with anything. By using SETUID (giving a process that normally takes root privileges standard user access) you create gaping security holes on your machine. Run those commands as SU instead. This will create only a temporary hole—and temporary is much better than permanent!

Reducing the threat of viruses

By Brien M. Posey, MCSE

With all the hype in the news lately about viruses such as Chernobyl and Melissa, there's been increased awareness among computer users about the threat of viruses. In the past, virus prevention meant following safety precautions such as avoiding downloading files from questionable sources and scanning floppies before use. However, although it's still a good idea to take such precautions, the world of computers is much different today than it was five to 10 years ago when most of the basic virus-prevention rules were developed. Not only have computers changed, but so have viruses.

To deal with viruses in today's world, you need to use more advanced techniques. In this article, we'll show you some techniques you can use to help protect your network.

Why the increased threat?

There are three basic reasons why viruses are more of a threat today than they were in the past. First, practically everyone is connected to the Internet. The Internet lets people share files, ideas, and viruses with other people all over the world at record speed.

Second, software is more complex today than it has ever been before. Because many programs—such as the Windows operating system and Microsoft Office—are designed to be expandable through scripts and add-on modules, it's easy to write viruses that the system will mistake for legitimate code.

Finally, more viruses exist than ever before. New viruses are discovered every day. Presently, there are thousands of known viruses.

The first step in preventing viruses is to determine how they're loaded onto your network. Once you know how they get in, you can prevent them from doing any harm.

E-mail

In most environments, e-mail is by far the most common method of transmitting viruses. For example, how many times has someone sent you a joke or a cartoon that you forwarded on to 20 of your best friends? If an e-mail message contains an attachment, it's possible that the attachment contains a virus. For example, one such virus is called Happy99. This virus appears to be a harmless cartoon with some animated fireworks and the words *Happy New Year 1999*. While the unsuspecting user is watching the show, the virus is at work in the background destroying Windows and Exchange Client (or Outlook).

The easiest way of preventing e-mail viruses is to implement an anti-virus program on your mail server that scans all inbound messages for viruses. If a virus is detected, the virus is quarantined before it ever reaches the intended recipient. You can acquire such a program from Symantec (www.symantec.com).

Client/server

As you've probably already figured out, scanning inbound e-mail messages isn't enough by itself. Viruses can come from sources besides e-mail. Therefore, you need to install an anti-virus program on each workstation and each server. Such programs should run in an autoprotect mode that scans each file as it's accessed. Keep in mind, though, that scanning all files can take a serious toll on system performance. Unless you're extremely paranoid, you can set your virus checker to monitor program files only.

For example, in Symantec's Norton AntiVirus, using the Program Files Only setting will monitor most types of files that are capable of being infected. Such types include .exe, .com, .bat, .dll, .ovl, .doc, and .xls files, just to name a few. However, if you tell your anti-virus program to monitor all files, you'll check files that aren't even capable of carrying a virus. For example, we've never seen a .wav file carry a virus.

You should also keep in mind that no virus protection program is perfect. Because a virus can slip through a detector, it's sometimes a good idea to run one brand of anti-virus program on your servers and a different program on the workstations. That way, if a virus slips past the anti-virus program on the server, the program on the workstation will probably catch it.

Service packs

As we said earlier, many viruses are designed to exploit weaknesses in common programs.

For example, many macro viruses pose as legitimate Microsoft Word or Excel macros, but actually contain malicious code. One defense against viruses aimed at exploiting a weak program is to keep up with the latest service packs and hot fixes.

Although a service pack won't directly protect you against a virus, many times it will remove certain vulnerabilities from a program. This is especially true of the Windows NT operating system. To date, Microsoft has issued five service packs for Windows NT version 4. Microsoft also creates hot fixes that you can download each time a new vulnerability is discovered; these hot fixes are designed to remove the security threat. When a new service pack is released, it contains all previous hot fixes and bug fixes.

Anti-virus updates

With new viruses being released every day, it's important to keep your virus checker up to date. One way of doing so is to use its live update feature, which will automatically download anti-virus updates from the Internet and install them. One downside of live updates is that sometimes the Internet becomes bogged down with traffic, making a live update slow or

impossible. One way to get around such a problem is to schedule the update to run at 3:00 A.M. on the weekend. By picking a time when Internet traffic will be very light, you'll increase your chances of completing a successful update.

Is DOS dead?

In a large organization, you'll always find one idiot who removes or disables virus protection. It's also inevitable that this person will infect his or her PC with a virus that's so bad Windows won't even boot. In such a situation, you need to have an alternative means of removing the virus. For example, you can have an anti-virus program that runs in DOS and that doesn't have to be installed to the hard disk. The DOS version of F-Prot by Data Fellows is such a product. (You can download the DOS version for free from www.datafellows.com.) When an infection occurs, boot the damaged system from a write-protected DOS disk or a write-protected Windows 9x repair disk. When you reach the command prompt, insert your write-protected F-Prot disk and begin disinfecting the system. The main downside with this method is that because F-Prot is a DOS program, you must manually download the updates. ◆

When viruses attack

By Talainia Posey

If you're a computer user, then having your hard work wiped out by a virus has to rank as one of life's most frustrating experiences. Although it's relatively easy to protect your computer from viruses, most people outside the IT community don't have a clue about how to do so. The concept of viruses is constantly exaggerated by media hype and urban legends. In this Daily Drill Down, I'll discuss viruses in detail. I'll describe the anatomy of a virus and then examine methods of virus prevention and removal.

Where do viruses come from?

A virus is nothing more than a computer program. Although most viruses are written with malicious intent, some viruses simply display a message or a cartoon. One example of such a

virus is the Cookie Monster virus, which was common about ten years ago. The Cookie Monster virus displayed a picture of Cookie Monster at random times, along with a message that said something like "Give me a cookie." If you typed the word "COOKIE," the picture would go away for a while. You could remove the virus completely by typing "OREO."

Other viruses are more hostile. They may do things like delete or corrupt data, destroy executable programs, or prevent your computer from booting. There are many types of viruses, and they all have at least two things in common: They're annoying, and they're nothing more than a simple computer program that's designed to attach itself to or overwrite your normal programs.

How common are viruses?

Viruses are much more common than most people realize. It's always amusing to watch some clueless anchorperson on the news freak out over some new virus that just happened to catch the attention of the media. The media focuses so strongly on such viruses that they totally overlook two crucial facts. First, whatever virus they're making people paranoid about is usually no more destructive than any other virus. Second, several new viruses are created every single day.

As you probably guessed from that last statement, there are thousands of known viruses in circulation. Companies, such as Symantec and McAfee, have employees who do nothing but write antidotes to every new virus that comes along.

Anatomy of a virus

As I mentioned earlier, there are several types of viruses. Before you can truly prevent a viral infection, you need to understand at least a little bit about how these viruses work. The major types of viruses are:

- boot sector viruses
- executable file viruses
- macro viruses
- e-mail viruses

Boot sector viruses are probably the most common. As the name implies, a boot sector virus infects the boot sector of a hard disk or a floppy disk. When the computer is booted, the virus loads into memory. Once the virus is resident in memory, it can inflict damage, even if you've removed it from the hard disk. Typically, the memory-resident portion of the virus contains instructions for the virus to copy itself to any floppy disk that's inserted into the computer. It usually contains instructions to do some sort of damage to the hard disk. These instructions may include doing anything from erasing files over time to setting up a time bomb algorithm that will eventually prevent the computer from booting after it has been booted a specified number of times.

Other viruses infect executable files. These viruses automatically attach themselves to target files. Usually, such a virus makes the executable file unusable. When someone tries to execute an infected file, the virus is loaded into memory.

Once in memory, the virus will infect any other executable file that you try to run.

Macro viruses infect document files, such as Microsoft Word and Excel documents. These viruses use the macro functions that are built in to the various applications to attack your documents. For example, one such macro virus goes through your Microsoft Word documents and boldfaces random letters. Typically, a macro virus is contracted by opening an infected document. When such a document is opened, the macro is executed automatically. Code within the macro damages your document and usually appends the menacing macros to your master document template. All future documents created with the now infected program will also be infected—and will have the ability to infect other computers.

E-mail viruses are one of the newest types of viruses. Typically, an e-mail virus is attached to an inbound e-mail message in the form of an executable file. If you try to execute this file, the virus will be activated. Many e-mail viruses examine the contents of your address book and spread automatically by e-mailing themselves to names from your address book. Your friends will receive the virus attached to a message from you that says something like, "Hey, check out this cool file that I found." Obviously, if they open the file, the virus will spread to everyone in their address book. As you can imagine, e-mail viruses can spread very rapidly.

Of course, there also are hybrid viruses. For example, viruses exist that can infect executable files and boot sectors. There are macro viruses that spread automatically via e-mail. Although these hybrid viruses exist, it's important to understand that the same basic concepts apply to the way that such viruses function.

Getting the virus

Now that I've discussed the various types of viruses, let's take a moment to review the ways that viruses spread. The most common ways of contracting a virus are by downloading files from the Internet and through software piracy. Any time that you download a file from the Internet, there's a chance that the file could be infected. Likewise, if you acquire software through dubious means or use disks in someone else's PC, there's a chance of getting a virus.

Protecting your PC

With thousands of viruses floating around, it's easy to come into contact with one. After all, few people avoid downloading a needed file just because there's the remote possibility that the file may be infected. It's much more practical to protect your PC. You can do so with one of the antivirus programs that exist. Some of the better ones are Norton AntiVirus by Symantec, McAfee's antivirus suite, and the Panda antivirus program.

How do antivirus programs work?

With the wide array of viruses that exists, you may be wondering how an antivirus program can protect your PC. There are several things that an antivirus program must be able to do in order to be effective.

At the time that you install the antivirus program, it must test the integrity of your system to make sure that it's not already infected. Usually, this procedure is done by scanning your memory for memory-resident programs that behave in a manner that's typical of a virus.

Once the PC has been verified as being clean, the program begins installing. One of the first things that happens as the antivirus program installs is that the boot sector of your hard disk is inoculated. This process usually involves copying the boot sector to a compressed file and noting the dates and sizes of the files involved. Each time the computer is booted, the antivirus program compares the boot sector against the record that was made during the antivirus install. If any files involved in the boot sector have modified dates or sizes, the antivirus program will alert you and may give you the opportunity to revert to the backup copy.

Once the boot sector has been verified, many antivirus programs will run a scan against the main Windows files by comparing the contents of each file against a virus signature file. Each virus has unique characteristics. A virus's signature is composed of a few bytes that uniquely identify that virus. Therefore, a virus signature file is a collection of the signatures from thousands of different viruses.

Once the low-level Windows files have been verified, Windows loads. Then, the antivirus

program goes into auto-protect mode, which means that the antivirus program stays in memory and scans certain types of files against the signature file each time they're accessed. If a virus is encountered, the file is immediately isolated and optionally disinfected.

That takes care of keeping an eye on the system, but you may be wondering about e-mail. Some antivirus software includes server-side plug-ins for the e-mail server. These plug-ins will scan and disinfect e-mail before the recipient ever gets the messages. Such programs may even send a message to the sender of the infected e-mail and inform that person of the infection. If you don't have or can't afford this type of protection, the auto-protect feature will still protect you. The only difference is that it won't delete infected e-mail automatically.

One final way that the antivirus programs can protect you is by constantly scanning for new viruses. All three of the antivirus programs that we mentioned earlier have the ability to connect automatically to the Internet and download updated signature files. You can set the program to download these updates weekly or daily—or whatever schedule meets your needs.

If you get a virus that you don't have a signature file for, all is not lost. The programs we mentioned earlier have some capacity to monitor your system for virus-like activity. If the program suspects an unknown virus, it may alert you to the condition and/or send the code to the company that made the antivirus program so that the company can make an antidote for the potential virus.

If your computer gets a virus

Even with an antivirus program installed, it's still possible to get a virus. For example, if you boot your computer from a floppy disk, your antivirus program isn't in effect. If you encounter a virus while working, your PC is unprotected. Fortunately, you can still protect yourself. The next time you boot your computer normally, the computer will scan for boot sector viruses and file viruses as it encounters each file. If you want to make absolutely sure that your system is clean, then you can use your antivirus program's manual scan function to scan every file on the hard disk. ◆

Chapter 5—Encryption

Encryption

Chapter 5: Encryption

Chapter 5 focuses on the subject of encryption. This chapter examines just what encryption is and what tools are necessary to employ its use.

In chapter 5 we will examine such tools as:

▶ Secure Shell

▶ GNU Privacy Guard

▶ Public key encryption

All of these are great tools for enabling a more secure networking metaphor on any level.

A highlight of this chapter is Vincent Danen's series on Secure Shell—an invaluable tool for transmitting data securely across a network. You should come away with a sound knowledge on how to set up, configure, and use this powerful encryption tool.

Don't rely solely upon encryption for data protection

By John McCormick

An enormous security problem is looming over our heads, but it's receiving little or no attention. This problem involves too much reliance on data encryption.

We congratulate ourselves that we're past the days when users wrote passwords on pieces of paper and taped them to the bottom of desk drawers, and we now force them to change passwords regularly. But many of us feel that our most sensitive files are safe just because they are encrypted. In fact, a lot of companies have a relaxed policy about encrypted files, even sending highly sensitive data over the Internet. The thinking is that if all other security measures fail, the data will still be safe. After all, even if someone gets the files they can't read them. But is this really true?

Don't buy into the myth

Should we be complacent just because we use data encryption? We are told that it would take years of computer analysis to break even the simplest encryption schemes, but as someone familiar with the underlying mathematics, I never bought into this myth, and neither should you.

What people conveniently forget is that computers keep getting faster. What would have taken years of analysis just a decade ago can now be accomplished by hacker groups more quickly.

Data that was thought to be secure even five years ago—and thus wasn't stored or transmitted with any great concern for access security—can now be decrypted. You must presume that any data you encrypt today will eventually be readable by people working with home computers, to say nothing of competitors with a strong economic incentive to learn what's in your files.

Control access

Realistically, this means that the only effective, long-term way to protect your data is to prevent access to the files, no matter how well encrypted they are by today's standards. Of course, if you can accurately determine how long data needs to be protected, then encryption may offer the best, lowest-cost protection. If data will be sensitive only for a short period, encryption provides sufficient security.

But you have to remember that you can't trust any level of encryption for those really sensitive, never-to-be-disclosed documents. If you need to show upper management that this threat is real, check out distributed.net, an association of thousands of individuals who link their computers to crack algorithms, such as those in 56-bit RSA, DES II, or DES III challenges.

Until recently, the 56-bit key was the only one approved for export—and this also applied to branch offices outside the United States and to Internet security. For many years, this scheme was thought to be secure enough for most purposes, but by the end of 1997, there were at least four publicly known cracks.

The 56-bit encryption scheme had 72 quadrillion (72 followed by 15 zeros) possible keys, but several groups took the time to break a meaningless message recorded in it. If you've distributed long-lived and highly sensitive data using the 56-bit key or lesser encryption schemes, you have a real reason to be concerned.

Keys get cracked

On June 24, 1997, Netscape received federal permission to export a browser with 128-bit encryption, so we now have better protection—but for how long? An encryption scheme thought secure for years is now known to be too weak, and the Data Encryption Standard (DES) III has also been cracked. Can the 128-bit key be far behind?

Do you feel confident about your file encryption because only a supercomputer could possibly break your system—and no competitor would spend $10 million on a supercomputer just to learn your secrets? Perhaps you haven't heard about the scientists at Los Alamos National Labs who couldn't wait years for a new supercomputer, so they built one they called Avalon, capable of 20 giga-flop speeds. That's not so surprising, but it took them only 30 hours to build the world's 315th fastest computer and it used off-the-shelf Intel components. They could easily have built an even faster version at first, but they had to wait for a new power line to be installed. IBM is even working on quantum-based computers that could eventually factor large primes incredibly quickly—that's the heart of modern cryptography.

I could go on detailing the threats, but it should be obvious that any complacency about the security of encrypted e-mail or data is misplaced. Remember, just because no one else can read your files today doesn't mean that everybody won't be able to read them soon. Failure to view any encryption scheme as merely temporary protection can come back to haunt you and your company. Don't make that mistake. ◆

Secure Shell: Protecting data in transit

By Vincent Danen

If you're a network or systems administrator, one of your top considerations for any computer should be security—whether it's local security or network security. Since Linux is a networked operating system by design, chances are that the computer is being used in a network environment as a simple firewall or as a server providing such services as HTTP, FTP, and Telnet.

Why Secure Shell?

Often, it's convenient to administer remotely, and Linux supports remote administration. With such programs as Telnet and rlogin, an administrator staying at home can work on and configure a remote Linux machine at the office across the Internet. With more and more companies choosing Linux as a server, as a component of their Internet sites, or even as their gateway to the Internet, remote administration happens all the time.

Linux is very secure. With a little bit of work and through the use of firewalls, IP masquerading, and TCP Wrappers (which prevent unwanted guests from launching services), you can make a computer that runs Linux virtually invulnerable to any attacks across the Internet. Unfortunately, the same cannot be said about the Internet itself.

Most protocols transmit data in clear-text format, which means that there is no encryption or "scrambling" of the network data. Anyone who's curious can "listen" to your network traffic as it goes from point A (let's say the system administrator at home) to point C (the server at work). Because of the nature of the Internet, without a direct dial-in connection to

your server, your network traffic will probably be routed through point B (a host out in the Internet) or even multiple point Bs. It's possible that you'll have a few, or even a few dozen, hops between your system and the one you're trying to reach. To find out how many hops exist between you and any given destination, give the program traceroute a try (which is usually located in /usr/sbin). It will tell you how many hops and how long of a delay between hosts it will take to reach your final destination.

Keep in mind that, if there are a dozen hops to the machine you're trying to reach, there are also a dozen points of interception. Anyone with a packet sniffer or other network-monitoring tool can see and intercept your network data. If this is the case, not only can they view your network data, but they can maintain a local copy of it, view it later, and possibly glean passwords from it. If you think that you are protected just because you require a password for access, think again. Once this type of interception occurs and someone has obtained a user password to your system, your entire system could become compromised. As regular users, they may not get very far, but once they have access to your system, there are a number of holes they may exploit, like programs that are *suid* or *sgid* other users (like root). They may even make attempts to learn the root password of the system. Once an unwanted guest has access to your system, you should view your entire system as compromised. What if they installed a packet sniffer or keyboard monitor on your system? The root password could then be obtained quite easily.

But by then, it's too late. You can plug the hole and change the user's password, but the exposure has already occurred. Your system is compromised. The best way to deal with this situation is to prevent it from happening in the first place. Clear transmission is fundamentally a bad idea, and it should be avoided like the plague. Conscientious system or network administrators should avoid it even on local networks. The Internet is not the only place that harbors curious individuals.

Just what does Secure Shell do?

To guard against vulnerability and to protect your day-to-day network data, I highly recommend installing and using Secure Shell (SSH). SSH is a client/server suite of programs that encrypts data prior to sending it and that unencrypts data once it is received. Every packet in transit, whether across a local LAN or from point A to point C in the earlier illustration, is encrypted and safe from packet sniffers and other network monitors that may pose a security risk to similar programs. SSH is a suitable alternative for programs like *Telnet, rlogin, rsh, rcp,* and *rdist*. SSH was designed to provide strong authentication and secure communication over insecure networks (as noted in the Secure Shell RFC).

Secure Shell supports a number of encryption algorithms, such as:

▶ **BlowFish**—A 64-bit encryption scheme developed by Bruce Schneier

▶ **Triple DES**—The Data Encryption Standard, which was developed in 1974 by IBM and is used by the U.S. government for encrypting nonclassified data

▶ **IDEA**—The International Data Encryption Algorithm, a powerful block-cipher encryption algorithm that operates with a 128-bit key, which makes it far more secure than Triple DES

▶ **RSA**—The Rivest-Shamir-Adelman algorithm, a widely used public-key/private-key cryptographic system

SSH's multi-algorithm support is quite extensive and user-definable. If you feel more comfortable using IDEA than using RSA, you can use IDEA quite easily without changing how SSH works.

Besides providing encryption for network data, SSH can also be used to protect against IP Spoofing, which occurs when a remote host sends out packets that pretend to come from another (trusted) host. It can protect against IP Source Routing, which involves a host pretending that an IP packet comes from another (trusted) host. It protects against DNS Spoofing (when an attacker forges name server records). It prevents manipulation of data by people in control of intermediate systems (the hosts through which IP packets "hop"). And finally, it can also protect against attacks based on listening to X authentication data and spoofed connections to an X11 server.

Despite all of this functionality, using SSH for remote connections does not require an enormous learning curve. Using it is quite similar to using simple Telnet. Authentication and session encryption are completely transparent, and there is no apparent slowdown of information in transit beyond perhaps the seconds when the session authenticates.

How does it work?

SSH is a suite of programs designed to secure connections between two computers, one as client and one as server. To accomplish this task, it comes with a number of programs, including the client program, *ssh*. The client program is very much like a Telnet client in every respect, and it allows you to perform any console-based commands on the server. The server itself, *sshd*, listens on TCP Port 22, and when it receives a connection request from a valid SSH client, it starts a new session. There is also a copy program called *scp*. Secure Copy provides a secure means to copy files from one machine to another, much like the *rcp* program. Since SSH is based on keys to authenticate between client and server, it includes some key management programs like *ssh-add,* which will register new keys for the *ssh-agent* program. This program is used to perform RSA-style authentication over networks when you're using SSH. In other words, it allows remote hosts to access and store your RSA private key. Finally there is *ssh-keygen*, which is the key generator for SSH. It generates an RSA key that is used by *sshagent* to authenticate both locally and remotely.

As you can see, SSH can offer a complete replacement for insecure programs like Telnet and rlogin. In its most basic form, SSH provides a method to secure remote logins and in-transit data and provides a way to protect files and documents transmitted from one machine to another. SSH is, however, quite versatile and can be used for more than that task alone. SSH can be used as an effective "tunneling" mechanism and can secure far more than just remote logins and file transfers. The only catch is that, because SSH is client/server-based, both the remote host and the local machine must use SSH. SSH for Linux is a freely available program. You can obtain the binary programs from ZEDZ or the source code itself from the SSH home page.

The benefits to compiling your own version of SSH are the various options that you can set during compilation and that you can customize to secure your network further. A number of the compilation options can be set in the configuration files if you choose to go with a binary distribution.

An important configuration option that can be specified only at compilation is whether or not SSH will use TCP Wrappers. There are two different schools of thought on this issue, but it boils down to how your system is configured and how you want to customize things. SSH can be independent from the rest of your system in terms of which hosts are allowed to connect, or it can use TCP Wrapper support, which enables SSH to allow and disallow connections based on the hosts defined in /etc/hosts.allow (specified authorized hosts) and /etc/hosts.deny (specified unauthorized hosts). TCP Wrappers is an excellent security tool that works similar to a firewall. The two configuration files are used to select services and to authorize or "unauthorize" specific hosts or domains from using those services. SSH can use this tool, or it can use its own form of allow/deny authorization (when compiled without TCP Wrappers support).

What are the specifics?

Once you've decided which method you're going to use (source or binary) and you have installed SSH, the suite of programs will become available to you. To any systems administrator, I recommend disabling all running Telnet servers completely. This disabling can be done by commenting out the Telnet field in /etc/inetd.conf so that the Inetd super-daemon will never open a Telnet session when an incoming request on TCP Port 23 is received. By the same token, you should also disable the rlogin and rsh suite of programs (*rshd*, *rlogind*, *rexecd*, and *rexd*). The system will not be secure until all of these programs are disabled or, preferably, removed completely.

You can then decide whether *sshd* will be a persistent service (started on its own and continually running) or whether Inetd will start it upon request. If you want Inetd to start the SSH daemon when required, add the following to your /etc/inetd.conf (if you have TCP Wrapper support enabled):

```
ssh stream tcp nowait root
/usr/sbin/tcpd sshd -i
```

or if you have TCP Wrapper support disabled:

```
ssh stream tcp nowait root
/usr/bin/sshd sshd -i
```

There is little real benefit to running *sshd* from Inetd. The SSH daemon does not take much memory or CPU when idle, so there is no need to worry about wasted resources if it is not used very often. The side effect to using Inetd, however, is that SSH must generate a server key prior to responding to the client, and this action can take a few seconds because it has to generate the key immediately before it can authenticate a session. Consequently, the session initiation will take a few seconds longer than necessary. Normally, *sshd* keeps a generated RSA key in memory so that it can respond to client requests immediately. The RSA key is usually re-generated hourly (which can be changed in the configuration), and it is never written to the disk—so as to preserve the key's integrity. Because of this added security, running the daemon stand-alone is recommended.

There are a number of other options that can be used by the SSH daemon on the command-line. These options include the number of bits to use in the server key (by default, it's 768 bits), how often *sshd* regenerates the server key (by default, it's once an hour), alternate ports to listen to (by default, it's TCP Port 22), and more. The configuration file for the daemon, /etc/sshd_config, permits more options to control how the daemon operates.

The SSH client program, *ssh*, also has a number of command-line options, as well as its own configuration file, /etc/ssh_config. Some of the options on the command line allow you to select which cipher (encryption method) to use, which user to log in as (if not the current user), and so forth. It will connect to the remote SSH server and initiate an interactive Telnet-like session. In fact, it is so transparent that, beyond the login, you will think that you're sitting in front of the server itself.

The Secure Copy program should be used whenever you need to transfer one file to another. It is not an interactive copying program, like FTP, but it's very similar to the *cp* program that's used locally. It allows you to select which cipher you want to use on the command line, but it uses a unique syntax to copy files. The syntax is:

```
scp user@host1:[/path/filename]
user@host2:[/path/filename]
```

or it can be abbreviated to

```
scp [/path/filename]
user@host2:[/path/filename]
```

SSH can also be used as a tunneling program to create rough Virtual Private Networks or to allow remote users to access a remote X11 server securely. Beyond that, however, the uses for SSH are virtually endless because of its built-in tunneling and forwarding capabilities. It can be used to provide secure RPC sessions, which are useful in securing NIS services. It can be used to run encrypted PPP sessions on top of a standard SSH session. It can also be used to communicate with outside entities from behind a firewall, because of its TCP forwarding options. It can be used to provide encrypted access to POP3 servers so that, by tunneling it via SSH, you can securely download e-mail that would otherwise be transferred in clear-text (unless the server supports APOP or a similarly encrypted POP3 protocol and only if your client program supports the same protocols).

To Linux and beyond

For the Linux user, Secure Shell is an excellent suite of programs. Unfortunately, in the real world, not everyone uses Linux. So, does this fact limit SSH's usefulness at all? Definitely not! Within a heterogeneous network, or even for the administrator who uses Linux as a server at

work and runs Windows at home, there are SSH clients for other platforms, as well. You can obtain various commercial SSH client implementations (called F-Secure SSH) for Windows and Macintosh systems from DataFellows. However, commercial alternatives have an associated cost.

If you want a free alternative for Windows, Tera Term Pro is useful. It is a popular Telnet client for Windows, but it doesn't come with SSH support natively. Robert O'Callahan, however, wrote an excellent SSH extension for Tera Term Pro that makes the Telnet client fully SSH-compliant. TTSSH (the SSH extension) can be obtained from the TTSSH home site. There are also two ports of SSH (command-line) to Windows from the SSH site and from Gordon Chaffee. There is yet another SSH client for Windows in the works, and it's called Free FiSSH. It is not currently available to the public but should be soon. You can find more information on the official FiSSH site.

For Macintosh, there is Nifty Telnet, which supports SSH natively and can be obtained free of charge from Jonas Walden.

For OS/2, there is a port of SSH available. This port looks a little dated; however, it may still work as a client against the current release of SSH.

For those who use Java, there is also a Java-based SSH client called MindTerm that can run stand-alone or within a Web browser. This free program would be useful for operating systems that come without a direct version of SSH but that use Java.

It should be apparent that SSH is not only a useful solution to many security issues, but almost a necessary one. SSH has been quite popular for many UNIX and Linux system administrators for years, and the ever-increasing number of clients for other operating systems proves that the usefulness of SSH is not limited to UNIX and Linux alone. Unfortunately, there are no free servers for many operating systems, so anyone who plans on using SSH needs to do so with a UNIX or Linux server. That is yet another reason for using a stable and free platform, like Linux, in a networking environment. ◆

GNU Privacy Guard brings industrial-strength encryption to Linux systems

By Bryan Pfaffenberger

Does your organization have a need for secure, encrypted communications? Perhaps you're working with sensitive business strategy documents that in the wrong hands, could cause your employees and stockholders no end of grief. Perhaps you need to exchange e-mail with off-site business partners—and you need to do so without the fear that your messages are being intercepted and read while they're en route. If so, you should take a look at GNU Privacy Guard, a public key cryptography system created by the GNU project, with assistance from the German Federal Ministry of Economics and Technology.

In this Daily Drill Down, I'll explain the fundamental concepts underlying GNU Privacy Guard. After a brief introduction to the program, you'll learn the essential concepts of public key encryption, the technology that underlies GNU Privacy Guard. In plain English, you'll learn how to decode this technology's confusing terminology, and you'll learn ways that you can apply GNU Privacy Guard to the sensitive and confidential tasks your organization undertakes.

Introducing GNU Privacy Guard

Why look at GNU Privacy Guard? In brief, GNU Privacy Guard—or GnuPG, for short—is a full implementation of OpenPGP, a public Internet standard. Unlike PGP, GnuPG does not rely on patented algorithms. What's more, GnuPG isn't a U.S. product, so it's not subject to U.S. export restrictions. In addition, GnuPG is available for a huge variety of platforms, including virtually all UNIX-like systems, Windows 95, and Windows NT. In sum, GnuPG stands a good chance of becoming the de facto standard for encryption technology.

What can you do with GnuPG? Here's the short take: You can use GnuPG to encrypt files on your computer—and what's more, you can do so with a level of encryption that is, for all practical purposes, unbreakable. You can also digitally sign your files so that, whether or not they're encrypted, you'll be able to tell whether someone has tampered with them. The same

goes for e-mail: You can use GnuPG to send and receive secure, encrypted messages, and you can digitally sign the messages so that it's immediately apparent whether they've been altered en route.

Understanding public key cryptography

All encryption boils down to some technique to scramble a readable message (called plaintext) so that its contents, if intercepted, look like gibberish. The scrambled message is called *ciphertext*. To read the ciphertext, the intended recipient needs the *key*, the formula that decodes the message and restores the readable, plaintext version. As this section explains, the encryption techniques prevailing until the 1970s had a serious flaw, which public key encryption remedies in a way that has revolutionary implications—and as you'll see, these implications extend to the technology's social as well as technical impact.

Symmetric key encryption: The old, insecure way

Until the 1970s, the prevailing encryption techniques (called *symmetric ciphers*) had a serious flaw. This flaw comes into play when you're trying to send a secret message from one place to another: You must send the decoding key as well as the message to the intended recipient. For this reason, you couldn't initiate secret communications with someone unless you'd made prior arrangements. Worse, you had to send the key through an insecure channel. Banks and military intelligence organizations often rely on human couriers for this purpose. But what if the courier is compromised by bribes from the bank's competitor—or turns out to be a double agent?

Public key encryption: The new, highly secure way

Public key encryption, the technology underlying GnuPG, solves the problems of previous encryption technologies. In brief, public key encryption uses two keys, not one: the *public key* and the *private key* (also called the *secret key*). You can freely give the public key to anyone; in fact, you can post it on the Internet. Anyone who wishes to send a secret message to you employs your public key to encrypt the message; once this is done, it cannot be read until it is decoded using your private key.

Similarly, when you wish to send a secret message to someone, you obtain this person's public key and use it to encrypt the message. The message cannot be read until it is decrypted using the recipient's private key. As this example illustrates, public key encryption eliminates the major vulnerability of single-key encryption techniques in that the decoding key is *never* sent to anyone. Of course, public key encryption is viable only as long as the private key cannot be determined by analyzing the public key. Experience to date suggests that, as long as you use a key of sufficient length (at least 1,024 characters), brute-force (repetitive-guess) techniques cannot be used to break messages encrypted with public key technology.

Is public key encryption a threat to public safety?

Public key encryption is nothing short of revolutionary—and that's true for its social as well as its technical implications. Security agencies worry that foreign adversaries will obtain public key technologies and use them to their advantage. For these reasons, the U.S. government defines public key encryption technologies as a *munition* and imposes crippling restrictions on

their export. These policies seem ludicrous in view of the fact that strong encryption technologies are easily available anywhere in the world. In fact, you'll need to obtain GnuPG from *outside* the United States; if GnuPG were made available from the GNU Project's home system in Cambridge, Massachusetts, it would be subject to the same, crippling export restrictions that have kept U.S. companies out of the encryption market.

In addition, U.S. law enforcement officials worry that drug dealers, terrorists, child pornographers, and other unsavory types will use public key encryption to evade detection. For this reason, the U.S. government is pushing for the mandated use of *key recovery* schemes, in which encryption software would include a built-in trap door that would enable law enforcement personnel to decode an encrypted message. Experts believe that such a trap door could introduce grave vulnerabilities, which attackers could exploit. The burgeoning world of electronic commerce depends on strong, reliable encryption, and key recovery systems won't fill the bill. For example, banks are solidly opposed to the government's key recovery proposals, and they're not enthusiastic about the U.S.-designed Pretty Good Privacy (PGP), which is designed to enable the type of trap door that the government wants. In fact, PGP's shortcomings in this area helped spur the GnuPG project. GnuPG contains no code that would enable a third party to decode an encrypted message.

It's inevitable that crooks, terrorists, and child pornographers will use public key encryption, but let's face it: The cat's out of the bag. It's too late to stop the dissemination of this technology. For law-abiding citizens, the only remaining question is whether you'll learn how to use it to your best advantage for legitimate, lawful purposes. GnuPG has all the answers.

Just how secure is GnuPG?

GnuPG is safe enough to protect you from all but the most concerted efforts to break your code, but much depends on you. For example, there's a trade-off between execution speed and key length; if you choose a lengthy encryption key (more than 1,024 characters), you decrease the chance that an attacker could decrypt your messages using brute-force techniques, but you also increase the load on your system. (With public key encryption, CPU usage increases exponentially with every increase in the length of the encryption key you're using.) Generally, you'll be safe enough with an encryption key length of 1,024 characters. As far as anyone knows right now, keys of that length are operationally secure, in the sense that the time and expense involved to break messages encrypted with such a key almost certainly exceed the value of the encrypted messages.

But key length can't protect you against carelessness. If an attacker is intent on decrypting your data, there are much easier methods available than trying to determine the cipher you're using. For example, perhaps you've written down your passphrase somewhere in your office, where an intruder can find it. Memorize your passphrase and don't write it down! Worse, suppose you've left your secret key on the hard disk of a system connected to an insecure network, where it's accessible to electronic intruders. Always protect yourself by writing your private key to a write-protected floppy disk or a CD, and don't leave these disks in your office when you're away from your desk.

Hybrid encryption

Although public key encryption solves the courier vulnerability problems of previous encryption techniques, it introduces a problem of its own: inefficiency. Public key technologies require much more CPU horsepower than symmetric ciphers. For this reason, GnuPG uses *hybrid encryption:* The program uses public key encryption to distribute symmetric cipher keys in a secure channel. It then relies on symmetric ciphers for most of the grunt work of encrypting and decrypting files and messages.

Here's how hybrid encryption works: When you send someone a message, GnuPG uses your recipient's public key to encrypt the *session key,* a symmetric key that varies for each message you send. The session key is then used to encrypt the rest of the message. When your message reaches its destination, the recipient's software decodes the session key using the private key, and then uses the session key to decode the rest of the message.

Digital signatures

Public key encryption technology also supports *digital signatures.* In brief, a digital signature enables a recipient to judge whether a given message is really from you, and whether it has been altered while it was en route. You don't need to encrypt a document in order to sign it digitally; encryption is optional. However, your recipient does need your public key in order to verify your signature.

Key management

Because you'll be working with your own key pairs and your correspondents' public keys, you need *key management* capabilities. GnuPG provides a number of tools to help you manage your *key ring,* where the various keys are stored. To help you manage keys, GnuPG enables you to associate each key with a user-friendly user ID, which consists of the person's real name and e-mail address. You can use GnuPG's key management capabilities to examine the keys on your key ring. You can perform actions such as adding new keys, editing user IDs, and deleting unneeded keys.

When you create your key pair with GnuPG, the program automatically creates two kinds of private keys: a *master key,* which is used for digital signatures, and a *subkey,* which is used to decode incoming messages. The program makes this distinction for the following reasons. You do not want your master key (also called *signing key*) to change very often; if you change it, your correspondents will have to update their key rings in order to tell whether your messages are really from you. However, it's wise to change your subkey from time to time. This key is used to decode the encrypted messages that are sent to you. By changing the key, you gain protection against attackers who may have obtained your private key, perhaps by breaking into your office and copying information off your computer. To safeguard yourself against such attacks, it's wise to store your subkey on a write-protected floppy disk, which you keep in your personal possession at all times.

Web of trust

To prevent man-in-the-middle attacks that involve the use of forged public keys, GnuPG applies your digital signature to your public key. When you send your public key to others, the recipients can immediately discern whether the key has been altered in some way. However, there's still a chance that the key isn't really from you. Perhaps someone has broken in to your office and discovered that you wrote your passphrase on the bulletin board. GnupG cannot provide total security because human behavior comes into play.

To include some measure of protection against users who fail to use the technology properly, GnuPG implements the *Web of trust* system. In this model, you attach your own digital signature to the public keys you receive. When you do, you attest your level of confidence that the key is, in fact, genuine, and that the person who created the key is a responsible and trustworthy user of GnuPGP technology. If you know the correspondent well and you are certain that the key has not been compromised, you can affirm a high level of trust. This attestation is visible to others. A given public key may receive several such attestations, which inspires confidence that it is, indeed, genuine.

Keyservers

To facilitate the distribution of OpenPGP-compatible public keys, volunteers have created a worldwide system of *keyservers*. In brief, a keyserver is a database-linked Web site that performs two functions: It enables users of GnuPG (and other OpenPGP-compatible programs) to submit their public keys, and it enables site visitors to search for and download a person's public key. For example, suppose I upload my public key to a keyserver. Once I've done so, you can visit the keyserver, search for my name, and download my public key. Then, you can send me a secret, encrypted message—even though we've never previously exchanged messages.

Several OpenPGP keyservers exist, and they're designed to periodically refresh each other's databases so that in time, all keyservers have copies of all the keys users have contributed. For this reason, you should visit a keyserver close to your area. Currently, there are keyservers in Austria, Belgium, Finland, Germany, Thailand, and the United States. For more information on keyservers, visit Open PGP Keyserver.

Obtaining and installing GnuPG

To obtain GnuPG for Linux, visit one of the following sites:

▸ If you would like to compile GnuPG using source code tarballs, grab them from the official GNU site.

▸ To obtain RPM packages for the Linux version of GnuPG, go to this gpg directory via FTP. Currently, up-to-date RPMs are available for Intel 386 and 686 systems running Red Hat Linux 5.x and 6.x.

▸ A Windows 95/98 version is available from the GNU site. Note that this is an alpha version and shouldn't be used for mission-critical purposes.

What you'll need

To run GnuPG on your Linux system, you'll need the random devices files—specifically, /dev/random and /dev/urandom. To determine whether these devices exist, do the following: In a terminal window, type *cd/dev/random* and press [Enter]. Do the same with *cd /dev/urandom*. If these devices exist, you'll see these pathnames echoed at the terminal. If they do not exist, create them. Switch to superuser, type *mknod /dev/random c 2 3 ; mknod /dev/urandom c 2 4*, and press [Enter].

Installing GnuPG from the RPM binary

To install GnuPG from RPM binaries, type *rpm -ivh gnupg*rpm*.

Installing GnuPG from the source code tarball

If you've downloaded the GnuPG tarballs and are planning to install the software by compiling from the source code, follow these steps:

1. To verify that the version of GnuPG you have downloaded is genuine, type the following: *md5sum gnupg*.gz.* You'll see a checksum on-screen. Verify that this checksum is identical to the one published on GnuPG's download page.

2. In the directory where you've downloaded the GnuPG tarball, type the following: *tar -xvzf gnupg*.gz*, and press [Enter].

3. Switch to the directory tar created by typing *cd gnupg** and pressing [Enter].

4. Type *./configure*, and press [Enter].

5. Assuming the configure utility exits without error, type *make* and press [Enter].

6. Switch to superuser (Type *su* and press [Enter].)

7. Type *make install* and press [Enter]. ◆

Getting started with GNU Privacy Guard

By Bryan Pfaffenberger

GNU Privacy Guard implements public-key encryption based on the OpenPGP protocol. In this Daily Drill Down, you'll learn how to get started with GNU Privacy Guard (abbreviated GnuPG) by using the program's text-mode interface. By the time you've finished working through this step-by-step approach to GnuPG, you'll be ready to take full advantage of all the benefits strong encryption technology can give you, including secure, confidential storage and transmission of sensitive documents, as well as digital signatures that can reveal whether anyone has altered an important file. Specifically, here's what I'll cover in this Daily Drill Down:

▶ Choosing a passphrase

▶ Generating the key pair

▶ Exporting your key to keyserver

▶ Creating a revocation certificate

▶ Encrypting files

▶ Wiping the original file

▶ Decrypting files

▶ Encrypting and signing files

▶ Clearsigning files

▶ Creating a detached signature

▶ Verifying a signature

▶ Exporting your public key

▶ Importing and validating public keys

If you're new to the basic concepts of encryption technology, be sure to read "GNU Privacy Guard brings industrial-strength encryption to Linux systems." In particular, note that use of GNU Privacy Guard isn't legal in some countries.

Choosing a passphrase

Your first task with GnuPG involves creating your *key pair,* including the *private key* that you never divulge to anyone and the *public key* that you make available to others. Your correspondents use your public key to encrypt messages to you, and you use your private key to decode these messages.

Generating a key pair is a simple process, as you'll see, but you should give some thought to your passphrase before starting. GnuPG's technology won't give you much protection if you choose an easily guessed passphrase.

In brief, a *passphrase* is a multiword password of unlimited length. A good passphrase consists of several strings separated by spaces. Each string should contain a mixture of numeric and alphabetical letters. You shouldn't use dictionary words, which are easily guessed by passphrase-cracking programs.

There's a trade-off involved in coming up with a good passphrase: The worst ones are easy to remember, while the best ones are close to impossible to remember. Bear in mind, too, that you won't be able to access your files if you encrypt them and then forget your passphrase! Ideally, you shouldn't write down your passphrase. In practice, most people will do so, fearing that they'll forget it. If you choose to write down your passphrase, be sure to keep it in a secure place—preferably, in a location separate from that of the computer that's running GnuPG.

Generating the key pair

Once you've chosen a suitable passphrase, you're ready to generate your key pair. Follow these instructions to do so:

▶ Log on to your ordinary user account and switch to your home directory, if necessary.

▶ Open a terminal window, type *gpg -- gen-key,* and press [Enter]. You'll see a prompt asking you to select the kind of key you want. You can choose DSA and ElGamal (the default), DSA (sign only), or ElGamal (sign and encrypt). The best choice is the default, so just press [Enter]. (If you choose DSA, you can't use the keys for encryption; if you choose the other option, ElGamal, you'll be using the less efficient public key encryption algorithm for all encryption purposes.)

▶ Next, you'll be prompted to select a key size. The default option, 1024, is a good trade-off between CPU demand and security, so just press [Enter].

- You'll now be asked to choose an expiration date. Since you don't want your public key to expire, press [Enter] to accept the default here (0 = key does not expire).

- In the next three steps, you'll create your user ID, which consists of your name, your e-mail address, and a comment. In response to the Real Name prompt, type your first name and last name, then press [Enter].

- In response to the E-mail prompt, type your e-mail address and press [Enter].

- In response to the Comment prompt, enter your nickname or your initials.

- Next, you'll be asked to specify your passphrase. Type your passphrase and press [Enter]. You'll be asked to type it again for confirmation. If you make a mistake when you type the passphrase the second time, you'll be asked to repeat the whole process.

Caution: It's wise to store your private key on a floppy disk or CD rather than your computer's hard drive. You can then take this disk with you when you're away from your computer.

Exporting your key to a keyserver

To make your exported key available to others, you can send the binary version of your key as an e-mail attachment. You can also send the ASCII-armored version of the key within the text of an e-mail message. Additionally, you can export your key to a *keyserver,* an Internet-based service that maintains a database of public keys. Since keyservers belong to a network that exchanges the new keys that are uploaded, you need do this only once; after you've sent your key to a keyserver, all the keyservers on the same keyserver network will have a copy of your key. Anyone who wishes to send you an encrypted message can do so without first contacting you; they need only visit the keyserver, search for your name, and obtain your key.

GnuPG's -- *send-key* and -- *keyserver* options enable you to upload your keys to a keyserver. To send your key to the keyserver for example, you'd type *gpg -- keyserver search.keyserver.net -- send-key* followed by your user ID; you'll need to be connected to the Internet in order to use this command. See the keyserver for the latest information on OpenPGP-compatible keyservers.

Creating a revocation certificate

After you've successfully generated your key pair, you should create a *revocation certificate.* Sign it with your digital signature, and use this certificate to warn your correspondents that your private key has been compromised.

To create your revocation certificate, type the following and press [Enter]:

```
gpg —output revoke.asc —gen-revoke
userID
```

(For *userID,* type any part of your user ID that will identify your key pair.) This command writes a revocation certificate to the file revoke.asc, which is located in the working directory. The GnuPG documentation recommends that you print the certificate, store the certificate in a secure location, and delete the file. Otherwise, an intruder could render your private key useless by obtaining and publishing your certificate. (The revocation certificate isn't very long, so you won't have a tough time copying from hard copy, should the need ever arise.)

Encrypting files

To encrypt files with GnuPG, remember that you're using a public key encryption program—you're encrypting with the intended recipient's public key. If you're encrypting files on your own system and intending to decrypt them yourself, you need to encrypt them using *your* public key. If you encrypt the files with someone else's public key, you won't be able to decrypt them, unless you have that person's private key!

To encrypt a file so that you can decrypt it later using your private key, do the following:

1. At the Linux prompt, type *gpg -- encrypt* followed by the name of the file you want to encrypt, then press [Enter]. You'll see a prompt asking you to identify the recipient.

2. Type any part of your user ID (your first or last name, your e-mail address, or your comment) and press [Enter].

GnuPG encrypts the file and writes the output to a new file with the .gpg suffix.

Wiping the original file

There's not much point in encrypting a file on your local system if you leave the original file intact—and that's just what GnuPG does. What's more, it's not sufficient to delete the file using ordinary file-deletion techniques, such as the *rm* command; a knowledgeable intruder can easily restore deleted files. Using a technique known as Magnetic Force Microscopy (MFM), an intruder can even recover data that has been overwritten two or three times.

For better security, you should erase the original file using a file-wiping utility, such as Wipe. Be aware, however, that utilities such as Wipe have known (and unknown) imperfections that may leave traces of the original data intact, especially on SCSI drives. Don't use Wipe to safeguard your nation's military secrets; here, we're talking about keeping your data safe from snoops, such as employees who are hoping to find something of value to sell to a competitor. You can use GnuPG and Wipe to keep confidential data out of the hands of minor-league intruders, but Wipe might not protect you from a well-funded, professional investigation.

Once you've downloaded and installed Wipe, it's easy to use. Just type *wipe* followed by the name of the file you want to delete, then press [Enter].

Decrypting, encrypting, and signing files

To decrypt a file, use the *-- decrypt* option, as in the following example:

```
gpg —output output-file —decrypt
input-file.gpg
```

This command decrypts the file specified by *input-file* and writes the file to *output-file*. You'll be prompted to enter your private key password. When you've entered the password successfully, GnuPG decrypts the file and writes to the output file you specified.

If you're encrypting a file for a recipient other than yourself, consider signing it as well as encrypting it. When you sign a file, the file contains your digital signature. It also contains a timestamp indicating when the file was signed. In addition, the recipient can use your signature to verify that the file has not been tampered with since you signed it. To verify your signature, the recipient will need your public key, so be sure to send this along with the document.

To sign as well as encrypt a file for a recipient other than yourself, do the following:

1. Type *gpg -- output output-file.gpg -- sign input-file*, where *output-file.gpg* is the name of the signed

file and *input-file* is the name of the source document. Press [Enter] to sign the file. You'll be prompted to enter the passphrase for your private key. This key is used to create the digital signature.

2. Type any uniquely identifying part of your user ID (first name, last name, e-mail address, or comment) and press [Enter].

3. Now encrypt the file you just signed, the one with the .gpg suffix. To do so, type *gpg -- encrypt* followed by the name of the signed file (*output-file.gpg*, from step 1). You'll be prompted to enter the user ID of the recipient.

4. Type any uniquely identifying part of the recipient's user ID and press [Enter].

GnuPG creates the signed and encrypted file with the .gpg suffix.

Clearsigning files and creating a detached signature

You can sign files without encrypting them. Although the file can be read by anyone, your signature attests that the file is really from you—and what's more, the recipient can apply your public key to the file to determine whether it has been altered in any way. Signing a file without encryption is called *clearsigning*.

To clearsign a file, type *gpg -- clearsign* followed by the name of the file, then press [Enter]. GnuPG will create a new file with the .asc suffix.

If you examine a clearsigned file, you'll see that it has been enclosed in an ASCII "wrapper," which includes an ASCII version of your digital signature. Your recipient won't be able to use the file without removing this information. To make life easier for your recipients, you can use a *detached signature*. A detached signature provides the same function as a clearsign signature; it attests that you are indeed the file's sender, and it enables the recipient to verify that the file hasn't been altered since you signed it. However, the signature, timestamp, and verification information is stored in a separate file.

To create a detached signature for a file, first type *gpg -- filename.sig -- detach-sig filename*, where *filename* is the name of the file you want to sign. Then, press [Enter]. For example, to create a detached signature for proposal.doc, you'd type *gpg -- proposal.sig -- detach-sig proposal.doc*.

Verifying a signature

If you receive a file that has been digitally signed, you can verify it by using the -- *verify* option. To verify an encrypted file that incorporates the signature, you must first decrypt it; verification is automatic.

To verify a clearsigned file that incorporates the signature, type *gpg -- verify* followed by the name of the file. If you're verifying a clearsigned file called proposal.doc, type *gpg -- verify proposal.doc*.

If the document was signed with a detached signature, you must supply the name of the signature file as well as the name of the document. For example, suppose you've received budget.doc and the signature is in a file named budget.sig. To verify the signature, type *gpg -- verify budget.sig budget.doc*.

Exporting, importing, and validating your public key

To exchange encrypted and digitally signed documents with other GnuPG users, you'll need to export your public keys to a disk file that you can exchange with others. You can export your public key to a binary file or an ASCII-armored file.

To export your public key to a binary file, type *gpg -- output filename.gpg -- export user-ID*, where *filename* is the name of the public key file you're creating and *user-ID* is any uniquely identifying part of your user ID. To export my user ID, I type *gpg -- output bryan.gpg -- export Bryan*. This command creates a file containing the public key in binary format.

If you'd like to include your public key in e-mail messages, you'll need to create an ASCII version of your public key. To do so, use the -- *armor* option, as in

```
gpg —armor —output bryan-asc.gpg —
export Bryan
```

This command creates an ASCII version of my public key and saves the output in the file named bryan-asc.gpg.

If you've received a public key from a correspondent, you need to import the key before GnuPG can use it. To import the key, type *gpg -- import* followed by the name of the binary or ASCII-armored file that contains the key.

Before you use someone's public key, you should first make sure it is valid. To do so, you

should read the key's *fingerprint,* an identifying code. You can access a public key's fingerprint by doing the following:

1. Type *gpg -- edit-key* followed by the public key owner's user ID, then press [Enter]. You'll see information about the key and a GnuPG command prompt.

2. Type *fpr* and press [Enter]. You'll see the fingerprint code for this key. Don't exit the GnuPG command mode yet; in step 4, you'll sign the key.

3. Call the person who sent you the key, read the fingerprint, and ask this person whether the fingerprint is valid. The fingerprint code should be exactly the same as the one displayed on your correspondent's screen.

4. If you're satisfied that the public key is valid, you can sign the key. (You can still use the key even if you don't sign it.) To do so, type *sign* at the GnuPG command prompt. Caution: By attaching your signature to this person's key, you're attesting that it's valid. Don't do this unless you've verified the fingerprint, as described in step 3.

5. You should now define the key's trust level, a number from 1 to 4 that expresses your confidence that the key is indeed a valid one that originated from the stated owner. The trust level you assign is for your purposes only; trust information isn't exported or accessible to others. To assign a trust level to the key, type *trust* at the GnuPG command prompt and press [Enter]. You'll be asked to indicate the trust level (1 = Don't know, 2 = I do NOT trust, 3 = I trust marginally, 4 = I trust fully). If you followed the instructions in step 3, you can type *4* and press [Enter]. If you skipped step 3 and didn't sign the key, type *1* and press [Enter].

6. Type *quit* to exit the GnuPG command mode.

GnuPG horizons

In this Daily Drill Down, you've learned all the basics of using GNU Privacy Guard. You've generated your key pair, encrypted and signed documents, and managed public keys.

With GnuPG-compatible utilities, you can make GnuPG easier (and more fun) to use. If you're running KDE, you'll want to download Geheimnis, a well-conceived front-end program that works with recent versions of PGP as well as GNU Privacy Guard; GNOME users should take a look at GnomePGP. Both of these utilities simplify key-management tasks and enable drag-and-drop for point-and-click encryption, decryption, digital signing, and document verification.

What's missing from the GNU Privacy Guard picture? To use GnuPG conveniently with e-mail, you need a GnuPG-compatible e-mail program. Unfortunately, they're scarce; for the latest information on compatible software, see the GnuPG home page. Scripts and patches for the Emacs and pine e-mail utilities are available now, but there's a dearth of GnuPG support for GUI-based mail packages. Here's the good news: Such support is indeed on the way. For example, KDE users will be able to use GNU Privacy Guard transparently within the KMail utility. In the GTK+/GNOME world, the Archimedes project is once again under way. ◆

Jargon Watch: Encryption

By Mary Ann Fitzharris

When you start to buy and sell over the Web using the highly convenient netcheque, you might wonder what encryption methods are in place to protect your transactions.

Netcheque

If you're registered to use netcheques, you can pay other registered users through e-mail or the Internet, thus authorizing the funds to be transferred from your account to theirs. This type of transaction will allow the smooth payment of bills online. Netcheque uses Kerberos and conventional cryptography.

Kerberos

Kerberos is a complex authentication system, developed at the Massachusetts Institute of Technology (MIT), that is used in networks to determine that you are who you say you are. Essentially, you log in to a network, and an authentication server opens a session based on your password.

RSA

RSA (named for its inventors, Ronald Rivest, Adi Shamir, and Leonard Adleman) is an Internet encryption and authentication standard that uses a complex mathematical algorithm to determine two numbers, or "keys." One will be private and the other made public. The private key decodes text that has been coded with the public key. The RSA algorithm is included as part of the Netscape and Microsoft Web browsers.

DES

DES (data encryption standard) is another encryption and authentication standard that uses a mathematical algorithm developed by IBM and the National Security Agency. DES breaks the message into 64-bit blocks, codes it quickly, and then sends it over a network to the recipient. A new key—or identifying number—can be generated each time, or a key can be reused. New keys are sent to the recipient through public key or RSA method. DES can be standard (which uses one key) or triple (where three keys and three decodings are used), thus providing additional security.

Cryptography

When sending a secret code over a public network, the original text is converted into code with an encryption algorithm, which uses a binary number key to "lock" the data. When the message is received, the encrypted code is decoded or "unlocked" and turned back into the original text.

Cryptography can be done in one of two ways: secret key vs. public key. The secret key uses the DES standard. Because both the sender and recipient use the same key to lock and unlock the message, this is faster but less secure.

The second way is public key cryptography, such as RSA, which combines the use of a private and public key. The recipient has both a private and public key, and senders use the public key to send a message. The recipient, however, uses the tightly held private key to decode the message. Since the recipient is the only one with the private key, and since the key is never sent over the Internet, this message is more secure.

Digital envelope

When both DES and RSA are used at the same time—because DES is fast, and RSA is convenient—the message is coded using DES (the public key), and the secret key is sent via RSA. This so-called "digital envelope" transmits across the network both the DES-encoded message and the secret key needed to decode it.

Steganography

When cryptography goes one step further—and you can't detect there's an encoded message in a seemingly innocent document—it's called steganography (for "covered writing" in Greek). The encrypted data is first inserted into an unneeded piece of data that is part of a file format (such as a JPEG file)—for example, color pixels repeated in a row inconspicuously, where the encrypted data is added and appears to be a parrot of the pattern. When files are hidden this way, scanners looking for encrypted data will not discover it. Watermarks and other symbols are often hidden in software code. Programs that allow you to hide and then decode messages in JPEG files include JPHIDE, JPSEEK, and OutGuess. ◆

Public key encryption: And they said it couldn't be done

By Mark Leon

Anyone who has used a browser to buy a book from Amazon.com has made use of the public key encryption system. In fact, this two-key security system has become prevalent in buying on the Web.

Of the keys involved, one is there to authenticate the merchant while the other protects your credit card number. The basic idea is simple, but the execution is more involved.

Public key infrastructure (PKI) refers to all the machinery that the trusted public key encryption entity must maintain and protect.

This complex system is changing the face of e-commerce, making it more trustworthy than ever—a necessary movement for the survival of the dot com breed. But this complexity of PKI was almost its early downfall. The breadth of such a system had convinced early critics that the system would never be more than an academic curiosity—or the property of the government.

In this article, we'll look at the history of this security technology, which, all in all, has proved its critics wrong.

A skeptical start

Twenty-five years ago, when a young Stanford University computer science professor named Martin Hellman started talking about a new encryption scheme, his colleagues told him he was nuts.

"When this [public key encryption] was first proposed," says Eric Holstege, chief technology officer with ReleaseNow.com, an e-commerce outsource provider for digital goods in San Carlos, CA, "people said it would never work since it would be way too complicated to administer."

Critics felt that if such a thing were possible, there was another group that would have created it.

"They said," Hellman recalls, "'The National Security Administration has a billion-dollar budget, so how can you hope to come up with anything they don't already have? And if you do, they will just classify it.'"

Hellman ignored the sage advice and went on—with the aid of two students: Whitfield Diffie and Ralph Merkle—to create public key encryption, a method that turned out to be both new and highly successful outside the dark dungeons of national security.

The technique has spawned a new industry, that of the PKI vendor. It is, according to Abner Germanov, analyst with International Data Corp., still a fledgling industry, worth about $122.7

million in 1998. Germanov predicts it will be worth $1.3 billion by 2003. Firms such as VeriSign, Entrust Technologies, and Baltimore Technologies have built successful businesses on top of Hellman's creation. It is difficult to imagine e-commerce today without it.

PKI basics

Hellman's breakthrough insight was to separate the process of disguising a piece of data (encryption) from that of revealing it (decryption).

"Traditionally, ciphering was a symmetric process," explains Holstege. "This means you use the same key to unscramble a message that you use to scramble it. The weakness here is that you must transmit the key with the message."

Hellman designed a system that uses not one key but two: a public key that is available to everyone, and a private key that remains with a single party.

"It can be used in a number of ways," says Hellman. "To send you a private message, for example, I could just look up your public key and scramble the message using that. Then I send it to you, and you can use your private key to unscramble it."

The advantage to this system is that it is asymmetric. Anyone can encode a message, but only the one who is supposed to read it can do the decoding, since that requires the private key, known only to the recipient. And, since the private key does not need to travel, it stays nice and secure.

These key pairs are also commonly used for authentication. "This is where the digital signature comes in," says Hellman. "In this case, you use the private key to scramble a piece of data that is the signature. Now anyone can decipher this since that is done with the public key. But only the private key holder can encode the right signature that verifies identity."

The security of public key encryption does come at a price. The asymmetry of the model creates some real logistical problems. Key pairs and certificates that authenticate keys must be created and issued by a trusted entity, the certificate authority.

And the very existence of the industry, no matter how fledgling, must give Hellman at least some small measure of satisfaction. "When I first proposed public key cryptography, people said it was computationally unfeasible," says Hellman. Now, as professor emeritus and board member of Confinity, a firm that leverages public key technology, Hellman can relax and watch his unfeasible creation flourish. ◆

Notes

Chapter 6—Tips

Tips

Chapter 6: Tips

Chapter 6 is a heavy-duty helping of shorter tips that include such gems as:

▶ Keeping passwords unique

▶ Locking out accounts

▶ Improving your company's security

▶ Disabling administration shares

▶ Hiding drives

▶ Hiding servers

▶ VPN security

▶ Antivirus settings

▶ Password policies

▶ Locking NT workstations

Many of these tips focus on the training aspect, as well as hole patching and passwords.

The primary OS dealt with in these tips is Windows, but don't be surprised to find a Linux tip here and there.

Chapter 6 may be the most useful chapter you will read. These quick tips just might save your security as well as your sanity.

Keeping passwords unique with domain account policies

A solid password aging policy can help secure network resources by forcing users to select different passwords periodically. Not only does this make it more difficult for intruders to guess user passwords, it also limits the amount of time that a cracked password can be used for illicit purposes. To access the password age configuration, open User Manager For Domains and select Account from the Policies menu.

The first setting is Maximum Password Age, which forces users to change their passwords when the passwords reach a certain age. You can choose either the Never Expire Pass-words or Expire Passwords After One To 999 Days options.

To the right of these settings are the Minimum Password Age settings. Here you can choose to Allow Changes Immediately or require that a password be from one to 999 days old before allowing changes. The latter option ensures that users can't change their passwords back to previous passwords after being forced to choose new ones due to the Maximum Password Age configuration. Using these two password policies together can help keep your network resources secure. ◆

Locking out accounts to keep strangers off your LAN

Windows NT's Account Lockout feature allows an administrator to lock out a particular account if the admin suspects that someone is trying to guess a user's password by repeated logon attempts. These settings are effective only for regular logons, not logging on to a locked workstation. To access the Account Lockout configuration, open User Manager For Domains and select Account from the Policies menu.

Select Account Lockout from the Account Policies window. Once lockouts are enabled, you can choose to lock an account out after one to 999 failed logon attempts. You can also reset the count after one to 99,999 minutes to accommodate normal user error. Finally, the Lockout Duration can be customized to one to 99,999 minutes, or accounts can be locked out forever. ◆

Use NTFS permissions to guard open systems

Even in a tightly administered environment, you may still want to enable shared folder or file permissions for some networked resources. In such an environment, remember that NTFS permissions work cumulatively—that is, the most restrictive permission applied to a resource is enforced. However, it's important to remember that shared folder permissions *apply to networked resources only*, so you can't rely solely on them to protect resources on systems with open user access.

Let's suppose you use the NTFS Security tab to assign a user Full Control to a resource but then use the Sharing tab to assign the same user Read permission to that resource. If the user tries to access the resource across the network, she or he will only have Read access, since that access level is most restrictive in use. However, if the same user tries to access the resource on the system where it resides, only the NTFS permission of Full Control will be in force, leaving the door open to unwanted user access. ◆

Tuning the server service to suit your needs

Since Windows NT Server offers the interactive user interface, it's important to tune your server for optimal performance. To access the interface, open Network Properties and double-click Server on the Services tab.

Under the Optimization selection you'll find four settings.

- Select the Minimize Memory Used setting if the server will accommodate 10 or fewer simultaneous connections.

- Use the Balanced setting for 11 to 64 connections. (This is also the default setting for NetBEUI applications.)

- Select Maximize Throughput For File Sharing for a file server on a larger network.

- Choose Maximize Throughput For Network Applications if the server will host a heavily used client/server application.

You'll also find the Make Browser Broadcasts To LAN Manager 2.x Clients at the bottom of the Server Properties screen. This setting facilitates backward compatibility. ◆

Members choose their favorite security links

By Paul Baldwin

Security issues always receive a high ranking when IT professionals discuss the industry. But security, as any CIO knows, is an ever-changing problem with multiple sides and various courses of action. We'd like to share with you some of the security sites our members have suggested.

Members say?

TechRepublic member James Jankovich offered these three sites as his favorite security resources:

- Gibson Research Corp. offers an online test to help determine security flaws.

- Zone Labs offers free firewall software to individual users. The freeware, ZoneAlarm, monitors all the activity on your computer, including each time an application tries to access the Internet.

- Trend Micro Inc. provides tools to detect blocked viruses, malicious code, and other Internet security threats. The site's home page has a link that sends users to products designed for corporate use. Steven Thompson, IT director for Boston-based Newman Communications, Inc., recommended Security Systems, which specializes in network security management and features industry leaders such as Internet Scanner and SAFEsuite software.

Here are some of the links that TechRepublic member James King recommended:

- Security offers its clients a network security assessment as well as a review of hardware, software, architecture, and designs. It also deploys Public Key Infrastructure, establishes security policies, and offers design services for applications, systems, and networks.

- Packet Storm, a division of Security, provides news and free security services to users. It also includes a list of security resources.

Other TechRepublic members recommended Sans Institute online, a cooperative that provides security alerts and news updates, research, and other publications.

Microsoft's security page was also recommended. The page has a link to Microsoft security bulletins, as well as checklists and other evaluation guidelines for Microsoft products. ◆

Hide user-created shares

Any share that you create can be hidden from the network browser with a simple keystroke. Just as you can hide the IPC$, C$, and other administrative shares, you can also hide a user share by simply adding a $ at the end of the name. By doing so, you hide the share from anyone browsing in Network Neighborhood, but you can still map to the share by typing its name directly. This same trick can be used for hiding an NT printer share. ◆

Permanently disable the Hidden Administration shares

The C$, D$, etc. shares can pose a security risk on your systems, since they're widely known among NT hackers. The problem is that when you delete these shares, they're re-created after every reboot. To disable the shares altogether, you must edit the registry. (Remember that working with the registry does include risks, so make sure you have a verified backup before beginning.)

First, locate the following key:

HKEY_LOCAL_MACHINE\SYSTEM\ CurrentControlSet\Services\LanManServer\ Parameters\AutoShareServer

Then, change the value of this key to 0. For workstations, the key is AutoShareWks. ◆

Hiding drives from "motivated" users

Preventing accidents is what network administrating is all about. Given that, you might want to hide certain drives from users if they don't absolutely need access. NT enables you to hide drives from the obvious access points (Explorer and My Computer), although a motivated user could still access them from Start | Run. But you can change that.

Start up the Registry Editor and follow these steps:

1. Go to HKEY_CURRENT_USERS\ Software\ Microsoft\Windows\ CurrentVersion\Policies\Explorer.

2. Right-click within the right pane and choose New/DWORD Value.

3. Name the new key Hidden and press [Enter] twice.

4. Within the Edit DWORD Value dialog box, select Decimal.

5. Enter the number corresponding to the drive you want to hide (A: 1, B: 2, C: 4, D: 8, E: 16, etc.). If you want to hide more than one drive, add the numeric values assigned to the drives. For example, to hide drives D and E, enter 24.

6. Exit the registry.

The next time the PC boots up, the drives will be hidden from casual browsers. ◆

Use IPC$ to administrate

It can be a major security risk to always be logged on as a domain administrator. When you walk away from your machine, even for a short time, you open yourself up to security breaches. Instead, log on to your workstation as a regular user and connect to a server with the IPC$ share when you need administrative privileges.

The syntax is as follows:

```
Net use \\thePDC\IPC$
/user:domain\AdminAcct AdminPasswd
```

When you've finished with your administration task, issue the following command:

```
Net use \\thePDC\IPC$ /d
```

This will get you back to your user-level account. ◆

Hiding the last logon

If you work in a security-minded environment, you may want to disable the default setting in NT 4.0 that displays the name of the last person who logged on to the system. It's often far too easy to guess a user's password from his or her username or from the logon environment.

To do so, you'll need to launch Regedt32 and follow these steps:

1. Select the HKEY_LOCAL_MACHINE key.

2. Find subkey \Software\Microsoft\ WindowsNT\CurrentVersion\Winlogon.

3. Go to Edit | New | String Value.

4. Enter *DontDisplayLastUserName* for the string's name.

5. Double-click the new string to edit the value.

6. Change the value to 1.

7. Click OK.

8. Exit the Registry Editor.

Note: Please remember that editing your registry can be risky; be sure you have a verified backup before you begin. ◆

Hide the server from the world

Occasionally, you may need to hide a server from the browse list. This may be because you don't want to open the server up to hackers or just because the server is intended for personal use, and you want to keep unknown factors out. Here's a registry change that lets you hide your server from the rest of the world but lets you still access it through command methods.

To begin, find the key:

```
HKEY_LOCAL_MACHINE\SYSTEM\
CurrentControlSet\Services\
LanmanServer\Parameters
```

and then make the following change:

```
"Hidden"=dword:00000001
```

Note: Editing your registry carries potential risks, so always have a verified backup before you begin. ◆

Securing and testing passwords

Your NT network is only as secure as its weakest password. NT provides a great utility for controlling passwords called the User Manager. To access this utility, go to the Start menu and select Administrative Tools | User Manager. In the User Manager window, select the user or group you want to work with and then go to the Policies menu and choose Account. NT will display an Account Policy dialog box where you can control the maximum age of a password, its minimum length, and uniqueness. By limiting the life of passwords and requiring at least eight characters (NT allows passwords up to 14 characters) you can reduce your system's susceptibility to brute-force attacks.

You can test how your system holds up under a brute-force attack with a password cracking utility called L0phtCrack. This utility works by grabbing passwords as they move across a network or by extracting the NT passwords from the system registry or an emergency repair disk. L0phtCrack uses a dictionary to guess passwords but also attacks the full key space by systematically searching letter, number, and symbol combinations. You can download L0phtCrack at the L0pht Heavy Industries Web site (www.l0pht.com). ◆

Auditing failed logons to track hacker activity

Hackers often gain access to a system by setting up an automated program that bombards a server with thousands of possible password combinations. Windows NT provides an auditing utility that can help you recognize these hacking attempts by tracking events at the system and object level. By default, this auditing option is turned off. To configure NT to audit events, go to the Start | Programs | Administrative Tools | User Manager. In the User Manager window, go to the Policies menu and select Audit. In the resulting Audit Policy dialog box, click the Audit These Events radio button to activate auditing and use the check boxes to track successful and failed events for

▸ Logon And Logoff

▸ File And Object Access

▸ Use Of User Rights

▸ User And Group Management

▸ Security Policy Changes

▸ Restart, Shutdown, And System

▸ Process Tracking

When you select one or more of these items, NT tracks occurrences of the events and stores them in the security log, which you can view in the Event Viewer. (Go to Start | Programs | Administrative Tools | Event Viewer.)

To watch for failed logons, for example, select the Logon And Logoff check box, and click OK. With this configuration, periodic checks of the Event Viewer should quickly provide evidence of a high frequency of failed logon attempts that could indicate a hacker trying to break in to your system. ◆

Securing company laptops with CompuTrace

Keeping information on an NT network secure from hackers is difficult enough without having to worry about mobile NT workstations. A user that travels with a laptop is susceptible to a different kind of threat— theft. Just a few distracted moments in an airport and the entire system's gone, and with that system a lot of sensitive information about your network. There is, however, a security system that can provide a considerable amount of protection for critical NT-based workstations on the move.

Absolute Software Corp. has developed a software/service called CompuTrace that can track down stolen laptops with great accuracy. CompuTrace is a security software utility that uses the Internet or a telephone network to regularly make automatic contacts (about once a week) to the CompuTrace Monitoring Center to update the system's status. When a computer is stolen, all you have to do is report it to CompuTrace. Absolute Software's Recovery Service then monitors incoming calls for your computer's next contact. The Recovery Service traces that call and contacts the appropriate law enforcement agency or company security department in order to recover the PC.

You may be thinking, "What if the thief erases the hard drive, obliterating the utility?" CompuTrace will still be on the job. The utility doesn't show up on a computer's regular directory listing and is protected against reformatting and disk partitioning, making it very difficult to remove from a system. Even better, when CompuTrace dials in to the CompuTrace Monitoring Center, the utility is designed to turn off the computer's modem sound, reducing the odds that the thief will realize something is happening. CompuTrace is available for Windows NT systems, as well as Windows 9x and W2K. ◆

Exterminator: AppleShare has its share of problems

By Ed Engelking

Cisco issues
Regarding: Cisco Router and IOS
Posted: May 3, 2000
Patch URL: http://www.securityfocus.com/vdb/bottom.html?section=solution&vid=1161 has patch information.
Information URL: Go to http://www.securityfocus.com/bid/1161 for more information.

SecurityFocus.com recently reported a vulnerability in the Cisco Router Online Help. According to SecurityFocus, under certain revisions of IOS, multiple Cisco routers have information leakage vulnerability in their online help systems. For more information, visit the Information URL above.

Apple issues: AppleShare
Regarding: AppleShare IP 6.1 through 6.3
Posted: May 2, 2000
Patch URL: http://www.securityfocus.com/vdb/bottom.html?section=solution&vid=1162 has patch information.
Information URL: Go to http://www.securityfocus.com/bid/1162 for more information.

SecurityFocus.com recently reported a vulnerability in Apple's AppleShare software.

According to SecurityFocus, requesting a URL containing a range exceeding the physical limit of a file will cause the Web Server in Apple-Share IP to return an extra 32 KB of information taken from RAM. The additional data will appear appended to the file requested and may contain sensitive information. For more on this issue, visit the Information URL above.

Linux issues: Linux Kernel

Regarding: Linux Kernel 2.3.x, 2.2.x, and 2.1.x
Posted: May 1, 2000
Patch URL: No known patch at this time.
Information URL: Go to
http://www.securityfocus.com/bid/1155
for more information.

SecurityFocus.com recently reported a vulnerability in the Linux Kernel, versions 2.1.x through 2.3.x. According to SecurityFocus, a denial of service exists in the Linux kernel. Due to inconsistencies in differentiating between signed and unsigned integers within the program, it becomes possible for a remote, unauthenticated use to cause the knfsd and the NFS service to be unavailable.

Linux issues: S.u.S.E

Regarding: SuSE 6.3 and 6.4
Posted: April 29, 2000
Patch URL: No known patch at this time.
Information URL: Go to
http://www.securityfocus.com/bid/1155
for more information.

SecurityFocus.com recently reported a vulnerability in S.u.S.E. versions 6.3 and 6.4.

According to SecurityFocus, a vulnerability exists in the handling of the display variable in versions of Gnomelib shipped with S.u.S.E Linux. By supplying a long buffer containing the machine executable code in the display environment variable, it is possible to execute arbitrary code with the permissions of the user running the binary. For more information, visit the information URL given above.

Virus Alerts from Trend Micro

Posted: April 26, 2000 through May 3, 2000
The following virus updates have been posted on Trend Micro's Security Info page:

- W97M_CONCON.A
- FEC
- TROJ_MUIE
- TROJ_ANTI-RS
- VBS_KILLMBR
- TROJ_SPYDER
- BAT_FORK.A
- TROJ_WIN32SYS
- W97M_BRIDGE.A
- W97M_MARKER.DB
- TROJ_WINSOUND
- VBS_FREELOVE.A
- VBS_BREAKER.A
- W97M_VISOR.A ◆

Exterminator: Windows NT receives tighter permissions

By Ed Engelking

Microsoft Security Bulletin (MS00-024)

Regarding: Microsoft Windows NT 4.0
Date Posted: April 12, 2000
Patch URL: http://www.microsoft.com/
Downloads/Release.asp?ReleaseID=20330
for the x86 patch

Patch URL: http://www.microsoft.com/
Downloads/Release.asp?ReleaseID=20331
for the Alpha patch

Microsoft posted a patch providing improved permissions in Windows NT 4.0. The default permissions could allow a user to compromise the cryptographic keys of other users who log on to the same machine. For more information, visit the Microsoft Web site.

Microsoft Security Bulletin (MS00-023)

Regarding: Microsoft IIS 4.0 and 5.0
Date Posted: April 12, 2000
Patch URL: http://www.microsoft.com/Downloads/Release.asp?ReleaseID=20292 for the 4.0 patch
Patch URL: http://www.microsoft.com/Downloads/Release.asp?ReleaseID=20286 for the 5.0 patch

Microsoft posted a patch for security vulnerability in its Internet Information Server. The bug could allow a user to slow a Web server's response, or prevent it from providing services altogether. For more information, visit the Microsoft Web site.

Microsoft Security Bulletin (MS00-022)

Regarding: Microsoft Excel
Date Posted: April 3, 2000
Patch URL: http://www.officeupdate.com/downloadDetails/Xl8p9pkg.htm?s=/downloadCatalog/dldExcel.asp for the Excel 97 patch (requires SR-2)
Patch URL: http://www.officeupdate.com/2000/downloadDetails/O2kSR1DDL.htm for the Excel 2000 patch

Microsoft recently posted a patch for their Microsoft Excel program due to vulnerability within the software. The hole could allow a macro to be run without generating the proper security warning. For more information, visit the Microsoft Web site.

BeOS Update

Regarding: BeOS 4.5 and 5.0
Date Posted: April 10, 2000
Information URL: http://www.security-focus.com/bid/1098 for more information

SecurityFocus.com posted information regarding BeOS and a security hole that can cause the OS to crash. If a user makes a direct system call using invalid parameters through int 0x25, BeOS will crash. A reboot is required to operate normally.

Virus Update

Regarding: TROJ_IRCFLOOD
Date Posted: April 10, 2000
Information URL: http://www.antivirus.com/vinfo/virusencyclo/default5.asp?VName=TROJ_IRCFLOOD for more information

Trend Micro posted an alert in their virus encyclopedia for the TROJ_IRCFLOOD Trojan. The Trojan allows for a denial of service (DOS) flood attack by a client machine. The Trojan specifically floods dal.net servers. For information on how to delete the Trojan, visit the Information URL above. ◆

There's a new Trin in town

By Erik Eckel

According to an Internet Security Systems report, a new version of Trin00 is on the loose. The new incarnation runs on Windows-based systems and can be used to coordinate Denial of Service attacks.

The Windows Trin00 variant is similar to its UNIX counterpart. The daemon service with the Windows version listens to port 34555, but it does not attempt to contact a master server.

ISS believes Trin00 is being used in conjunction with BackOrifice and SubSeven to launch attacks. More information is available from ISS.

NetWare 4.1 updates

LIPUP4J.EXE is available for NetWare 4.1 networks. The new file, released Feb. 23, 2000, updates CLIB and DSAPI v4.11r libraries.

According to Novell, the following fixes are included with the update:

▶ **CLIB:** Fixed calculations for out-of-range month days in NormalizeStructTM().

▶ **NLMLIB:** NWRConvertLocalFileHandle now returns the correct handle for a remote file handle.

You'll find more information on Novell's Web site.

ManageWise updates

Virus signature updates have been published for ManageWise for both the Windows 9x and Windows NT platforms. You can download the signatures, available for ManageWise versions 2.5 and 2.6, directly from Novell.

Linux vulnerabilities

The CERT Coordination Center is reporting that multiple vulnerabilities exist in the Cron clock daemon software developed by Paul Vixie. Increased hacker activity related to these vulnerabilities prompted CERT to distribute an advisory to UNIX administrators.

Multiple patches and security reports have targeted these vulnerabilities. For a list and for more information, visit the CERT Coordination Center.

Holy FreeBSD!

Two holes have been identified in FreeBSD.

The U.S. Department of Energy's Computer Incident Advisory Capability (CIAC) site is warning that the third-party Delegate Proxy Server software may permit hackers to execute arbitrary code. There are no patches currently available. More information can be found on the CIAC site.

A pair of vulnerabilities has also been discovered in the *asmon* and *ascpu* utilities published by Afterstep. These holes could also allow hackers to execute arbitrary code, according to CIAC. Upgrading the software can eliminate the security risk, which CIAC rates as low. ◆

DoS: Have you presented a welcome mat to a bunch of hacks?

By Erik Eckel

Coordinated, distributed denial of service (DoS) attacks paralyzed Web systems at eBay, CNN, E*Trade, and others, including Yahoo!. The latter is particularly surprising, as Yahoo! is a popular site and possesses more computing power than almost every other Web site on the planet.

Of course, a coordinated, distributed DoS attack, which brings a Web site to its knees by flooding it with bad requests, relies upon "zombie" machines that have been infected by the hackers staging the attack. It's possible you administrate one of these "zombie" machines.

System administrators can work to prevent such flare-ups by ensuring they've loaded, and are maintaining, current antivirus software on their machines. According to Internet Security Systems, the following tools are being used to launch the prevalent DoS attacks:

▶ Trin00

▶ Tribal Flood Network (TFN)

▶ Tribal Flood Network 2K (TFN2K)

▶ Stacheldraht

The eradication of such programs on compromised machines could prevent similar attacks. Administrators might want to monitor their network traffic, too, in the event that they're suspicious of malevolent behavior.

Microsoft Security Bulletin (MS00-004), take two

Back in January, Redmond released MS00-004. At the time, the bulletin targeted a hole affecting RDISK creation on Windows NT 4 Server Terminal Server Edition. The bulletin has been updated to also address issues on Windows NT Server 4.0.

The problem is that RDISK creates a temporary file during creation of an emergency rescue disk, and that file can contain sensitive security information. However, access to that security information isn't properly restricted.

You can download a patch, which addresses the issue, from Microsoft's Web site.

Trend Micro reports new backdoor Trojan on loose

Trend Micro is receiving reports of the proliferation of a new backdoor Trojan program. TROJ_SUB7GOLD.21 permits hackers to remotely control an infected machine. The program arrives as an executable.

TROJ_SUB7GOLD.21 isn't believed to have played a role in the recent DoS Web attacks, but it can be used to steal confidential information, such as credit card numbers.

Trend Micro has more information about the Trojan on its Web site. ◆

Hole found in MS Clip Gallery: Nip it in the bud

By Erik Eckel

Microsoft Security Bulletin (MS00-015)

Do your users work with Microsoft Clip Gallery? Maybe you use it on your own machine. Either way, you'll want to beware.

A security hole has been found in Microsoft's clip art program. According to Microsoft Security Bulletin (MS00-015), additional clips can be downloaded from Microsoft to complement those included with the original-issue software. A .cil file format is utilized for this purpose. Under certain conditions, an extra long field embedded in one of these .cil files could trigger a buffer overrun. In turn, this buffer error could cause a crash or execution of "hostile code."

According to Redmond's bulletin, the Microsoft Clip Gallery is included with the following products:

▶ Office 2000

▶ Works 2000

▶ Picture It! 2000

▶ Home Publishing 2000

▶ Publisher 99

▶ PhotoDraw 2000 Version 1

A patch, and more information, are available at http://cgl.microsoft.com/clipgallerylive/pss/bufovrun.htm.

Novell client update

Novell has released NT47PT2.EXE, an update for Client 4.7 for Windows NT/2000, on its site. The Novell client for Windows NT fixes several problems and errors. Among the fixes is a correction of the contextless login window being displayed before the GUI login.

More information is available on Novell's site.

ManageWise updates

New virus updates have been released for ManageWise versions 2.5 and 2.6. New files are available on Novell's site for both the Windows 9x and NT platforms.

More information on the version 9.20 updates can be found at http://support.novell.com/misc/patlst.htm. ◆

Exterminator: Windows 2000 has IP limitations

By Ed Engelking

Microsoft bug issues

Regarding: Windows 2000 Server

Date Posted: April 5, 2000

Information URL: http://www.msnbc.com/news/388430.asp?0m=T23F has more information from MSNBC.

MSNBC recently reported a problem within Windows 2000 regarding Internet Protocol (IP) addresses. The report states that Windows 2000 limits the number of IP addresses assigned to any combination of network interface cards (NICs) to 51. Once 52 or more IP addresses have been assigned, Active Directory misplaces all of its directory objects. For more information, visit the Information URL given above.

Microsoft Security Bulletin (MS00-019)

Regarding: Internet Information Server 4.0 and 5.0

Date Posted: March 30, 2000

Patch URL: http://www.microsoft.com/downloads/release.asp?ReleaseID=18900 for the Intel 4.0 patch

Patch URL: http://www.microsoft.com/downloads/release.asp?ReleaseID=18901 for the Alpha 4.0 patch

Patch URL: http://www.microsoft.com/downloads/release.asp?ReleaseID=19982 for the 5.0 patch

Microsoft has released a patch that fixes vulnerability in IIS version 4.0 and 5.0, as well as the products that are based on it. Microsoft states, "under certain fairly unusual conditions, the vulnerability could cause a Web server to send the source code of .asp and other files to a visiting user." For more information, visit Microsoft's Web site.

Microsoft Security Bulletin (MS00-021)

Regarding: Windows NT 4.0 and Windows 2000

Date Posted: March 30, 2000

Patch URL: http://www.microsoft.com/Downloads/Release.asp?ReleaseID=19884 for Windows 2000 Server and Advanced Server

Patch URL: http://www.microsoft.com/Downloads/Release.asp?ReleaseID=20015 for Windows NT 4.0 for Intel

Patch URL: http://www.microsoft.com/Downloads/Release.asp?ReleaseID=20016 for Windows NT 4.0 for Alpha

Microsoft has released a patch that eliminates vulnerability in the Transmission Control Protocol/Internet Protocol (TCP/IP) Printing Services for Microsoft Windows NT 4.0 and Windows 2000. If this service is installed on your system, the vulnerability could allow users to disrupt printing services. A specific malformed request could cause the service to crash, causing several other services, such as Dynamic Host Configuration Protocol (DHCP), to stop. For more information, visit Microsoft's Web site.

Linux bug issues

Regarding: Linux Kernel 2.2.x, RedHat 6.x, Debian 2.x

Date Posted: March 29, 2000

Information URL: http://www.securityfocus.com/vdb/bottom.html?vid=1078 for more information

SecurityFocus.com reports that there is vulnerability in the IP Masquerading code present in the Linux 2.2.x kernel. The site states, "due to poor checking of connections in the kernel code, an attacker can potentially rewrite the User Datagram Protocol (UDP) masquerading entries, making it possible for UDP packets to be routed back to the internal machine." For more information, click the Information URL given above.

Virus Alert

Regarding: BAT_CHODE911 a.k.a. 911 Virus

Date Posted: April 3, 2000

Information URL: Go to http://www.antivirus.com/vinfo/virusencyclo/default5.asp?VName=BAT_CHODE911 for more information.

OS Affected: Windows 9x, Windows NT, Windows 2000

Trend Micro recently reported a new virus known as BAT_CHODE911, more commonly referred to as the 911 Virus. The virus has several payloads, some of which can be destructive. When activated, the virus randomly chooses a payload to execute. For more information on this virus, check TechRepublic's Virus Alert. ◆

Exterminator: New vulnerabilities plague SQL Server 7.0

By Ed Engelking

Vulnerability in Microsoft SQL Server 7.0

Regarding: Microsoft SQL Server 7.0
Date posted: March 14, 2000
Information URL: http://xforce.iss.net/ alerts/advise45.php3

According to an alert posting on the XForce Web site, there is a hole in the Microsoft SQL Server 7.0 encryption step used to store administrative login ID. The vulnerability, reported by Internet Security Systems, is caused by a weak encryption value stored in the Windows registry. For more information, visit the XForce Web site by using the information URL above.

Microsoft Security Bulletin (MS00-014)

Regarding: Microsoft SQL Server 7.0 and Microsoft Data Engine 1.0
Date posted by Microsoft: March 8, 2000
Patch URL: http://www.microsoft.com/ downloads/release.asp?ReleaseID=19132

Microsoft recently released a patch for its SQL Server 7.0 and Microsoft Data Engine 1.0. The patch eliminates a vulnerability that could allow the remote author of a SQL query to take actions on a SQL Server or MSDE database without authorization. For more information, visit Microsoft's Web site.

Microsoft Security Bulletin (MS00-008)

Regarding: Microsoft NT 4.0
Date posted by Microsoft: March 9, 2000
Patch URL: Intel - http://www.microsoft.com/ downloads/release.asp?ReleaseID=19172
Patch URL: Alpha - http://www.microsoft.com/ downloads/release.asp?ReleaseID=19173

Microsoft recently released a tool that gives tighter permissions on three sets of registry values in NT 4.0. The original permissions could allow a user to gain privileges on a machine that they are able to log on to interactively. This bug does not have an effect on Windows 2000. For more information, visit Microsoft's Web site.

Novell update

Regarding: NetWare Administrator 5.19
Date posted: March 14, 2000
Patch URL: http://support.novell.com/cgibin/ search/download?sr&/pub/updates/cp/cpdid ompr/admn519f.exe

Novell has recently updated its NetWare Administrator program. This patch addresses a problem that occurs when NWAdmin runs out of Thread Local Storage (TLS) handles due to the amount of DLL snap-ins it loads. The symptoms occur on workstations that load NWADMN32.EXE from a server with multiple products installed, which in turn use snap-ins to NWADMN32. Symptoms include the messages "C++ Runtime Error" or "dll is missing or corrupt" when loading NWADMN32. For more information, visit the Novell Web site.

Novell update

Regarding: ManageWise—Virus Signature 9.31 Update
Date posted: March 13, 2000
Patch URL: http://support.novell.com/cgibin/ search/download?sr&/pub/updates/man/ mwise/mwinoc2j.exe (NT Only)

Novell released a virus signature update and service pack for its InocuLAN version 4.0 for both Windows NT and 9x. The patch may be used for either ManageWise 2.5 or 2.6. For more information, visit the Novell Web site.

Virus Update: KALI virus doesn't need to be cured

Regarding: KALI, a.k.a. Let's Watch TV
Date posted: March 8, 2000
Status of virus: Hoax
Risk: Low

Network Associates released a statement on March 8, 2000, describing the KALI virus as a hoax. Also known as "Let's Watch TV," the hoax is sent in e-mail by concerned users who may be tricked into believing there is such a virus. This e-mail hoax is not related to the existing known virus named "Kali-4." For more information, visit Network Associates Web site. ◆

Block those ports!

By Ed Bott

When setting up a firewall or proxy server, one of the most important tasks is to block undesirable incoming and outgoing ports and allow only the ones you need. Besides being time-consuming, this task can also be frustrating, because the basic information isn't readily at hand. Recently, I asked TechRepublic members to help me compile an authoritative and comprehensive list of TCP/IP and UDP ports. Boy, did you all come through!

Delivering a succinct analysis of the problem, **huba** writes, "In the perfect scenario, you would deny all connections (any connection from anywhere to any port) and allow only those connections to ports that you find out you really need to open up. Of course, this perfect security world is an unusable system from a user's perspective…Your best bet is to find a peer at an organization that does similar work and ask them what they block, what they allow, and why." Excellent advice.

Suggested links

The most popular link, by far, is the official list of port numbers maintained by the Internet Assigned Numbers Authority, or IANA. (Save this bookmark, because it takes far too many clicks to get to this important resource from the IANA home page.) By definition, of course, this list is authoritative, but it lacks even the most basic ease-of-use features or any sort of explanation to accompany its terse listing. Every Windows NT/2000-based machine includes a Windows-centric excerpt from the IANA list in a file called Services (no extension). You'll find this file in the %systemroot%\system32\drivers\etc directory.

I was impressed with the sheer number of unofficial sites that TechRepublic members suggested. After reviewing most of them, however, I offer this caution: Most such sites are poorly maintained and do little more than duplicate the information found elsewhere. Among the suggested links, I found sites that were last updated in mid 1999, 1997, 1996, and even 1995. Needless to say, any port listing that doesn't get an update at least a few times a year is likely to contain some significant gaps.

Of all the "volunteer" sites, I was most impressed by the source that **calves** suggested. Richard Akerman's list of TCP/IP ports for Internet services comes from the Great White North. It's an excellent compendium, and the site is updated frequently. While not comprehensive or especially authoritative, it does do a good job of covering the ports used by popular messaging programs (NetMeeting, AOL Instant Messenger) and data-streaming applications (Liquid Audio, VDOLive). I especially enjoyed Mr. Akerman's wry sense of humor—he titled the page "Any Port in a Datastorm." And his mission statement is spot-on: "It seems like every day there is a new Internet service that uses some new set of poorly documented, unregistered ports. I created this page to gather together all the information I could find about the ports used by these new services, for use by firewall administrators and other network monitors."

Two TechRepublic members offered pointers to sites that help you keep the forces of darkness at bay. As **pshannon** points out, there's no substitute for recent experience. "I have three offices connected in a VPN using Netscreen's product, and I'm in the process of blocking the unused ports myself." Besides the authoritative IANA list, he recommends the full list of ports maintained by NetworkICE, makers of the BlackIce Defender security software. Mixed in with the well-known ports (FTP, SMTP, and the like) are ports commonly used by Trojan horses and other malware.

An even more extensive list of ports used by trojans is available courtesy of a Swedish firm called Simovits Consulting. The list was updated as recently as March of this year, and the author includes a link for e-mail. ◆

IPSec and L2TP lead the Windows 2000 security lineup

By John McCormick

You've heard all the hoopla, and there's only going to be more. Windows 2000's improved security features are already making the rounds.

Why? As I mention in the following article "New Virtual Private Network security options coming with Windows 2000," much of the hype is due to enhanced security in the new OS, including support for Internet Protocol Security (IPSec) and the Layer 2 Tunneling Protocol (L2TP).

L2TP is essentially a merger of Cisco Systems' L2F (Layer 2 Forwarding) and PPTP (Point to Point Tunneling Protocol, developed by Microsoft, U.S. Robotics, and others). L2TP was developed through the IETF (Internet Engineering Task Force) standards process. One of its chief functions is to provide a mechanism for remote users connecting to a local ISP to tunnel to a remote network.

It's important to remember that L2TP does not conflict with or replace IPSec. L2TP can and should be used in conjunction with IPSec tools to secure a virtual private network.

IPSec overview

IPSec operates in two modes. Transport mode secures existing IP packets between source and destination. Tunnel mode encapsulates the existing IP packet inside another packet. In either mode, the packets can be encapsulated in Encapsulated Security Payload (ESP) or Authentication Headers (AH).

IPSec's transport mode offers security, replay, and authentication protection between systems. IPSec's tunnel mode operates between one private IP network (router or gateway) and another, including over the Internet.

In basic terms, IPSec addresses server-to-server tunneling, not client-to-server tunneling. That's L2TP's job.

Of course, that's a simplification, but it gets us started in looking at the virtual private network features found in Windows 2000. According to Microsoft, Win2K is the only "operating system-integrated solution for securing end-to-end communications within a private network.

Windows 2000 integrates IPSec with the Active Directory directory service to deliver central control of policy based security administration."

Microsoft claims that the OS will support client/server PPTP- and L2TP-based virtual private networks running over IPSec, as well as server-to-server tunnels based on PPTP, L2TP, and IPSec.

L2TP overview

L2TP is a protocol that defines a method of encapsulating and transporting multi-protocol data packets in point-to-point links. It extends the Point-to-Point (PPP) protocol by allowing the layer-2 and PPP endpoints to exist on different devices connected by a packet-switched network.

L2TP manages data frames (PPP), which are sent over IP, ATM, X.25, or frame-relay networks, and includes support for non-Internet Protocol (IP) packets, including AppleTalk and NetWare IPX (a feature taken from PPTP).

Control and data messages in any L2TP implementation are, by default, checksum protected. UDP checksums can optionally be disabled for data messages. However, this can weaken the security.

The L2TP payload and header are held within a UDP datagram. The frames themselves can be either compressed or encrypted and, since they can be sent as IP packets, standard IPSec-compatible security can (and should) be applied. This means L2TP data can use standard authentication, privacy, and replay protection.

As usual, there is fresh jargon to go with the new technology. Here are some brief definitions of terms you'll be hearing, if you haven't heard them already:

- **NAS**—Network Access Server

- **LAC (L2TP Access Concentrator)**—a PPP- and L2TP-capable device with telephone system or ISDN connections

- **LNS (L2TP Network Server)**—the server side of the L2TP protocol that terminates calls originating at PPP calls

> **NOTE**
> It's important to remember that Microsoft has its own definition of VPN, which may vary from yours. Microsoft considers VPNs to include:
>
> ▸ Secure remote access from client-to-gateway, either through Internet connections or within private or outsourced networks.
>
> ▸ Secure gateway-to-gateway connections, across the Internet or across private or outsourced networks.

The tunnel in L2TP is created between the LAC and LNS. For more basic definitions, see the mini-glossary below.

In a typical L2TP session:

▶ Remote user contacts the NAS using PPP connection.

▶ After the NAS determines that the user has authorization, the NAS/LAC component attempts to connect to the LNS through a tunnel.

▶ LNS authenticates user and completes the tunnel connection.

▶ LNS and user device exchange PPP negotiations.

▶ Data is now exchanged between user and LNS through the tunnel.

We don't need no stinking tunnels!

Before you decide that you do or don't need L2TP, it helps to know just what an L2TP tunnel is. **Figure A** illustrates an L2TP session. The L2TP tunnel is an L2TP frame encapsulated in a User Datagram Protocol (UDP) packet placed inside an IP packet carrying the tunnel origin and destination address. It looks roughly like this:

(IP packet(UDP(L2TP)UDP)IP packet)

You also need to know what an LT2P tunnel isn't.

Strong authentication control is available when the L2TP tunnel is initiated, but that only applies to the endpoints. There is no authentication for the individual data packets and, therefore, no way to know if someone has altered the data. This can leave the connection open to denial-of-service attacks, which close the tunnel by faking control packets.

L2TP tunnels are an important component of secure low-cost remote access. But, as we mentioned earlier, IPSec is also needed to provide enhanced security. Together they make a strong combination.

IPSec, L2TP, PPTP, and L2F

A Microsoft FAQ compares IPSec and PPTP this way:

IPSec offers Compression and Encryption. PPTP offers MPPC (Microsoft Point to Point Compression), Address Allocation, Multi-protocol support, MPPE (MS PTP Encryption), Flow Control, and Token Cards (in Windows 2000).

There are several differences between L2F and L2TP, but the most important is that L2TP offers vendor interoperability and isn't limited to Cisco users.

Mini-glossary

▶ **UDP**—User Datagram Protocol is a TCP/IP protocol generally used instead of TCP for streaming data such as audio and video, where it doesn't matter if a few packets are lost (or at least there is nothing you can do about it because there's no time for retransmission of lost packets).

▶ **SSL**—Secure Socket Layer, a security protocol operating at Layer 4. IPSec operates at Layer 3.

▶ **Layer 2**—the data-link layer (also MAC, or Media Access Control, layer) that contains the actual physical address of the server or client. MAC (e.g., CSMA/CD for Ethernet or Token Ring passing protocols) is built in to the network adapter.

▶ **Layer 3**—the network layer that contains the physical IP, IPX, or other address used by routers to forward packets.

▶ **Layer 4**—that part of the OSI model that controls the establishment of a connection. ◆

Figure A

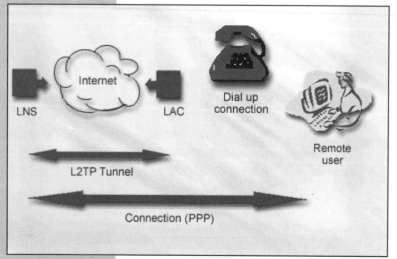

This is an L2TP Session Diagram.

New Virtual Private Network security options in Windows 2000

By John McCormick

Look for an explosion of trade publication hype about Virtual Private Networks (VPNs) over the next year. Why? Because administrators will find many new VPN security options and tools in Win2K.

A lot of admins are already struggling to make a VPN work, but Windows NT managers in particular may need a refresher course. They'll encounter some new tools when upgrading to Windows 2000—tools that will make implementing a VPN much more practical.

First, just what is a VPN?

Everybody talks about taking a company on the 'net, referring to e-commerce, or a connection between the sales force and customers. But, unless you're a retail business, this doesn't matter very much to your business plan. The importance of the Internet to many companies is the way it can be used as a backbone to extend local office applications and data to branch offices. Of course, this is nothing new for giant corporations, which have long used leased lines and dial-up, modem-to-modem connections to share data between distant offices.

My first experience with leased lines was decades ago when we used them to link the WGBH-TV [PBS, Boston] remote cameras and sub-station to local control and master control rooms. This approach was used to move video signals in the days before satellite links, but the concept is the same whether you're moving accounting data or video signals.

What's new is the "virtual" part, which refers to the use of secure technologies to let companies use the extremely public (and extremely cheap) Internet to replace dedicated and relatively secure connections used in what you might call "real" private networks.

If you've never had serious security concerns before, the mere thought of your company's daily business transactions and precious accounting or engineering data being passed around the Internet second-by-second on a 24/7 basis should be a real wake-up call!

Not only do you have to worry about outsiders getting a peek at your confidential information (the way you do when they dumpster dive or gain access to tape or floppy diskette copies of some of your computer files); you now have to make certain that they don't modify data between the time it leaves one office and the time it arrives at another distant office, possibly insinuating false information into your system undetected. In other words, to run a safe VPN and realize the cost savings from giving up leased lines or not having to set up entirely new systems at each branch office, you must find ways to prevent copying, deleting, modifying, or even falsifying entire files—and you must do all this over an extremely public communications system.

In five years, almost anyone who's interested in your data will be able to build a supercomputer in a few days. So, although encryption is an important tool in protecting the data you send over a Web-based VPN, it's only the beginning.

New tools for Windows 2000

Windows 95, Windows 98, and NTW/S (workstation and server) 4.0 support Microsoft's PPTP (Point to Point Tunneling Protocol), which provides for encrypted communication sessions between a PPTP client (all Windows platforms, or even Macintosh, with third-party tools) and a PPTP (Windows NT) server. That works for the Microsoft universe, but it leaves out a very large part of the world.

Cisco Systems' Layer 2 Forwarding (L2F) was developed in the mid-'90s, about the same time as PPTP. What's new for Windows 2000 is Layer Two Tunneling Protocol (L2TP), a combination of the best parts of both. L2TP is actually a mature Internet Engineering Task Force protocol.

Working together

IPSec (Internet Protocol Security) provides tools for encryption, authentication, and more. IPSec is a network layer security protocol and, although it has been used to support server-to-server tunneling, it's not intended for client-to-server tunneling. Thus, IPSec and PPTP or L2F, and the combined L2TP, are complementary.

Microsoft says it will support client/server PPTP/L2TP-based virtual private network sessions running over IPSec in Windows 2000 (NT 5), but it will continue to support server/server tunneling based on PPTP to ensure a smooth transition.

For information on all active IETF security working groups, check out http://www.ietf.org/html.charters/wg-dir.html#Security_Area. ◆

Simple security tips for Windows NT servers

By Ed Engelking

Windows NT Server provides a number of security measures to protect your organization, from simple things, such as ensuring the correct use of passwords, to sophisticated measures, such as screening calls upon dial-in. Are you using all of the necessary features to keep your network secure?

What to do with old user accounts

Do you have a user who has recently left your organization? Your position as the system administrator requires that you terminate access to that account on the network. You have two ways to go about doing this: the hard way or the easy way.

▶ **Deleting user accounts:** This is a permanent action to take when a user has left your organization. Once the account is deleted, the information stored within that account, such as permissions and security identifier (SID), is erased. Once the SID is erased, an administrator can't reinstate the account simply by creating a new account with the same name. It will require a different SID, and NT will consider it a different account.

Table A: *Settings for various security needs*

User property	Minimal security	Moderate security	High Security
Hours of access	No restrictions	Restrict temporary employees to office hours	Restrict all users to office hours only
Logon To	No restrictions	Restrict temporary employees to computers they normally work on	Restrict all users to one computer
Account Expiration	Temporary employees	Temporary employees only	Set expiration date for temporary employees only
Dial-in (RAS)	No restrictions	Limit to the Callback number set by the caller	Limit to the preset Callback number
Rename the administrator account			

▶ **Disable user accounts:** This is the safe way to go when an employee leaves the organization. You can disable the account rather than deleting it, which can save you the effort of starting from scratch when you hire a new employee. By doing this, you will not have to create a new user account, reassign appropriate access permissions, user rights, and group memberships. The only work required is to rename the account. Note, however, that some permissions may have to be changed, unless the network is set to grant permissions via groups instead of individuals.

Controlling users via User Properties

In a moderate- to high-security environment, it is advisable to control certain aspects of user access via the User Properties dialog box. **Table A** suggests settings for various security needs.

Another important step in securing your network is to rename the administrator account with a less obvious name. The administrator account offers an easy way for unauthorized users to break in to the network by guessing passwords. Unauthorized users like to hack the administrator account for three reasons:

1. The account name, Administrator, is a given, so it is easy to try to access that account by guessing the password.

2. It is impossible to disable the Administrator account.

3. You can't lock out the Administrator account even after repeated logon attempt failures.

While renaming the administrator account on Windows NT 4.0 doesn't present a problem to the administrator, doing so on NT 3.5x could keep certain utilities from operating correctly because they depend on the name being unchanged. In addition, international versions of NT could also be adversely affected by a name change.

Passwords are a great thing if used correctly

One of the hardest things to do in an organization is to get users to comply with policies requiring hard-to-guess passwords and frequent password changes. To set up a hard-to-guess password, it is suggested that users use the following guidelines:

▶ Passwords should be at least six characters long.

▶ Passwords must not contain the user's name or any part of the user's full name.

▶ Passwords should contain at least three of the following four classes: English uppercase letters A-Z, English lowercase letters a-z, westernized Arabic numbers 0-1, and special characters such as *, ?, and #.

There are some additional steps that may help keep the passwords safe:

▶ Educate users not to write down their passwords.

▶ Have users avoid obvious passwords, such as the names of the user's children or spouse.

▶ Do not distribute user accounts and passwords in the same communication. For example, if you were to send users their password in e-mail, send it separately from the account name that they must use.

Use NT to your advantage

Using hard-to-guess passwords is a step in the right direction, but you can also bolster Windows NT Server security by using the account lockout feature. This will make it extremely difficult for a person to break in to an account.

When this feature is enabled, the account will lock if someone makes a certain number of incorrect logon attempts. Once this occurs, only the administrator can take off the block, or a certain time period must pass before access to the account is permitted once again.

Keep Windows NT holes patched

Microsoft offers security enhancements by offering service packs and security patches from its Web site. It's a good idea to monitor the site for the newest upgrades and to implement them when they're suitable for your organization. ◆

Make sure your hardware doesn't walk out the door

By Jeff Davis

We spend a lot of time trying to defend our systems against attack from software viruses, worms, and hacks, but we shouldn't limit ourselves to software protection. In some shops, the threat of hardware theft is real and shouldn't be ignored. If you've been looking for some way to lock down your machines, start your shopping at the home pages of Securityware and Innovative Security Products.

Get your cables and padlocks here

Securityware is a California-based manufacturer of anti-theft devices for computers, printers, fax machines, and other electronic devices. Its products not only lock a machine in place but can also prevent unauthorized access to a computer's interior components.

The firm offers products specially made for Apple computers as well as lock-down solutions for tower PCs and desktop machines. It even sells the equivalent of a bicycle lock system—a metal cable and a lock—for laptop owners to use when they're traveling and want to prevent their laptops from being swiped.

One thing I like about the site is the abundance of high-quality pictures of the products. You get a good idea of how the products will look if you attach them to furniture in your offices. For your convenience, there's a secure online order form.

Pick up alarms and ultraviolet marking pens here

Innovative Security Products is a Kansas-based company that offers many products similar to those you'll find at Securityware. In addition to lock-down products, Innovative Security Products has a product that creates a loud, shrill alarm if someone tries to tamper with the device to which it's attached.

It also has an interesting product that lets you or the police identify stolen furniture, computer components, and even compact discs—a special ultraviolet marking pen that writes on glass, paper, plastic, metal, wood, and cloth, and cannot be washed or rubbed off.

One nice feature is the ability to request a brochure and price list by clicking a link and completing a form. In addition, there's a pretty good white paper on the site that covers the basic principles of securing systems in your enterprise. ◆

How to avoid getting an $80,000 long-distance phone bill for Christmas

By Jake Necessary

"T was the nightmare before Christmas; the workplace was a loss; everyone was at home except for the boss."

The following is a true story, but the names have been changed to protect the innocent (and the guilty).

If no one's in the office, the lines shouldn't be busy

James Wafflehouse, the owner of a small telemarketing company, had dropped by the office to wrap up a few things. Scrooge was downright charitable compared to this executive. Although Christmas was a company holiday (a day off) this year, no trees or other decorations were allowed.

Before leaving the office, Wafflehouse decided to call his children, who live across the country, when suddenly there arose a clatter (inside the phone, that is). Wafflehouse had cursed these particular phones for years and was by no means technically skilled.

Fumbling through his wallet, he found the system administrator's business card. Billy had only worked for the company for about two months. When his cell phone began to ring, he was at home enjoying the holiday with his wife, daughter, and little Tim. Billy answered the call and talked with a frustrated Wafflehouse, who described a fast busy signal and the inability to make a long distance call.

Billy was instantly worried. This problem had arisen a few times during peak hours. He knew the symptoms well. His outgoing phone lines were busy. But how? No one but Wafflehouse was at the office.

Suddenly, Billy realized he had big trouble. The company's phone system was lighting up like a Christmas tree. There appeared to be many users on the system. The only answer? *The company's phone system had been hacked!*

Jake's take

I wish that this were just a "nightmare before Christmas" story, but this is a serious problem for technicians. Without the proper security measures, hackers will break inside and wreak havoc. If they don't use the phone system to get into the computers, they still can run up the company phone bill in no time.

A few hours of hacker mayhem can result in thousands of dollars in unwanted phone charges. For example, my company has nearly 100 phone lines. If all lines were busy with activity for one hour and a generous rate of eight cents an hour was applied to our bill, the total bill for just one hour would come to nearly 500 dollars. And that number doesn't include costs that might be incurred from dialing 900 numbers.

The plain truth is a hacker's one-night stand can cost thousands of dollars. Who is the fall guy? You, the phone administrator!

To help secure your phone system, you must understand three basic processes: discovery, prevention techniques, and periodic maintenance. Here's the scoop.

Discovery

Discovery is the documentation stage, or the process by which an IS team establishes a starting point for analyzing phone system security issues. As in any goal-setting activity, you must set the baseline. To do so, you need to determine the current state of your system security.

You will need this pre-assessment of the phone system in order to document the system on paper. I recommend getting a three-ring binder and setting up several tabs for lists, including the following: Trunk Groups, Hunt Groups, Class of Service, Class of Restriction, Dial-Plan, Digit Analysis, Stations, Agents, Vectors, VDNs, and various system feature configurations. Having documentation handy will help during day-to-day operations, troubleshooting, system recovery, and security.

The telephone system manager must have proper training on phone system operations and programming in order to do a decent job in the discovery process. If you're an administrator who's new to the phone system, hire an outside consultant to perform the discovery process. Your phone system vendor may be willing to assist you in the discovery process free of charge or at a reduced rate.

Prevention and maintenance

Once you've documented your phone system, the administrator can figure out if there are any security loopholes. Administrators must tighten the reins on phone system security and not be

DON'T BE FOOLED BY THIS SCAM

The following problem has been reported throughout the nation. Some criminals have been calling large corporations, stating that they are technicians from the local phone company or the particular corporation's long-distance provider. Once the receptionist has been conned into believing their story, they state that

some problems have been reported and that, in order to fix the problems, they need to be transferred to a specific extension, usually beginning with "9." What the receptionist is actually doing is transferring them to an outside line. These criminals are then making their long-distance calls on the company's dime! An ounce of

training can prevent this type of criminal activity. Normal phone users would have the ability to perform this off-net transfer. If administrators follow the most restrictive form of administration, however, the phone system will prevent these kinds of transfers from non-receptionists.

afraid to restrict access to certain features for all users.

Here's one way to prevent a breach in phone security: Limit the functions available to all users. Let your phone system users start out with very few rights to advanced features. Then, slowly and selectively, you can give your users access to functions that they need. Never allow rights to a user if they do not need them.

This restrictive attitude should be especially followed with call forwarding, off-net dialing, and out-dial functionality. These features are the ones that can cause security holes.

Prevent conference call trickery

Another example of off-net usage is personal use of conference calls (to call relatives who are long distance) on the company's dime. To prevent this activity, use call accounting codes or Call Detail Recording (CDR). CDR is software that monitors outgoing phone calls and traces them back to individuals. Typically, the thought

that "Big Brother" is watching every phone call made is enough to prevent users from making these kinds of calls.

Phone system security is similar to network security, so borrow from the network security measures. One of the best practices is to frequently change the administration passwords. This practice is absolutely necessary if you're the new administrator on the telephone block. You don't want your predecessor or any disgruntled employees to be able to dial in to the phone system. Change the administrator's password frequently, and always disable the passwords and accounts of employees who have left the company.

Finally, utilize all the reporting power of the phone system. Develop a routine for reviewing phone system activity. Through time you will become accustomed to your phone system's usage.

Any activity that appears to be "out of the norm" will be easily identified if you've been watching your reports. ◆

HOW'S YOUR PHONE SYSTEM TODAY?

Phone security is a big deal! There are millions of ways hackers can attack. We must keep our security ball caps in place. Through the process of discovery, we can develop a layout of our phone system. The utilization of training, reporting, prevention, and maintenance techniques will make your phone system a safe communications tool.

Keeping those nasty LOVE bugs off your Linux servers

By Jack Wallen, Jr.

With the onslaught of the newest bugs, viruses, and Trojan horses cutting down desktops and servers left and right, it's imperative that we all have our systems set up with the highest possible security in place.

In a perfect world, we wouldn't have to deal with these situations, and in a perfect network-

ing setup, we wouldn't have to take precautions. Unfortunately, no one has found the perfect networking setup—so we're bound to precaution and locked into paranoia.

As long as Microsoft products are going to dominate the networks, we Linux folk know that there will be problems—it's inevitable.

The Microsoft model is *open for business* when it comes to security issues. IT professionals know it, and they've (seemingly) come to accept it. People using Linux as their servers know better.

With the attitude of hackers leaning toward the flagrant guerilla attempts to take down all Microsoft machines and applications, more and more people are hopping on the Linux wagon for their server needs. Linux can be used as an amazing Web server, FTP server, mail server, file server, and print server. It's simple to set up and painless to administer.

But what happens when you have to serve up files to a Windows farm? Imagine this: You're using one Red Hat 6.2 box as a mail server and another for a file server. One day, an innocent user allows the ILOVEYOU virus into his or her system, and all of a sudden you have an entire barnyard of sick Microsoft cows and pigs. Yes, the Linux server happily chugs along the food trough, but the stock is simply dying. What do you do? Fortunately, you're using Linux, so the solution is simple.

Filtering mail attachments with procmail

The solution is to use *procmail* to filter your mail attachments. By using the amazing *.procmailrc* file, you can add entries that will keep all those nasty ILOVEYOU's out of your system. A very simple recipe for the *.procmailrc* file is the following:

```
:0:
* ^Subject:.ILOVEYOU
/dev/null
```

The above recipe will delete only e-mail with the subject *ILOVEYOU*. Of course, the problem lies with all the variants you'll inevitably encounter.

Another approach (and less invasive) would be to mark each e-mail suspect. To do this, add the following to your *.procmailrc* file:

```
:0
* ^Content-Type: multipart/mixed;
* B ?? \\.vbs
{
 :0 c:
 /var/mail/attachments.vbs
```

```
:0 h f
| /bin/sed -e 's/^Subject:/Subject:
[ALERT: MAY CONTAIN A VIRUS
ATTACHMENT]/'
}
```

This code will check the entire body of the message for *.vbs* and, if *.vbs* appears in the body of the message, mark the message suspect. Unfortunately, this is not a true cure. We still need to be able to get rid of the suspect e-mail before it gets into the target's inbox.

There is another way to deal with these possible threats. An attached file can do no harm to a Microsoft machine *unless* it is executed. If, with *procmail*, you mangle that executable's extension (change it from .vbs to BROKEN-vbs), the user can no longer *mistakenly* execute the corrupted file.

The script for this process is quite large and can be found at ftp://ftp.rubyriver.com/pub/jhardin/antispam/html-trap.procmail. Download this file and add it to your *.procmailrc* file.

Cleaning a Linux server

What if your Linux file server happens to be currently doling out files with the corrupted attachment? A very simple solution would be to put the following script in your root *cron* (preferably */etc/cron.daily*):

```
0 4 * * * find / -name *vbs -exec rm
{} \;
```

With this job in place at 12:04 A.M., all files with the extension .vbs will be deleted.

Of course, this brings up yet another problem. What if there are necessary files with the .vbs extension on the server? In that case, you could place those files on a separate partition and exclude them from the above search.

Conclusion

Yes, it's a crazy world out there, and crazy things are happening! The IT industry is up in arms, desperately trying to find a solution for this madness. Until a perfect solution is discovered, your best bet is to avoid the issue altogether: Delete your enemy! ◆

Changing network logon passwords—simple skill, big payoff

By Jody Gilbert

Changing passwords is one of those computer housekeeping chores that most of us handle routinely—although maybe not as often as we should. But a lot of users aren't aware of the importance of periodically setting new passwords—or worse yet, are unaware that they *can*.

It may seem like a minor shortcoming, but companies that want to prevent IT resources from being siphoned off into minor support tasks are demanding a higher level of user self-reliance. Picture an enterprise that's in the midst of rolling out new network server software. Users need to change their logon passwords, but administrators shouldn't have to go from desktop to desktop, helping them through the process.

Fortunately, you can teach your students to update their logon passwords regularly as a common-sense measure and whenever a network upgrade demands it. Here's a simple walk-through of the steps for changing the NT logon password on a Windows 98 machine that will get your students up to speed on this basic skill.

▶ Click the Start button on Windows' taskbar, choose Settings, and select Control Panel.

▶ When the Control Panel window appears, double-click the Passwords icon to open the Password Properties dialog box.

▶ In the Change Passwords tab (the default), click the Change Other Passwords button.

▶ In the Select Password dialog box, choose the appropriate service from the list box (Microsoft Networking, in this example).

▶ Just click Change and then type the old password, the new password, and the new password again for confirmation. (If you're teaching a basic-level class, be sure to explain that the asterisks are merely Windows' way of hiding the characters they type from prying eyes.)

▶ Click OK. Windows will present a message telling you that the password has been changed.

▶ Click OK again, then click Close to exit the Password Properties dialog box. ◆

Figure A

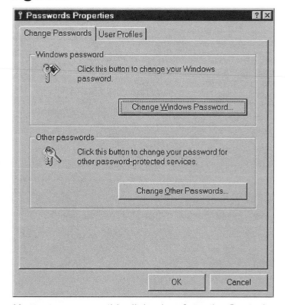

Users can access this dialog box from the Control Panel window.

Figure B

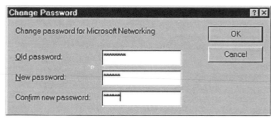

Windows will ask for the old password once and for the new password twice.

Don't let the cat erase your password

By Jeff Davis

A funny thing happened to my home computer recently. I tried to connect to my Internet service provider (ISP) and kept getting kicked out during the username and password verification process. Unfortunately, the password wasn't one I had created—it was set for me by my ISP—and I couldn't remember it. And I had never written down the password, so I had to call with my billing credit card handy in order to get the ISP to divulge the password over the phone.

The cat did it

I'm pretty sure my cat erased my password. My theory is that I left the desktop shortcut selected, the cat stepped on the [Enter] key on the end of the keyboard, which launched the connectoid, and then stepped on another key. That misstep left one asterisk where there used to be eight in the password field.

Of course, the Save This Password option was activated, so the connectoid saved the single-character entry. The net effect was that I had no Web access until I made the call to the ISP.

Moral of the story: Write down your passwords somewhere. I realize this tip falls under the category of "incredibly obvious, commonsense things to do." But if you take time to document your passwords today, you'll thank me the next time you need one of them.

The challenge, of course, is documenting your passwords without making them accessible to snoops. Put them in your little black book? Put them in your wallet? Maybe you should print a list of passwords and put the list in a double-secret file drawer somewhere.

For now, I'm going with the "yellow sticky note stuck under the monitor" approach, but there's got to be a better way. ◆

Increase security by adding password protection to your screen saver

By Jeff Davis

Can people off the streets—job applicants, customers, delivery people—stroll through your offices unattended? If so, your users may be using a screen saver to hide sensitive data when they're at lunch, on break, or in a meeting.

However, if someone taps the spacebar or jiggles the mouse, that sensitive data is now available to a casual snoop. That's why many support pros recommend that their users enable password protection to get past the screen saver. It requires the user to do a little extra typing to get back to work, but in many cases the extra security is worth the effort.

Creating a screen saver password

In Windows 98, you activate the screen saver password by right-clicking on the desktop, choosing Properties, and clicking the Screen saver tab. To enable password protection, one of the screen saver options must be selected—that is, you can't apply a password if your screen saver is set to "None."

Then click the Password Protected check box, and select Change. That step will display the Change Password dialog box, which lets you create or change the password that allows you to get past the screen saver and back to the desktop.

The power-saver password is the Windows password

If your users activate the power-saving settings, they can tell Windows 98 to require a password when the machine comes out of standby mode. To enable this protection, right-click on the desktop, choose Properties, and then click the Screensaver tab. This time, click the Settings button in the energy-saving features section to open the Power Management Properties dialog box. Click the Advanced tab, click the Prompt For Password When Computer Goes Off Standby check box, and then click OK.

The thing to note about this process is that you don't get a chance to define a separate password for the screen saver. So if you teach your users to activate this kind of screen saver protection, remind them that the screen saver password is the same as their Windows logon password. ◆

Don't let users take your password policies lightly

By Jeff Davis

Back in my days in the Army National Guard, those of us who had "secret" security clearance were taught how to use security codes that changed daily or sometimes hourly. You had to know the secret paradigm and have the little yellow book of codes to correctly identify yourself and confirm the identity of the person on the other end of the radio or telephone. If you didn't receive the correct responses, you assumed you were talking to the enemy.

In a networked corporate environment, changing user passwords on a daily or hourly basis may sound like a ridiculous idea. After all, most network administrators build in alerts that remind users to change passwords on a periodic basis—anywhere from once a week to once a year.

Hopefully, whatever interval you choose to require users to change passwords will be often enough to keep the corporate data safe from intruders. The bigger risks come into play when your users don't take seriously enough your password-protection policy, especially during service calls.

Changing passwords on service calls

You arrive in person to troubleshoot a problem or perform some maintenance on a workstation. Under what circumstances do you make the user change the password?

▶ If the user has left you his or her password on a note stuck to the monitor, the password needs to be changed. Anybody strolling through the office could have seen the note.

▶ I once asked a user to come log in to the system for me, and she shouted across the room, "Oh, you can do it. My password is ********." If a user dictates the password aloud for you, the password must be changed before you leave. Anybody who overhears the conversation might misuse that password.

▶ If your service call requires you to change the user's password, make sure the user changes the password again before (or immediately after) you leave. That way, you can always credibly say, "I don't know what that user's password is," and you can never be accused of misusing someone else's access.

Make sure users know how to change their passwords

Why don't users change their passwords more often? One reason is that people don't like to have to remember a new password. They get into the habit of typing the old password, and it's hard for them to change their routine. Another reason is that they don't know *how* to change their passwords.

Moral of the story: When you remind users of the importance of changing their passwords, make sure they know the correct procedure for making that change. ◆

Teach your users how to automatically lock their NT Workstations

By Jake Necessary

Do you work for a company that, due to security concerns, requires its employees to lock their Windows NT 4.0 Workstations when they're not at their desks? In my company, some employees have the authority to issue check amounts in the tens of thousands of dollars. For a dishonest employee, this means that an unlocked workstation has the potential to become a fancy ATM machine.

In order to prevent unauthorized access, we've instructed our users to lock their workstations when not in use. Unfortunately, I've found that most users often forget. They walk away from their computers for a few minutes and wind up taking a three-hour tour. To combat this bad habit, we're teaching our users how to activate an "automatic" locking mechanism, an operating system setting that turns on the "lock" after a certain period of time. (In a Novell network environment, you might want to use NetWare Administrator to force these changes on a user's profile; however, you should get management's approval before you take that step.)

Spell it out for them

The following is the document I sent to my users. Feel free to borrow this format for use in your shop. (I refer to a flowchart for NT shutdown options, and you can get a copy of that document in the article "Help users understand the importance of network security" at www.techrepublic.com/article.jhtml?id=/column/r00320000126nec10.htm)

Important message to all users

Recently, I distributed a flowchart that illustrates your startup, shutdown, and locking options for Windows NT. For security reasons, everyone must lock their workstations when away from the computer.

I have been a culprit of forgetting to lock my workstation. Frankly, sometimes a problem arises, and I rush off to correct it without locking my workstation.

Figure A

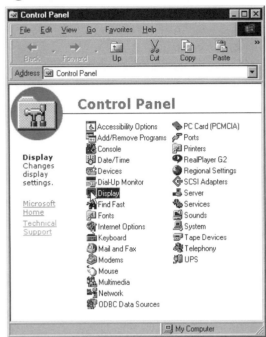

Select and double-click the Display option from the Control Panel.

I use a trick, however, to automatically lock the workstation, and you can use it, too. By making a small change in your screen saver settings, you can configure a pre-set time when the system will start the screen saver and "lock" the station automatically.

Locking your workstation is NOT optional

We must lock the workstations to meet internal audit requirements and protect our interests. Use the following procedure to configure the automatic locking procedure and screen saver on your workstation:

▸ **Launch the Control Panel**. Click the Start button, select Settings, and then choose Control Panel.

▸ **Open the Display Properties window.** Double-click the Control Panel's Display option, as shown in **Figure A**.

▸ **Click the Screen Saver tab.** Familiarize yourself with the Screen Saver Tab, shown in **Figure B**. Pay careful attention to the Password Protected, Wait, and Screen Saver options. Password Protected is really the "automatic locking" check box. If you select this box, the computer will automatically lock after a certain period of time. You set that period of time by entering a number of minutes in the Wait field. In a nutshell, when this box is checked, the computer will wait for the specified number of minutes of inactivity and then lock the station. I recommend setting the waiting time to 15 minutes.

Be creative with your screen saver

Windows NT offers a number of standard screen savers. You can explore the various screen savers by selecting them from the drop-down list box. Click the Settings button to customize the screen savers. Please note that the settings options are different for each screen saver.

When you've customized your settings, click Preview to test the screen saver configuration. Click OK to finish and save your settings.

Unlocking the station

As you probably know, you deactivate the screen saver by moving the mouse or pressing any key on the keyboard. To unlock the workstation, press [Ctrl][Alt][Delete], and then enter your *network* password (not your mainframe password).◆

Figure B

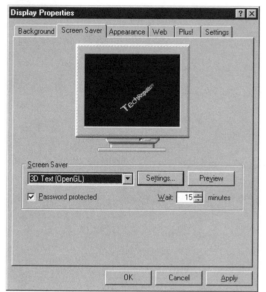

The Screen Saver options let you configure your machine so it automatically shuts down after a certain amount of inactivity.

Chapter 7—Gartner Notes

Gartner
Research

Chapter 7: Gartner Notes

Chapter 7 is a compilation of the latest Gartner security research.
In Chapter 7, we examine:

▶ Implementing Internet credit card payment processes

▶ Security precautions for small and midsize businesses

▶ Security features unique to the Linux operating system

▶ Review of the CA-ACF2 access control system product

▶ Analysis of CA-Top Secret for OS/390 software security features

▶ The strengths and limitations of IBM's Resource Access Control Facility (RACF)

R-10-3503   Context Overview Report
K. Kerr   14 February 2000

Enabling Retail Payments on the Internet

Management Summary

Enabling an Internet site to conduct e-commerce requires establishing a method for receiving payment information. Managing payment processes is not usually viewed as being central to a company's core business, so parts of the process are often outsourced. Yet, whether it is done in-house or it is outsourced, an effective and low-cost Internet payments process is essential to conducting successful Internet commerce. Merchants conducting Internet commerce need to find the solution that best fits their current and future needs. To help find the best solution, this report covers the key issues related to Internet retail payments. These issues include the following:

- Credit cards are the dominant payment method used for Internet purchases and currently account for about 95 percent of electronic Internet retail transactions. Credit card advantages include: they are the most common electronic payment method used for in-store purchases, they require no new security device for online use and they allow consumers to buy on credit. Other payment methods such as online debit cards offer greater security and lower processing fees for merchants, but security, standards, infrastructure and regulatory hurdles stand in the way of immediate adoption and widespread usage.

- Merchants need a new Internet merchant account to receive payments on the Web and should expect to pay discount fees that are one-half percent to one percent higher than those paid for in-store sales.

- For Internet sales, the liability with chargebacks rests solely on the online merchant. While card issuers and merchant acquirers (banks or processors) are not liable for fraudulent or other chargeback transactions on the Internet, they do incur significant handling costs for chargebacks and thus charge higher discount rates for Internet sales.

- To authorize (and sometimes settle) payments in real-time, merchants need to establish gateway connections from their Web storefronts to the card processing networks. Merchants pay fees for online gateway services that are in addition to, although much smaller than, the fees (discount rate) paid to the merchant's acquiring bank. Real-time connections allow the merchant to close sales at the time of purchase since they provide for immediate transaction acceptance just as customers receive and expect with in-store purchases. Real-time connections also give merchants access to fraud detection services and digital certificates networks used to authenticate the buyer.

- Merchants can create online gateway connections to the processing networks either in-house, by building custom connections or purchasing payment processing software, or by outsourcing the process to third-party gateway services. Merchants should consider the expected volume of online.

transactions and the level of internal e-commerce capabilities in selecting a solution. Except for the largest online merchants, most will want to outsource this activity.

- Online merchants need to secure online payment instruction information using a protocol such as SSL. They should also consider other mechanisms, such as digital certificates, for authenticating online buyers.

- Since only card information and not the actual cards are presented online, the risk of fraud is significant. Current online fraud rates are at least five times higher than those for in-store purchases. Merchants who sell digital goods or high-dollar items that can easily be resold are most at risk for online fraud. Fraud detection services can be purchased; these can dramatically reduce losses due to fraud.

- E-wallet is a tool to help reduce customer frustration with online purchasing. Current adoption is low but is likely to grow with increased distribution by financial institutions. Merchants should make their sites compatible with the Electronic Commerce Modeling Language (ECML) standard for facilitating the use of e-wallets.

- Merchants with low-priced digital goods that could be sold on the Internet can partner with new micropayment vendors who leverage credit cards for economically enabling payments of low-priced items.

Enabling Retail Payments on the Internet

CONTENTS

GartnerGroup RAS Services

R-10-3503

Copyright © 2000

14 February 2000

FIGURES

Enabling Retail Payments on the Internet

1.0 Introduction

Receiving payments is an essential though often overlooked part of enabling a Web storefront to conduct Internet commerce. Proper functioning of the payments mechanism is critical not only to receiving funds but also to producing a successful customer experience and to the financial success of the e-commerce initiative.

Few enterprises have core competencies in e-payments systems. Even fewer view payments as a strategically important part of the business and rightfully so. Online merchants should be free to concentrate on growing sales and building relationships with their customers, with payments operating smoothly as a back-office function. Yet, an ineffective payments process can damage a merchant's e-commerce initiative. What most enterprises need is a cost-effective payments solution that functions smoothly, integrates with back-office systems and is all but transparent to their customers.

This report focuses primarily on retail transactions (i.e., on business-to-consumer sales) or on small dollar sales to business customers that can be handled using standard retail payment methods. Internet trade between businesses increasingly involves arrangements made in industry-specific trading communities and allows for different methods for authenticating participants. While procurement is moving to the Internet for B2B e-commerce, payment instructions are often sent using pre-existing payment channels, such as file transfers over private networks. For large-dollar purchases, lines of credit are extended and used by businesses instead of the point-of-sale payments.

This report covers the mechanics, issues and strategies related to retail Internet payments. It is intended as an overview of a range of topics that can be used to assist enterprises in initiating an Internet payments strategy or in making adjustments to their current strategies.

2.0 Internet Payment Methods

Several methods for enabling payments specific to the Internet have been proposed and are discussed in Section 2.2. Some have been piloted or implemented without success, such as the e-cash programs promoted by several vendors (see Section 10.0). Others are being proposed or are in early stages of implementation, such as those offered by the new micropayment vendors. But these methods require sellers, buyers and intermediaries to all adopt new payment methods, These requirements present enormous hurdles for gaining adoption.

New Internet payment methods are being developed, but today credit cards are the dominant method used for Internet purchases.

2.1 Current Payment Methods

Over 90 percent of payments made electronically for Internet retail purchases are made with credit cards. Checks are also used for some Internet purchases, but they have limitations relative to card payments. As most check payments are mailed in by the customer and since most merchants will not ship goods until payments are received, delays occur in receiving funds and in the shipping of purchased items. Merchants can use a check guarantee service if their processor is allied with one (as Signio is with Telecheck) that guarantees payment to the merchant. The other common method used for in-store purchases —cash— is obviously not a viable option for the Internet.

With credit card payments, merchants can obtain the necessary card information from customers at the point of purchase online. Some merchants allow customers who prefer to telephone in credit card information to do so. When information is entered online, merchants receive payment information.

GartnerGroup RAS Services

Copyright © 2000

R-10-3503

14 February 2000

immediately and can have the card payment authorized by the cardholder's issuing bank in seconds (see Section 4.1.1).

Credit cards are the simplest payment type to process electronically over the Internet. They have several advantages that have positioned them as the current leader in Internet payments:

- Credit cards are the leading electronic method of payment for in-store purchases.
- Use of credit cards is not a new payment method that customers must learn. The lone difference between online and in-store use is that customers need to enter the card information (or optionally, they can automate the process by using an e-wallet; see Section 9.0) rather than simply having the card swiped as with in-store transactions.
- Credit cards allow customers to buy now and pay later, as opposed to bank debit transactions, which result in funds being debited from a customer's bank account in one to three days.
- Customers are liable for only the first fifty dollars of unauthorized purchases should the card or card information be stolen and used by thieves. In reality, some customers have suffered damage to their credit ratings when victimized by card theft, but this fact is not commonly known. Many customers remain more comfortable with sending their credit card information than using other options.
- Although the use of security codes (e.g., digital certificates or PINs) would increase transaction security and reduce the risk of identify theft, they are not necessary to enable reasonably safe transactions.

The general acceptance of credit cards by customers today has precluded the necessity for merchants to invest in proprietary Internet payment schemes.

2.2 Future Payment Methods

While credit cards dominate as the payment method of choice on the Internet today, other payment mechanisms will be available to both merchants and their customers in the future. These include:

Debit Cards: Currently, debit cards face security, standards, infrastructure and regulatory hurdles, but once these are eliminated, both merchants and consumers will begin to accept and use debit cards for online purchases. The increased use of debit cards for in-store purchases attests to their growing popularity with consumer customers. Merchants will begin accepting them due to the lower process fees, which mirror the lower fees paid in the physical-world environment. Also, debit cards will be attractive to sellers since the security architecture needed to entice consumers to use the cards online will at the same time authenticate the identity of the buyer and thus reduce fraudulent transactions.

The networks of automated teller machines (ATMs) are positioned to provide the infrastructure to enable Internet debit transactions, but if they continue in their slow pace to bring a solution to market, other players will offer alternative architectures. Solutions for enabling online debit transactions include the introduction of new products, such as readers for PCs that will solve the problem of providing adequate encryption for a customer's PIN. But asking consumers to pay for a new device, or even install it for free, creates an enormous barrier to mass adoption.

A more promising method for enabling debit cards is being launched by NYCE. Similar to being issued an ATM card and a PIN for physical-world transactions, consumers will receive an Internet debit "card" that is actually a CD-ROM disk, along with an e-PIN from their financial institution. To use this debit option, consumers insert their "card" in their computer's CD-ROM drive and enter their e-PIN. The product is portable to any computer, which bodes well for its future. The PIN provides consumers with a level of.

security currently unavailable for Internet purchases. Yet, consumers who are given this payment method will be able to use it only at participating merchant sites.

E-Check: An e-check is an electronic version of a paper check. The main difference is the medium — e-checks are sent through e-mail and require a way to provide a digital signature. E-checks are actually best-suited for B2B payments, particularly for small and midsize companies that want to conduct B2B payments and remittance processing, without the steeper setup costs of Financial Electronic Data Interchange (FEDI) processes suitable for large-scale and repetitive trading operations. They use the same data and flow and business processes, and they conform to the same legal and liability that apply for paper checks.

E-checks face stiff challenges in gaining acceptance. To write and read e-checks, users need a smart-card reader kit and browser access to an e-check program, which requires both users and banks to be e-check-enabled. To the extent that e-checks have a retail application, they are in a race with debit card schemes to capture merchant and consumer adoption. While they may coexist due to differing consumer preferences, both link to a customer's bank account and expose merchants to a lower incidence of fraud than do credit cards.

E-Cash: Previous e-cash models have been tried and have failed. New micropayment solutions (see section 10.0) will keep any new e-cash solutions on the shelf for the near future. E-cash systems may emerge again in another ten years when other Internet-based financial payment infrastructures are built and commonly used, providing the pathway for consumers to easily load cash to an e-wallet-like device or smart card from their financial accounts.

Other Initiatives: With current payment methods, several unique schemes will emerge to ease customer concerns over privacy and security. An example is one at Citibank. Addressing consumer concerns over Internet security, the bank is setting up credit card accounts for their cardholders that are for Internet-only payments. Thus customers' physical-world card accounts are protected from damage should they encounter problems with Internet purchases.

New Channels: In addition to these new payment methods, consumers will buy and pay for goods and services on the Internet through devices other than their computers. These will include a variety of handheld devices, such as cell phones and personal digital assistants (PDAs), as well as through their television monitors.

3.0 Establishing Internet Credit Card Capability

Whether an organization currently has a physical-world retail presence wherein it receives credit cards or is a new Internet startup selling for the first time, it will need to take two initial steps to process credit card payments online. The merchant will need to establish (1) an Internet merchant account with a financial institution and (2) a gateway connection from its Web site or storefront to the processing networks.

3.1 Internet Merchant Accounts

To accept credit cards on the Internet, merchants need to establish an Internet merchant account with a merchant/acquiring bank. Merchants that already have a merchant account for in-store sales or through other sales channels will need to acquire a separate merchant account that is specific to Internet sales.

The merchant acquirer performs the function of processing the card transaction through the card networks and then deposits the funds in the merchant's bank account. Merchants with an in-store retail sales history can usually obtain a merchant account from their current acquirer with little trouble. Internet-only and mail-order-only merchants may have a more difficult time locating an acquirer from which they can

Enabling Retail Payments on the Internet

obtain a merchant account. Acquirers offer varying discount rates (the fees paid to process transactions) so merchants that are concerned about the size of processing fees should shop around for the best rates.

3.2 Internet Gateway Connections

These connections will enable merchants to gain authorizations of their customers' credit cards in real-time. Some enterprises with existing sales channels capture payment information presented by customers on their Internet sites and re-key it into existing in-store payment systems. This bypasses the need for an Internet gateway connection, but this method is inefficient and expensive with any significant level of transactions; it is not advised for most merchants. Gateway connections can be made by purchasing and installing software solutions, developing in-house solutions or by contracting with an outsourced gateway provider (see Section 5.2).

3.3 Acquiring Bank Processing Charges

Some acquiring banks (also referred to acquirers or merchant banks) charge merchants an initial setup fee of several hundred dollars for establishing an Internet merchant account. To process transactions, merchants pay a set of fees, or a discount rate, to their acquirer for each payment transaction. The discount rate is stated as a percentage of each transaction. For Internet transactions, the rate is typically in the range of 2 percent to 3 percent. In addition, a transaction fee, usually 20 to 30 cents, will be paid for each sale. Some acquirers charge a monthly minimum fee for new merchants.

Internet sales are regarded as card-not-present transactions, since the buyer provides only the card information and not the card itself. A credit card thief need only steal the card information from its rightful owner — and does not need the card itself — to use it fraudulently online. The discount rate quoted for Internet transactions will usually be the same as the bank's rate for mail order or telephone order (MOTO) catalog sales. These card-not-present rates are significantly higher than those for in-store transactions due to the increased risk. In-store discount rates are typically in the 1.5 percent to 1.75 percent range, with transaction fees also around $0.30 per transaction (see Figure 1).

Channel	Low discount rate	High discount rate	Transaction fees
In-store	1.5%	2.0%	0 to 35 cents
Internet	2.0 %	3.5%	0 to 40 cents

Source: GartnerGroup

Figure 1. Discount Rates Compared

In addition to the fees paid to its acquiring bank, merchants pay fees to Internet payment gateway outsourcers, or shoulder additional technical and personnel costs if choosing to establish gateway connections in-house (see Section 4.0)

3.4 Chargeback Liability for Internet Sales

A chargeback is a transaction for which the card-issuing institution will not be paid. This results either because a customer disputes a transaction (e.g., customer claims that the transaction never occurred or that the goods were never delivered) or because the purchase was fraudulent (i.e., the buyer was not the owner of the card). For Internet sales, the liability with chargebacks rests solely with the online merchant. Acquirers are willing to extend merchant accounts to sellers for card-not-present sales, but due to the much higher chargeback rate for these transactions, the liability for chargebacks shifts from the card issuer to the seller. For in-store transactions, the issuer is liable for chargebacks once the card authorization is given.

While card issuers and merchant acquirers (banks or processors) are not liable for fraudulent or other chargeback transactions on the Internet, they do incur significant handling costs for chargebacks, which explains the higher discount rate charged. Acquirers will stiffen terms or cancel the Internet merchant account if chargebacks remain at a high level. In addition to not receiving funds for chargebacks, merchants will be charged a fee in the range of $10 to $15 for each payment chargeback. This is a concern for merchants selling goods that attract online card fraud perpetrators.

4.0 Mechanics of Internet Credit Card Processing

The processing of Internet credit card transactions is the same as for face-to-face credit card transactions at the point of sale, except that the transaction that takes place at the Internet storefront needs to be routed into the payment networks.

4.1 Card Authorizations

The first step in accepting a credit card transaction is the authorization. This is done to gain acceptance of the transaction by the issuer (the institution that issued the card). The issuer will return an authorization code if the cardholder has not gone beyond his or her credit limit and if the supplied card information (cardholder name, address and account number) matches the information held by the issuer. This authorization does not however, authenticate the buyer, that is, verify that the buyer is in fact the true owner of the card.

The customer initiates the transaction by entering the credit card and other information on a Web-based online order form and submits the information for transmission to the merchant's Web server over the Internet. This transmission of the customer's credit card information over the Internet should be secured and is typically done using the Secure Sockets Layer (SSL) protocol (see Section 7.1). If the merchant is set up to authorize transactions in real-time mode, the information is sent from the merchant's Web server to the acquiring bank and/or its third-party processor via the merchant's payment processing software or through the merchant's outsourced gateway provider. For a MasterCard or Visa card, the processor transmits the credit card and sales draft information through the appropriate national credit card network, which then routes it to the card-issuing bank. (For a Discover or American Express card, the card is sent directly to these card clubs). The card-issuing bank (or card club) either approves or disapproves the transaction based on the status and limitations of the customer's account. If the transaction is approved, an approval code and a reference number is transmitted back through the national credit card network to the acquiring bank and then back to the merchant. An authorization message is displayed on the payment page for the benefit of the customer. The entire authorization process happens in seconds (see Figure 2).

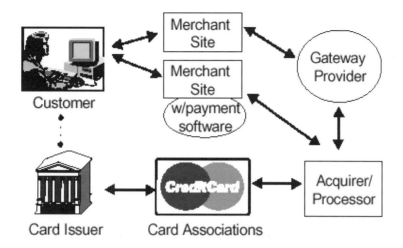

Source: GartnerGroup

Figure 2. Credit Card Authorization and Settlement Process

Real-Time vs. Offline Authorizations: Customers are given real-time authorization for in-store purchases and will expect the same immediate acceptance of their transactions on the Internet. Real-time connections to the processing networks also give merchants access to systems (such as fraud detection services and digital certificates networks) used to authenticate the buyer. With rising Internet fraud rates, authentication services have become increasingly valuable. One of the biggest hurdles that Internet merchants face is in converting online visitors from shoppers to buyers. Industry studies indicate that even when potential customers reach the payments page during the purchase cycle, they abandon the purchase nearly two-thirds of the time. Not finalizing the payment authorization at time of purchase further jeopardizes the closing of online sales.

Authorization attempts fail when customers enter incomplete or incorrect information, but merchants can usually gain authorizations on legitimate payment attempts by asking customers to correct or provide additional information. When this is done in real-time, the rate of sales loss is minimized. When done offline, customers must be contacted at a later time, sometimes with difficulty; and some customers will reconsider the purchase (particularly for impulse buys) and may stop the transaction. Additionally, a transaction delay will annoy some customers, which could cause damage to a brand image that is emerging or has been developed over time in the physical world.

Merchants that do not conduct real-time authorizations use a batch procedure instead. These merchants print reports of the sales and credit card information entered by customers on their Web sites and manually re-key the information using their existing in-store connections to the processing networks to gain authorizations. This is often done at the end of business, but it is sometimes done periodically throughout the day.

4.2 Transaction Settlement

Once an authorization is acquired, the merchant must initiate a second process to receive payment. This actually includes three steps, referred to as the capture, clearance and settlement of the transaction.

Capture: After the purchased products have been shipped to the customer, the sales draft information from the authorization of the Internet credit card transaction is "captured" and transmitted to the acquiring bank and/or its third-party processor for clearance and settlement of the transaction. According to the bank credit card association rules, a merchant cannot "capture" a transaction until the purchased merchandise is shipped.

Clearance: Clearance is the process by which a credit card company collects data about a transaction from the acquiring bank and delivers the data to the card-issuing bank. The bank will use the information to post the transaction to the cardholder's account.

At the end of the business day, the Web merchant or the acquiring bank's third-party processor electronically submits all credit card transaction data for that day to the acquiring bank. This process is usually done in batch mode, rather than in real-time as with card authorizations. The acquiring bank credits the merchant's account for the total amount of the transactions. The acquiring bank then seeks settlement with the card-issuing bank, and the merchant is out of the process.

The acquiring bank is responsible for getting paid by the card-issuing bank. The acquiring bank sends the card payment instructions through the national credit card networks (e.g., Visa). These national credit card companies sort all of the credit card transaction data and transmit the data to the appropriate card- issuing bank. The national credit card companies also determine the amount of money owed by each card issuing bank, which is the net settlement amount.

Settlement: The transaction is settled when the credit card company collects funds from the card-issuing bank and pays funds to the merchant's bank for the cleared transactions.

The card-issuer pays the national credit card company using Fedwire as the payment channel, transferring funds by authorizing the Federal Reserve to electronically debit its account at the Reserve Bank for the net settlement amount and to transfer the funds to the national credit card company's settlement bank account. This bank then pays the acquiring bank, again using Fedwire as the channel. This occurs one calendar day after payment from the card-issuing bank to the national credit card company.

However, if a bank is both the card-issuing bank and the acquiring bank, then settlement is handled entirely within the bank as an "on-us" transaction. The credit card company is therefore not involved in settlement.

Automatic and Delayed Settlement: If goods are delivered immediately on purchase as with digital goods (e.g., as software products), merchants can request "automatic settlement." Payments are authorized and captured for settlement in a single step. In reality, the authorization and capture are done immediately, while the actual settlement is batched and submitted at the end of the day.

More typically, goods are shipped some time after the purchase occurs. Merchants then use delayed settlement, in which the transaction is only captured for settlement after the goods have been shipped.

5.0 Options for Enabling Internet Payments

Online connections are replacing the batch procedures used by many e-commerce site operators. With batch processing, merchants gather up credit card purchase data entered on their e-commerce sites, and at the end of the day they manually re-key it into separate point-of-sale credit card systems to request authorization and settlement.

To provide real-time payment processing, merchants must establish an electronic connection from their e-commerce sites to their acquirer, which then connects to the card-processing networks. Online merchants have three options:

Enabling Retail Payments on the Internet

- Develop in-house transaction processing capability, either by building the connections with in-house resources or purchasing payment-processing software, which will still require some in-house customization

- Outsource the process to third-party gateway services while retaining most e-commerce functions

- Outsource payment processing as part of an outsourced e-commerce solution

The merchant selects the most efficient way to handle payment processing, largely by considering two factors: the expected volume of online transactions and the level of internal e-commerce capabilities, particularly the level of dedicated e-commerce personnel available (see Figure 3). In most cases, online merchants view payments as a nonstrategic activity and should outsource this activity.

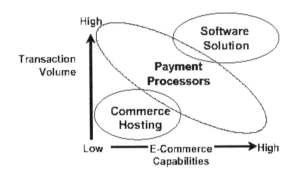

Source: GartnerGroup

Figure 3. Selecting Type of Internet Payment Solution

5.1 In-House/Software Solution

Online retailers planning both robust internal e-commerce capabilities and high transaction volumes should consider using a software system for payment processing. Payment software routes payment data directly from the business's e-commerce site to the card networks. This is a best fit for users with in-house, e-commerce expertise and the extensive infrastructures required to support payment processing. With software, an online retailer plugs the payment product system into its e-commerce site and establishes the required telecommunications links with the card and/or bank-processing network with which the company has chosen to work.

Organizations must compare the fixed costs of a product solution to the expected fees from a service solution to determine which makes more economic sense. Products range from $100,000 at the low end to over $500,000 for high-end platforms. When hardware, personnel and communication costs are added, the total investment could be a million dollars over two years. Product costs should be compared with service fees that range from five cents to 50 cents a transaction, depending on volume, and the value-added services used (e.g., fraud detection).

Vendors: Providers of payment processing software include: IBM, Trintech, HP Verifone, PaylinX, Atomic Software, Spyrus and ICVerify and Tellan (both owned by CyberCash).

Advantages: The organization maintains control of the process in-house and is not vulnerable to potential outages by outsourced processors; the solution may be cost-effective with high transaction volumes.

GartnerGroup RAS Services

Copyright © 2000

R-10-3503

14 February 2000

Disadvantages: The solution has high initial costs; it takes time to implement; it requires in-house e-commerce expertise for installation and resources for system maintenance; and 24 x 7 system monitoring.

5.2 Outsourced Payment Gateway Solution

Merchants with moderate to large transaction volumes who lack resources for the operation of a robust payment systems infrastructure should outsource to a payment service provider. Most service providers charge a fee for each transaction, regardless of the size of the transaction. Merchants with high transaction volumes will usually receive volume discounts. Some providers are moving toward a single monthly pricing fee for unlimited transactions.

A business can plug service vendor software directly into its e-commerce site or access it as a module in a larger e-commerce package available from e-commerce application vendors. The service provider maintains connections to the credit card and/or bank networks, along with real-time credit card authorization and batch settlement. Both commerce server and e-commerce software vendors provide payment plug-ins as value-added applications integrated with their offerings.

Selecting a service provider with connections to a large number of processors gives a merchant flexibility in choosing an acquiring bank. Merchants will not be locked into a relationship with a particular acquiring bank and can price shop if their discount rate is raised.

Outsourced Internet gateway providers all provide basic authorization and settlement of transactions. Some of these providers also offer related payment services that merchants can purchase, usually on a per transaction basis, such as tax calculation and fraud detection.

Vendors: Providers of outsourced Internet payment gateway services include CyberCash, Signio CyberSource, iTransact, Vitessa, SkipJack, ATS Gateway, WorldPay, Authorize.net and First Ecom.com.

Advantages: The solution has low start-up costs; it is quick to implement; customers pay only for transactions that are processed; solution requires few in-house resources for installation and maintenance; solution will scale as transaction volume increases, technical enhancements are handled by outsourcer; flexibility exists for selecting acquiring bank.

Disadvantages: Control is in the hands of the outsourcer, with vulnerability to possible system outages; the solution may be costly over time when transaction volumes become large and merchant is paying on a per transaction basis.

5.3 E-Commerce Hosted Solution

Merchants with low online transaction volumes or those without a cadre of e-commerce experts should look to a full-service commerce service provider (CSP) to outsource payments as part of a larger outsourced e-commerce workload. CSPs provide payment processing bundled with front-end commerce functions, including hosted catalogs, site wallets and shopping carts. In some cases, CSPs make use of a payment service on the back end, then mark up the wholesale cost or offer a bundled offering. CSPs take care of integrating the front-end e-commerce function along with payment-processing connections to the credit card and/or bank networks.

Vendors: There are many ISPs and ASPs that provide merchant e-commerce and payment hosting solutions and the number is growing rapidly; Earthlink, PSINet, Mindspring and ICOM are just a few.

Advantages: The solution has low initial costs; nonstrategic functions are outsourced.

Disadvantages: Control and customized applications are limited. Transaction costs may be high.

GartnerGroup RAS Services
Copyright © 2000

R-10-3503
14 February 2000

6.0 Criteria for Evaluating Internet Payment Solutions

Most e-commerce payment solutions accommodate basic requirements, such as credit card support, and provide acceptable system performance. Some providers distinguish themselves with additional forward-looking services designed to accommodate a merchant's expanding e-business. These services range from sophisticated fraud detection, to support for multiple payment types, to tools that enable integration across delivery channels.

Basic Requirements: These include:

- Card Authorization Support: All major credit cards should be supported. Online credit card authorization should be immediate, but merchants will want the option of immediate and delayed settlement (see Section 4.2).
- Performance: While system performance depends on the speed of user communications and equipment, payment systems should support a credit card authorization response to online consumers within 10 seconds.
- Architecture, Scalability and Redundancy: Merchants should look for "thin" software, or tightly bound executable code, that manages their payment processes. Some solutions require the installation of dozens of software libraries that are cumbersome to maintain. The payment solution should sit on a scalable platform with multiple levels of redundancy (e.g., for data, system, I/O channels and power supplies), as is required by mission-critical systems. Protocol and system management support is crucial. To ensure future flexibility, payment solutions should operate on different system platforms (e.g., Unix and NT, with Java or ActiveX/ASP applications).
- Reporting: Users should demand flexible reporting and simple account reconciliation that supports business and inventory management. Users should be able to reconcile one complete transaction log to their bank statement.

Service and Support: As with any software product or service, installation and customer service support are critical to a successful venture.

- Implementation Support: Application architecture determines ease of implementation, which should take less than a day (as opposed to weeks, as required by some cumbersome applications). Programming templates make it easier to integrate payment solutions with existing e-commerce applications.
- Customer Service: Optimally, users should get round-the-clock customer service directly from the payment solution vendor. Some vendors delegate this critical task to the acquiring bank or ISP and customer service can suffer.
- Certification: Payment solutions should be certified by at least one major credit card processor (e.g., FDC). Processors impose stringent certification procedures that ensure a robust payment process. If a solution is not certified, normally the transactions run over someone else's service that is certified.

Differentiators: Some, but not all, providers offer additional service features. These include:

- Security: Some solutions require merchants to be responsible for security; others rely on the payment solution vendor. Merchants should be careful about hosting credit card and other sensitive consumer payment information on their own Web sites unless they are able to handle stiff security requirements. Customers selling items that are in high-risk categories for fraud should look to solutions that offer fraud detection services.

- Multiple Payment Types: Credit cards are now used to pay for most purchases over the Internet, but as more secure Internet payment solutions evolve, merchants will want to offer them as well. Internet payment solutions should support multiple payment types or have an architecture that can easily add new payment mechanisms.

- Integration With Other Service Channels: Enterprises with other service channels, such as call centers and point of service (POS) systems, will eventually want a payment solution that integrates with all of their delivery channels because integrated enterprise solutions reduce the total cost of ownership. Merchants looking to quickly establish a Web presence can first select a low-cost, Internet-only solution and look for an integrated solution at a later time.

- International Support: Merchants may want to sell goods in currencies other than U.S. dollars. Buyers that can purchase in their own currencies will know exactly what the purchase cost is and avoid fluctuations in currency exchange rates. Some providers now offer the ability to sell goods in multiple currencies.

- Bill Payment Support: Payment solutions are geared for Internet sales, but some can "plug in" to Internet bill presentment applications. This is relevant to companies that are presenting bills at their own Web sites and need a vendor to process bill payments.

- Processor Connections: Software connections for Internet credit card payments are not standardized, so acquiring banks may only accept certain types of software. This lack of standardization means that a relationship between a merchant and his acquiring bank or third-party processor may be unique, making it difficult for a merchant to change his acquiring bank once an account has been set up.

7.0 Payment Security Issues

Connections between parties on the Internet can be routed through dozens of independent systems, any of which can easily be monitored and messages that are not secured can be intercepted. To send and receive payment instructions on the Internet, merchants must deploy a secure protocol to protect their transactions.

Web merchants that accept customers' credit cards over the Internet, need to consider security in three basic areas:

- **Receiving the customer's credit card data from their PC (or other device) to the merchant's Web site**

- **Sending the card information to the card networks for processing**

- **Protecting the consumer's credit card information from theft**

The third point is a matter of storage. If customers' card numbers are to be retained by the merchant, they should be stored in a secure database that cannot be accessed via the Internet and should be left in encrypted form, which will provide some protection against internal theft.

Several security systems have been devised to secure the transmission of Internet payment transactions. In the United States today, Secure Sockets Layer (SSL) is the primary standard in use for credit card transactions. Digital certificates, which provide a much greater level of security due to their ability to authenticate parties, may eventually become commonplace, even in the United States. Secure Electronic Transaction (SET) is a certificate-based system that has had successful implementations in Europe and in Asia, but has made no progress in the United States.

7.1 SSL

SSL was developed by Netscape for transmitting private documents via the Internet. It is a connection-based protocol that uses channel encryption to offer authentication, integrity and nonrepudiation. It can be installed relatively quickly and the process does not slow transaction speed.

SSL works by using a private key to encrypt data that is transferred over the SSL connection. Specifically, SSL encrypts data between a customer's Web browser and the merchant's Web server. Since the card information is encrypted, a message that is intercepted must be decrypted before it can be read. The major Web browsers, including Netscape Navigator and Microsoft Internet Explorer, as well as most e-mail programs, are SSL-capable. A customer using one of these applications can determine if a payment session is secured by SSL by checking for a closed lock or key that appears on the bottom left corner of his or her browser software. Another indication is that the URL of secure Web pages will display https instead of the more common http.

To receive online payments, merchants need a secure server with an SSL certificate for their e-commerce platforms. While 40-bit keys can be used, 128-bit key encryption is recommended and is most commonly used for receiving payment instructions. SSL provides message privacy, message integrity and merchant authentication with secure online transactions.

- Message privacy: SSL encrypts all information exchanged between the merchant Web server and the customer's browser, such as credit card numbers and other personal data, using a unique session key. To securely transmit the session key to the consumer, the server encrypts it with the merchant's public key. Each session key is used only once, during a single session (which may include one or more transactions) with a single customer.

- Message integrity: When a message is sent, the sending and receiving computers each generate a code based on the message content. If even a single character in the message content is altered enroute, the receiving computer will generate a different code and then alert the recipient that the message is not legitimate. With message integrity, both parties involved in the transaction know that what they are seeing is exactly what the other party sent.

- Authentication: Customers can check that the merchant site is legitimate by examining the server ID, or can at least be comforted by simply seeing the security firm's logo on the merchant site. This will reduce hesitation by some customers who are concerned about supplying card information over the Internet.

7.2 Digital Certificates for User Authentication

While SSL can protect the delivery of payment instruction messages, it does not authenticate the parties in a transaction. This means that it cannot ensure that each party is who he or she claims to be. A knowledgeable thief can use a stolen credit card or credit card number that is still active for purchases in an SSL-only environment.

Digital Certificates, also called digital IDs, are encrypted codes or signatures, issued to both buyers and sellers to ensure the identity of both parties. A digital certificate is the digital equivalent of an ID card used in conjunction with a public key encryption system. The certificates must be issued and managed by a Certificate Authority (CA), which may either be a financial institution or a third-party security vendor.

The digital certificate is actually the owner's public key that has been digitally signed by the CA. The digital certificate is sent along with an encrypted message to verify that the sender is truly the entity identifying itself in the transmission. The recipient uses the public key of the CA, which is widely publicized; to decrypt the sender's public key attached to the message. Then the sender's public key is used to decrypt the actual message.

The most vulnerable aspect of this method is the CA's private key, which is used to digitally sign a public key and create a certificate. If the CA's private key is uncovered, then false digital certificates can be created.

A security protocol for Internet payments based on a digital certificate, known as SET, has been in existence for four years and has had the backing of the major card associations and other financial-service companies.

SET: SET is a protocol that uses digital certificates to authenticate the various parties involved in an online transaction. SET encrypts all transaction details, authenticates each of the parties involved in a transaction, fully records transaction acknowledgments and ensures that customer payment details are made available only to the bank. SET uses encryption for securing the payment details and makes use of digital certificates for consumer, merchant and bank identification.

In 1995, SET was conceived to overcome fraud arising from Internet-based payment transactions. Since then, SET has slowly gained momentum, with pilot programs around the world. Despite the benefit of significantly reducing fraud from online transactions and despite the backing of a large number of banks, credit card companies and vendors, SET has not gained widespread usage.

Visa and MasterCard have promoted SET several times, but it has failed to gain acceptance, particularly in the United States. It faces several hurdles in gaining merchant and consumer adoption:

- SET requires the participation of merchants, consumers, banks and a certificate authority

- consumers need to subscribe to a certificate authority and then download an e-wallet to their PCs to store the certificates

- merchants must build complex architectures

- the system's complexity slows verification response times

- the system is not inexpensive to maintain

Thus far, neither merchants nor consumers have demanded this type of security protocol.

Merchants would benefit from reduced fraud rates if digital certificates were commonly used. But lacking a critical mass of customers or merchants that currently use digital certificates, coupled with the technical investments needed, merchants are not demanding such a solution. With SET, in addition to implementing it on the Web site, the merchant has to subscribe to a certification authority and support the necessary communications to the certification body, the customer's bank and the merchant's own bank. In many cases, this requires the installation of an additional infrastructure.

While it is not currently used in the United States, several large banks in Europe and in Asia invested in and implemented SET. However, low demand from consumers and merchants and the lack of a certification framework will keep the acceptance of SET low there as well.

8.0 Online Fraud and Other Chargebacks

The rate of credit card fraud on Internet purchases is at least five times higher than that on purchases made at in-store retail locations, where both the customer and the card are present and the card is swiped in a reader.

Without a deployed system for authenticating buyers, online merchants will continue to accept credit cards and continue to face the risk of increasing fraud and chargeback rates. Industry estimates place online fraud rates as high as 15 percent. A recent survey of its own customers by CyberSource, a leader in fraud detection software, showed that fraud was at the 5 percent level. Still, this compares with a rate of less than one percent for POS transactions.

Nearly all online merchants are at risk for fraudulent transactions. But they are a significant concern for merchants selling particular types of goods. These include merchants that sell digital goods, such as software, online for which the items are sent immediately and are not shipped to physical location. Also, at major risk are merchants that sell high-dollar items, particularly those that can easily be resold illegally. In addition to not receiving payments for delivered products, merchants face bank chargeback fees, penalties from credit card associations and the administrative expenses of investigating and processing disputes and chargebacks. For smaller merchants, the ability to accept credit cards can be revoked if a high chargeback rate is maintained.

Merchants should consider defensive options for avoiding fraud and limiting the cost of customer chargebacks. Fraud detection methods available to help verify that the online buyer is the legitimate owner of the card include Address Verification Service and rules-based and fraud-scoring services.

- Address Verification Service (AVS): The address provided by the buyer at the time of purchase is matched against the address registered with the card issuer. The result of this check (match/mismatch) is sent back to the merchant, but a mismatch does not result in automatic transaction denial. Since there are valid reasons for a mismatch, merchants are left to consider a variety of factors (e.g., size of the transaction) to determine whether to accept the purchase. Most real-time card payment providers offer this service, which should be used by merchants with transaction volumes greater than what can be checked manually.

- Fraud-Scoring Services: Some Internet payment companies offer more sophisticated fraud detection services than AVS. These include: 1) screening credit card numbers against databases of previously misused card numbers; 2) pattern fraud screens, in which several criteria are examined against a rules-based knowledge store to create a risk score; and 3) experiential fraud screens, using criteria that can be customized by merchants based on their own selling experiences. Rule-based detection systems vary in sophistication, from those based on simple rules to credit scoring schemes based on changing individual and group consumer activity patterns.

CyberSource and ClearCommerce are two firms offering a fraud detection service as an add-on to merchants' payment gateway services. HNC, a provider of credit card fraud detection systems that serve banks and merchants, launched an Internet version of its Falcon fraud detection product (E-Falcon) in the second half of 1999. This type of service is too costly for small purchases (less than $10), but is cost-effective for high-ticket items, which are the usual fraud targets. CyberSource charges in the range of 20 cents to 40 cents per transaction for the service, depending on transaction volumes.

The introduction of card verification codes by the card associations is another method developed to reduce fraud.

- Card Verification Codes: Credit card associations are implementing this method of verification protection for Internet and mail order purchases. A security code of extra digits is imprinted on the back of the card and embedded in its magnetic stripe. This code is read by POS readers for in-store purchases, but does not appear on written receipts, from which numbers are often stolen. The numbers can be given by cardholders for card-not-present purchases, but are unavailable to thieves.

not in possession of the actual card. This will be useless, however, in stopping fraud when cards are stolen. This method requires consumers to enter another piece of information to initiate a purchase but adds no cost to the merchant.

Both Visa's Card Verification Value (CVV2) and MasterCard's Card Verification Code (CVC2) are beginning to provide this verification protection. Starting this year, Visa will begin requiring banks and processors to send and receive the CVV2 responses as part of the authorization messages. All of Visa's cards are projected to carry the CVV2 code by year-end 2000.

A large share of chargebacks on Internet purchases is not the result of fraud, but is simply due to disputes filed by customers. Internet merchants can take steps to reduce these rates. To limit customer disputes, merchants should:

- provide in-depth descriptions of sale items

- deliver goods promptly

- fully disclose all charges, including taxes and shipping costs, involved with each purchase

- provide customer care contact information

Actions by merchants to reduce fraud and chargebacks on the Internet should be guided by such factors as volume and dollar value of online transactions and by how goods are delivered. High-risk merchants who do not address the potential growth in costs associated with Internet fraud and chargebacks will facelosses that may threaten the viability of their e-commerce initiatives.

9.0 E-Wallets

E-wallets were developed to replicate the functions of physical wallets for use on the Internet. They are software programs that hold information about credit cards and other payment instruments, such as account numbers, expiration dates and billing addresses, needed by users to conduct online purchases. Most e-wallets can store information for multiple types of cards and can store e-cash, loyalty points gained online, user names and passwords to specific merchant sites and even personal pictures.

One of the key attractions of e-wallets is their ability to autopopulate payment forms, which differ from merchant to merchant, eliminating the need for online buyers to re-key information for each new online purchase. In addition to autopopulating payment forms, consumers can use the wallet to track and organize purchases, specify product preferences, allow specific incentive offers to be received and createlinks to customer service departments.

Rather than simply being extras, these features are key to producing revenue for e-wallet vendors, as most vendors are giving their wallets away for free. Vendors plan to leverage their e-wallet user base with merchants, contracted merchants to make offers to e-wallet users based on users' self-selected product preferences. E-wallet vendors will receive affiliate commissions for goods sold through this relationship. Vendors will also offer merchants fee-based access to their customers for marketing initiatives. Vendors may also produce revenue through bounties paid by financial institutions for new credit card subscribers produced through the e-wallet relationship.

E-wallets are sometimes confused with the term e-purse, which is a store of currency. A smart card may have several e-purse applications, or stores of money for different uses. An e-wallet, in contrast, typically stores multiple payment instruments.

GartnerGroup RAS Services

Copyright © 2000

R-10-3503

14 February 2000

Enabling Retail Payments on the Internet

Although early e-wallets found few users, new e-wallets use improved business and technical models worthy of merchants', consumers' and financial institutions' attention.

9.1 Consumer E-Wallet Adoption

Consumer interest in early e-wallets was very weak. Early versions required heavy software downloads, were not intuitive to use, were used by few merchants and could autopopulate few payment forms. Also, until recently, few consumers were active online purchasers and so the demand for the product was low. But the current online purchasing abandonment rate has raised the need for the functions that E-wallets serve. Industry sources report that up to two-thirds of consumers who select items for purchase at an online site never finish completing the payment form and finalizing the transaction. In industry surveys, online consumers have cited the hassle of completing the form as the top reason for not completing transactions.

Recent technical improvements, new standards, increased online purchasing levels and growing interest from some financial institutions are raising the chances for consumer adoption.

Consumer use of e-wallets will increase when:

- online purchasing increases, heightening the need for the convenience that e-wallets provide

- financial institutions distribute and promote them, providing the trust and familiarity needed to overcome consumers' security and privacy concerns

- they are easy to install and simple to use

- a single e-wallet can be used at many merchant sites

9.2 Migration From Client to Server-Side Wallets

Early versions and some current versions of e-wallets require consumers to download heavy client-side software to their PCs. Download times tend to be long and consume several megabytes of hard drive space. As a result, consumers have found them inconvenient. Also, vendor upgrades require additional downloads by consumers.

A perceived advantage of storing the wallet on the PC is security — the consumer's personal information is stored on his or her PC rather than residing on a remote server of an e-wallet vendor. Some new e-wallet releases have kept the client-side architecture, while attempting to create a thinner piece of software. But most new e-wallet releases have moved away from this client-side version.

A new architecture places both the user's wallet and data on a server maintained by the wallet vendor. This shift from a PC to a server offers these benefits:

- payment forms of connected merchants can be autopopulated

- time-consuming downloads and upgrades are eliminated

- users can access their wallets from any Web-enabled PC

- stored e-cash is protected which might otherwise be lost due to PC failure

Recognizing that thick, client-side e-wallets were cumbersome, early e-wallet pioneer CyberCash initially reduced the size of its client-side wallet, but is now distributing a server-side wallet. Other vendors that introduced server-side e-wallets in 1999 include Qpass, Trintech and Brodia.

9.3 Interacting With Merchant Sites

Lacking common standards, each individual online merchant has designed his payment form to suit his individual preferences. The result is that there is no uniformity across merchant sites in the way that payment information is collected, either in the type of information collected, the formats used or in the naming of field names.

For an e-wallet to autopopulate the fields in a payment form at a merchant site, it must be able to correctly identify and read the fields at the various merchant sites. To do so, vendors have typically installed code at a merchant's Web site, which requires merchant acceptance of the solution and software installation at the merchant's site. But this approach limits the usefulness of any given wallet solution, since it can be applied only at participating sites. To expand the number of Web sites with which a wallet can be used to autopopulate payment forms without merchant integration, new techniques are being used that do not require merchant acceptance of a given e-wallet.

Qpass (in partnership with HNC Software) engineered an e-wallet that uses intelligent text processing to recognize the fields on a merchant payment form without any physical integration at the merchant site. When the wallet cannot recognize a field, the user must manually input the data. Being a server-side e-wallet, the server "learns" from the information provided and attempts to identify the field. If successful, any future wallet user encountering this or a similar field will have the field autopopulated. Other e-wallet vendors, such as Brodia, are simply profiling the sites of major Internet merchants and hard coding the maps of their payment forms into the server-side software. This will enable their e-wallets to communicate with most e-commerce sites that their users will encounter.

9.4 ECML

As with most technologies, the lack of industry standards can stifle acceptance and market penetration. Addressing the need for some uniformity in payment form, a standard called ECML was developed and released by industry leaders in June 1999. Once applied, any ECML e-wallet that encounters an ECML-compliant merchant site will be able to autopopulate the payment form without having to learn the elements of the form.

ECML was developed collaboratively by three major credit card associations — Visa, MasterCard and American Express — and by e-wallet makers and other technology vendors, including IBM, Microsoft, Sun Microsystems, Compaq, Trintech, CyberCash, Brodia and SETCo. Several merchants with active e-commerce sites were early endorsers of ECML, including Dell, Beyond.com, fashionmall.com, healthshop.com, reel.com and Nordstrom. A standard such as ECML has broad online merchant support. In an industry survey, 76 percent of merchants agreed on the need for interchangeable e-wallets.

ECML provides standards both for merchant Web page payment forms and for how information is stored in a digital wallet. ECML is an open standard, rather than a programming language. It will function with any security protocol (e.g., SSL or SET) and support any type of consumer payment card. E-wallet vendor competitors were willing to cooperate to produce the standard, each knowing that few consumers would use their e-wallets without the universal usability that a standard could provide.

ECML defines a uniform set of internal field names to be used by merchants for the information fields on their Web order/payment forms. The standard sets uniform field names that can be recognized by e-wallet software that includes fields for customer name, card account information, billing and shipping addresses, order ID numbers and payment protocols. It does not require merchants to order the presentation of fields, or to include or omit any particular fields. Also, only the internal field names affect the field descriptions that consumers see.

GartnerGroup RAS Services   R-10-3503

       14 February 2000

Merchant Compliance: Merchants that apply the ECML standard to their sites are able to support all e-wallets that also use the standard. Until the introduction of this standard, merchants that wanted to enable their sites to communicate with e-wallets needed to support each of the many e-wallets on the market. Conforming their payment forms to the ECML standard enables them to communicate with all e-wallets without building the code of each vendor into their sites, as all e-wallet distributors will likely abide by the standard. Merchants just need to make changes to the code of their existing Web pages to conform to the standard. Wisely, this standard was designed with simplicity in mind. No new technology was introduced, and merchants do not need a license to use the standard.

Since the task of conforming to the standard takes little time and expense, online merchants should conform their payment forms to the ECML standard to reduce a barrier to purchasing at their sites. Financial institutions and vendors should build the standard into their e-wallet products. ECML's simplicity and strong industry support gives it a strong chance for industry-wide adoption.

Several issues were not addressed by this initial ECML release (v.1.0), such as the use of corporate purchasing cards, the use of non-card-payment mechanisms, privacy-related issues and the completion of fields that merchants set as mandatory. Future versions will address these issues and will likely be implemented in XML.

9.5 Branding of E-Wallets by Financial Institutions

Some banks (and credit card issuers) are recognizing value in offering e-wallets to customers. This product can increase their online brand presence and can be used to promote the use of the bank's credit card by designating it as the default card within the wallet software. When consumers download e-wallets directly from technology vendors, banks lose an opportunity to expand their customer relationships and leverage the trust that consumers feel toward banks.

Banks can use e-wallets to offer customers discounts and loyalty points with merchant partners, offer access to account balances online and use the online connection to build an e-commerce relationship with their customers.

Trintech introduced an E-wallet-type product, called EZCard, which can create a virtual copy of a customer's existing credit card and install the virtual image on the toolbar of the user's browser. The physical representation may give some users a greater sense of security and privacy.

10.0 Enabling the Sale of Digital Goods

While credit cards account for nearly all e-payments currently made for online purchases, they are not practical for handling payments for low-priced transactions on the Internet. Credit card processing fees for purchases of low-priced goods, those selling between a penny and $10, make credit cards uneconomical. A widely used micropayment mechanism to handle these transactions has not yet developed.

A large untapped market exists for the purchase of digital goods on a pay-per-use basis. Digital products typically sold for under $10 include music, video clips, financial reports, news articles and other reports, pictures and software. Instead of a pay-per-use method, some providers offer users monthly subscription plans. However, these miss the larger market of occasional users who seek to purchase only specific items, such as single articles and have no need for a regular service. Also, monthly subscription fees require a commitment by users, which runs counter to the typical Internet information surfing experience. Lengthy subscription plans block more potential buyers than they capture. Also, purchased documents containing hyperlinks to documents available from other content providers (with their own subscription fees) will frustrate consumers who want to search those documents.

Some online consumers will be slow to accept paying for low-priced Internet items that had previously been free. Should an effective method for enabling payment acceptance of low-priced items gain common acceptance, the currently minuscule sales volume of low-cost digital goods could exceed $1 billion within three years.

E-Cash: Early e-cash methods designed to address the micropayments space have failed. First Virtual left the business. DigiCash failed to attract interest in its architecture, and CyberCash terminated its CyberCoin e-cash program. Each needed the coordination and simultaneous adoption by consumers, merchants and financial institutions prior to the existence of a proven market. The models proved too cumbersome. DigiCash required online users to establish accounts with banks that issued e-cash, install bank-issued e-purse software and transfer funds to these PC-based accounts before making a first purchase. Merchants needed to establish new connections and install software on their Web sites. Doubting the viability of this process, few financial institutions became e-cash issuers.

While several micropayment methods have been deployed with little success, some new methods are promising.

Single-Click Purchasing: New outsourced payment schemes have simplified user requirements for completing low-cost transactions. Designed to enable simple, fast and frequent purchases, these methods usually require a password and one mouse click to make a purchase. While they are free and simple to use, most of these solutions still require vendors to individually register merchants to enable the micropayment service. Users can only charge purchases at registered merchant sites.

The vendors of these micropayment solutions typically receive a 10 percent to 35 percent share of the purchase price for each transaction. Because the fixed cost of digital content is negligible, profit margins in the sale of these goods will be very high. Merchants who do not currently have effective outlets for their products will not likely view the percentages required by third parties as high. There are several variations of the single-click model:

- QPass gathers charges for a user's purchases into a single monthly credit card charge. As with several other services, users can view their monthly purchases at the QPass site.

- Cha Technologies uses preloaded accounts, billing an amount (typically $20) to a consumer's credit card account. Deductions are made from these loaded accounts with each purchase. Merchant membership is free and no software installation is needed. Merchants send URLs offering goods for sale to Cha for hosting and order processing. This prepaid scheme, however, is not likely to be adopted by many consumers. Paying in advance runs counter to the card payment experience. Also, although the prepaid amount is small, some consumers will be concerned about storing funds with a little-known start-up company.

- Trivnet and iPin are signing up ISPs to bill their customers for Internet purchases. ISPs track individual purchases, add the total to the consumer's monthly ISP fee and make one charge to the credit card account. The simplicity of this method should appeal to consumers and also to ISPs since they will be offered a share of the vendor's revenue. The method, however, still requires that merchants be signed up individually. Also, if free Internet access becomes ubiquitous, using ISPs as billing centers will be a problem. A similar method used by eCharge places charges onto a customer's telephone bill.

Related Purchase Methods: In addition to the e-cash and one-click solutions, several other payment-related methods have emerged for facilitating online purchases and activities. Loyalty points for online purchases are offered by companies such as CyberGold, online gift certificates are offered by

ExpressGold.com and an Internet-only currency that can be earned as well as spent online is offered by Beenz.com.

Current Options for Merchants: These new micropayment methods are simpler to use than e-cash systems and do not require users to store cash for purchases. These vendor solutions will enable the early development of the micropayments market, but other solutions will likely follow. Merchants who want to deliver digital goods should look to partner with micropayment vendors who have low up-front costs and are developing a growing list of clients.

Future Solutions: E-wallet solutions are maturing and banks will likely offer their own micropayment methods within bank-branded e-wallets. E-cash for Internet payments may be revived when it is downloadable onto smart cards, offering the advantage of stored-value usability in both the physical and virtual worlds. Smart cards show no sign of gaining widespread consumer adoption in the United States and e-cash will likely have to wait to be an add-on to a multiapplication card rather than as a leading application.

11.0 Conclusions

To enable payment in an e-commerce storefront, merchants should look to establish online connectivity to the processing networks to enable immediate authorization of customer purchases. This gives customers immediate acceptance of their purchases which will aid sales completions. It also gives merchants access to systems that can reduce their exposure to high online fraud rates. Most merchants will want to outsource the process of connecting to the processing networks. Merchants wanting to maintain control of the process in-house can build or buy software to send the process transactions directly to the processing networks.

Credit cards are the current method of choice for Internet retail payments. While they are a relatively easy method to use and process, most merchants accept them without any authentication of the purchaser. Merchants are liable for chargebacks for online sales and should consider buying online fraud detection services if they are selling items that place them in a high-risk category for fraud. In the future, digital certificates should become more common to reduce fraud risks and new payment methods, such as the use of debit cards for online purchases, will provide greater security and lower processing fees for merchants.

IGG-05102000-01

J. Browning, J. Pescatore

Article

10 May 2000

CIO Alert: Many Small and Midsize Enterprises Need Tightened Security

Small and midsize enterprises, which often do not have the security resources of large enterprises, must take steps to ensure that their networks are not exposed to security breaches.

All enterprise executives are keenly aware of the potential havoc that can be wreaked on their enterprises by hackers or virus attacks. The recent ILOVEYOU virus attack was a resounding warning to CIOs, security officers and other enterprise executives. Executives clearly want to know what measures their enterprises are taking to secure Internets. Moreover, small and midsize enterprises, which often do not have the security resources of large enterprises, are doing more business on the Internet, so their networks are increasingly exposed to security breaches. Gartner discusses the defensive actions required to protect such enterprise networks.

Any server connected to the Internet makes it and the rest of the network vulnerable to access from unauthorized and malicious users. An issue faced by small and midsize enterprises is that many cannot afford, or do not attract, experienced security personnel. As a result, part-time employees or personnel with less than top-notch qualifications manage key enterprise servers (i.e., Web, e-mail). Moreover, small and midsize enterprises often use regional Internet service providers that provide unknown levels of security.

By 2003, 50 percent of small and midsize enterprises that manage their own network security and use the Internet for more than e-mail will experience a successful Internet attack (0.7 probability). More than 60 percent will not know they have been penetrated. Gartner identifies potential security holes and provides advice on how to plug them.

Start With a Security Checkup

Small and midsize enterprises connected to the Internet should consider contracting with an outside security company to conduct an audit and risk-assessment of their networks. The effort should include an internal network security audit and an external penetration test. Consulting companies should have certified their security consultants (see the sidebar, "International Information Systems Security Certification Consortium").

External vulnerability assessments should be performed whenever an enterprise makes major changes to its Web site or firewall, at a minimum on a yearly basis. Increasingly, security vendors will offer low-cost "self-service" vulnerability assessments, such as the offering by myCIO.com, which labels itself as "Your Chief Internet Officer." Those types of tests can be cost-effective for small and midsize enterprises but will require experienced support to address reported security problems.

First Line of Defense

Precautions must be taken to ensure a proper firewall configuration to offer the best possible protection for the enterprise. Firewalls are deployed to prevent unauthorized "external" users from accessing the enterprise network, while permitting "internal" users to communicate with "external" users and systems. Firewalls also provide a central point for logging and auditing Internet traffic. Enterprises should focus on firewall appliances such as Watchguard Firebox, Nokia FW-1 and SonicWall that provide a base level of security without requiring detailed security knowledge.

CIO Alert: Many Small and Midsize Enterprises Need Tightened Security

By 2003, the dominant means of deploying network security technology will be through the use of appliance technology (0.9 probability). Enterprises should request quotes for managed firewall and intrusion detection services from their own Internet service providers and companies such as ISS/Netrex, RIPTech and GTE Internetworking. Those services will generally cost less than the equivalent salary of a half-time firewall administrator.

Other Safeguards to Consider

Other safeguards include:

- Boundary Services: Virus scanning of incoming e-mail is a critical security control. It can be done by using desktop antiviral protection; but it is often difficult to keep desktop signature virals current. Server-side antiviral protection (e.g., from Trend Micro or FinJan) provide protection against incoming viruses and hostile ActiveX or Java applets. Enterprises should take immediate action to disallow relay and halt the entry of spam into their environments.

- Web Security: The major vulnerability in Web servers is attacks against Common Gateway Interface scripts and other active code. It is generally impossible for enterprises to assure that active server code does not contain security vulnerabilities. Enterprises that develop and host their own Web servers should deploy products such as Tripwire by Tripwire Security or Entercept by ClickNet to detect and prevent hacker attacks.

- Consolidated Remote Access With Strong Authentication: Enterprises that provide dial-in access to e-mail and other corporate systems should eliminate desktop modems and use consolidated modem pools and remote access servers. Enterprises should require the use of hardware tokens such as RSA Security SecurID or Axent Defender to authenticate remote users.

- Extra Protection: The measures identified so far will satisfy the security needs of two-thirds or more of small and midsize enterprises that use the Internet. Small and midsize enterprises that must manage more highly sensitive environments must plan for additional precautions.

Additional Security Measures

Additional security measures include:

- Virtual private networks for secure remote access over the Internet

- Intrusion detection to alarm the enterprise of internal and external attacks

- Firewall log analysis and e-mail content filtering to detect misuse of the Internet connection by employees or business partners.Small and midsize enterprises often have too low a usage level for managed services to be cost effective. That makes small and midsize enterprises candidates for implementing remote access virtual private networks with the firewall acting as server.

Dealing With Emergency Security Situations

The ILOVEYOU virus, which spread so rapidly throughout the world, is a derivative of the Melissa virus and affects only Microsoft e-mail systems. That incident highlighted why enterprises must have a plan for responding quickly to malicious code incidents. The plan should include a coordinated team, particularly the antivirus, firewall and backup people involved, and predefined procedures, including emergency powers such as blocking Internet e-mail, and — as a last resort — shutting down e-mail servers.

CIO Alert: Many Small and Midsize Enterprises Need Tightened Security

Gartner outlines standard security measures for enterprises dealing with emergency security situations:

- Have a security response team in place. Gartner's security team is organized into two main areas of expertise to facilitate immediate response, the virus team and the firewall team.
- Block all Internet e-mail until the virus fix is applied.
- Have communications and security response team procedures in place. Each hour counts in identifying and stopping viruses and hackers. Early detection and communication are vital. Enterprisewide e-mails and warnings about the event rapidly restore an infrastructure to a secure state. Enterprises must have specific responses mapped to either virus or hacker attacks.
- Connect the security response team with the rest of the IT department. When the security response team is in place and reports directly to the CIO or chief security officer, other IT teams that maintain the supply chain and customer relationship management systems can be updated immediately about any impact to vendors and customers.

Bottom Line

- The amount of security required should be weighed against the degree of risk associated with doing business on the Internet.
- The sensitivity of information, productivity of users and impact on revenue should all be assessed to determine the safeguards required. Enterprises that fail to pay attention to Internet security issues will experience significant losses as a result of attacks on their networks (0.8 probability).

International Information Systems Security Certification Consortium

The International Information Systems Security Certification Consortium (ISC2) is a nonprofit organization that administers the Certified Information Systems Security Professional (CISSP) certification program (www.isc2.org/isc2faq.html). While passing a CISSP exam is no guarantee of performance, it does establish a minimum body of knowledge.

The System Administration, Networking and Security organization has established a similar program, System Network Assurance Program, consisting of a standard series of briefings, courses and tasks used to demonstrate a more detailed technical body of knowledge (www.sans.org/giactc.htm).

Written by Edward Younker, Research Products

Analytical sources: Jim Browning and John Pescatore, Enterprise Network Strategies

For related articles published in "Inside GartnerGroup This Week," see:

- "CIO Alert: Modems on the Desktop Can Put Important Enterprise Elements at Risk," 8 December 1999
- "CEO and CIO Alert: Web Security — Sin in Haste, Repent at Leisure," 7 July 1999

GartnerGroup RAS Services   IGG-05102000-01

Copyright © 2000   10 May 2000

Linux Security: Perspective   **October 28, 1999**

Datapro Summary

Linux security includes all the traditional essentials--a security policy, tools, and rigorous system maintenance. However, Linux is different than any other operating system because security flaws are found and fixed as fast as it takes one of the thousands of contributors to find them, fix them, and post them on the Web. Also, there are a plethora of tools, most are freely available to help make your Linux system bulletproof.

—By Mary Hubley

Technology Basics

Making A Linux System Secure

The system administrator is the key behind a Linux system's security--the better this person performs his or her job, the more secure the system will be. By putting in the time to make and maintain the system security, most break-ins can be avoided. This person ensures there is a useable security policy in place, performs regular security maintenance procedures, and has the competence to quickly act upon attacks that do happen. The Linux community offers a wide array of software packages to help the administrator perform his or her job better. Many tools are included with the Linux system, while others are freely downloadable from the Web.

Starting with the basics, points to consider when setting up a secure Linux system include the following:

- Do not give regular users access to the server.

- Physically secure PCs.

- Use encryption software.

- Check for changes. Do regular network checking to look for software that should not be there and review the process table and open ports. (Lots of third-party software is available for this).

- Use BIOS passwords.

- Ensure that the server boots from the its hard drive only.

- Use a password for the LILO prompt.

- Do not give regular users root access or access to interactive shells such as bash and pine. Also, minimize user privileges.

- Use firewalls.

- Have a written security policy.

- Remove all unneeded software.

- Segment the server with different services to minimize single points of failure.

- Make backups.

Linux Security: Perspective

As with any security program, remember the following steps:

- Balance intrusiveness with usefulness--The most secure systems are also intrusive. Determine how to make the system easy to work with, while still enabling enough security for your organization.

- Establish a security policy--Include how much security and auditing should be required. Determine threat level, intruder risks, and vulnerability. If the user is just starting out, build a simple, generic policy for the system that is easily understood and followed. Determine who has access to the system, who can install software, who owns the data, disaster recovery, and appropriate system use.

Account Security

Linux account security is the same as that of UNIX. When assigning account access, follow these guidelines:

- Give users a minimum of privileges--only what they need. Consider giving users only menu access rather than a full shell environment.

- Remove inactive accounts.

- Ease maintenance by using the same user IDs on all systems.

- Do not use group user IDs; the user should only use user accounts to ensure accountability is maintained.

- Encourage users to choose hard-to-guess passwords.

Root IDs Avoid using root or super user IDs, as the superuser provides authority over an entire computer or network. Problems occurring under a regular user account are an annoyance, but they happen as root and can compromise the entire network. Except for essential root tasks, most operations should be run as a normal user in a user shell. Allow the root user to be accessed only from the system console, and limit access to the console.

Disable Unnecessary Services

The most important thing to do after installing a new Linux system is to disable unnecessary services and daemons. Many network services are automatically enabled in most Linuxes, including Red Hat, Slackware, and Debian, making it easy to set up servers. However, many of these services are unnecessary and could cause serious security problems. It is simple to disable services the user does not intend to use. Follow these guidelines:

- To see what services are running on a system, issue netstat .tua or netstat .tnua.

- Then, edit /etc/inetd.conf and comment out unneeded services.

- Remove or delete boot-time Linux processes if they are not being used; processes such as sendmail, named, routed, and hppd (in /etc/rc.d.) are often considered for removal. Remove daemons running standalone in /etc/rc.d (inetd and syslogd are necessary services and should not be eliminated).

- Consider disabling nntp (news), uucp, r-commands (rsh, rlogin, and rexec), and finger. Services to leave in tact are ftp (configure to not allow anonymous), telnet, the remote access user interface, and auth.

- Find all setuid binaries and decide which ones are needed; remove unwanted setuids with chmod ug-s /path/to/filename.

GartnerGroup RAS Services
Copyright © 2000

Linux Security: Perspective

- Review syslogs, messages, and .log files in /var/adm directory.

- Keep up with new releases and apply patches.

- Use add-on security software.

Passwords

All UNIX/Linux systems have the /etc/passwd file as a standard authentication tool. For passwords to work, UID files need username mappings, GID files need groupname mappings, and user passwords are needed. In Linux, passwords are not crypted. Rather, Linux systems use a hashing algorithm such as DES or MD5, along with a shadow password. Users are allowed in after the login program generates the hash and verifies it against the passwd or shadow file.

Red Hat Software implements the PAM facility for authentication to make shadow passwords easier to maintain. Shadow passwords involve the tedious job of the system administrator ensuring all programs have shadow-password support. With PAM, however, administrators simply add a PAM module, edit the config file for a program, and PAM allows it to use the module to do the authentication without recompiling.

Even with hashed passwords, it is possible for crackers to retrieve them by hashing a list of words and comparing them. Thus, it is recommended that users should be encouraged to choose random passwords not found in the dictionary. However, be aware that non-random passwords are easier for users to remember, who tend to either write random passwords down or use the same passwords on several systems. Using mkpasswd can automatically generate random passwords, although mkpasswd is not available on all systems. If not, try head .c 6 /dev/random |mmencode.

Controlling User Access

Linux is bundled with many utilities that can control user access, essentially preventing users from getting into a system and creating havoc. The system administrator should ensure that users have a quota on disk usage and then monitor users. In addition, it is important to make sure users are prevented from having an interactive shell account. Utilities inherent in Linux to control user access include.

- PAM--Linux systems generally include PAM, which sets the environment, such as limiting a user's memory. Configure Red Hat and Caldera in the /etc/security/ directory. The /etc/security/limits.conf file allows you to set user and group rules, define soft or hard rules, and whether it applies to CPU, memory, maximum filesize, etc.

- Bash--If a Linux system is use that does not come with PAM, Bash commands can be used as an alternative. Bash provides a built-in limiter (ulimit), enabling the user to enforce hard limits (defined in /etc/profile or .bash_profile) on users with the Bash shell. Bash only works if users are restricted from changing their login shells.

- Quota--This restricts users' disk usage. Most Linux distributions include Quota.

Monitoring Users

There are several Linux resources, downloadable for free from the Web, which can help system administrators monitor users:

- ttysnoop--Monitors and records what a user is doing. Download it from http://uuscan.cjb.net/.

- UserIPAcct--Monitors bandwidth usage by user. This software consists of a kernel patch; it adds user IP accounting to the kernel. Rules can be set up that monitor the amount of data a user's programs send or receive. Download it from http://zaheer.grid9.net/useripacct/.

Logs

Linux logging can be simply accomplished by sysklogd and klogd. The default file logging is in /var/log/. The bash command shell and Apache handle their own internal logging. Sendmail uses syslogd for logging or can log SMTP transactions to a file. Do not let users see or modify log files.

- Syslog--This is the default log for Linux systems. The klogd facility handles kernel messages and passes most to syslogd. Syslog logs messages to a remote host running syslog; logging can be centralized to a single host. Standard log files in syslog.conf include messages (user logins, tcp wrappers, IP firewall packets), secure (events--users changing UID/GID, failed password attempts), maillog (pop/imap connections, email headers), and spooler (for usenet and uucp). Most default Linux syslogd files are not secure--they are easily manipulated or destroyed. To make them more secure, set the files to append only. Also check our list of third-party software, which includes several more secure versions of syslog.

- Bash--As default Linux shell, most basic logging variables can be configured within bash at run time or during use. Variables to be aware of include HISTFILE (history file), HISTFILESIZE (maximum number of commands to keep in the file), and HISTSIZE (the number of commands to be used).

Table A: *Web-Based Downloadable Network Intrusion Scanners*

Program	Description	Internet Address
Nmap	Includes TCP/IP fingerprinting, TCP scans, SYN scans	http://www.insecure.org/nmap/index.html
icmpinfo	TCPdump that works with PING	ftp://hplyot.obspm.fr/net/
Portscanner	Port scanner	http://www.ameth.org/~veilleux/portscan.html
Trinux	Network security/monitoring	http://www.trinux.org/
Queso	Determines what OS a remote host is running.	http:// www.trinux.org/
Saint	One of the better tools; gathers network and security flaws about remote hosts and networks by examining network services such as finger, NFS, NIS, ftp and tftp, rexd, and statd. Easy output, problems are graded by priority. Next-generation Satan model.	http://www.wwdsi.com
SARA	Supports multiple threads for fast scans; stores data in a database, generates HTML reports. Based on Saint model.	http://home.arc.com/sara/
Nessus	One of the better tools; supports port scanning and has over 200 attacks. Can search through network DNS and attack related hosts.	http://www.nessus.org
Ftpcheck	Scans hosts and networks for FTP and anonymous FTP archives.	http://david.weekly.org/code/
Firewalk	Scans firewalls and execute tests. Uses traceroute style techniques to analyze firewall filter rules. IP packet responses. Determines gateway ACL filters and maps networks.	http://www.packetfactory.net/firewalk/

Linux Security: Perspective

- Change Attributes Command--Do not allow regular users access or the capabilities to manipulate a server's log files. The superuser and group own most log files, and permission is not available for individual users..Use the 'chattr +a filename' command to set the log file for append only, thus preventing people from overwriting the file. 'chattr +i filename' will prevent changes.

File System

The Linux ext2 file system is a traditional UNIX system with the same chown, fdisk, mkfs, fsck, du, setuid, setguid, and chmod commands useful to secure the system. However, as of this writing, Linux does not yet have journaling or Access Control Lists (ACLs) that are available in commercial UNIXes. ACLs allow the user to control file access more granularly than with the standard user, group, and other.

Security Holes and Threats

The best way to work around security problems is to check the security advisories on the Web and then upgrade with the latest patches. Many of the advisories also define specific workarounds, such as which files should be disabled, where to find upgrades, and how to install them. Viruses and worms are controllable by simply keeping the software upgraded to the latest releases, and only using software from trusted sites. Many people believe it is unnecessary to purchase antivirus software for Linux because it is not prone to viruses. If a user does experience an attack, it is important to have a good backup of the data so that it can be reinstalled on the system.

- Viruses--UNIX and Linux systems are not as susceptible to viruses as Windows and Mac systems. Because of the almost fool proof UNIX permission system and the fact that users are not allowed to write to any memory location they want, viruses have a difficult time replicating in UNIX systems. Viruses must insert code somewhere, such as in a boot sector, so they can be executed. Unless the code has purposely been given permission, UNIX systems automatically prevent code execution. The user actually has to tell UNIX to run something. This is in contrast to Windows systems, which run and execute code automatically. Nonetheless, there have been a few cases of Linux viruses, and there are many virus scanners available. These scanners are useful to filter e-mail and to scan Linux file servers accessed by Windows clients (which are susceptible to inactive viruses that may be sitting in the Linux server).

- Worms--Worms are more common for UNIX/Linux systems. The last big UNIX worm took place years ago; the infamous Morris Worm that took advantage of a vulnerability in sendmail. There are several current Linux worms that infiltrate imapd, sendmail, BIND 4.x, WU-FTPD and.other daemons. There are fixes to all, so it is important to keep updating software.

- Trojan Horses--Trojan horses are occasionally experienced in Linux. In a recent break in at ftp.win.tue.nl, TCP_WRAPPERS and other packages were changed, providing passwords via e-mail to an anonymous account.

Back Door Threats

Back doors are one of the biggest threats for Linux systems. Examples include:
- Buffer overflows or overruns--These problems are the most commonly mentioned in Linux security alert lists. Buffer overruns include setuid/setgid programs and daemons running as privileged users. Problems have happened with xterm (in libXt), sperl (setuid), lpr, and sendmail. A remote attacker, who can gain super user privileges on a host, can exploit these buffer overrun problems. Networking daemons such as sendmail create the most havoc, because they can allow users to obtain the root login and access to an entire system.

Linux Security: Perspective

- Environment variables--Environment variables affecting library functions, such as setuid and setgid program behavior can be controlled by user input.

- Executing arbitrary commands--Networking daemons can execute arbitrary commands. This is more commonly seen in poorly written CGI scripts and scripting languages such as tcl and perl than with programming languages such as C and C++.

Detecting Intrusions

With careful monitoring, intrusions can be detected and contained. Use the following tools and hints to help.

- Baselines--make a profile of the system. Include its resource usage in normal operation. Tools to help include free, df, and du. The user should make full system backups; regularly backup config files, and log files to help determine when an intrusion occurs.

- Monitor Servers--track down break-ins and determine legal issues. Monitoring tools include syslog and auditd.

- Scanning and Detection--firewalls are an essential line of defense. Packet filters need to be used on all Internet accessible machines. In.addition, useTCP-WRAPPERS and automated logging software that examine logs and bring problems to the attention of the system administrator.

- In addition to a plethora of third-party packet sniffers (packet sniffers capture network data not destined for the machine), Linux ships with tcpdump, which is very useful although not as advanced as most third-party packet sniffers.

The following checklist can be used to determine if the site has been compromised:

- Review log files for unusual activity.

- Examine configuration files for unauthorized entries.

- Examine for unusual or hidden files.

- Know where all the setuid and setgid files are to avoid unauthorized copies allowing unauthorized entrance to the system.

Table B: *Administration Tools*

Program	Description	Internet Address
SSH (secure shell)	Commercial product. Allows secure remote access to servers. Supports password, rhosts based, RSA key authentication, redirects ports, and configures user logins.	http://www.ssh.fi/
LSH	Under development; GNU free version of SSH	http://www.net.lut.ac.uk/psst/
NSH	Commercial product. Automates administration of multiple systems. Encryption and Perl.	http://www.networkshell.com/
Fsh	Uses encrypted tunnel using SSH or LSH	http://www.lysator.liu.se/fsh

GartnerGroup RAS Services

Copyright © 2000

Linux Security: Perspective

- Look for unauthorized services, especially in /etc/inetd.conf.

- Check any modifications to /etc/passwd; look for unauthorized new accounts.

- Compare system binary files with original installation copies to ensure they are not altered. Check login, su, telnet, netstat, ifconfig, ls, find, du, df, libc, sync, binaries referenced in /etc/inetd.conf, and others.

- Look for sniffers--unauthorized use of network monitoring to avoid intruders looking for user accounts and passwords.

- Make sure cron and at jobs are not running unauthorized files that might open back doors. Ensure the jobs are not world-writable.

- Look through all the network computers, not just the server.

Technology Analysis

As a member of the UNIX family, Linux has very similar security concerns as UNIX. However, because Linux is not tied closely to traditional commercial vendors, there have been concerns among corporate users that Linux may not be as secure as UNIX. Actually, Linux is proving to be a stable, secure operating system. However, as in any other UNIX system, Linux is only as secure as the administrator makes it. One of the basic concerns with Linux is that the more services are.working, the more chance there is to introduce a security hole. However, the administrator can remove services to reduce security weaknesses. The rule of thumb should be to only install the minimum, essential services, and remove any unused services.

One of the big differences between security in Linux versus security in other operating systems is the speed in which problems are found, and fixes are accomplished. With Linux, these fixes have happened much faster than in other operating systems because thousands of volunteers find it,

Table C: *Logging Packages*

Program	Description	Internet Address
ssylog	Implements a cryptographic protocol allowing remote system log audits.	http://www.coresdi.com/english/freesoft.html
Nsyslogd	Supports TCP, allows for encrypted network-wide delivery of syslog messages.	http://coombs.anu.edu.au/~avalon/nsyslog.html
Abacus -- Psionic Logcheck, Psionic PortSentry	Reviews logs and e-mails reports of suspicious activity	http://www.psionic.com/abacus/logcheck/
WOTS	Collects log files. Generates reports, executes actions based on log findings.	http://www.vcpc.univie.ac.at/~tc/tools/

announce it, and offer immediate fixes. These volunteers are the Linux development group--a worldwide group of volunteers, much larger than traditional vendors' development groups; Traditional vendors have small development groups that take many months to find and fix security bugs. Thus, while Linux security may not yet be as advanced as the high-end proprietary or UNIX systems, it has taken Linux much less time to get where it is now, and bug fixes happen much faster than in the traditional model.

Linux is in the middle of the Internet revolution, which is marked by increased security risks. For example, because the Internet redirects data through several points, it allows malicious users the opportunity to intercept data. Intruders or "crackers" can more easily steal data if the user is connected to the Internet.

Another factor to take into account is that the more secure the system is, the more intrusive security is on users. The system administrator must balance usability versus security. For instance, the system could require everyone dialing into the system to use a callback modem to call them back at their home phone numbers. This is very secure, but if someone is not at home, it makes it difficult for

Table D: *Intrusion Detection Packages*

Program	Description	Internet Address
Tripwire	Commercial product. Detects variances in file integrity. Determines if files have been added to or deleted from protected system directories.	http://www.tripwiresecurity.com/
AIDE	Alternative to tripware. Freely downloadable.	http://www.cs.tut.fi/~rammer/aide.html
Gog&Magog	Lists system file properties, compares and notifies you.	http://www.multimania.com/cparisel/gog/
confcollect	Collects system info	http://www.skagelund.com/confcollect
Sxid	Checks and tracks setuid and setgid for changes	ftp://marcus.seva.net/pub/sxid
Pikt	Monitors, reports and fixes problems, and manages system configurations.	http://pikt.uchicago.edu/pikt/
DTK	Emulates typical services to provide false readings to attackers	http://all.net/dtk/
TCP-WRAPPERS	Restricts connection to services and configures response	ftp://ftp.porcupine.org/pub/security/
NFR	Packet sniffer. Logs data, detects attacks, and scans	http://www.nfr.com
sniffit	Packet sniffer. Filters, ASCII and graphical modes.	http://sniffit.rug.ac.be/~coder/sniffit/sniffit.html
Ethereal	Protocol analyzer/packet sniffer.	http://ethereal.zing.org
Snort	Lightweight packet sniffer/logger. Detects attacks.	http://www.clark.net/~roesch/security.html
SPY	Commercial product. High-end LAN multiprotocol analyzer.	http://pweb.uunet.de/trillian.of/Spy/
Ksniffer	Packet sniffer. Collects network statistics	http://ksniffer.veracity.nu/
Sophos	Commercial virus scanner.	http://www.sophos.com
AntiVir	Commercial virus scanner	http://www.hbedv.com

Linux Security: Perspective

him or her to login. The user could also setup a Linux system with direct dial access only and provide no network or connection to the Internet, but this also limits its usefulness.

One of the nice things about Linux and UNIX systems is that the basic operating system structure makes it almost impervious to viruses, unlike Windows and NT systems. The recent worldwide virus and worm epidemic that include the infamous Melissa virus have deeply affected Windows and Windows NT systems, but not UNIX or Linux. Even running the new beta 3 version of Windows 2000, the 17,000-user Microsoft campus was hit by the June 10 (1999) worm.

Nonetheless, Linux is still prone to other security problems. One of Linux's biggest security flaws is its preponderance for buffer overruns or overflows (which have also been plaguing UNIX for many years and is also inherent in Microsoft operating systems). Buffer overflows open up the system to attack by allowing someone to overrun a program variable and introduce and execute new code as the root user. Buffer overflows happen when a program inputs more data into a buffer than the file has.room for. If the attacker can accomplish a buffer overflow, then he or she can insert the "/bin/sh" command in root, allowing the attacker unlimited access to the system. To avoid these overflows, stay up-to-date with the latest security patches and regularly check the vendors' web sites for new occurrences.

Business Use

Businesses can experience many different attacks from crackers for many reasons--to entertain, to cause harm, to alter data, or to crack other hosts. Businesses must take precautions to avoid malicious or mischievous activity by maintaining a good security policy and performing strict security system management. Without developing rigorous protection schemes, the greatest risk is in losing all of a corporation's data. It may be time consuming to take precautions, but the risk is catastrophic.

Technology Leaders

Caldera OpenLinux
www.calderasystems.com
Caldera publishes an extensive security advisory--a list of bugs, along with the descriptions and solutions. Caldera has several extra utilities that are worthwhile for security. Its lizard graphical installation forces the user to create a user account, which should encourage users to not log in as root. In addition, the sulogin in /etc/inittab eliminates the capability to get into the root command prompt at the lilo boot prompt, without first entering the root password.

Debian
www.debian.org
Debian claims that most security problems brought to its attention are corrected within 48 hours. Debian's security web page addresses Debian's status to known security holes. Debian tracks security bugs until a version with the fix is released. Thus, the company recommends using the latest version to avoid security problems. For more information, subscribe to the Debian Security Announce mailing list at.http://www.debian.org/MailingLists/subscribe. Archives are available. Report bugs to security@debian.com.

Red Hat Linux
www.redhat.com
Red Hat 6.0 allows the user to use shadow passwords and MD5 passwords.

Linux Security: Perspective

S.u.S.E.
www.suse.de

The Harden SuSE utility cleans up file permissions and turns off daemons. The SuSE security check provides scripts that check password files and regularly lists installed software.

Linux Security: Perspective

TurboLinux
www.turbolinux.com

TurboLinux comes with Tripwire on the companion CD, in addition to other security facilities such as the Amanda backup program and the ipchains firewall.

Datapro Insight

Security basics are applicable to any operating system, and Linux is no exception--start with a policy and maintain the system with sound security practices. Basic Linux security procedures are similar to UNIX. However, Linux does not have the same high level of security as operating systems that have been around for years, simply because it is newer than anything else, and many facilities are still being developed. Nonetheless, Datapro believes Linux does have several advantages over every other operating system on the market. Most important is the fast bug identification and remediation that happens as a result of Linux's being an open source product. Unlike traditional software, where a user has to wait months for the company to release patches for bugs and holes, Linux security problems are found and posted on the net sometimes within hours after the problem is found. Also, because of the open source nature of Linux, a great abundance of free security tools and problem lists have quickly emerged for the operating system.

Table E: *Other security packages*

Program	Description	Internet Address
John the Ripper	Password cracker; detects weak passwords	http://www.openwall.com/john
Crack	Password cracker	http://www.users.dircon.co.uk/~crypto
VCU	Password cracker	http://wilter.com/wf/vcu/
Wipe	File wiper; erases data	http://gsu.linux.org.tr/wipe/
PGP	Public encryption	http://www.linuxsupportline.com/~pgp/default.htm.
GnuPG	Encryption alternative to PGP	http://www.gnupg.org/
CIPE	Encyrption for IP routers	http://sites.inka.de/~W1011/devel/cipe.html
CFS	Data encryption on the hard drive	http://www.cryptography.org
TCFS	Data encryption; integrated with NFS	http://tcfs.dia.unisa.it/
PPDD	Encrypted disk device driver	http://linux01.gwdg.de/~alatham/
Encrypted Home Directory	Encrypted directory	http://members.home.net/id-est/
StegFS	Hides data on hard drive	http://www.nollan.pp.se/computer_security.html
qmail	Secure alternative to sendmail	http://www.qmail.org/
pidentd	Secure alternative to identd	ftp://ftp.csc.ncsu.edu/pub/security/
rhosts dodgy	Checks rhost entries	http://gopher.metronet.com:70/0/perlinfo /scripts/admin/rhosts.dodgy.pl

GartnerGroup RAS Services
Copyright © 2000

Computer Associates Intl. CA-ACF2 for OS/390

April 21, 1999

Datapro Summary

CA-ACF2 for OS/390 is a comprehensive access control system for the IBM mainframe-compatible and extended environments. There are versions of CA-ACF2 for all major mainframe operating systems: OS/390 (MCS), VSE, and VM. There is also a version that operates with IBM's DB2 relational database management system (RDBMS) and Compaq's Alpha/OpenVMS and VAX/VMS environments. One of the three most popular security systems on the market, CA-ACF2 has been consistently maintained to support all new technologies and standards for open systems and client/server environments. CA-ACF2 for OS/390(MVS) has a B1 security trust status rating. CA-ACF2 WorkStation combines a Windows NT GUI for single-point administration of all CA-ACF2 for OS/390 (MVS) systems with centralized monitoring and reporting of security events throughout an entire enterprise.

—By Herb Gepner
—Analytical Source: Ed Cowger

Note: Computer Associates Intl.'s (CAI's) CA-ACF2 for OS/390 (MVS) Release 6.2 expands existing support for the Sysplex environment; supports interfaces between OS/390 (MVS), VM, and VSE (IBM does not support VSE with RACF); and enhances full OpenEdition Distributed Computing Environment (DCE), CICS Transaction Server for OS/390, and PassTicket support. In addition, CA-ACF2 continues support of non-IBM platforms.

Corporate Headquarters

Computer Associates Intl., Inc.
One Computer Associates Plaza
Islandia, NY 11788, U.S.A.
Tel: +1 516 342 5224; +1 800 225 5224
Fax: +1 516 342 5734
Internet: http://www.cai.com

Overview

CA-ACF2 for OS/390 is designed around the concept of "default protection"; the entire computer system is protected automatically at all times. Sharing of data among users is allowed only when it has been explicitly authorized. Default protection also means that company policies and procedures regarding computer facility use can be applied automatically, with no risk of undefined areas evading or bypassing management controls and procedures.

Overview

Product Name	CA-ACF2 for OS/390
Product Type	A data set, system resource, and system access control system for IBM mainframes and Compaq VAX/VMS systems.
Platform Supported	Any IBM OS/390 (MVS), VM, or VSE (as a guest system) system. CA-ACF2 WorkStation can be installed on a Windows NT workstation. Also provides extended support for DB2 and Compaq Computer VAX/VMS and Alpha/VMS platforms and Sysplex configurations.
Current Installed Base	Over 5,000 (Datapro estimate).
Price Range (US$)	A license for CA-ACF2 for OS/390 (MVS) starts at approximately $26,028. See Pricing section for other pricing information.

CA-ACF2 Enhancements

CA-ACF2 for OS/390 (MVS) Release 6.2 Enhancements

Release 6.2 includes the following enhanced features:
- Special privileges can be controlled through standard resource rules.
- Access and Resource Rules were expanded to 32KB.
- Sysplex and Coupling Facility support that includes XCF for CA-ACF2 operator commands to be routed to other CA-ACF2 systems.
- A batch utility (ACF Rule Cleanup) can automatically identify "dead" rules.
- Access rules and resource rules can include the date on which the rule will automatically become effective.
- CA SAF enhances performance with the creation of Fastpath logic for the SAF calls issued most frequently in the system.
- Utilizes Message Services (MMS) to permit the use of alternate language messages. National-language profiles can be created.
- Expanded "List If" support to include any defined logonid field.

CA-ACF2 for VM Release 4.0

Enhancements
MVS Compatibility
Enhancements

The ACF Commands LIST, CHANGE, and SET TERSE subcommands now provide extended capabilities.
The access rule compiler and decompiler supports the $RESOWNER control statement used for OS/390 (MVS) data sets controlled through DFSMS.
The resource rule compiler and decompiler supports the $RECNAME control statement used for record-level protection.

CA-ACF2 for VSE Release 3.0

Enhancements

Can communicate with OS/390 (MVS) and VM versions and can also inherit login ID information for batch jobs from these environments. Default resource protection enables automatic access control over programs and files.

Basic Product Characteristics

Internal Logic

Each version of CA-ACF2 is logically similar but distinct depending on the operating system supported.
Allows the user to establish a single security interface regardless of the version(s) being employed.

Currently, versions are available for:

- OS/390
- System/390 Parallel Sysplex and Coupling Facility
- VM/SP, VM/ESA, and VM/VSE (all VSE versions through VSE/ESA 2.3)
- Compaq Alpha/OpenVMS or VAX/VMS configuration (when tied to an IBM OS/390 (MVS) centralized host)
- DB2

Computer Associates Intl. CA-ACF2 for OS/390

System Authorization Facility (SAF) Support	Uses the industry-standard security interface to IBM operating systems. With CA-ACF2 OS/390 (MVS) Release 6.0 and above, the SAF interface provides trace control facilities to aid in troubleshooting and implementation.
Profile Support	OS/390 (MVS) uses Profiles to maintain information regarding how components process data. An Information Storage class determines the record type. Structured Information Storage Profile segment records contain detailed information on the individual segments of the Profile. Processing information for OS/390 (MVS) components, such as DLF, SMS, and APPC can be stored in Profiles.
Sysplex Support	Uses the Cross Systems Communications Facility (XCF) to automatically notify and process updates on other processors in the Sysplex/390 environment when a change has occurred. This feature also promotes automatic synchronization of security changes throughout the Sysplex environment.
Partitioned Data Set (PDS) Protection	Provides member-level security for PDSs by controlling access to individual PDS members. PDS security includes protection against channel programs that attempt to read the PDS directly.
User Interface CA-ACF2 Command Language	An interactive command language with full ISPF support defines users, resources, and their relationships. Provides protection at the data set name level for all data sets residing on direct access storage devices (DASDs) and mass storage system (MSS) volumes designated as resident or data sets on magnetic tape.
Logon Identifier (ID)	Each user possesses his or her own logon ID, and each logon ID is protected by a password known only to the owner. Uses one-way encryption to ensure that the password cannot be disclosed by the system or discovered by other means.
SECTRACE Facility	Enables the user to view the OS/390 (MVS) system as a whole and look at all SAF calls.
The Command Propagation Facility (CPF) Command-Level Security	Enables a security officer to administer the network's CA-ACF2 clusters from a single node. Provides security for the system programmer interface (SPI) subset of CICS command-level commands. A CICSKEY resource called XCMD is used to protect the SPI commands. The SERVICE keyword in resource rules can be used to further restrict access between inquiry and update functions.
General Interface System Access Control	CA-ACF2 interfaces with all common sign-on and logon procedures (e.g., CICS, TSO, and CMS). Users are validated at the system level during logon, JES2 Job Control Language (JCL) conversion processing, or JES3 input services processing. In a VM/VSE system, validation occurs when a batch job is submitted through CMSBATCH, VMBATCH, the POWER/VSE

subsystem, or when a user issues a sign-on request to access a CICS region.

Optional validations can be made to determine whether a requested physical device(s) is an authorized job input source for the requesting user or whether the shift (time of day) or even date/day of week is appropriate for access to the system.

Security records are maintained in a logon ID database, a rules database, and an information storage database.

Subsystem interface support includes TSO, CICS, IMS/DB, CA-Datacom/DB, CA-IDMS/DB, CA-Roscoe, and DB2.

The Mandatory Access Control (CA MAC) Facility	Provides disclosure protection as prescribed by the National Computer Security Center (NCSC) for eligibility for B1 security clearance. Provides antivirus protection.
Logon ID Database	Contains user identification, logon, and password data information. The privileges section contains directives relating to authority control actions. An access and statistics section maintains statistics relating to access counts and time and date of last system accesses.
Rules Database	Contains all data set access rules. Resource rules, which govern all system and subsystem resources, are stored in the Information Storage Database.
Information Storage Database	A few of the record types stored in this database include the following: • CICS rules, • DB2 rules, • Administrative guidelines and limitations, • System and source controls, and • IMS rules.
Data Sharing and the Coupling Facility	For users with the Coupling Facility Option, CA-ACF2 places heavily used security information in the Coupling Facility list structures, making this information accessible to all processors.
Extended User Authentication	Used with the CA-ACF2 for OS/390 (MVS) to provide an additional safeguard to protect the system from unauthorized access by prompting the user for input that only that user should know and validating that input with information stored in the database.

Recovery Features

Backup Features	In the CA-ACF2 for OS/390 (MVS) system, VSAM clusters can be backed up by an operating system utility. VM or VM/VSE databases can be formatted as either standard CMS files or as VSE/VSAM clusters. CA-ACF2 databases are copied from the resident DASD to a scratch file and then dumped to permanent data sets..Dumping is initiated either through an automatic time setting generated into the CA-ACF2 system or through an interactively entered operator command.

Computer Associates Intl. CA-ACF2 for OS/390

Recovery Operation — Uses the IBM SMF file. Generates a copy of each modified record in the backup clusters. A utility program uses a forward-recovery technique with these clusters. In the VM and VM/VSE environments, CA-ACF2 logs each insertion, modification, or update made to a database record. The backup copies of the databases and the log records are used to forward-recover the databases.

Data Access/Data Bridge

Data Access Control — Intercepts operating system activities that control data set allocation, open, scratch, and catalog processing and determines whether further verification must be performed.
If rules do not exist, or if the level of specified access is not sufficient, the user request is aborted and a record of the attempt is entered into both the System Management Facility (SMF) log and the job log, the CA-ACF2 for VM logging file, or the CA-ACF2 for VSE log.

Generalized Resource Rules — Allows the user to define installation-unique resources that require access validation.
Generalized resource rules and algorithmic methodologies are similar to the data access control rules. They determine whether access via a system resource should be allowed, denied, or allowed and logged to a history journal.

Resource Rules Command — Users with the proper authority can be allowed to change rule line information only within a Rule Set, but are restricted from changing the control information.

Communications/Connectivity

Subsystem Support — CA-ACF2 for OS/390 (MVS) supports IBM's IMS/DC, CICS/VS, and MVS/TSO online environments. A security subsystem supports all DL/1 databases. A networked administration capability between CA-ACF2/Secman for VAX exists.

CA-ACF2 CICS Security Subsystem — Protects multiple CICS regions and includes validation for Multiple Region Operation (MRO), Intersystem Communication (ISC), and Interregion Communication (IRC).

CA-ACF2 CICS Master Terminal Transaction Facility — Helps the CICS administrator to maintain and fine-tune CA-ACF2 CICS.

Network Administration — Centralized, decentralized, single-point, or mixed network administration is available.

CICS Transaction Server — Support Designed for use in the OS/390 environment utilizing CICS TS architecture. Provides:

- VSAM record-level sharing (RLS) allowing VSAM files to be shared among CICS regions.
- Temporary storage sharing allows applications running in different CICS regions to share queues.
- Supports the MVS System Logger for CICS logging. Information from multiple CICS regions can be merged, allowing for enhanced recoverability.

Computer Associates Intl. CA-ACF2 for OS/390

Security Features

Access Rules | An access rule contains the following:
- A description of the data or files that are to be shared.
- A description of the system user(s) to be allowed access.
- A description of the circumstances under which the sharing will be allowed.
- The particular type of access that will be allowed in any given circumstance.

Access Types | CA-ACF2 supports several discrete access types:
- No Access,
- Execute-Only Access,
- Read-Only Access,
- Write-Only Access, and
- Allocate Access.

Rule Sets | Can be added or deleted dynamically, and elements of a set can be added, deleted, or modified.
Access types can be combined as required.

Reporting Features

CA-Easy Access Report Language (EARL) | An English-like, high-level language with charting and arithmetic capabilities that allows users to format reports locally and to customize special reports. Allows users to generate programs to produce lists and reports on all actively CA-ACF2 monitored and controlled operations.
Inputs are provided by the CA-ACF2 databases and either the SMF or a CA-ACF2 SMF-like file.
Output can be hardcopy or viewable at a terminal.

CA-ACF2 for VM

Operating System Support | Supports VM/ESA Releases 2.1 and 2.2 and Version 2 Release 1.0 and above.
Idle Terminal Time-out | Monitors terminal activity in order to limit security exposure when unattended.
Basic Facilities | Exploits and provides security for VM/ESA Data Spaces.
Full-screen administration of resource rules.
An extension of the shared group logon feature which allows someone in the designated group to log on under a given ID.
A REXX language interface.
Audit data is recorded under a single SMF record number making it compatible with CA-ACF2 for OS/390 (MVS).
Provides an emergency database maintenance capability.
Provides security for APPC VM communications.
Provides security for Shared File System.

CA-ACF2 VSE Release 3.0

VSE/ESA Feature (optional) | Extends functionality by supporting activity surveillance in both static and dynamic partitions.
Extends IUCV to dynamic partitions to allow communication among systems operating as guests under VM.
Exploits VSE/ESA Data Spaces.
Allows CA-Earl report writer work areas to be placed in Data Spaces. Data Space support is available in both 370 and ESA modes.

Computer Associates Intl. CA-ACF2 for OS/390

Options

CA-ACF2/Secman for VAX
Provides integrated security for Compaq Computer Alpha/Open VMS and VAX/VMS systems in an IBM network.

Provides a single, centralized, coordinated security administration point for networked VAX machines.

IBM's VTAM and Compaq's DECnet handle intersystem communications. Security administrator can secure remote Alpha/OpenVMS and VAX/VMS users and resources using the same panels and line commands of CA-ACF2 for OS/390 (MVS).

CA-ACF2 databases are automatically synchronized with each VMS-resident User Authorization File (UAF) and Network Authorization File (NETUAF).

All standard VAX/VMS and Alpha/OpenVMS control options for Access Control Lists (ACLs) and Access Control Entries (ACEs) are supported.

CA-ACF2 for DB2
Extends security to the entire IBM DB2 database system. It enables users to control access to DB2 resources and provides the same enterprise-wide security solution provided with other CA-ACF2 products.

DB2-specific resource types protected through CA-ACF2 for DB2 include:

- System privileges,
- Databases,
- Table spaces,
- Tables/views,
- Plans,
- Collections,
- Packages,
- Storage groups, and
- Buffer pools.

Frees the user from the DB2 GRANT/REVOKE security table facility and makes it easier for the security administrator to control user access and create objects.

CA-provided conversion utilities allow users of DB2's internal security to convert to CA-ACF2/DB2 while preserving their investment in existing security implementation solutions.

Enhanced Facilities
- Single-point security linking CA security to DB2.
- Access controls in DB2 conform to the standard DB2 enforcement approach.
- DB2 security table synchronization.

CA-ACF2 WorkStation
Functions with CA-ACF2 for OS/390 (MVS) Release 6.1 and above and Windows NT Version 3.1 and above.

Provides a fully windowed graphical environment that enables administrators to more quickly enable security administration using standard CA-ACF2 functions.

Provides a central point of administration. All information retrieval and updating occurs in realtime.

Allows administrators to extend their capabilities with Unicenter TNG to manage other enterprise management applications.

Provides realtime notification of critical security events on all OS/390 platforms.

Computer Associates Intl. CA-ACF2 for OS/390

Analysis

With CA-ACF2's "default protection" approach to system and data protection, the entire computer system is protected automatically at all times. Data sharing among users is allowed only when explicitly authorized. Additional CA-ACF2 capabilities are label dominance, object sensitivity, and user clearance. Features, such as Cross System Communication Facility (XCF) and the Coupling Facility Option which enhance use of the Parallel Sysplex capability; the Command Propagation Facility (CPF), which provides full recovery of all commands and passwords propagated to remote nodes; and Partitioned Data Set (PDS) member-level protection greatly enhance security in the OS/390 operating environments.

Security is a major component of CA's Unicenter TNG product line. CA-ACF2 is now integrated with Unicenter through an offering called CA-ACF2 WorkStation that runs on Windows NT platforms. This product enables CA-ACF2 user records and rules to be administered from a workstation. Integrated with Unicenter TNG, CA-ACF2 WorkStation adds additional functions including network-wide, realtime security event monitoring and security reporting.

With either CA-ACF2 or CA-Top Secret installations, total enterprise-wide security can be administered from a single workstation. With Unicenter TNG Single Sign-On (SSO), Windows-based end users are provided with an easy point-and-click access facility to enterprise-wide network applications, including UNIX, PC, and mainframe-based services. For existing RACF MVS users, CA has the Unicenter TNG RACF Option, a set of advanced reporting and monitoring facilities that combines a Windows-based GUI for all OS/390 systems and Unicenter platforms with centralized monitoring and reporting of security events throughout a heterogeneous, multivendor environment

In the IBM mainframe area, there are three major security products that dominate the market. Two of these are provided by CA: CA-Top Secret and CA-ACF2. The third is IBM's RACF. Taken as a group, the CA products undoubtedly control the largest percentage of the IBM OS/390 mainframe security market, with CA-ACF2 usually ranked first and CA-Top Secret second. RACF comes in a valiant third. CA-Alert, another CA product that supports the VSE, CICS, and VM environments, does not directly compete with any of the aforementioned products.

Pricing

Product	Starting Price (US$)
CA-ACF2	
CA-ACF2 for OS/390	26,028
CA-ACF2 for VSE	15,558
CA-ACF2 for VM	16,176
CA-ACF2/Secman for VAX	636
CA-ACF2 for DB2	10,932
CA-ACF2 VAX/NET	8,196
CA-ACF2 VSE/ESA Option	3,882

GSA Pricing
No.

Computer Associates Intl. CA-ACF2 for OS/390

Competitors

As noted in the Analysis section of this report, there are three major OS/390 security products that dominate the mainframe marketplace: CA-ACF2, CA-Top Secret, and IBM's RACF. CA-Top Secret is an alternate choice to CA-ACF2 for those who wish to install a user protection scheme as opposed to CA-ACF2's rules-based philosophy. Also, CA-Top Secret also supports native-mode VSE.

RACF provides most of the functionality found in CA-ACF2 for OS/390, but has a tendency to be more complex to implement, especially when implementing a DB2 environment. RACF and CA-ACF2 for OS/390 cannot coexist in a single OS/390 processor, but a Unicenter TNG RACF Option permits RACF security event logs to be combined with CA-ACF2 for OS/390, CA-Top Secret, and Unicenter TNG logs.

In the VM environment, Sterling Software offers VM:Secure, a utility-type product that goes to make up Sterling's total VM disk and data management support applications. Those users with the Sterling group of products make up the majority if its user base. VM:Secure is also a rules-based product that can be tailored to meet installation requirements.

Strengths

What CA-ACF2 offers the IBM mainframe market is a cornerstone for enterprise-wide security administration. Its flexible structure allows for policy-based security definition. For open systems support, Unicenter TNG, through its interconnection with CA-ACF2, provides extensive Windows and UNIX support. The Windows capability allows the security system to interact with the Unicenter TNG Single Sign-On Option (SSO). CA-ACF2 WorkStation products further expand the applicability of CA-ACF2-type security throughout the enterprise environment. Centralized security of Compaq's Alpha/Open-VMS and VAX/VMS systems is achievable through CA-ACF2's OS/390 host environment. CA-ACF2 also was the first security system on the market to provide security at the internal DB2 level.

CA-ACF2 for VM provides full support of VM/ESA along with full-screen administration functions and the REXX language interface so that users can write their own REXX language applications. In addition, CA-ACF2 for VM provides Shared File System security as well as VM/ESA Data Space exploitation and security.

CA-ACF2 for VSE can support either VSE/SP or VSE/ESA. The VSE/ESA feature is optional and supports all VSE/ESA operating system enhancements.

Limitations

CA-ACF2 for VSE was an extension of the original MVS version of the product. The original implementation supporting the VSE platform prohibited its use in native-mode VSE. Instead, CA-ACF2 for VSE can only be used in the VSE environment when VSE is running as a guest in a VM configuration. This differs from its CA-Top Secret for VSE counterpart and CA-Alert which do support native-mode VSE. However, in the VM mode, security databases from any one of the major systems (OS/390 (MVS), VM, or VSE) can be shared.

Computer Associates Intl. CA-ACF2 for OS/390

Datapro Insight

Although the industry recognizes the existence of the three major IBM mainframe security products—CA-ACF2, CA-Top Secret, and RACF—CA is considered the dominant software supplier of software for this marketplace, with IBM's RACF bringing up the rear. The main choice that users have in selecting which CA product to install is based on the security approach the installation wishes to implement.

CA has expended a great deal of effort in maintaining its security products, not only for use with mainframes, but also through the use of enterprise elements that go to make up a fully functional corporate entity. Through the use of Unicenter TNG and the WorkStation options, security can be extended throughout the enterprise. The ability to incorporate information from non-IBM systems gives these products an even further reach. Then there is the DB2 database support, which is easier to implement than IBM's user-exit approach. On the whole, it goes without saying that Computer Associates not only enjoys leading this segment of the software industry, but also works hard at maintaining that lead.

Computer Associates Intl.

CA-Top Secret for OS/390   April 20, 1999

Datapro Summary

CA-Top Secret is a software security product that secures the IBM mainframe operating systems (OS/390, MVS, VM, and VSE) along with related subsystems and applications. CA-Top Secret interacts with other CA products to secure DB2 applications as well as Compaq Computer VAX/VMS and Alpha/OpenVMS processors that are networked with an IBM OS/390 system, providing user authentication; resource access control; and security administration, logging, and reporting. In conjunction with Unicenter TNG and CA-ACF2 for OS/390, CA-Top Secret for OS/390 can provide enterprise-wide distributed security capabilities. With CA-Top Secret WorkStation, an installation can implement a windows-based GUI to provide single-point control and monitoring of mainframe environments. CA-Top Secret is also an integral member of CA's enterprise-wide Security Solution.

—By Herb Gepner
—Analytical Source: Ed Cowger

Note: The most current version of CA-Top Secret for OS/390 is Release 5.1. Some of the enhancements in this release include Record Level Protection (RLP), further performance improvements by increasing the Command Processors, Accessor ID (ACID) refresh, masking all resources, the introduction of calendars, and password reverification. In addition, Releases 5.0 and 5.1 provide Digital Certificate support.

Corporate Headquarters

Computer Associates Intl., Inc.
One Computer Associates Plaza
Islandia, NY 11788, U.S.A.
Tel: +1 516 342 5224; +1 800 225 5224
Fax: +1 516 342 5734
Internet: http://www.cai.com

Overview

CA-Top Secret provides access control for OS/390, MVS, VSE, or VM operating systems and their subsystems or facilities. This includes, but is not limited to, JES2, TSO, CICS, IMS, DB2, CA-IDMS/DB, CA-Datacom/DB, and CA-Roscoe. It also supports the Sysplex environment. CA-Top Secret controls who accesses what resources, how, when, and through which facilities. In addition, it supports the latest version of OS/390, including UNIX System Services (formerly OpenEdition/MVS) and Digital Certificate Support.

With the Command Propagation Facility (CPF), remote security synchronization is automatic. The CA-Top Secret WorkStation product simplifies enterprise-wide security management and advanced graphical administration, auditing, reporting, monitoring, and automated response.

Overview

Product Name	CA-Top Secret
Product Type	Mainframe resource access security system.
Platform Supported	Any IBM OS/390, MVS, VM, and VSE systems. Also includes extended support for DB2, OS/390s, and Compaq VAX/VMS and Alpha/OpenVMS platforms and Sysplex configurations.

CA-Top Secret for OS/390

Current Release Levels

CA-Top SecCA-Top Secret for OS/390¾Release--5.1.
CA-Top Secret for VSE--Release 2.3.
CA-Top Secret for VM--Release 1.4.

Current Installed Base

Over 4,000 (Datapro estimate).

Price Range (US$)

A CA-Top Secret for OS/390 license starts at approximately $26,028. See the *"Pricing"* section for other CA-Top Secret product pricing information.

Overview

With few exceptions, all versions of CA-Top Secret have the same logical features and functions. In the following descriptions, any feature unique to a specific version is identified as such.

Highlights of CA-Top Secret for OS/390 Release 5.1

Product Enhancements

- Record-level protection for CICS.
- Screen-level protection for CICS.
- Single command refresh of the security environment.
- CPF recovery.
- Password reverification on ownable transactions (OTRANs).
- Support for the use of x.509 Digital Certificates.
- Extended administrative and performance enhancements.

Basic CA-Top Secret Structure

Security File

CA-Top Secret stores its user profile information in a security database called the Security File. This file can be shared among all OS/390, VM, and VSE CPUs at any single site or among multiple VTAM-networked sites using the Command Propagation Facility (CPF). CA-Top Secret for VSE requires a different file. Each system user is assigned a Security Record. Using the Top Secret System (TSS) command, all user attributes and access control parameters are defined in this Security Record or in a Profile (a record used to group similar access authorizations).

Global security authorizations and default protection for both data and resources are also provided (except in the VSE environment). Both batch and online resource protection can be established from a single system.

Security Components

CA-Top Secret's architecture offers a security scheme built around the concept that security can be defined in terms of the user and what resources he or she may access.

The logical components of CA-Top Secret are Users, Profiles, Departments, Divisions, Administrators, and Zones. System administrators and auditors can belong to Departments, Divisions, or Zones or can be defined globally.

CA-Top Secret for OS/390

PDS Member-Level Protection	Controls access to individual members within a partitioned data set (PDS). Users can be given read access to an entire PDS, but restricted to updating only certain members.
	Within a single PDS, programmers responsible for a certain application can be restricted to just the source members that make up their applications.
	Provides unique access levels that enable reading, writing, deleting, or renaming of PDS members and provides an audit trail of activity against selected PDS members.
Site-Definable Security File Fields	A Field Descriptor Table (FDT) enables administrators to dynamically add site-defined fields to ACIDs within the Security File. FDT fields can be retrieved and modified by the use of TSS commands.
Accessor IDs (ACIDs)	Define the logical components. Resources can belong to Users, Profiles, Departments, Divisions, Administrators, or Zones and are generally accessed only through User or Profile ACID authorizations.
	A user may be allowed to administer his or her own resources. The number of ACIDs that can be defined is unlimited, regardless of the ACID type.
Virtual Storage Constraint Relief (VSCR)	VSCR enables CA-Top Secret to maintain some Accessor ID (ACID) and PROFILE information in storage, reducing the amount of I/O in multiuser address spaces.
Support for OS/390 Facilities	• Supports UNIX System Services (USS) MVS, including the Hierarchical File System (HFS). • Supports the Secured Sign-on function of the IBM Network Security Program (NSP) and PassTicket applications. • Persistent Verification allows CA-Top Secret to keep an ACID's sign-on information in memory, reducing I/O and password transmissions during APPC/MVS conversation processing. • Provides enhanced security for the Sysplex/390 Coupling Facility.
Sysplex/390 Support	This release supports: • OS/390 Release 2 • USS DCE • SystemView • NetView 3.1 • OS/390 Internet Connection Server (OS/390 Bonuspack) (Lotus Domino Go Webserver) • WebSphere Application Server • CICS Transaction Server (CTS) • Component Broker Series • MQSeries
21st-Century Support	All CA-Top Secret products now support dates for the 21st century.

Operations

Job/Session Initiation Verifications and Resource Validation	When a user's job initiates, or the user signs on to an online facility, CA-Top Secret verifies the user and validates the password, ticket, or token. It stores pertinent Security Record information and then verifies attempts to access a protected resource based on this information.
	If a user attempts to access information for which he or she has not been authorized, CA-Top Secret immediately terminates the request and writes a record of the event, which may be reviewed by the security administrator either in batch or online.
	As an option in the event of repeated attempts, CA-Top Secret notifies the TSS Administrator and suspends the user's access to the system. Administrator can centrally monitor events for multiple CA-Top Secret systems in realtime.

Security Administration Functions

Control	CA-Top Secret control can be customized to meet installation requirements. Control can be established in a centralized, decentralized, or mixed mode. System control options can be set and changed dynamically by the security administrator.
	TSS Administrators have the responsibility for identifying users, resources, and access to resources. All maintenance of ACIDs and associated definitions is the responsibility of TSS Administrators.
System Access Protection CA	defines a facility as any service that processes work on behalf of users or jobs. CA-Top Secret supports the following facilities:

- TSO
- Batch and Started Tasks
- IMS/VS and IMS/ESA
- DB2
- CICS/VS and CTS
- CA-Datacom/DB
- CA-IDMS/DB
- CA-Roscoe
- Other CA and non-CA services
- Site-defined services

The ACID information determines whether CPU access will be allowed. Upon logging on to the system, the user must provide a password, ticket, or token that positively identifies him or her. Several access authorization criteria are also checked.

Users may optionally change their own passwords.

Support for sign-on authentication can come from devices such as fingerprint readers, magnetic bar cards, decoder devices, and external key boxes.

Security is provided for work received from other systems via RJE, NJE, and APPC/MVS.

GartnerGroup RAS Services

Copyright © 2000   20 April 1999

CA-Top Secret for OS/390

CICS Support	Several CICS enhancements are available with CA-Top Secret for OS/390 and VSE. CICS/ESA Release 4.1 is supported in the OS/390 environment; CICS/VSE 2.3 is supported in the latest CA-Top Secret for VSE release. The TSS function can establish protection of access to IMS databases when accessed via CICS, and a CICS debugging utility permits online verification of critical control blocks and parameter settings.
	CICS Transaction Server 1.1 and 1.2 are supported in CA-Top Secret for OS/390R l 5 0 d 5 1 CTS13 illb t d h itb.OS/390 Releases 5.0 and 5.1. CTS 1.3 will be supported when it becomes generally available. Full Multiple Region Operation (MRO) and Intersystem Communications (ISC) session security is provided, as well as support of CICSplexes. ISC link support also applies to both the OS/390 and VSE systems, allowing transaction routing between the OS/390 and VSE CA-Top Secret environments.
Support of Advanced Peer-to-Peer Communications (APPC)/MVS	APPC uses the CA-Top Secret security database to perform resource checks, to retrieve information associated with users, and as a repository for logical unit (LU) information, such as distribution codes. Provides conversation security specifically oriented to limit individual inbound user access to APPC communications paths and transaction programs.
Protection of Resources	Any type of ACID can own resource types protected by CA-Top Secret. In order to access a resource, the user ACID must either own the resource or have been previously given permission to access it.
	An access technique allows a group of similar resources to be defined by one generic prefix. Profiles are also used to establish access to both like and unlike resources in groups.
	Once a resource is owned by an ACID, explicit authorization can transfer ownership, allow access permission, and assign various restricted levels by which the resource can be accessed. Time-of-day, day-of-week, facility, etc., can also restrict access.
Command Propagation Facility (CPF)	CPF is a feature that allows sites to maintain multiple, separate Security Files across a VTAM networked environment, while keeping common information, including passwords, completely and automatically synchronized (OS/390 and VM).
Command Propagation	Password synchronization between CA-Top Secret and CA-ACF2 in Facility (CPF) Extension the OS/390 environment has been extended to include Unicenter TNG and provides enterprise-wide password synchronization across OS/390 and distributed platforms, including Windows NT, UNIX systems, AS/400, NetWare, and others.

CA-Top Secret for OS/390

Phased Implementation	Supports implementation of full security over time through security processing "MODES." MODES determine how strictly security is to be enforced. They range from no control over access, to control with warning messages upon violations, to full security for all resources.
	MODES can be set system wide, for each facility, by user or group of users, by particular resource authorizations, and by type of resource access violation.
Cache Facility	Designed for retrieval and storage of user and profile information. Options are available to tailor cache operations to site-specific needs and to evaluate and tune performance.

Reporting and Recovery

Activity/Violation Logging and Reporting	This function reports on violators. If a user's request to access a resource is not authorized, CA-Top Secret logs a record of the event to the System Management Facility (SMF) file and/or a shared Audit/Tracking File and optionally notifies the TSS Administrator via the security console.
Recovery Capabilities	Information in the Security File is automatically backed up once a day. When changes to the Security File occur, the system records the change into the Recovery File, which can be used to reconstruct the Security File if it becomes damaged or unusable.
File Analysis Routine (TSSFAR)	This utility is available for examining and diagnosing problems in the Security File. There are options for checking allocations and chainings.
TSSRPTST Utility	Available to generate reports of SAF SECTRACE output data sent to SMF.
TSSOERPT Utility	Generates reports of security events logged in a USS environment.

CA-Top Secret for VM Features

Control Program (CP) Protection	Each CP command is treated as a separate resource that can be permitted or denied. Certain CP commands have been limited to specific groups to protect the integrity of the individual virtual machines.
	In the host-guest environment, the CP Diagnose code can be protected on an individual basis to improve performance. In a shared direct access storage device (DASD) environment, protection is provided for OS/390 and VSE data sets.
	Both VSAM and non-VSAM data sets can be protected from VM/CMS users when opened, and non-VSAM data sets can be protected from direct CP-level access.
Shared File System (SFS)	Supported for VM/ESA Release 1.1 and above.
Data Space Protection	Supported for VM/ESA Release 2.0 and above.

CA-Top Secret for OS/390

APPC/VM Support	Communications path for the transfer of data between virtual machines and the Control Program (CP) is supported at connect time.
Release 1.4 Added Features	• Compatible with CA-Top Secret for OS/390 Release 5.0. • Alternate AUDIT file permits switching between two AUDIT files. • The Audit Tracking File supports up to 256 byte resource names.

CA-Top Secret for VSE Facilities

Environment	Provides basic support for VSE/ESA environment. Optional VSE/ESA Feature exploits this environment. A security interface between CA-Top Secret for VSE and the CA-RAPS print management system gives CA-RAPS sign-on, command, and queue file access control. A conversion routine that automatically converts a CA-Top Secret for VSE security file to a CA-Top Secret for OS/390 security file is available.
Cache Option	Saves the results of successful resource validations and utilizes those results for repeated access attempts of the same resource.
Security Inheritance	Submitted jobs inherit the submitter's authorizations, eliminating the need for explicit ID statement processing.
RESET Vector Facility	Provides realtime update of most product options without the need for an IPL (Initial Program Load).
Resource and Facility Security Extensions	Checks the Accessor CPU ID and partition ID before granting access.

Options

CA-Top Secret VSE/ESA Feature Release 2.3	Uses storage above the 16MB line. Provides the following: • VSE/ESA Data Space support in System/370 and ESA modes. • Exploits dynamic partitions. • Allows installation to monitor job activity in both static and dynamic partitions as Secured Files. • Supports over 20 concurrently active CICS partitions.
CA-Top Secret/Secman for VAX Features	Allows for the installation of centralized security administration and auditing control. A single communications platform can monitor security events throughout the entire OS/390-VAX/VMS or Alpha/OpenVMS network of remote and/or local systems. Supports continued use of local administrators. CA-Top Secret for OS/390 permits VAX/VMS and Alpha/OpenVMS security administration through its full-screen command line facilities.

GartnerGroup RAS Services

Copyright © 2000   20 April 1999

A DECnet-to-VTAM connectivity component provides a two-way communications interface to automatically send and receive administrative commands and audited event alarms between OS/390 and VMS.

In addition to all CA-Top Secret administration controls, CA-Top Secret/Secman for VAX also supports all standard VMS user authorization options. All VAX-resident Access Control Lists (ACLs) and Access Control Entries (ACEs) are automatically stored in the OS/390 Security File.

CA-Top Secret for DB2	Enables CA-Top Secret for OS/390 to fully secure IBM's DB2 relational DBMS. It permits the TSS Administrator to control and audit DB2 resources. All DB2 controls are defined and enforced via standard CA-Top Secret for OS/390 definitions.
	Links CA-Top Secret for OS/390 security to DB2, eliminating duplication of security administration across multiple DB2 subsystems.
	Can coexist with subsystems using native DB2 security.
	Supports the Distributed Data Facility (DDF), which enables remote data access.
	Eliminates the need to maintain secondary AUTHIDs.
	Maintains synchronized security definitions in both the CA-Top Secret Security File and DB2 Catalog to accommodate products that rely upon the catalog to retrieve this function.
CA-Top Secret WorkStation	A Windows NT-based security management extension that provides advanced graphical administration, auditing, reporting, and monitoring facilities.
	Provides single-point, enterprise-wide security management.
	Provides security administrators with a system-wide, top-down view of events.
	Presents map-based geographic views of the enterprise, components, and events and consolidates reports from multiple platforms.

Analysis

Security software has always been a major product type in CA's vast repertoire of data and systems management, and CA-Top Secret and its sister product CA-ACF2 have been major elements of the mainframe and enterprise computing corporate environment. Along with IBM's RACF product, these three are considered the major players in the marketplace. Not to say that there are no niche suppliers for the VSE and VM market. In addition, CA has not forgotten all those corporate PC users out there who interact with the mainframe. For these environments CA provides CA-Top Secret WorkStation and CA-ACF2 WorkStation. Unfortunately, IBM does not provide any form of integrated PC support for RACF.

CA-Top Secret for OS/390

CA's proactive approach to security software resulted in the introduction of CA's recent enterprise-wide security solution, featuring interoperability between mainframes and distributed systems. These capabilities permit CA's OS/390 mainframe solutions (CA-Top Secret and CA-ACF2) and its Unicenter TNG to communicate changes and other security-related events such as enterprise-wide password synchronization, enterprise-wide userID suspension propagation, and enterprise-wide monitoring and reporting. Security can be propagated between mainframes and distributed platforms such as Windows NT, UNIX, AS/400, NetWare, and others.

In the IBM mainframe area, there are three major security products that dominate the market. Two of these are provided by CA: CA-Top Secret and CA-ACF2. The third is IBM's RACF. Taken as a group, the CA products undoubtedly control the largest percentage of the IBM OS/390 mainframe security market, with CA-ACF2 usually ranked first and CA-Top Secret second. RACF comes in a valiant third. CA-Alert, another CA product that supports the VSE, CICS, and VM environments, does not directly compete with any of the aforementioned products.

As this report was being compiled, CA announced a projected acquisition of PLATINUM technology Intl., another major supplier of data and systems management. With still more products to add to its vast compilation of mainframe-oriented products, and with CA's history of product integration, CA clients could benefit from a single-vendor, one-stop-shopping situation.

Pricing

Product	Starting Price (US$)
CA-Top Secret	
CA-Top Secret for OS/390	26,028
CA-Top Secret for VSE	15,558
CA-Top Secret for VM	16,176
CA-Top Secret/Secman for VAX	612
CA-Top Secret for DB2	10,512
CA-Top Secret VAX/Net	7,884
CA-Top Secret VSE/ESA Option	3,732

GSA Pricing

No.

Competitors

IBM's RACF, as noted earlier, ranks number three in the mainframe marketplace after both CA-ACF2 and CA-Top Secret. It provides most of the same functionality as the CA offerings but has a tendency to be much more complicated to implement and install. It also does not provide the level of DB2 support that either of the CA products do, which is surprising when one considers that DB2 is a major DBMS in the industry. Also, the PC support for large corporate enterprises is practically nonexistent in integrated form.

One of the niche suppliers alluded to earlier is Sterling Software and its VM:Secure product. This VM-only security product is functionally similar to the CA product for VM, but does not offer the wide range of features to be found in the CA products. VM:Secure is one of a family of utility products that Sterling markets to the VM installation and is not designed to interact with an enterprise-wide environment. In most respects, VM:Secure cannot be truly compared with any of the leaders.

CA-Top Secret for OS/390

Finally, the other mainframe security product from CA--CA-ACF2--is an alternate choice to CA-Top Secret. CA-ACF2 is designed for those who wish to install a rules-based philosophy as opposed to CA-Top Secret, a user-based protection scheme. Also, CA-Top Secret supports native-mode VSE; CA-ACF2 does not.

Strengths

CA-Top Secret can be used in a fully centralized, fully decentralized, or a combination of centralized and decentralized administration schemes. Individual departments may be given as much or as little autonomy over security for their areas as organization policy allows. There are default options that ensure protection and security for resources not even known to the administrator. Also, administration operations can be performed from a range of the most popular platforms, including the use of a single-point GUI management workstation capability that operates in a heterogeneous, enterprise-wide environment.

CA-Top Secret comes with utilities that can be used to extract and report on security violations and log records, and a preprocessor to make formatted security information available to any standard report writer. Decentralized reporting is available with complete enforcement of what information a department administrator can see. Realtime monitoring is available to track security events as they occur. Filters can be used to limit output to selected events of particular interest. Security system trace information is also available to help resolve access problems and difficulties with integrating new products that use CA-Top Secret facilities.

Another major benefit afforded by CA-Top Secret for OS/390 is its capability to interact with CA-Top Secret for DB2 to secure DB2 systems and applications, replacing the internal security of IBM's DB2 database system. It enhances native DB2 security, eliminates the cascade effect associated with the WITH GRANT option, and provides for centralized security through the familiar CA-Top Secret for OS/390 mechanism.

The CA-Top Secret Resource Descriptor Table (RDT) is a tool that clients can use to secure resources used by their own in-house-developed or proprietary applications. The Static Data Table (SDT) is a security file repository which can be used to provide calendars and time functions, as well as record-level and screen-level protection.

Limitations

Although CA-ACF2 for OS/390 does support full Mandatory Access Control (MAC) B1 security, CA-Top Secret for OS/390 capabilities have not yet been delivered. Although probably not as important a factor to commercial customers, B1-level security is very important to certain mainframe government customers who require the controls of MAC protection. CA is currently working on achieving this level of security and has targeted this support for a future release.

Although the VSE version of CA-Top Secret is now syntactically compatible with the OS/390 or VM versions, there are some differences when employing a shared Security File. According to CA, CA-Top Secret VSE Release 3.0 will be a superset product that will address the shared Security File issue as well as provide VM and OS/390 affinity. No formal release date is available at this time.

Datapro Insight

Never before in the history of information processing has the topic of security been of greater concern than it is today. With the introduction of the Internet and the incidence of "hacking" into ultraconfidential systems taking on potentially dangerous proportions, security has become the major point of concern at all levels of government and business. Security now entails data security, application security, and overall system security. Therefore, it is understandable that products such as CA-Top Secret, as well as its sister product CA-ACF2, are considered mainstays in so many medium- to large-scale operations. It is also understandable that these products draw a lot of attention from users who, sometimes, are impatient for the vendor to keep enhancing the product as technology needs grow and change.

In response to this growing need, CA has instituted a formalized demand Analysis Request (DAR) client review prioritization process, wherein each user-submitted enhancement request is reviewed by the responsible CA development team for technical feasibility. Those requests that are deemed reasonable and feasible are submitted back to the clients, through organized user groups, to be prioritized. Clients are notified when the requested enhancement is delivered, and this information is published as part of the product documentation.

Datapro Summary

One of the several elements of the SecureWay Security Server for OS/390 is RACF, which works within OS/390 to protect its vital resources. Building from a strong security base provided by the RACF component, the Security Server is able to incorporate additional components that aid in securing a system. Other elements of the SecureWay Security Server for OS/390 include the OS/390 Firewall technologies, the OS/390 Lightweight Directory Access Protocol (LDAP) Server, the OS/390 Distributed Computing Environment (DCE) Security Server, and the Open Cryptographic Enhanced Plug-Ins. RACF also creates and supports client authentication via digital certificates. All of these elements come free with the acquisition of SecureWay Security Server for OS/390 Release 2.8.

RACF administers security, records access attempts, and reports violations. It can be used to maintain a single image of security access across a sysplex of S/390 processors, provide remote sharing capabilities, and support open client/server and distributed computing environments.

—By Herb Gepner

—Analytical Source: Ed Cowger

Note: RACF has been substantially enhanced since 1997. Since then, RACF has introduced support for access control of DB2 objects (DB2 Version 5 required), digital certificate support (mapping certificates to MVS user IDs), generation of certificates, and additional support for Unix System Services.

All releases of RACF after RACF 2.2 were shipped as an integral element with OS/390. The current release of OS/390 is Release 8. The current release of RACF is 2.8, duplicating the SecureWay Security Server for OS/390 release number.

Corporate Headquarters

IBM
Old Orchard Road
Armonk, NY 10504, U.S.A.
Tel: +1 914 765 1900
Fax: +1 914 765 4190
Internet: http://www.ibm.com

Overview

Among IBM mainframe users, the Resource Access Control Facility (RACF) has been a dominant security control system. In 1996, RACF was incorporated with IBM's Security Server for OS/390, becoming a dominant component of that environment's security offerings. Recently, IBM has expanded its overall security umbrella with its SecureWay environment, and RACF/Security Server for OS/390 is a major component of that coverage.

RACF/VM Version 1, Release 10 (not a component of SecureWay Security Server for OS/390) has not significantly changed since 1996. In it, IBM provided OpenEdition for VM/ESA support for registration of users and groups in the RACF database. It also provided shared file system (SFS) support that enables RACF file-level protection, simplified product installation and service, and SMF data unload, allowing advanced analysis of audited events using the relational data manager of choice.

**IBM SecureWay Security Server for OS/390--
Resource Access Control Facility (RACF)**

Overview

Product Name	IBM—Resource Access Control Facility (RACF)
Product Type	An IBM licensed program that provides data security through mainframe system and resource control.
Current Release	RACF/MVS 2.8; RACF/VM Version 1, Release 10 (not a component of SecureWay Security Server for OS/390).
Platforms Supported	IBM and compatible mainframes running MVS, OS/390, and VM/ESA.
Current User Base	Estimated to be well over 3,500 MVS, OS/390, and VM installations.
Price Range (US$)	Estimated monthly license fee averages range from $1,396 (Base Group 40) to $2,205 (Base Group 80-100). Frequently, licenses are based on the MIPS configuration of the installation.

RACF
Enhancements to RACF 2.8

Protected User ID	Allows the definition of a new type of user ID called the Protected User ID. A Protected User ID will not have a password assigned and cannot be used to log on to TSO/E, sign on to CICS, or log in from a workstation. They can be used to help protect the user ID assigned to OS/390 Unix, Unix daemons, and other important started tasks and subsystems from being used for other purposes.
Administration Enhancements	User ID administration has been enhanced by providing the ability to reset passwords, resume user IDs, and list users without requiring the SPECIAL or group-SPECIAL attribute. This support is provided via a RACF APAR.
Connecting Enterprise Environment	Tivoli Security Management for OS/390 and Tivoli Users Administration for OS/390 provides centralized control over widely distributed cross-platform systems.
More Controls for Unix Users	The RACF component of OS/390 Release 8 Security Server allows for selective assignment of Unix System Services Security. RACF access controls can be used to grant specific superuser privileges to specific users.

Other SecureWay Security Server for OS/390 Elements

Lightweight Directory Access Protocol (LDAP)	With OS/390 Release 7, the LDAP Server can be used to retrieve RACF database information for LDAP client applications, both on and off of the OS/390 platform. User ID and password authentication of LDAP client access to OS/390 LDAP Directory Server can be optionally handled by RACF rather than by accessing user IDs and passwords stored within the server Directory.
Open Cryptographic Enhanced Plug-In OS/390 Firewall Technologies	Greatly assists with support for SSL calls. Enables safe, secure e-business by controlling all communications to and from the Internet. IBM developed this firewall technology back in 1985. Unlike most other firewalls, the IBM firewall contains all three critical firewall architectures: • Filtering • Proxy • Circuit level gateway IBM also offers a Firewall for AS/400 facility.
Java Resources	Access to Java resources can be controlled using RACF.

IBM SecureWay Security Server for OS/390–
Resource Access Control Facility (RACF)

Basic Environment

Working Environment
Any processor that supports IBM's Enterprise Systems Architecture (ESA). All models of the S/390 Parallel Enterprise Servers or S/390 Parallel Transaction Servers. Other models with appropriate engineering changes can also be supported.

Basic Security Features

Overview
RACF supports two access control approaches: discretionary access control and mandatory access control.

Discretionary Access Control
The resource profile facilitates resource ownership and access control at the discretion of the resource owner.

Mandatory Access Control
RACF uses a combination of security levels and categories for users and resources. Resources are assigned a security label, and the user's security label must include that of the resource. Access Profiles RACF maintains sets of profiles to define system users and their ability to access system resources. They include the following:

- User profiles, which are included in the Base segment of the multi-segment control facility, include user name, a unique identifier, the password, the owner ID, the security classification, and any attributes assigned to the user. Other segments control TSO, DFP, Operations, CICS, Natural Language, and MVS OpenEdition access.

- Group profiles, with all RACF users assigned to at least one group. Groups can own resources, users, and other groups or subgroups, and each group has a group owner. The group owner has authorization to add or delete members from the group to authorize their access to resources, etc.

- Data Set and General Resource Profiles contain the access list and user group, auditing options, and the Universal Access Authority. Data Set profiles contain security information about data sets stored on tape or disk. Resource Profiles contain definitions of more generalized RACF-protected resources. RACF has predefined resource classes, including DASD, tape volumes, terminals, CICS, and IMS transactions.

Attributes
Security Classification
These define the authorities or limits that each user has while logged on. The security classification has two types of user information. The first is the category to which the user belongs; this is an installation-defined name corresponding to a department or area within an organization with similar security requirements. The second type of user information is a security label, an installation-defined name, such as "secret," that corresponds to a security level. Labels may also be assigned to users and resources within their profiles.

Security Level and Category Checking
By classifying users and resources, an installation may either use security levels and categories in place of, or in addition to, normal RACF access list checking.

MVS Performance
RACF/MVS uses the MVS/ESA VLF, CSA caching, and the CF of a Parallel Sysplex environment to hold security information in virtual storage, reducing I/O to the RACF database. Authority checking is speeded through the process.

GartnerGroup RAS Services

Copyright © 2000

17 February 2000

IBM SecureWay Security Server for OS/390--
Resource Access Control Facility (RACF)

Security Administrator Facilities

Administrator Interface | The RACF system is accessed through ISPF screens. The various panels show definitions of groups, users, and resources to be protected. RACF commands and service options are listed in a menu-like format for ease of use. RACF functions can be entered as a background job or interactively during a TSO session. The ISPF-help feature includes a comprehensive set of RACF tutorials. RACF supports the Hiperbatch function in MVS/SP JES2 and JES3 Version 3 Release 1.3 and beyond.

User Interface

User Access Procedure | Access is given when a user enters a unique ID and password or a Pass Ticket. Passwords are encrypted using the Data Encryption Standard (DES). There are also access exits available so the installation can customize RACF processing if desired.

Resource Access Procedure | When a user accesses a resource through an MVS, CICS, TSO, IMS, or VM.interface, the request is passed from the System Resource Manager (SRM) to RACF for consideration. When access to an RACF-protected resource is requested, RACF uses information about the user from the user profile and information about the resource from the resource profile to determine if the user has authority to access the resource.

Network Job Entry | RACF can determine if a job submitter is authorized to enter work with a particular name from a certain node.

Operator Control | MVS operators can be required to log on. Certain console commands can be limited to defined operators.

General Interfaces

Database Management | Since the availability of OS/390 Security Server Release 4, RACF users have had the ability to control access to DB2 objects using RACF profiles. This function is provided by a fully supported exit load module called RACF/DB2 External Security Module.

DB2 Access Control Authorization Exit Point | Provided in DB2 Version 5, this function provides administration and auditing of control from a single point, the ability to define security rules before a DB2 object is created, and more.

Resource Controls | RACF encompasses all resources in a mainframe-based SNA environment, including multiple mainframe systems. Attached personal computers, either stand-alone or in a local network configuration, are included in the RACF security scheme if they are emulating LU2- or 3270-type devices. APPC/MVS connectivity support is also provided.

Various levels of access may be specified--such as execute, read, or update--and resources may be assigned a default level of access called a Universal Access Authority, which relates to all users not covered by an individual or group permission.

Communications and Connectivity

Devices Supported | RACF supports VTAM, SNA, LU2, and LU6.2 devices.

VTAM Security | VTAM calls RACF to verify the authority of certain users or programs to open VTAM control blocks.

IBM SecureWay Security Server for OS/390–
Resource Access Control Facility (RACF)

Connectivity Support

Connects to traditional 3270-type devices or computers emulating 3270 machines. Supports APPC/MVS.

Reporting Functions

Audit Logging

The owner of an RACF-protected resource may specify, through the AUDIT parameter, which processing activities are to be logged. Options include writing an SMF record for each unauthorized access attempt, each successful attempt, or all attempts to issue RACF commands.

Audit Reports

RACF creates summary reports from the audit trail that show the use of sensitive files, files subject to repeated unauthorized access attempts, the identity of users who tried unauthorized actions, and the activities of security administrators and selected users.

Audits may be done on a security-label basis. Resource class, providing a more detailed trail and greater control, can also do global auditing.

Year 2000 Support

With the latest available versions of RACF, the product now considers a date with a yy value of 70 or less to be in the year 20yy, and a date with a yy value greater than 70 to be in the year 19yy. RACF provides a module to allow customers to convert a 3-byte packed decimal date to a 4-byte packed decimal date.

RACF Support for
Digital Certificates

With the availability of OS/390 Version 2, Release 8, RACF can accept the digital certificate authenticated by WebSphere without requiring an RACF user ID and password for each client when Web pages are accessed.

RACF for VM

Architecture

Provides enhanced security through the use of security labels and Mandatory Access Control (MAC).

Provides improved availability through the support of multiple RACF service machines.

Virtual Machines

RACROUTE can become the single security-function server interface for VM and MVS resource managers. RACF services are available to resource managers in virtual machines.

VM Security Console

Administrators can define which users are security operators. These operators can send and receive messages from the RACF service machine.

Shared File System
(SFS) Support

VM shared system files and directories at the file level are secured through resource classes.

VM Performance

VM and VM/HPO installations can set up multiple RACF service machines to spread the workload and make more efficient use of virtual storage while.avoiding virtual storage constraints.

VM Command Interface

An interface that allows customers to define their own RACF/VM command names and syntax rules.

VM Logonby

Allows an authorized appointee to act as a surrogate for a designated authorized user.

OpenEdition For
VM/ESA Support

Provides the capability to register OpenEdition for VM/ESA users and groups in the RACF database and offers security for files and directories residing in the OpenEdition byte file system.

GartnerGroup RAS Services

Copyright © 2000   17 February 2000

**IBM SecureWay Security Server for OS/390--
Resource Access Control Facility (RACF)**

SMF Data Unload	Allows for the advanced analysis of audited events using the relational data manager of choice.
Download or Browse	Allows users to get a copy of the program directory for RACF 1.10 for VM by browsing or downloading a PDF file.

Analysis

From 1976, when RACF was introduced, it has frequently set the standard for security products. From the beginning, the RACF development team has delivered a premier product for securing the most valuable corporate data on mainframe systems. Working closely within the operating system's existing features, the RACF licensed program provides improved security for an installation's data. It also protects vital system resources and controls what users can do on the operating system. RACF has since been incorporated in larger, more encompassing enterprisewide security environments, initially as a key component of the OS/390 Security Server, which, in turn, is now part of the overall SecureWay Security Server for OS/390.

RACF is the primary element of the total enterprise environment offered by IBM. It is an active product, being maintained to meet the security needs of growing corporate demands as well as adhering to changing governmental needs in a timely fashion with such enhancements as Firewall Protection and the LDAP Directory.

There are two major competitive products, both from Computer Associates Intl. (CA). The first is CA-ACF2 and the second is CA-Top Secret. The security methodology of CA-ACF2 most closely approximates that used within RACF, but CA-Top Secret differs significantly. CA's "User-addressed" strategy in CA-Top Secret associates resources with users and stores user authorization information in one place for a "rules-based" strategy. Despite the different implementation methods, both RACF and CA-Top Secret offer similar external security features and functions, including user identification and authorization and data access control. Both products are also compliant with the SAF and provide peer-to-peer communications security. On the other hand, RACF and CA-ACF2 use a "resource-based" strategy, which requires separate user and resource profiles.

At one time, the CA products provided more enterprisewide security features, but with the introduction of later releases of RACF and its enhancements and now the further introduction of Tivoli product adjuncts, The all-inclusive RACF offering is as robust as the CA products, which rely heavily on extra-cost adjuncts.

Pricing

Prices for a monthly license for the base RACF product vary widely depending on hardware configuration. The price would start at approximately US$1,396 (monthly license fee for a Group 40 system).

GSA Pricing

Yes.

Competitors

• Computer Associates Int'l. CA-ACF2 and CA-Top Secret

IBM SecureWay Security Server for OS/390–
Resource Access Control Facility (RACF)

Strengths

RACF provides all the primary security functions required to secure data and resources in the mainframe environment. These include:

- Identification and verification of system users.

- Identification, classification and protection of system resources.

- Authorizing the users who need access to the protected resources.

- Controlling the means of access to these resources.

- Logging and reporting unauthorized attempts to gain access to the system and to the protected resources.

- Administer security to meet an installation's security goals.

Limitations

At one time, the major criticisms of RACF were the complexity of integrating RACF with the various operating systems and the myriad of subsystems required to meet an installation's needs. With the introduction of OS/390 Security Server and, subsequently, SecureWay Security Server for OS/390, all of these complexities have faded into the background. With RACF being an integral part of the operating system, there is no need to go through a major configuration exercise. However, if users do not want to change their existing operating system level, but do want RACF features available only in a higher level of the operating system, they have to make the choice: one or the other.

Also, some distributed, client/server extensions require the inclusion of some of the Tivoli products.

Datapro Insight

RACF has been, and will continue to be, IBM's primary mainframe security product. It competes very favorably with the two CA product offerings and, according to IBM, is installed in more than 70 percent of all OS/390 installations, both commercial and governmental. It has met all the government-established guidelines for security software and has been maintained judiciously for almost 24 years.

Although the security software market has, for the most part, stabilized, there are still OS/390 sites migrating to IBM's SecureWay Security Server for OS/390. Therefore, it is.important that software suppliers maintain their products to meet the ever-changing needs of their clients, as IBM seems to be doing. Addressing the changing enterprise makeup, expanding distributed security capabilities, and encompassing the Internet needs for security are the current challenges for both IBM and its competitors in order to satisfy its user base.

Notes

Notes